"Thiagi has done it again! The man you love to listen to has created a book that brings HPI interactive strategies down to a level that everyone can use."

—George M Piskurich, principal, GMP Associates

"Though there are many collections of training and simulation games, only a few are able to give you the understanding and guidance you need to take full advantage of the power of games as learning tools. Of those few, none is more comprehensive, more fun, more practical than Thiagi and Son's Templates—a master trainer and master player who has been bringing new levels of functioning fun to business and education for more than thirty years. His son Raja has taken the best of his father's wisdom, and added both clarity and humor."

—Bernie DeKoven, author, DeepFUN.com, *The Well-Played Game*

"At various meetings over the years, Thiagi has been sharing his innovative approaches to action learning and we've all been taking notes. Now, in *Design Your Own Games and Activities*, Thiagi and Raja provide us with do-it-yourself templates. My working life just became easier, better, and a lot more fun! Thanks."

—Glenn Parker, team-building consultant and author, *Team Depot: A Warehouse of 585 Tools to Reassess, Rejuvenate, & Rehabilitate Your Team*

"Teachers, trainers, church and community leaders will want this collection of inexpensive, highly creative, useable games. Suggestions and aids for helping the participants gain the most value from each experience are included for each game. It's truly a valuable work."

—R. Garry Shirts, Simulation Training Systems.

"The Thiagarajans are the grand masters of games for training. In their new and richly-illustrated book they tell all you need to know to become your own game master."

—Danny G. Langdon, partner, Performance International

"This is 'Thiagi in a box!' A comprehensive resource of highly-interactive, performance-improvement strategies. This book is in Thaigi's tradition of sharing wisdom at it's best."

—Chris Saeger, chair, North American Simulation and Gaming Association

"Once in a lifetime a book like this comes along. As a trainer, I'm going to make sure this book stays within reach on my desk. Is there anyone who would want to take this opportunity to learn from a master?"

—Sandra Mumford Fowler, editor, *Intercultural Sourcebook: Cross-Cultural Training Method, Volumes 1 & 2*

"A Thiagi *tour de force*—people who understand performance will find practical templates for rapid development of training that supports performance-improvement projects. At minimum, the templates, examples, and guidelines will excite expert facilitators, guide novices, and bring smiles to the lips of participants."

—Dale Brethower, coauthor, *Performance-Based Instruction: Linking Training to Business Results*

DESIGN YOUR OWN GAMES AND ACTIVITIES

Thiagi's Templates for Performance Improvement

SIVASAILAM (THIAGI) THIAGARAJAN
WITH
RAJA THIAGARAJAN

JOSSEY-BASS/PFEIFFER
A Wiley Imprint
www.pfeiffer.com

Published by Pfeiffer
An Imprint of John Wiley & Sons, Inc.
989 Market Street, San Francisco, CA 94103-1741   www.pfeiffer.com

For additional copies/bulk purchases of this book in the U.S. please contact (800) 274-4434.

Pfeiffer books and products are available through most bookstores. To contact Pfeiffer directly call our Customer Care Department within the U.S. at (800) 274-4434, outside the U.S. at (317) 572-3985 or fax (317) 572-4002.

Pfeiffer also publishes its books in a variety of electronic formats. Some content that appears in print may not be available in electronic books.

Printed in the United States of America

ISBN: 0-7879-6465-4

Library of Congress Cataloging-in-Publication Data
Thiagarajan, Sivasailam.
Design your own games and activities: Thiagi's templates for
  performance improvement / Sivasailam Thiagarajan.
      p.   cm.
    Includes bibliographical references and index.
    ISBN 0-7879-6465-4 (alk. paper)
    1. Management games. 2. Games—Design and construction. I. Title.
HD30.26 .T485 2003
658.4′0353—dc21
2002014804

Acquiring Editor: Martin Delahoussaye
Director of Development: Kathleen Dolan Davies
Editor: Rebecca Taff
Senior Production Editor: Dawn Kilgore
Manufacturing Supervisor: Bill Matherly
Interior Design: Bruce Lundquist
Cover Design: redletterdesign.biz

Printed in the United States of America

Printing   10   9   8   7   6   5   4   3   2

Contents

How to Use This Book

To get the maximum benefit from this book, we suggest that you begin with a real-world performance challenge that you are currently facing. Follow this sequence:

1. Read the introductory chapters on framegames and simulation games.

2. Select one or more interactive strategies that are appropriate for your needs.

3. Study the chapter to explore possibilities. Study the sample activity and play it with a representative group.

4. To help you with Step 2, the indexes in the back of the book include two navigation aids. These tables allow you to immediately locate complete ready-to-use activities and brief descriptions of other activities. You may use the first table to select possible interactive strategies according to type of activity, number of participants, and time requirement. You may use the second table to locate core ideas that can be developed into full-blown activities.

The best way to learn how to design interactive strategies is to design interactive strategies. Reading a chapter and thinking about activities is a good place to begin. But the sooner you get some hands-on experience in designing the activity, the more you will learn. Once you have designed an activity, the sooner you try it out with participants the more you will learn.

Remember, it's all about interactive experiential strategies. So go ahead: Interact and experience the strategies.

Introduction:
Toward Serious Playfulness

This book explores the "how" of designing interactive strategies for improving human performance. But first, this chapter explores the "why" and the "what" of interactive strategies.

To answer the question "why," I will briefly describe some of reasons the time has never been better to use interactive strategies for training and performance improvement. As for the "what," I will offer my own experience as a template for understanding how to use and design interactive learning strategies. This introduction ends with an overview of what is in this book and how to use it.

WHY?

The fact that you are reading the book suggests that you are already familiar with interactive learning strategies and believe in their effectiveness. (If you need additional information, please refer to the Resources section at the back of the book.) Here is a brief review of related information that you can use to present a persuasive case to others.

Psychological Rationale: The Intelligent Choice

Major support for the use of training games and other interactive strategies comes from recent research on the nature of human intelligence.

You are of two minds. Professor Seymour Epstein (1993) at the University of Massachusetts offers a theory of intelligence called *Cognitive Experiential Self Theory* (CEST), which suggests that we have an experiential mind and a rational mind. Our experiential mind learns directly, thinks quickly, pays

attention to the outcome, and forgets slowly. Our rational mind learns indirectly, thinks deliberately, pays attention to the process, and forgets rapidly. Epstein's contention is that you need both your minds. Games and interactive strategies appeal directly to the experiential mind. When combined with debriefing discussions, they provide a powerfully balanced approach to whole-brain learning.

You have three intelligences. Robert J. Sternberg (1997), IBM professor of psychology and education at Yale University, has demonstrated that someone can be highly creative and practical but score low on traditional intelligence tests. According to Sternberg's research, practical and creative intelligence are better predictors of job effectiveness than analytical intelligence measured by IQ tests. Interactive, experiential techniques can develop your practical and creative intelligence and enhance your success.

You may have eight types of intelligences. Professor Howard Gardner (2000) at Harvard University developed the revolutionary concept of multiple intelligences. According to this theory, you have several types of intelligence, including linguistic intelligence (thinking in words and using language), logical-mathematical intelligence (quantifying and working with hypotheses), kinesthetic intelligence (acquiring physical skills), spatial intelligence (three-dimensional thinking), musical intelligence (working with pitch, rhythm, timbre, and tone), interpersonal intelligence (interacting with others), and intrapersonal intelligence (understanding one's self). Traditional training caters almost exclusively to the first two intelligences. However, jobs demand other types of intelligence. Games and experiential activities tap into all of your intelligences and get you ready for the real world.

Your EQ is more important than your IQ. In his recent best-selling books, Daniel Goleman (1997) has shown that being smart goes beyond your IQ. You need emotional intelligence with self-awareness, impulse control, persistence, motivation, and empathy. The principles and procedures related to emotional intelligence are best learned by interactively experiencing the factors and analyzing their impact. Traditional training fails miserably to sharpen our emotional intelligence. Experiential and interactive approaches are obvious strategies of choice.

In summary, traditional strategies appeal to and utilize only a limited range of your intelligence. Interactive strategies help you exploit other types of intelligence.

Seven Laws of Learning

Many people are desperately seeking research evidence to prove that training games are more effective than traditional strategies. This is a futile search because there is no clear definition of *training games* and *traditional approaches* or clear specification of what constitutes *effectiveness*. A more logical approach will be to identify how interactive strategies relate to proven laws of learning.

Here is a quick recap of seven universal laws of learning. After a brief statement of each law, I discuss its application to interactive strategies:

1. Law of Reinforcement: *Participants learn to repeat behaviors that are rewarded.* Most interactive techniques provide opportunities for earning frequent rewards. They require participants to make frequent decisions and responses. The scoring system rewards people for correct responses.

2. Law of Emotional Learning: *Events that are accompanied by emotions result in long-lasting learning.* Boredom is not conducive to learning. Training games, simulations, and role plays add emotional elements to learning. By conducting a debriefing discussion after emotional activities, we can help players analyze their feelings and learn from their reactions.

3. Law of Active Learning: *Active responding produces more effective learning than passive listening or reading.* Interactive strategies provide participants with ample opportunities to respond by asking questions, encouraging them to ask questions, answering their questions, and questioning their answers.

4. Law of Practice and Feedback: *Learners cannot master skills without repeated practice and relevant feedback.* Understanding a principle or reciting the steps in a procedure is not the same as the ability to apply new skills and knowledge to real-world challenges. In contrast, interactive strategies provide repeated practice and feedback and improve effective transfer.

5. Law of Previous Experience*: New learning should be linked to (and build upon) the experiences of the learner.* Interactive strategies are useful for checking the entry level of participants. These strategies also help us incorporate the variety of rich experiences that learners bring to the training classroom.

6. Law of Individual Differences: *Different people learn in different ways.* Interactive strategies accommodate a variety of learning styles. These strategies require participants to respond by writing, speaking, drawing, and acting out. They also permit participants to learn individually, in pairs, and in teams. Team-learning activities ensure that participants receive individual attention from their peers.

7. Law of Relevance: *Effective learning is relevant to the learner's life and work.* Simulations and role plays increase the link between the learning situation and the real world. Interactive techniques incorporate realistic problems and challenges from a variety of workplace situations. After the activity, the debriefing discussion invites participants to come up with action plans for applying what they learned to their real-world context.

Both common sense and empirical research support these laws of learning. They apply to all types of learning by all types of learners.

Ten Workplace Trends

Let's leave aside the psychological rationale for interactive strategies for a moment and explore additional factors that suggest the timeliness of these strategies. Here are ten global trends in the workplace that are relevant to the use of interactive strategies:

1. Large-Scale Participation. Everyone wants a piece of action. All around the world, citizens want to participate in making political decisions. In the workplace, employees want to have a say in the way they are being managed. Computer and communication technologies support these demands for increased participation. Such participation not only makes moral sense but also business sense. New team techniques are evolving to involve large masses in real-time strategic changes.

2. Teamwork. Every week, more and more organizations are being flattened. During the past decade, traditional bureaucracies have been replaced by team-based structures. The complexity of knowledge work requires collaboration among members of cross-functional teams. If employees are going to work in teams, it makes sense to train them in teams. Therefore, individual instruction is being increasingly replaced by team-based learning.

3. Learning Organizations. Peter Senge's (1994) conceptual framework that organizations can suffer from fatal learning disabilities has now become an accepted truth. More and more people are using operational strategies related to the five disciplines Senge identifies as systems thinking, personal mastery, mental models, building shared vision, and team learning. Interactive experiential approaches provide effective tools for acquiring and sharpening all five disciplines, especially those of team learning and shared vision.

4. Globalization. Technologies of travel and communication have reduced distance to an insignificant variable. Through Internet and video conferencing, virtual teams around the world interact instantaneously with each other. This has changed the nature of teams and teamwork. Interactive training tools provide an effective strategy for learning hard skills related to the use of technology and soft skills related to cross-cultural communication.

5. Changing Characteristics of Learners. People born after 1970 and raised on "Sesame Street," MTV, and video games have learning and performance characteristics that are different from those for whom traditional training is designed. As Marc Prensky (2000) points out, this twitch-speed generation prefers play to work, payoff to patience, icons to text, and active learning to the passive variety. These new learners have a shorter attention span and a greater ability to interact in an asynchronous mode. All these characteristics favor fast-paced games, virtual worlds, and experiential activities.

6. Increasing Diversity Among Learners. Students in formal educational programs and participants in corporate training programs are becoming increasingly heterogeneous. New learners differ from one another in terms of age, race, culture, gender, national origin, learning styles, personality styles, previous experience, and hundreds of other such variables. These learners are also proud and protective of their individual differences, and they are unwilling to accommodate themselves to centralized, standardized methods of instruction. Games and other interactive strategies enable us to exploit this diversity.

7. Self-Help Groups. People have discovered the advantages of receiving and giving training and therapy through the sharing of experiences, insights, and skills with each other—without the need for specialists and subject-matter experts. Self-help groups are now available in real and virtual communities to assist people with all types of needs. Games and other interactive techniques help these groups to better achieve their goals and objectives.

8. Virtual Participants. An unobtrusive and powerful benefit of the Internet revolution is its ability to encourage introverts to interact. With web-based training, participants in experiential activities do not have to make fools of themselves in public. The anonymity of chat rooms enables people to play different roles without self-consciousness. Similarly, people can participate in truly democratic brainstorming sessions without being intimidated by the ideas from high-status people, because all inputs are presented anonymously.

9. More Training. Train-the-trainer programs are being converted into train-the-facilitator programs. In the past, facilitator training was offered by a few organizations at inconvenient locations and times. The approach to facilitation was dominated by group therapy models. We now have more facilitator training offered by more organizations in more places with greater frequency. Also, facilitation models now incorporate an eclectic collection of strategies from creativity, instruction, organizational development, community action, quality control, application design, project management, systems thinking, future scanning, and team building. The availability of competent facilitators is a harbinger of more efficient use of games and other interactive techniques.

10. The Computers Are Here. Ten years ago, interactive approaches such as simulation gaming were constrained by the cost and complexity of communication and computation technologies. We now have computer power on everyone's desktop that is capable of providing interactive, high-fidelity, virtual-reality simulations in any complex area. For a mere $100, you can buy an authentic driver-education software program, complete with a steering wheel or a flight simulator, complete the latest aerial maps. Several companies offer computer game design templates that permit non-specialists to create multimedia activities.

WHAT?

Now that we have re-emphasized the rationale for using interactive strategies, let's turn our attention to exploring the characteristics of these strategies.

Here's a personal introduction: Forty years ago, I began using instructional games in my training sessions. Five years later, I moved away from using ready-made games toward designing my own training games. Five years later, I moved from *games* toward different interactive techniques in training. Five years later, I moved from training toward strategies for improving human performance.

This book is an attempt to share what I learned from my journey. I am a firm believer in the principle that sharing ideas will make all of us richer.

Beginning with Games

It all started with games. So what is a game? Here is the semi-technical definition that I use: A game has four critical characteristics: conflict, control, closure, and contrivance.

Conflict refers to the fact that the players have a goal to achieve and different obstacles prevent them from achieving it. Very often, conflict is in the form of competition among players or teams. But you can also have conflict with previous records, time limits, or the ingenuity of the computer.

Control refers to the rules of the game that specify how you take your turn, make your move, and receive the consequences. Some rules may be explicit, while others may be implicit.

Closure refers to the fact that the game has to come to an end. A special rule (called the *termination rule*) specifies when and how the game ends. Termination rules may involve time limits, target scores, or elimination. They also determine who won the game.

Contrivance refers to the built-in inefficiencies in a game. Obviously, there are more efficient methods for dropping a little white ball into eighteen holes than the rules of golf permit us to do. This characteristic of contrivance is what makes people say, "After all, it was only a game."

When we talk about training games, we add another critical characteristic (that also begins with the letter C: *competency*. A training game is intended to develop one or more specific competencies.

When I talk about interactive strategies, it includes some of the elements of games and leaves out some others.

From Using Games to Designing Games

Initially, I used training games that other people had designed. Very soon I began modifying and adapting these games to suit my training objectives, the preferences of my learners, and the local constraints. To paraphrase James Carse (1994), I moved from playing within the rules to playing with the rules. When I started training other trainers, I decided it is better to teach them how to design their own games rather than give them a specific game to use.

Playing with the Rules

Initially, I focused on designing pure games (that featured all four critical characteristics). While using these games with participants from different cultures, I began emphasizing or de-emphasizing different elements of games. Eventually, I decided that the critical element in effective training games was not the technical perfection but action and interaction among participants. As a result, I began designing game-like activities that resulted in improvements in learning and motivation.

My movement away from pure games was accelerated by a sloppy research project that I started on March 21, 1998. In the best tradition of introverted psychologists, the project has a single subject and a simple task: Every day (including weekends and holidays) I designed a training activity. After the first couple of weeks in this study, I added one more constraint that required that today's activity should be significantly different from the ones that I designed during the past six days. I added this constraint from recycling MONOPOLY® or JEOPARDY® in hundreds of variations. As a result of this constraint, I decided to explore a variety of interactive training strategies. As of today, I have identified sixty types of these interactive strategies. In this book, I discuss the design of thirty of these strategies.

Beyond Training

Long before performance consulting became a buzz word, I have been a human performance technologist who believes that training is only one of several strategies (I hate the pretentious term *interventions!*). Without any conscious effort on my part, I realized that all types of performance-improvement efforts can benefit from the type of interactive strategies that I used for training purposes.

Here are a couple of examples that demonstrate the use of playful approaches to performance improvement:

Improving a Reward-and-Recognition System with Playing Cards. The manager of a fast-food restaurant was plagued by employees arriving late for work. Having identified lack of incentives as the root cause, she created a reward and recognition system to reduce tardiness. Whenever a worker arrived on time, he or she received a fifty-cent bonus for that day. This intervention cost about $1,200 a month and worked effectively—but only for a couple of months. Faced with workers reverting to their tardiness, the manager added an interactive element to the incentive system. She randomly organized the workers into teams of five people. Every day that all the team members arrived on time, she gave that team a playing card from a shuffled deck. Every other Friday, the teams created the best poker hand from the cards they had collected during the two-week period. The team with the best poker hand received a bonus of $500, to be divided among its members. This minor addition of a team activity to the reward and recognition system reduced the system's cost and increased its effectiveness.

Improving Personnel Selection Through Role Playing. The manager of a retail store was troubled by performance problems at the customer- assistance desk. Having identified a poor match between employee characteristics and job requirements as the root cause, the manager hired a consultant to administer several test instruments to select the most suitable employees with appropriate attitudes, skills, and values for the customer-assistance job. This personnel selection intervention worked fairly effectively. However, because the job involved interpersonal interactions, the manager decided to move away from paper-and-pencil tests to actual interactive testing through role playing. In this approach, test situations were carefully selected to reflect different types of customer requests and complaints. The role plays were conducted in a setting that simulated an actual customer-assistance desk. A group of six professional actors from a local improv theater were employed to play the roles of different types of customers. These actors were briefed about the characteristics of customers and how they should behave. Each candidate for the job played the customer- assistance provider role to indicate how he or she would handle each of the six actor-customers. These role plays were recorded on videotape and later analyzed with a behavioral rating scale. The candidates with the highest scores on this rating scale were selected for the job.

That is a quick overview of just some of the ways interactive strategies are used today. The rest of this book will give you not only a better understanding of what they are and how they may be applied, but dozens of examples, including a ready-to-use activity, complete with handouts, visuals, and step-by-step instructions, for each type.

HOW?

The book is divided into two major sections, each identified with a label that uses *game* in the broadest sense of the term: structured activities that require interaction among participants.

The first section deals with framegames. A *framegame* is a template for the instant creation of a performance-improvement activity. Within this broad category, there are specific strategies classified according to the primary source of information (examples: *participants, subject-matter experts, lectures, videotapes, web pages,* and *assessment instruments*), format and materials (examples: *card games, board games, puzzles,* and *telephone games*), and timing (examples: *openers* and *closers*).

The second section deals with simulation games. A *simulation game* uses processes and objects that represent real-world counterparts in order to facilitate transfer of training. Within this category, there are specific formats arranged according to how closely the interactive exercise resembles the real-world processes. These strategies range from *action learning* in which real-world groups complete a real task and learn from their experience to *jolts* that present brief contrived experiences to offer metaphorical insights.

Each strategy in the framegame and simulation game sections is presented in a standardized format for ease of reference and application. While the exact content and sequence may vary from one chapter to another, depending on the nature of the strategy, these are the main topics in a typical chapter:

- Definition of the strategy
- An illustrative application of the strategy
- Explanation of the strategy
- Types of activities related to the strategy
- Advantages
- Disadvantages and limitations
- Additional examples

Each interactive strategy is followed by a complete, ready-to-use activity with information and instructions related to the following categories:

- Purpose
- Participants
- Time requirement
- Setup
- Materials
- Preparation
- Flow of the activity
- Debriefing

This ready-to-use section also provides reproducible master pages for all handouts used in the activity.

Part 1

Framegames

1 Introduction to Framegames

This section of the book explores several types of framegames. Framegames are templates for instant creation of training games. These generic shells are designed to permit easy replacement of old content with new content. You can use framegames to rapidly develop training activities that suit your needs.

The best way to understand the concept of framegames is for you to participate in a game. Are you ready for a vicarious experience? Then work your way through VALUES ENVELOPES to get a feel for how a framegame works.

VALUES ENVELOPES

You are attending an orientation session designed to explore the values of your corporation. You feel that the session is going to be a waste of time because you have already studied the colorful poster that explains the five core corporate values: *customer satisfaction, quality, teamwork, integrity,* and *employee empowerment.*

At the beginning of the training session, your friendly facilitator Sue organizes you and other new employees into five teams of four people each. Each team receives an envelope and four index cards. Sue explains that a different core corporate value is written on the face of each envelope. Your team has 3 minutes to brainstorm a list of examples of how this value can be incorporated into everyday behaviors and decisions on the job.

Your team's envelope has *integrity* as the core value. After a hesitant start, you and your teammates write down ideas such as these:

* *Don't make promises you cannot keep.*
* *Don't accept gifts from any customers.*
* *Be honest about the limitations of the products we sell.*

At the end of the 3-minute period, your team has recorded ten such ideas on both sides of the index card. Sue asks the teams to stop writing, place their index cards inside the envelopes, and pass the envelopes, unsealed, to the next team.

During the next round, Sue wants you to repeat the same process of recording brainstormed examples for the value written on the face of the new envelope given to your team. You have to do this without looking at the card inside the envelope.

The value on the new envelope is *employee satisfaction*. Your team is now on a roll and you record several examples called out by your team members.

The game proceeds in the same fashion during two more rounds. You receive new envelopes with new core values. You generate and record examples of everyday behaviors that incorporate these values.

During the fifth round, you receive another envelope with the core value of *teamwork*. Before your team begins to generate examples of this value, Sue announces a change in the procedure. Instead of creating more examples, your team's task is to review the four cards inside the envelopes, compare the examples in those cards, and distribute 100 points among the four cards to reflect their relative merits.

After a suitable pause, Sue instructs each team to read the items from the cards in ascending order of points. You listen eagerly when the other teams read the cards to find out where your team's list is placed. After this activity, you collect the cards that your team created and add up the score points. Your total is 217, which is the second highest score!

Deconstructing the Framegame

Your experience with VALUES ENVELOPES does not actually demonstrate the framegame concept. To explore this concept, we have to deconstruct the VALUES ENVELOPE game. If you ignore the content (*core corporate values*) and focus on the process of the game, you end up with the framegame, ENVELOPES. Here is the generic structure of this framegame:

* Topics explored in this game are written on faces of envelopes.
* Participants are organized into as many teams as there are envelopes.
* Participant teams write responses on index cards.
* The same procedure is repeated during several rounds.
* During the last round, teams compare different cards inside an envelope.

Ten Framegame Applications

As you have probably figured out, you can use the ENVELOPES framegame structure with different content areas. Here are ten examples of how we have rapidly generated new games by using the framegame approach.

Markets

Training Objective: How to position a product to appeal to different market segments

Topics on Envelopes: Different market segments (examples: *home office* and *small business*)

Response Requirement: Write a list of product benefits to be emphasized

Icons

Training Objective: To communicate through the use of graphics

Topics on Envelopes: Different types of merchandise (examples: *books* and *software*)

Response Requirement: Sketch a graphic that will clearly communicate what type of merchandise is located in different areas of the store

Participants from Hell

Training Objective: To handle disruptive behaviors of participants at a meeting

Topics on Envelopes: Types of disruptive behaviors (examples: *side conversations* and *personal attacks*)

Response Requirement: Write a list of ideas for reducing or removing the negative impact of the disruptive behavior

Prevention

Training Objective: To *prevent* disruptive behaviors of participants at a meeting

Topics on Envelopes: Types of disruptive behaviors (examples: *side conversations* and *personal attacks*)

Response Requirement: Write a list of guidelines for the facilitator to prevent this type of behavior from happening

Slogans

Training Objective: To identify the key concept and summarize it in the form of a memorable slogan

Topics on Envelopes: A rambling paragraph describing the vision of an organization

Response Requirement: Write a slogan that captures the key message.

Objections

Training Objective: To handle customer objections during a sales call

Topics on Envelopes: Typical customer objections (examples: *price is too high* and *need committee approval*)

Response Requirement: Write a suitable response to the objection

Forecasts

Training Objective: To explore industry trends

Topics on Envelopes: Predictions (examples: *market share will increase* and *competition will slash prices*)

Response Requirement: Write a list of supporting arguments on one side of the card and a list of refuting arguments on the other side

Change

Training Objective: To use suitable strategies during each stage of change management

Topics on Envelopes: Stages of change management (*awareness* and *installation*)

Response Requirement: Write a list of suitable techniques for use during the stage

Checklist

Training Objective: To identify behaviors associated with different management roles

Topics on Envelopes: Roles of a manager (*communicator* and *organizer*)

Response Requirement: Write a list of behaviors associated with each role

Types

Training Objective: To communicate more effectively with different people

Topics on Envelopes: Personality types (*introvert* and *linear*)

Response Requirement: Write a list of guidelines on how to communicate with a person with this type of personality

Your Particular Situation

By now, you should have a good feel for the concept of a framegame, especially of ENVELOPES as a framegame. The best way to reinforce your mastery of the concept is to apply it to your own situation. Take a few minutes now to come up with two or three ways in which you can use the ENVELOPES framegame. Be sure to think through the answers to these questions:

- What training objectives can you reach with this game?
- What topics should be written on the faces of the envelopes?
- How should your participants respond?

Benefits and Limitations

The most obvious benefit of a framegame is the speed with which you can design a "new" game. If you are a subject-matter expert, you can create an effective game to suit your training objectives in a matter of minutes. Because you are borrowing the frame from an effective field-tested game, you have a high probability of success. You can also explain the structure of a framegame to your participants and ask them to design their own versions. This will help participants gain an in-depth understanding of the topic.

Because the framegame approach is so easy to apply, you may be tempted to design inappropriate games for irrelevant purposes. Many participants can recount horror stories related to the play of innumerable versions of JEOPARDY and MONOPOLY in their training sessions. To avoid such abuse, it is important to make sure that the framegame that you are using is suitable for the type of training content and the preferences of your participants.

Types of Framegames

Framegames can be categorized into different types. A useful way of categorizing framegames is to focus on the source of the training content. Table 1.1 shows one possible categorization system.

Structured Sharing. In this type of framegame, the content is generated by participants themselves, based on their experience and logical thinking. VALUES ENVELOPES, the sample game that you vicariously played earlier, belongs to this category.

Table 1.1. Framegames Classified According to Source of Training Content

Framegame	Content Source	Ready-to-Use Game	Page
Structured Sharing	Participants	TOP TIPS	27
Creativity Technique	Participants	SEVEN SENTENCES	35
Interactive Lecture	Lecture	INSIDE STORY	47
Textra Game	Reading materials	TIME TRAVEL	55
Item Processing	Unorganized information	SILENT MOVIES	64
Video Vitamin	Videotape recordings	BOOSTERS AND BASHERS	76
Assessment-Based Learning Activity	Responses to assessment instruments		
WebQuest	Internet		
Debriefing Game	Previous experiences	THIRTY-FIVE	89

Creativity Techniques. These form a special type of structured sharing activity that enables participants to solve a problem or to utilize an opportunity in an innovative fashion. The traditional BRAINSTORMING technique, for example, can enhance a training session by focusing on the application of newly acquired skills and knowledge.

Interactive Lectures. In this type of framegame, the content is presented through a lecture presentation. IDEA MAP is an example of an interactive lecture. In this activity, you begin by training participants how to take graphic notes using the idea-mapping technique. Then start your presentation, inviting participants to take notes using the idea-mapping technique. Stop the presentation from time to time and ask teams of participants to spend 5 minutes collaboratively drawing an idea map of the topics covered so far. Continue with your presentation and repeat the idea-mapping interludes. At the end of the presentation, invite the teams to display their final products and encourage participants to review other teams' products.

Textra Games. In this type of framegame, the content is presented through a handout (or some other form of reading assignment). Participants read the content first and then use the framegame to review it. In a textra game called MINING THE LIBRARY, participants have access to a collection of books on the training topic. Each participant selects and reads one of the books, looking for immediately applicable techniques. After a suitable pause, each participant finds a partner and shares the technique. Later, each pair selects one of the two and shares it with another pair. Finally, each team of four presents one of the techniques to the entire group.

Item Processing. This is a special type of textra game in which the content is presented as an unorganized collection of short pieces of information (such as ideas, facts, questions, complaints, suggestions, or tips). In this type of framegame, participants organize the items into meaningful categories or logical sequences. In an item-processing framegame called IDEA FILTER, for example, different participants are given different pages of a handout, each containing seven to ten different items in a random order. During the first round of the game, participants individually select two best items in their page. During the second round, participants with the same page organize themselves into a team and reach consensus on the two best items. During the third round, participants with different pages form teams and select the top three ideas across these pages.

Video Vitamins. In this type of framegame, the learning content is presented through a videotape. Participants view the videotape first and then play the game to reinforce their mastery of the content. In a video vitamin called RASHOMON (named after Akira Kurosawa's 1951 classic Japanese movie), you assign different key roles from the video's story line to each participant and ask participants to watch the video from the assigned point of view. After the video, assemble participants into same-role teams and have them

reconstruct the story from that character's point of view. After a suitable pause, ask teams to present the different versions.

Assessment-Based Learning Activities. These activities require participants to complete a test, a rating scale, or a questionnaire and receive a score (and feedback) about their personal competencies, attitudes, or personality traits. Whenever appropriate, these activities encourage interaction and discussion among participants to analyze their responses and to apply the results to future action. For example, in BEGINNING WITH THE END, participants are given a copy of the final test. The facilitator explains that the actual test will use different items in the same format. Participants spend a few minutes checking off the test items for which they feel confident about being able to give the correct response. Participants anonymously switch their test sheets and help the facilitator identify.

WebQuests. In this type of framegame, created by Bernie Dodge, the content is found in different locations on the Internet. You ask participants to find the answers to a set of questions by surfing the Net. For more details about this type, visit the WebQuest Page (http://webquest.sdsu.edu/webquest.html).

Debriefing Games. In this type of framegame, the learning content comes from an experiential activity conducted earlier. The ensuing game encourages participants to reflect on their experience and to gain appropriate insights. In RAPID SURVEY, participants organize themselves into teams. Each team collects responses from all participants to a debriefing question (example: *How does experience in the simulation game resemble your real-world experience?*). After a suitable pause for data collection, teams summarize and present the information.

Another Approach for Classifying Framegames

We can also classify framegames on the basis of game formats and materials. Some types of framegames based on this classification system are listed in Table 1.2, each with an example.

Card Games. These games involve pieces of information (such as facts, concepts, technical terms, definitions, principles, examples, quotations, and questions) printed on cards. These games borrow procedures from traditional playing card games and require players to classify and sequence pieces of information from the instructional content. SLAPJACK is a typical card game that provides an effective introduction to any classification system. Here's how this game is played with cards from Glenn Parker's *Team Players* system, which categorizes members of a team into four types: goal-directed collaborators, issue-oriented challengers, task-oriented contributors, and process-oriented communicators.

Players seat themselves at a table, around a spoon. One of the players takes the top card from the deck and reads the item aloud. The first player to grab the spoon gets to announce the type of team player associated

Table 1.2. Framegames Classified According to Formats and Materials

Framegame	Format/Material	Ready-to-Use Game	Page
Card Game	Cards	TEN TRICKS	94
Board Game	Game board	EMPTY OR FULL?	105
Matrix Game	Matrix	APPLES AND ORANGES	114
Paper-and-Pencil Game	Paper and pencil	ONE-ON-ONE	128
Instructional Puzzle	Puzzles	CRYPTIC STRATEGIES	140
Audio Game	Audiotape recordings	INSERT AND DELETE	160
Telephone Game	Telephones	CONFERENCE CALL	172
Game Show	TV game show	COOPETITION	182
Computer Game Shell	Computers		
E-Mail Game	E-Mail	C3PO	192
Improv Game	Improvisational theater	QUICK DRAW	202

with the item. Other players check the response against the type given in the reference card. If correct, the player takes a poker chip from a bowl. If incorrect, the player returns a poker chip to the bowl. The game continues with different players taking turns to pick a card and read the item.

Board Games. These games borrow structures and play materials from popular recreational games to create highly motivating training events. Board games typically use cards and dice to encourage individuals and teams to demonstrate their mastery of concepts, principles, skills, and problem-solving strategies. INSTRUCTIONAL PARCHEESI is a board game modified for training purposes. Each player has two pieces that begin at the player's home base. Three decks of question cards are also used in this game: the first deck has 1-point questions, the second deck has 2-point questions, and the last deck has 3-point questions. When it is your turn, you draw two cards from your choice of decks. If you answer the questions correctly, you move one of your pieces forward. If you land on a square that contains another player's piece, you knock that piece back to the start. The first player to take both pieces all the way around the board and back to the home base wins the game.

Matrix Games. These games require participants to occupy boxes in a grid by demonstrating a specific skill or knowledge. The matrixes provide a structure for matching or classifying individual items or organizing and comparing a set of items. The first participant to occupy a given number of boxes in a straight line (horizontally, vertically, or diagonally) wins the game.

Matrix-1 games have the same set of headings for both the columns and the rows of the grid. In a game called ETHNICITY, for example, the columns are labeled with five different ethnic groups in the workplace. The same labels are also applied to the five rows. The boxes along the diagonals have the same column and row labels. To win a box along this diagonal, the two competing participants write statements that identify the most salient characteristic of the ethnic group. To win a box above the diagonal, participants write statements about the most important similarity between the two ethnic groups. Finally, to win a box below the diagonal, participants write statements about the most significant difference between the two ethnic groups.

Paper-and-Pencil Games. These require players to make their moves by writing or drawing something on paper. A typical game may involve participants working on a small piece of paper (example: *writing a key word in a tiny Post-it® Note*) or a large sheet of paper (example: *drawing a mural of the organization's vision on three yards of butcher paper*). These games may incorporate elements of role play, simulation, puzzle, or quiz contests.

Q & A & Q & A . . . is a game for four or more players. Each player writes a question at the bottom of a piece of paper and gives it to the next player. Players now write the answer to the question in the piece of paper and fold the bottom part of the paper so that the question is hidden but the answer is visible. Each player once again passes the piece of paper to the next player. All players now study the answer and write a question that would have elicited the answer. They write the question above the answer and fold the paper so that the answer is hidden but the most recent question is visible. Players repeat the process. The game ends after a suitable period of rounds when everyone opens the papers and reads all the questions and answers.

Instructional Puzzles. These puzzles challenge participants' ingenuity and incorporate training content that is to be previewed, reviewed, tested, re-taught, or enriched. Puzzles can be solved by individuals or by teams. CROSSWORD PUZZLES are the most frequently used types of instructional puzzles. Questions from a final test can be presented as crossword puzzle clues. Participants fill the puzzle grid with the answers arranged in a crisscross pattern.

Audio Games. These are activities that primarily depend on recorded audio messages (such as audiotape, MP3, digital recording, or computer recording) to provide the training content, structure the training activity, and collect players' responses. In AUDIO MEMORY, the recording recites the names and positions of the top ten playing cards from a shuffled deck (example: *one, six of diamonds; two, five of clubs*). After a pause, the audiotape asks for the names of playing cards associated with a position (or the position of a specific playing card). After a few rounds of play, savvy participants figure out the strategy of forming an informal team

and asking each member to remember the names and positions of just two cards in the ten-card sequence.

Telephone Games. These involve the play of interactive games using telephones and answering machines. These games usually incorporate elements of role play and teamwork. The object of GLOBAL REACH is to familiarize participants with international telephone procedures. Each virtual team is given the name of a city in another country (example: *Yangoon in Myanmar*). The challenge for the team is to conduct a telephone interview with a citizen of the other country who is a member of their own profession.

Game Shows. A game show is a contest modeled after popular TV programs. The format involves a contest among a few selected participants, watched by spectators ("studio audience"). The training version of the game show features questions from specific instructional content. JEOPARDY is a television show that is watched by eighteen million people around the world every day. This game usually involves three people competing to answer questions at six levels of difficulty selected from five topical categories.

Computer Game Shells. These are special types of framegames that are presented on a computer screen. The shells permit the loading of new content (usually in the form of questions) by the facilitator. The computer program creates the game and acts as a timekeeper and scorekeeper. FIX LIST is a computer game shell that presents a list of steps (related to a procedure or process) in a random order. Using the mouse, you rearrange these steps in the correct order while a timer is counting down. If you succeed in arranging the steps in the correct sequence before you run out of time, your name gets inscribed in the computer's *Hall of Fame* screen.

E-Mail Games. These games are electronic versions of interactive training games that permit participants to receive and send messages at different times. Typical e-mail games exploit the ability of the Internet to ignore geographic distances and involve participants in pooling their ideas and polling to select best ones.

101 FACTOIDS is a sample e-mail game that encourages players to collect, distribute, and review factual information related to any job-relevant topic. During the first round, players receive an e-mail note with factoids (brief statements of facts) related to the topic, organized under different categories. The e-mail note also identifies different sources of information about the topic and invites players to contribute up to five new factoids every day before 4 p.m. The facilitator reviews these contributions, awards 10 points for each contribution, updates a "Hall of Fame" list with the names of the players with the top five scores, and updates the list of factoids by adding edited items. The game continues day after day with the players contributing not more than five new factoids.

Improv Games. These are activities adapted from improvisational theater where the actors do not use a script but create the dialogue and action as

they perform. When used as an interactive training technique, improv games facilitate the mastery of skills related to such areas as creativity, collaboration, communication, and change.

In an improv game called THE PERFECT FOLLOWER one player takes on the role of a leader and the other a follower. The two conduct a discussion related to project planning. If the follower's behavior is not satisfactory, the leader claps his or her hands and explains the reason for dissatisfaction (examples: too obsequious, too assertive, or does not listen actively). The offending follower is immediately replaced by another participant who tries to do better and last longer.

Chronological Classification

Another way of classifying framegames is based on when in the training session they are used, as shown in Table 1.3.

Openers. Sometimes called *icebreakers*, these are activities for jump-starting a training session. An effective opener helps participants achieve a combination of objectives, including previewing the workshop objectives and content, getting acquainted with fellow participants, working collaboratively with others, establishing ground rules, sharing a common experience, sharing current knowledge, and getting energized.

DEMANDS is an opener that uses a playful spirit to establish ground rules. Each participants creates a placard with a demand of the trainer (examples: frequent breaks and straight answers to my questions). Participants hold up their demand signs and silently walk around the room. After a few minutes, ask participants to pair up and jointly decide which demand to keep and which to discard. Both partners now hold the selected demand placard by the opposite corners and silently walk around the room. After a few minutes, ask participants to form groups of four to six and select one of the demands. Ask participants to present their selected demands. Finally, the facilitator holds up three or four "counter-demands" (examples: return from breaks on time and turn off your cell phones and beepers).

Closers. These are activities for winding down a training session. An effective closer helps participants achieve a combination of objectives, including summarizing the content, reviewing major learning points, testing for mastery, providing feedback, planning for application activities, and celebrating the completion of the session.

Table 1.3. Framegames Classified According to Training Use

Framegame	Timing	Ready-to-Use Game	Page
Opener	Beginning	ROBOT	212
Closer	Ending	TRIPLE FEEDBACK	224

HIGHLIGHTS is a closer that helps participants to review the key elements of a training session. Participants work independently to create a storyboard that captures the highlights of the session in a series of rough sketches. After a suitable pause, participants form teams, and within each team, take turns presenting their storyboard sketches. After everyone has completed her turn, each team identifies the most frequently mentioned highlight.

BACK TO BASICS

We explored different approaches to classifying framegames, based on the *content source, game format,* and *chronological position.* These approaches are not mutually exclusive. For example, you may use a board game to enhance learning from any of the seven different content sources: participants, documents, lectures, web pages, assessment instruments, videos, and experiential activities.

It is not important to master different classification systems. What really matters is the fact that we can use any type of framegame to rapidly design a training activity to suit your needs, objectives, resources, and constraints.

2 Structured Sharing

Structured Sharing represents a special type of framegame that facilitates mutual learning and teaching among participants. Typical structured sharing activities create a context for a dialogue among participants based on their experiences, knowledge, and opinions.

THE BEST AND THE WORST

You are sent to a leadership training session and you expect to be bored with a pontificating lecture on the qualities of a true leader. You are pleasantly surprised when Vince, the trainer, announces that you are going to play a game called THE BEST AND THE WORST.

Vince asks you (and the other participants) to think of three personal nominees for the best leaders. You may think of any past or present, fictional or real, male or female leaders, but at least one of them should be someone who has directly influenced your life. You choose Stephen Hawking, Mother Theresa, and your grandfather. After a suitable pause, Vince asks you to think of three worst leaders—people who have been given a leadership role but failed miserably to fulfill that role. You are tempted to come up with the names of three U.S. presidents, but instead you select Adolf Hitler and two of your past managers.

Vince now asks you to pair up with another participant and take turns presenting your choices and explaining why you consider them to be the best and the worst leaders. You team up with Jan and have an interesting conversation. Later, Vince asks you and your partner to come up with a list of desirable leadership qualities.

After another pause, Vince invites you and the other participants to call out different leadership qualities and lists them on a flip chart. With everyone's input, he clusters these qualities into nine appropriate categories. He then briefly introduces *stewardship* and *integrity* as at least two leadership qualities that are missing from the list.

What Is Structured Sharing?

THE BEST AND THE WORST is an example of a *Structured Sharing* activity. A *framegame* is an instructional activity that is deliberately designed to permit the easy removal of old content and insertion of new content. *Structured Sharing* is a special type of framegame that facilitates the sharing and analysis of participants' experiences, knowledge, and opinions. The primary source of information in this type of activity is the participant group. The instructor's role is merely to facilitate the activity and to correct major myths, misconceptions, and stereotypes. *Structured Sharing* implements the often-espoused-but-seldom-practiced cliché that adult learners bring a wealth of experience to the training session.

More Examples of Structured Sharing

Here are compressed instructions for conducting four more *Structured Sharing* activities:

SHOUTING MATCH. Identify a controversial topic (example: *sexual orientation in the workplace*) where a sharing of opinions could be beneficial. Announce a proposition for debate related to the topic. Divide the participants into three teams and assign an extremely positive role to one, an extremely negative role to another, and a neutral role to the third. Ask the positive and negative teams to make a list of arguments in support of their positions while the neutral team prepares a two-column list of arguments on both sides. Conduct a debate among the opposing teams and ask the neutral team to decide the winner. Correct any misconceptions and provide objective information.

COMPARISON TABLE. Identify two to four contrasting strategies or processes (examples: *leaders versus managers* or *virtual teams versus face-to-face teams*). Prepare a set of questions that require a comparison of these strategies or processes along different dimensions (examples: *What is one major strength of a virtual team?* or *What type of facilitator is required for a face-to-face team?*). Distribute two or three questions to each participant and ask him or her to survey the others and summarize the responses. After a suitable pause, distribute copies of a blank table with the items to be compared as the column headings and the dimensions along which they are to be compared as the row labels. Work through each cell in the table, eliciting information from the participants.

BRAINSTORM. Prepare a series of brainstorming questions on a topic (example: *What do customers expect from us? What are the obstacles to delighting all the customers?* or *What strategies can we use to delight all customers?*)

Introduce the topic, ask the first question, and encourage the participants to brainstorm alternative responses. Paraphrase participant responses on a flip chart, commenting on them when there is a lull in the flow of ideas. Correct any misconceptions and add additional information. Repeat the process with the other questions.

CONCEPT ANALYSIS. Organize the participants into teams and specify a concept to be explored (example: *leadership*). Explain that the goal of the activity is to identify the critical features of the concept. Ask the teams to provide a variety of examples, ranging from clear-cut ones to borderline cases. Then ask the teams to identify superordinate concepts (example: *competencies*), coordinate concepts (example: *facilitation*), and subordinate concepts (example: *charismatic leadership*). Explore synonyms, antonyms, and related words associated with the concept. Finally, ask the teams to develop a comprehensive definition of the concept.

Ready-to-Use Structured-Sharing Activity
TOP TIPS

TOP TIPS is a framegame. You can easily pull out the content and plug in your content. In the Flow section below, the generic rules for TOP TIPS are printed in regular type. A specific example is also given.

Participants

Any number can play. The best game is for twelve to twenty participants.

Time

Best time is 30 to 45 minutes. The exact time requirement depends on the number of topics and the amount of time allotted to each round.

Supplies

- A handout summarizing the TOP TIPS procedure, as shown at the end of this chapter. Reproduce one copy for each participant.
- A timer and a whistle to help you stick to the schedule.

Preparation

Select a common task performed by the participants. Identify four to six topics related to this task. Prepare a handout similar to the sample on page 32. Replace the task and the topics in the sample handout with your content. Make any other changes to suit your needs.

In a recent gathering of facilitators, we conducted a TOP TIPS session on handling disruptive participants. Our list of topics

included domination, passive aggression, excessive seriousness, flippancy, side conversations, and emotional outbursts.

Flow

Work individually on the first topic. Announce the topic and assign a suitable time limit. Ask each participant to recall successful strategies that he or she has used in this area. Also invite participants to recall tips and shortcuts that they have heard or read about. Recommend that the participants jot down notes for personal use.

The first topic was domination. Here are some strategies that Pam noted:

- Interrupt the dominator with a question directed to someone else.
- Acknowledge the comment and ask someone else to respond to it.
- Explain that it is important to hear from everyone else.
- Call on others.

Work with a partner. After a suitable pause, blow the whistle and ask each participant to find a partner to share the tips. Warn the partners that they will have to recall and present the other person's tips at a later time. Roam among the partners, eavesdropping on their conversations.

Pam pairs up with Matt. They take turns sharing their tips. Here are three tips from Matt:

- At the beginning of the meeting, establish a ground rule that everyone gets equal "air time" during the meeting.
- Give each participant six poker chips, each worth 2 minutes of talking time. When a participant uses up all the poker chips, she or he has to keep quiet.
- Use the "talking stick" approach. Only the person holding the talking stick may speak.

Pam listens very carefully to Matt's tips because she is worried about having to present them to the others.

Work in quads. After a suitable pause to permit the sharing of tips between partners, blow the whistle again and ask each pair to join another pair to form a team of four called a quad. Ask all four members of the quad to share the tips from the previous round, each person recalling and reporting his or her partner's tips. Roam among the quads, eavesdropping on the conversations.

Pam and Matt join Andy and Janet and share their tips. Matt has no difficulty recalling and reporting Pam's ideas. During the conversation, the four participants discover that their ideas are very similar. Janet, however, reports a unique idea (which she attributes to Andy): One

Design Your Own Games and Activities

participant is given the role of Conversation Controller. He or she does not participate in the discussion but makes sure that everyone is given equal time.

Select the best tips. Blow the whistle again and ask each quad to select two or three of their tips for presentation to the entire group. Recommend that the participants select practical tips that are unique.

Pam's team selects the tips that involve the poker chips, the talking stick, and the Conversation Controller.

Present to the whole group. Blow the whistle again and randomly select one of the quads. Ask the spokesperson from this quad to present its best tip. Repeat the procedure with a few other quads.

The spokesperson from the first quad suggests that the facilitator should ignore the dominating team member. He claims that most teams are capable of handling problem participants on their own without outside intervention. Pam's team is selected next. Andy explains his tip about using a Conversation Controller. This is followed by useful tips from three other teams.

Take your turn. Comment briefly on the tips, adding suitable caveats about their use. Also, if you have useful tips that are different from those presented by the participants, share them with the group.

Vince, the facilitator, makes a supportive comment about the suggestion to trust the teams to solve their own problems. He briefly shares a strategy that he uses to prevent domination of the team discussion by an individual: Each team member takes turns making a statement related to the topic of discussion.

Repeat the procedure. Announce the next topic. Take the participants through the steps of individual reflection, partnership, quad formation, and whole group presentation as before. Repeat the same procedure with the remaining topics.

Participants work through the other topics (passive aggression, excessive seriousness, flippancy, side conversations, and emotional outbursts) using the same procedure. During the latter rounds, Pam pairs up with other participants. She also discovers that some of the strategies (example: *establishing initial guidelines for team members' behavior*) are applicable to all types of disruptive behaviors. She shares this insight with the members of her quad.

Conclude the session. Ask each participant to take a few minutes to recall the different tips and to jot down personal notes about two or three of them for immediate application. Thank all participants for their contributions.

Variations

Inconvenient number of participants? The game involves the participants working with a partner and, later, in teams of four. If you have an odd number of participants, join the group or ask one partnership to invite the extra participant to join them. Make similar adjustments when each pair joins another pair.

Not enough time? Speed up the activity by reducing the number of topics, reducing the time allotted to each round, asking the participants to work in pairs from the beginning, and skipping the formation of quads.

Schedule chopped up? Play the game in installments. Discuss a different topic during each meeting.

TOP TIPS Games

Here are seven examples of different instructional content loaded into the TOP TIPS frame:

MEETING MANAGEMENT

Topics: Agenda setting. Physical facilities. Making decisions. Keeping minutes. Concluding the meeting. Follow-up.

Sample Tips: Replace the minutes of the meeting with an action plan that identifies goals, due dates, responsible people, and required resources. Take notes on a computer and print out the action plan for distribution immediately at the conclusion of the meeting. Use computer software for facilitating collaborative decision making.

MANAGING AN OVERSEAS PROJECT

Topics: Cultural differences. Travel arrangements. Immigration and customs. Language problems. Contact between home office and field staff.

Sample Tips: Read the latest edition of the U.S. State Department Field Book on the country you are visiting. Use e-mail for all local and international communications. Work through local agents when handling immigration and customs requirements.

SELLING PROFESSIONAL SERVICES

Topics: Pricing. Marketing. Repeat sales. Working at the CEO level. Maintaining integrity.

Design Your Own Games and Activities

Sample Tips: Spend more time listening to the clients than talking to them. Focus on adding long-term value to the client rather than making short-term profits. Treat client's objections as opportunities for identifying additional needs.

HIGH-TECH TIME MANAGEMENT

Topics: Surfing the Internet. Electronic organizers. Virtual meetings. Managing e-mail. High-tech telephony.

Sample Tips: Make sure that your Palm® computer is compatible with your office computer. Avoid making paper copies of e-mail messages. Practice appropriate answering machine etiquette.

HANDLING MARGINAL EMPLOYEES

Topics: Identifying problem employees. Counseling and coaching. Seeking external assistance. Goal setting. Documenting performance deficits. Implementing corporate policies.

Sample Tips: Involve the employee in setting up written performance goals. Do not confuse the employee with the sandwich technique (positioning negative feedback in the midst of positive comments). Work with the employee in identifying suitable strategies for performance improvement.

USING WEB-BASED TRAINING

Topics: Getting additional information about web-based training. Selling the concept internally. Selecting appropriate software and hardware. Converting existing courses for Internet delivery. Designing new courses for the web. Delivering and maintaining the courses on the web.

Sample Tips: Surf the Internet for the latest information on web-based training. When talking to managers, highlight the at-your-place, at-your-pace access to training. Use web-based computer game templates to reinforce traditional training.

CREATIVE PROBLEM SOLVING

Topics: Computer-assisted creativity. Right-brain techniques. Team-based creativity. Tests of creativity. Supporting creativity in organizations. Creative collaboration.

Sample Tips: Use Inspiration® software for brainstorming. Ask people to generate ideas independently before joining a team. Discontinue monetary incentives for employee ideas. Instead, implement the ideas immediately.

TOP TIPS

How to Participate

The TOP TIPS activity is designed to help us share practical tips, ideas, and strategies related to a common task.

Today's task is **Handling Disruptive Participants in Team Meetings**

These are the six specific topics that we will explore:

1. **Domination:** *How do we handle people who talk too much and interrupt others?*

2. **Lack of participation:** *How do we handle people who are totally withdrawn and do not want to participate in the meeting?*

3. **Excessive seriousness:** *How do we handle people who are uptight about everything and always talk in a politically-correct fashion?*

4. **Flippancy.** *How do we handle people who use excessive humor and make fun of the important issues?*

5. **Side conversations:** *How do we handle people who whisper or pass notes to each other and conduct a separate discussion?*

6. **Emotional outbursts:** *How do we handle people who lose their temper, attack each other, or get excessively emotional?*

Procedure

To ensure that everyone gets maximum benefit from this activity, we will use the following procedure:

1. **Work by yourself.** Recall successful short-cut strategies that you have used in this task. Also recall tips and short cuts that you have heard or read about. Jot down notes for personal reference.

2. **Work with a partner.** Find a partner and share your tips and short-cut strategies. Listen carefully because you will have to recall and present your partner's tips to the others.

3. **Work in quads.** Join another pair to form a team of four called a *quad*. Share the tips from the previous round, each person recalling and reporting his or her partner's tips.

4. **Work with the whole group.** Select the best tip from your quad. Make a brief presentation of this tip. Listen to the tips presented by the other quads.

Repeat the same procedure with each of the six topics.

At the end of the session make a note of two or three short-cut strategies that you want to apply immediately.

Design Your Own Games and Activities

3 Creativity Techniques

Creativity Techniques represent a special type of structured-sharing framegames. They provide a structure that enables participants to solve a problem or to utilize an opportunity in a creative fashion. These techniques are useful not only for learning new skills and knowledge but also for improving the performance of a team. This creativity technique helps you generate a large number of ideas to solve a problem. Here is the technique in action.

DOUBLE REVERSAL

You are asked to participate in a focus group to explore employee empowerment in your organization. You are not too thrilled when Vince, your ubiquitous facilitator, announces that he will begin with a brain-storming session. However, he surprises everyone by identifying the brainstorming topic as ways to demotivate the employees. He repeats the topic and explains that the participants should come up with strategies for discouraging and frustrating employees. After a brief pause, you and the others call out such sadistic ideas as punish the employees, blame the employees in public, increase the workload of employees, assign dull, boring, and mechanical tasks, threaten to fire the employees, reduce employee salaries, and behave in an unpredictable fashion. Vince lists these ideas on a flip chart. Later he demonstrates how to reverse each of these ideas to achieve the opposite goals of motivating and encouraging the employees. As an example, he takes the demotivating idea of withholding critical information from the employees and turns it around

into the positive idea of sharing critical information with all employees. Vince also demonstrates how some demotivating ideas can be reversed into more than one positive idea. You and your teammates now work through all your demotivating suggestions and end up with a list of twenty-five effective motivation techniques.

More Sample Creativity Techniques

Here are condensed descriptions of four more creativity techniques:

THREE-PART BRAINWRITING. This creativity technique makes sure that your ideas are based on facts and that they contribute to reaching your goals. It is similar to the traditional brainstorming technique, except you write your ideas down instead of calling them out. You join a group with five to seven participants faced with a problem or opportunity (example: *taking telephone orders*). Each of you is given three cards labeled Facts, Goals, and Ideas, respectively. You write a fact (example: *most telephone orders involve credit card charges*), a goal (example: *customers should be able to order twenty-four hours a day, seven days a week*), and an idea (example: *encourage customers to fax their orders*), each on its appropriate card and leave the cards in the middle of the table. You pick up cards from the other participants, read their statements, and add additional statements that fit the label for the card. Working rapidly, you pick up any card, write a new statement, and replace it on the table. You and the other members of the group repeat the procedure to generate large numbers of statements of all three types. Finally, you review the cards with the other members of the group and select the best ideas that help achieve selected goals.

COMPUTERIZED CREATIVITY. In this technique, a computer program structures your creative thinking process. Several different creativity programs are available. You begin the guided problem-solving approach by typing a clear description of your problem. Next you prepare a wish list. The computer now displays each of your wishes and asks you to type several ideas for achieving that wish. Then you list the plusses and concerns about each idea. Select your biggest concern and type additional ideas to overcome this concern. When you get stuck, the software program offers different triggers to evoke additional ideas. Eventually, you end up with creative solutions to your problem.

MEETING YOUR MENTOR. This creativity technique uses visualization. Close your eyes, relax your body, and visualize a calm, peaceful setting such as a deserted beach. Invoke sensory impressions, feeling the cool breeze against your face, smelling the flowers, hearing the gentle murmur of the waves, and tasting the sweetness of chocolate. When you are completely relaxed, visualize meeting a real or imaginary mentor and calmly communicating a problem to this mentor. Wait for your mentor's guidance with an open and trusting mind. At the proper time, your mentor whispers a word or reveals an image. Open your eyes and work out different solutions to your problem suggested by the message from your mentor.

VISUAL SUCCESS. This creativity technique helps you clarify your goals. The facilitator identifies a problem or an opportunity to be handled creatively. Each participant draws a picture of what success would be like in this situation. You cannot use any words, but your picture can be symbolic, abstract, or realistic. The facilitator collects the pictures from the group at each table and redistributes them to the other tables. You and your table mates now work jointly and list indicators of success that you infer from each picture. You integrate this list into a specification of goals to be achieved.

Types of Creativity Techniques

Some creative techniques are based on structured, rational approaches. THREE-PART BRAINWRITING and COMPUTER CREATIVITY belong to this category. Other creative techniques reflect less structured intuitive approaches. MEETING YOUR MENTOR and VISUAL SUCCESS belong to this category. Creativity techniques can also be divided into individual and team approaches. COMPUTER CREATIVITY and MEETING YOUR MENTOR are individual techniques. You need a team to conduct the other sample techniques.

Ready-to-Use Creativity Technique
SEVEN SENTENCES

This activity provides an alternative approach to traditional brainstorming. Instead of rushing to generate ideas, why not think a little bit about the situation first? Of course, you don't need to spend several days on it. Just think of seven elements of the situation; then generate ideas based specifically on each of these elements. Here is how it works.

Participants

Four to seven.

Time

15 minutes to 2 hours. Best time period is about 30 minutes.

Materials

- Index cards
- You will also need sheets of paper and pencils if accommodating a large group, or the job aid at the end of this chapter if working with an individual.

Equipment

- Flip charts
- Felt-tipped markers

Flow

Specify the situation. Think of a problem. At the top of a flip chart, write a short phrase that captures the essence of this problem.

A small group from an insurance company wants to improve the support provided to agents in the field. Jo, the facilitator, writes the phrase "agent support" on top of a flip chart.

Write seven sentences. Invite participants to call out seven sentences related to the situation. These should be factual, descriptive sentences about the actual situation rather than ideas for solving the problem. Write down the sentences on the flip chart, editing them as appropriate. Make sure that each sentence contains only one basic concept.

Mick offers this sentence: There are five hundred agents and only three support staff.

Jo splits this sentence into two: There are three support staff members. There are five hundred agents.

Here are the next five sentences offered by participants:

- All the work is done through phone calls.
- Agents use laptop computers.
- Agents need help with the hardware.
- Agents need help with the software.
- All computers use Windows 98.

Jenny comes up with another sentence: All three support staff members are women.

Jo points out that they already have seven sentences and offers to keep Jenny's sentence in reserve for future use.

Use each sentence to generate ideas. Tape the flip-chart paper (with the seven sentences) to the wall. Ask participants to focus on the first sentence and come up with creative ideas to improve the situation, based on this sentence. Write the ideas on a fresh sheet of flip-chart paper, numbering each idea. When participants run out of steam, ask them to shift to the next sentence. Repeat the process until participants have generated ideas based on all seven sentences. Whenever a flip chart is filled with ideas, tear it from the pad and tape to the wall.

Here are some of the ideas based on the first sentence ("There are three support staff members"):

1. The staff members should work as a team.
2. They should have a common mission and goal.
3. They should keep in touch with each other.

Design Your Own Games and Activities

4. They should have periodic conference calls to coordinate their strategy.

5. They should help each other to solve problems.

6. They should share information about the agents.

7. They should share practical tips with each other.

8. If one of the three staff members gets sick, the other two should cover for her.

Participants come up with a few more ideas based on this sentence. Then they generate several other ideas based on each of the other sentences.

Generate additional ideas. Ask participants to combine the first two sentences and come up with new ideas suggested by the combination. Repeat this process several times with each of the twenty-one different pairs of sentences listed in the sentence combination table at the end of this chapter. Continue to record the ideas on flip-chart sheets, taping filled-up sheets to the wall.

When Jo combines the first two sentences, Kathy contributes this idea: The staff members should divide the five hundred agents among the three of them to ensure an equal workload.

Pat jumps in with a related idea: Each staff member should treat every one of the five hundred agents with equal care—without worrying about whether or not that agent is assigned to her.

The group comes up with several other new ideas as they work through different combinations of the seven sentences. Eventually the wall is covered with eight flip-chart sheets with a total of ninety-three different ideas.

Review the ideas. After you have listed a large number of ideas based on each of the seven sentences and each of the twenty-one pairs of sentences, ask each participant to silently review the ideas on the flip-chart sheets taped to the wall.

Reduce the number of ideas. Go through the list of ideas on the wall and with the participants' help remove duplicate ideas, combine similar ideas, and eliminate obviously trivial ideas.

Specify selection criteria. Tell participants that they will be reducing the list of ideas to a smaller set. Present a couple of sample criteria for selecting useful ideas (such as customer satisfaction or time requirement) and invite participants to suggest additional criteria. List these criteria on a new sheet of flip-chart paper. Divide the criteria into negative factors (such as time requirement) and positive factors (such as customer satisfaction). Point out that the best ideas have low levels of negative factors and high levels of positive ones.

Here are the six criteria listed on Jo's flip-chart sheet. The + or − sign in front of each idea identifies whether it is positive or negative:

1. − Cost
2. − Time requirement
3. + Field agent satisfaction
4. + Consistency with business goals
5. − Possibility of creating new problems
6. − Potential delays

Select the best ideas. Ask each participant to review the lists of ideas again and write down the numbers of the seven ideas that would provide the most benefits at the least cost. After everyone has done this task individually, give each participant a felt pen and ask him or her to place check marks in front of the selected ideas. Identify the top seven to ten ideas that received the most check marks.

Integrate the ideas. With the help of participants, edit the selected ideas and arrange them in order of priority. Prepare an action plan for implementing these ideas.

Variations

Not enough time? Begin with five sentences. Give a time limit for generating ideas based on each sentence. Skip the step of generating ideas based on pairs of sentences. Conclude the activity when a large number of ideas have been generated. Complete the remaining activities by yourself.

Have ample time? After the participants have generated a large number of ideas in a leisurely fashion, declare a break. While the participants are taking the break, copy the list of ideas from the flip charts onto index cards. When the participants return from the break, ask them to work as a team to cluster ideas into different categories. Combine suitable ideas in each category. Select the best ideas, then repeat the entire activity with another set of seven different sentences.

Cannot assemble the participants at the same place? You can conduct this activity through e-mail or even paper mail. Send a note asking a group of people to suggest a few factual sentences related to a situation that you have defined. Review the responses and select seven sentences (either systematically or randomly). Send another note (incorporating the instructions at the end of this chapter) asking the group members to generate ideas using individual sentences and pairs of sentences. After a few days, combine the responses and send them back to the group, asking each person to select the top seven ideas. Use this information to identify the final set of ideas for implementation.

Too many ideas? Here are two alternative suggestions for identifying the top seven to ten ideas. Give each participant seven colored dots and ask each participant to place them next to the ideas that he or she personally prefers. Alternatively, go through several rounds of elimination. During the first round, eliminate half of the ideas. During the next round, eliminate half of the remaining ideas. Repeat this process until you have seven to ten ideas.

Too many participants? Divide the group into teams of four to seven members. Ask each team to work independently at different tables, beginning with their own sets of seven sentences. Instead of using flip charts, ask them to use sheets of paper. When each team has completed the activity and identified the top ideas, review the lists from different tables. Remove redundancies and combine similar ideas. Alternatively, after each team has generated a lot of ideas, you can switch the lists of ideas among different teams. Ask each team to select the top ideas from some other team's list of ideas.

Too few participants? You can conduct this activity with just two or three participants. You can even ask an individual to use this activity. Just give this person a copy of the job aid that follows.

SEVEN SENTENCES:
Instructions for Individual Use

Get ready. Make sure that you have a large working surface, several index cards, and pens or pencils.

Specify the situation. Think of a problem. On an index card, write a short phrase that captures the essence of this problem.

Write seven sentences. On another index card, write seven sentences related to the situation. These should be factual, descriptive sentences about the actual situation, rather than ideas for solving the problem.

Use each sentence to generate ideas. Focus on the first sentence and write creative ideas suggested by this sentence to improve the situation. Write each idea on a separate index card. Place the cards with the ideas face up so you can refer back to them. When you run out of ideas, shift to the next sentence in your list of seven sentences. Repeat the process until you have generated ideas based on all seven sentences.

Generate additional ideas. Combine the seven sentences into the pairs shown in the combination table below. Come up with new ideas suggested by each combination. Continue to record the ideas on separate index cards.

Review the ideas. After you have listed a large number of ideas based on each of the seven sentences and each of the twenty-one pairs of sentences, review the ideas on the index cards. Remove duplicate ideas, combine similar ideas, and eliminate obviously trivial ideas.

Specify selection criteria. Think of different criteria (such as customer satisfaction or time requirement) that will help you select the best ideas. List these criteria on an index card. Divide the criteria into negative factors (such as time requirement) and positive factors (such as customer satisfaction). Point out that the best ideas have low levels of negative factors and high levels of positive ones.

Select the best ideas. Review the ideas on index cards again and select the best ideas, remembering that they have low levels of the negative factors and high levels of the positive factors that you identified earlier. Continue this activity until you have identified the top seven to ten ideas.

Integrate the ideas. Edit the selected ideas and arrange them in order of priority. Prepare an action plan for implementing these ideas.

Sentence Combination Table

1 & 2	1 & 3	1 & 4	1 & 5	1 & 6	1 & 7
2 & 3	2 & 4	2 & 5	2 & 6	2 & 7	
3 & 4	3 & 5	3 & 6	3 & 7		
4 & 5	4 & 6	4 & 7			
5 & 6	5 & 7				
6 & 7					

4 Interactive Lectures

The training method that receives the most complaints and ridicule is the lecture. However, it is also the most popular training method. The lecture method provides the instructor and the learners with consistency and efficiency. It also lacks two-way communication.

Interactive lecture formats (also known as lecture games) facilitate two-way communication. They are highly motivating games, yet they give complete control to the instructor. They are also flexible. You can shift between a traditional lecture and the interactive variety with very little effort. If you know your subject area and have an outline for your presentation, you can easily convert the session into a lecture game.

BINGO LECTURE

You are attending a session on retail sales to Asian customers. You anticipate a boring presentation, but the trainer, Vandana, surprises you by giving everyone a bingo card with a 5 × 5 matrix that has words in each of the squares. Jill is seated next to you and you notice that the words on her card are arranged differently. Vandana explains that the bingo cards contain answers to questions that she plans to ask from time to time during her presentation.

Vandana begins her presentation by pointing out that the label "Asian" is too broad and proceeds to identify different types of Asians. She talks about similarities and differences among these subgroups. After 10 minutes, a timer goes off and Vandana stops her presentation—in the middle of a sentence. She announces a pop quiz and reads a question: "During which festival do people from India exchange gifts?" Vandana wants everyone to

review his or her bingo card and put a small check mark next to the correct answer. From the presentation, you vaguely recall that the name of this festival begins with the letter D. Scanning your card, you recognize Diwali as the correct answer and place a check mark next to it. After a suitable pause, Vandana gives the correct answer and asks those who checked it to place a big, bold mark on the square. Vandana now asks her next question: "Which Asian country has the largest proportion of professionals among its U.S. immigrants?"

After asking seven questions, Vandana returns to her presentation and continues from where she left off. During the next pop quiz, John shouts, "BINGO!" and claims that he has five marked squares in a straight line. Vandana congratulates him and asks him to continue playing so she can determine who has the most marked squares at the end of the session.

Types of Interactive Lectures

Interactive lectures come in a variety of types, listed in Table 4.1. Here is a brief description of each type (in terms of what you, the lecturer, do) illustrated with a few examples.

Integrated Quiz

Some interactive lecture formats feature test interludes, as in the BINGO LECTURE described above. In another format of this type called TEAM

Table 4.1. Examples of Basic Types of Interactive Lectures

Types \ Examples						
Integrated Quiz	Bingo Lecture	Crossword Lecture	Dyads and Triads	Question Cards		
Interspersed Tasks	Intelligent Interruptions	Interactive Story				
Active Summary	Best Summaries	Essence	Fictional Case Study	Idea Map	Intelligent Interludes	
Diagnosis and Prescription	Questionnaire Analysis	Glossary	Slide Sets	True or False		
Teamwork	Idea Map	Team Teach	Multilevel Coaching			
Participant Control	Item Test	Bites	Fish Bowl	Press Conference	Talk Show	Two Minds
Debriefing	Superlatives	Rapid Reflection				

Design Your Own Games and Activities

QUIZ, you deliver the lecture in your normal style. When a timer goes off (after 7 to 15 minutes), you stop the lecture. Instruct participants to organize themselves into three to five teams and ask the members of each team to compare their notes and come up with three questions based on what they heard in this segment of your lecture. After a suitable pause, select one team at random and invite its representative to read a question and to select an individual member of any other team. If this person gives the correct answer, award 2 points to the team. If this person consults with the team and then gives the correct answer, award 1 point. Repeat the process with different teams. Briefly comment on participants' questions and answers and remedy any misconceptions. Continue with your presentation, warning participants that the next quiz session will be conducted after about another 10 minutes.

Here are three more examples of the *integrated quiz* approach:

CROSSWORD LECTURE. Pair up participants and give a copy of a test disguised as a crossword puzzle. Begin your lecture and stop from time to time to provide puzzle-solving interludes. Before continuing the lecture, provide feedback and clarification based on participants' solutions.

DYADS AND TRIADS. After your presentation, ask each participant to write a closed question and an open question. Invite participants to roam around the room, playing a review game using these questions.

QUESTION CARDS. After your presentation, ask participants to write twenty short-answer questions based on the content. Collect all questions, shuffle the cards, and conduct a quiz program.

Interspersed Tasks. In some interactive lecture formats, you interrupt the presentation and ask participants to perform a task that helps them process the information you presented earlier. In INTELLIGENT INTERRUPTIONS, you stop your presentation and pause 30 seconds for everyone to get ready to make an intelligent interruption. Specifically, participants can apply the content by presenting a personal action plan, disagree by raising major issues with some idea that you presented, illustrate by providing a real or imaginary example for one of your concepts, paraphrase by listing the key points, personalize by sharing reactions to your statements, or question by firing off five or more questions about—and beyond—the recent content. After the 30-second pause, select a participant at random and ask this person to make his or her interruption for at least 30 seconds and not more than 1 minute. Repeat the procedure from time to time throughout your presentation.

Here is another example of the *interspersed task* approach:

INTERACTIVE STORY. Present a case study in the form of a story. Pause at critical junctures and invite participants to figure out what happened, why it happened, or what should happen next.

Active Summary. In some interactive lecture formats, you ask teams to summarize the key learning points at periodic intervals. In BEST SUMMARIES,

you make a series of 10-minute presentations on the training topic. At the end of each unit, distribute blank index cards and ask each participant to summarize your presentation on one side of the card. After a suitable pause, organize participants into teams and collect the summary cards from each team. Give the packet of summary cards from the first team to the second team, from the second team to the third team, and so on. Ask members of each team to collaboratively review the summaries and select the best one. Finally, ask each team to read the summary that was rated as the best.

Here are some more examples of the *active summary* approach:

ESSENCE. Ask teams to prepare a sixteen-word summary of your lecture. After listening to different summaries, ask teams to successively reduce the length of the summary to eight, four, and two words. At the end of each round, provide feedback on participants' summaries.

FICTIONAL CASE STUDY. Tell a story that illustrates different steps in a process. Invite teams to create and present their own stories, using the process as the plot line.

IDEA MAP. Train participants to take notes using an idea mapping approach. Stop the lectures at logical junctures, and instruct teams of participants to consolidate their idea maps.

INTELLIGENT INTERLUDES. Organize participants into six teams. After your presentation, ask two teams to prepare a written summary, two other teams to prepare a visual summary, and two other teams to prepare a musical summary. Ask teams to present their summaries and to vote for the best summary in the other two categories.

Diagnosis and Prescription. In some interactive lecture formats, you begin by administering a test to identify participant characteristics or gaps in their mastery of the training objective. You then make a presentation to help participants understand and make use of their characteristics or to improve their level of knowledge and skills. In QUESTIONNAIRE ANALYSIS, for example, you administer a self-scoring version of the *Myers-Briggs Type Indicator* R. You then help participants to score their responses and identify their personality types. Make a presentation on the eight preferences associated with personality types and answer questions from participants.

Here are two more examples of the *diagnosis and prescription* approach:

GLOSSARY. Present a key term related to your training content and ask teams to come up with a real or imaginary definition. Collect the definitions, insert the "official" definition somewhere in this set, read these definitions, and challenge teams to identify the correct one. Use participants' definitions to identify training needs and present a mini-lecture on the relevant topic. Repeat the process with several key terms until you have covered the relevant content.

SLIDE SETS. Prepare a series of slides to outline the presentation. Run through all slides rapidly. Then return to the first slide and pause. Ask participant teams to prepare a presentation related to that slide. Choose a team randomly to make its presentation. Add additional information. Repeat the procedure with each of the remaining slides.

TRUE OR FALSE. Display a series of statements about the topic and ask participants to decide whether each one is true or false. Present background information related to each statement.

Teamwork. In some interactive lecture formats, you ask participants to work with one another to produce a product based on your presentation. In IDEA MAP, for example, you begin by training participants how to take graphic notes using the idea-mapping technique in which the main idea is placed inside a circle in the middle of a sheet of paper. Subsequent ideas are placed inside smaller circles and linked to the main idea with lines. Begin your presentation, inviting participants to take notes using the idea-mapping technique. Stop the presentation from time to time and ask teams of participants to spend 5 minutes collaboratively drawing an idea map of the topics covered so far. Continue with your presentation and repeat the idea-mapping interludes. At the end of the presentation, invite the teams to display their final products and encourage participants to review other teams' products. Briefly comment on the common themes among different maps, identify missing elements, and correct any misconceptions.

Here are two more examples of the *teamwork* approach:

TEAM TEACH. Divide participants into two or more groups and present different parts of a procedure to different groups. Organize teams with one member from each group. Give an application exercise for each group to complete by using the procedure.

MULTILEVEL COACHING. Demonstrate a skill to a small group of participants and test them to make sure that they have mastered the skill. Ask participants to coach others to master the skill.

Participant Control. In some interactive lecture formats you let participants dictate the content and the sequence of your presentation. In ITEM LIST, for example, you provide participants with a list of guidelines, rules, or principles related to the topic. Ask participants to independently review this list and select a few items that require explanation. Select a participant at random and ask this participant to identify the selected item. Present a brief and clear explanation, using suitable examples. Continue with the items selected by a few more participants. Ask a randomly selected participant to present supportive anecdotes from personal experience. Still later, ask participants to identify potentially controversial items. Conduct a good-natured debate with a randomly selected participant, giving this participant a choice of either side in the debate. Spend the last 5 minutes responding to questions and comments from participants.

Here are some more examples of the *participant control* approach:

BITES. Make a brief 99-second introductory presentation about a technique. Ask each participant to write a question on the technique. Randomly select two participants to read their questions and ask the rest of the group to vote for the better one. Briefly respond to the question. Repeat the question-and-answer procedure to progress through your presentation.

FISH BOWL. Conduct a Socratic dialogue with an individual participant. Invite other participants to observe and learn vicariously. Replace the selected participant with new people from time to time.

PRESS CONFERENCE. Make an introductory 99-second presentation identifying key topics related to the training objective. Organize participants into teams and write a set of questions on each topic. Respond to these questions in a press conference format.

TALK SHOW. Interview a panel of experts in the role of a talk-show host. Invite participants ("the studio audience") to contribute additional questions and comments.

TWO MINDS. Ask teams to prepare a list of questions about a topic. Invite two experts to give independent responses to each question. Ask the teams to identify similarities and differences in the alternative responses.

Debriefing. In some interactive lecture formats, the lecture is integrated with a debriefing discussion of a previous activity. In the JOLT LECTURE, for example, you begin with a short experiential activity: You ask teams to come up with suggestions for marketing a new product, but you keep changing the nature of the product and the definition of the market segment every 3 minutes. After sufficiently frustrating the teams, debrief participants through a discussion of strategies for coping with rapid and continuous change.

Here are two more examples of the *debriefing* approach:

SUPERLATIVES. Ask teams to think back on the earlier experiential activity. Ask them to identify the most important, the most disturbing, the most surprising, or the most complex event they experienced in the earlier activity.

RAPID REFLECTION. After an experiential activity, ask participants to write down on a card the one most important insight they gained from it. Invite participants to exchange their cards. Randomly select a few participants and ask them to read the insight from the card they received.

The Basic Idea

While exploring and using a variety of interactive lecture formats, you should not lose sight of the basic principle: You can combine the structure and the efficiency of the lecture method with the excitement and participation of interactive strategies. The interactive lecture format provides you

with a high degree of flexibility and you should make use of this feature by constantly monitoring participant reactions and switching between the passive lecture and the active participation modes.

Ready-to-Use Interactive Lecture
INSIDE STORY

An *interactive lecture* combines the control and structure of a traditional lecture with the interest and interaction of a game. This activity is an interactive lecture called INSIDE STORY. You can use this interactive lecture format to help participants master the steps in a process and apply them to their personal situation.

Purpose

To identify the steps in a process and to explore their application to a personal project. (Example: *In a recent workshop, we used INSIDE STORY to introduce the steps in the human performance technology process.*)

Participants

Any number can play. This activity works best with twelve to thirty participants.

Time

Generally, 30 to 45 minutes. The exact time required depends on the complexity of the process and the number of steps involved.

Supplies

- Copies of a handout that explains the process, such as The Human Performance Technology Process at the end of this chapter.
- Copies of a short case study illustrating a specific application of the process, such as How We Held On to Our Best Talent at the end of this chapter.

Preparation

Master the model. Your success in using this interactive lecture format will depend on your fluency with the process model. Carefully study the model and figure out what is happening in each step and how the steps are linked to each other.

Create a story. The best way to master the model is to make up a story that illustrates the application of the process. This is what you will be asking the participants to do, and you need a sample story. For the basic format,

review the case study at the end of this chapter. You can base your story on one of your own successful projects. If you do so, don't let facts get in the way of a good story that clearly tracks your progress through the steps in the process. If you are adventurous, create a story around some popular TV show. If you are fainthearted, plagiarize the case study.

Flow

In the following section, each step in the activity is illustrated with an example from one of my recent facilitated sessions.

Brief the participants. Using your own words, present some introductory comments about the process.

Here are the introductory comments about the HPT process:

- Human performance technology is a systematic strategy for solving problems or realizing opportunities related to the performance of people.

- HPT is based on a careful analysis of the problem, identifying its underlying causes, and selecting and designing a variety of interventions.

- The HPT process can be applied to solve any problem and to profit from any opportunity.

- The HPT process can be used to improve the performance of individuals, teams, and organizations.

- While learning about specific interventions (such as training or incentive systems) is useful, it is a better idea to begin by mastering the generic steps in the HPT process.

Distribute the handout that explains the process. Point out that the handout identifies the steps in the process and the relationships among them. Ask the participants to read and review the handout. Announce a suitable time limit for this activity.

I distributed copies of the HPT process glossary (end of this chapter) and announced a 3-minute time limit.

Tell your story. At the end of the time limit, announce that you are going to tell a story of the process in action to make the abstract model become concrete. Narrate your story, pausing at the end of each section to refer to the steps in the process.

I decided to use the story from the case study (page 51) rather than make up a new story. At the end of each "chapter," I paused and related the incidents in the story to the steps of the HPT process as described in the handout.

Design Your Own Games and Activities

Distribute the case study. Explain that this case study illustrates the application of the process. Suggest that the participants refer to this case study later—after you give them an assignment.

> I distributed the case study, How We Held On to Our Best Talent, and explained that it is a printed version of the story I told them earlier.

Assign the story-creation task. Divide the participants into teams of three to five members each. It does not matter if some teams have an extra member. Ask each team to create a story of a successful application of the process. The story may be based on a team member's experience, a historical event, or some popular TV show. The story should clearly illustrate the application of different steps in the process. The teams have 11 minutes to create the story.

Conduct a storytelling session. Give the teams a 1-minute warning. Ask the teams to make finishing touches to their story and select a representative to present it to the whole group. After another minute, randomly choose a team to send its storyteller to the front of the room. Ask this person to present the story. At the conclusion of the story, select another team. Repeat the process until all teams have presented their stories.

Conclude with a caveat. Briefly comment on the stories and congratulate the teams on their depth of understanding of the process. In your own words, explain the advantages of using the systematic process. Here are some comments I made:

> The HPT process ensures that you don't leave anything to chance. It forces you to pay attention to all the necessary steps. The HPT process liberates you to try creative approaches. You can build innovative ideas on a solid foundation. The HPT process prevents you from wasting time, figuring out what to do first and what to do next. You spend your time solving the problem rather than planning to solve it. The HPT process increases your confidence. Because you know what to do and when to do it, it gives you momentum to rapidly attack the problem or profit from the opportunity.

However, point out the inherent danger in using a mechanical, step-by-step process. Warn the participants against rigid, obsessive use of the process. Using your own words, explain how to modify the standard procedure. Here are some comments I made:

> Add, delete, revise, combine, split, and rearrange the steps. For example, split the analysis step into the two steps of analyzing the performance and analyzing the performers. Enter the procedure at any point and exit at any other point. In an emergency, skip the analysis and allocation step, proceed directly to design and development, and begin to implement the intervention immediately.

Reproduced from *Design Your Own Games and Activities* by Sivasailam (Thiagi) Thiagarajan with Raja Thiagarajan with permission of the publisher. Copyright © 2003 by John Wiley & Sons, Inc.

Variations

Too little time? Divide the players into teams and distribute both handouts. Immediately assign the story-creation task and announce a 5-minute time limit. Skip the storytelling session.

Ample time? Allow plenty of time for the teams to come up with their stories. During the storytelling session, ask different teams to comment on each story.

Too many players? Conduct the early parts of the activity as usual. However, select only two or three teams to tell their stories.

Too few players? If you have only two or three players, ask them to create a joint story. With fewer than seven players, ask them to pair up with each other and work on the stories.

Human Performance Technology (HPT) Process

The HPT process consists of eight individual activities. Because some of these activities are very closely associated with others, the HPT process presents them as four steps, each integrating a pair of associated activities. The paragraphs below briefly describe each step.

ANALYSIS AND ALLOCATION

The purpose of this step is to define the performance problem, identify the probable causes of the problem, and select one or more specific HPT interventions. This step begins with an intimation of an opportunity or a performance problem. It uses a variety of data-collection techniques (including testing, observation, interviews, and analysis of existing records). At the end of this step, we obtain a clear definition of the performance problem as a gap between what should/could be and what actually is, a list of causes of this gap, and suggested HPT interventions to remove or to reduce the impact of these causes.

DESIGN AND DEVELOPMENT

The purpose of this step is to systematically design and produce HPT interventions to solve the performance problem or to realize the performance opportunity. This step begins with a clear definition of the problem, a list of probable causes, and one or more suggested interventions. It uses strategies associated with the selected intervention to prepare a blueprint, design and produce components of the HPT intervention, and integrate the components into a total package. At the end of this step, we obtain a revised HPT intervention package consisting of materials and methods that are ready for implementation.

(*Continued*)

IMPLEMENTATION AND INSTITUTIONALIZATION

The purpose of this step is to manage the change effort associated with the HPT intervention. This step begins with an intervention package. It involves preparing a plan for implementation, training local managers, implementing the package, troubleshooting transition problems, and ensuring smooth operation of the new system. At the end of this step, we obtain improved performance, increased productivity, and local commitment and capability for continuing use of the intervention.

EVALUATION AND ENHANCEMENT

The purpose of this step is to improve different materials and methods based on expert review and user feedback. This step is used in conjunction with all three earlier steps of the HPT process, especially with the design and development step. It begins with draft reports and prototype products. The step involves collecting data through expert reviews, individual tryouts, and field tests and using these data to revise the materials and methods. At the end of this step, we obtain improved reports, methods, and materials, along with data on the effectiveness of the HPT intervention.

How We Held On to Our Best Talent

CHAPTER I. THAT'S NOT THE REAL PROBLEM!

I'm an independent performance consultant. A little while back, the personnel manager of a software design company called me with a problem. The CEO of the company was concerned about the high turnover among software engineers. The personnel manager thought this was an unavoidable problem troubling the entire industry. However, the CEO wanted a motivational seminar and threatened to take drastic action if "employee loyalty does not improve soon."

I interviewed several people. In addition to the CEO and the personnel manager, I talked to employees who quit after the first year, employees who stayed on the job for more than five years, and newly recruited employees. I also reviewed the company's employment records, exit interviews, and information about employee turnover in the software industry. By analyzing the information and probing for additional information, I came up with these conclusions:

- The turnover rate in this company is greater than the industry norm. It should be possible to reduce turnover by 50 percent.

- Most of the new software engineers are tempted away from other companies with a salary that is significantly higher than their current salaries. The candidates are treated like royalty during recruitment. They receive special bonuses when they join the company. Once they join the company, however, they are frequently given uninspiring tasks to "get them used to the company's way of doing things." The pay raise at the beginning of the second year is insignificant.

Based on this analysis, I identified the cause of the performance problem as an inappropriate incentive system. I tactfully communicated my findings to the personnel manager.

(Continued)

CHAPTER II. WE'VE GOT A SOLUTION

With the approval of the personnel manager, I worked with a team of compensation and benefits specialists. We carefully reviewed the system of salaries, bonuses, incentives, and non-monetary rewards. What we found out confirmed my earlier suspicion that employees leave their jobs at the end of the first year because the incentive system does not reward them for staying with the company. We came up with alternative pay-and-reward systems and, after suitable reviews and revisions, recommended the following package:

> Recruitment of new software engineers will be less aggressive. More attention will be paid to recruiting new graduates. Recruiters will stress long-term prospects of working for the company. The beginning salary will not be significantly higher than the industry standard. There will not be any signing bonuses. Instead, new employees will be given stock options at the end of the first year. Working conditions for the new employees will be significantly improved and they will receive more attention from top management. New employees will be invited to work a third of their time on their own projects, and all initiatives will be recognized and rewarded. Annual salary increases will be significantly higher than the industry standard.

CHAPTER III. LET'S GET THIS THING MOVING

Throughout the project, we kept the CEO and top management informed of our plans and progress. We explained how we can fund the new package by a redistribution of the recruitment budget and how we can save money by avoiding the costs associated with replacing and training software engineers who left the company. We received buy-in from the top management for all major decisions. We provided information on the new recruitment and retention system to recruiters and senior managers through a briefing conducted by the CEO and personnel manager. We provided additional information through the company's intranet. We supported the new recruitment strategy with attractive brochures outlining long-term prospects of joining the company. We accompanied the company personnel during their new recruitment efforts and provided feedback on their performance. We completed our project at the end of three months.

CHAPTER IV. CONTINUOUS IMPROVEMENT

We integrated evaluation activities during all phases of the project. For example, I asked an expert on incentive systems to review my analysis report and recommendations. I made suitable revisions to the draft report on the basis of this expert's suggestions. We designed different types of compensation and incentive packages and had them reviewed by senior managers and outside experts. More importantly, we tested alternative packages with focus groups of current employees and potential recruits. We continuously improved the system until fresh focus groups rated it as the best possible package. We also tested our new recruitment brochures and revised them on the basis of reader feedback. During the first two months of implementing the new system, we made minor changes based on recruiters' feedback. Although it is too early to prove the bottom-line impact of the intervention, most old and new employees predict that the turnover rate will be drastically reduced.

5   Textra Games

Textra Games are special types of framegames that combine the effective organization of well-written documents with the motivational impact of interactive experiential activities. Participants read a handout and play a game that uses peer pressure and support to encourage recall and transfer of what they read.

EACH TEACH

In a workshop on quality management, Vince, the facilitator, briefly demonstrates how to use a Pareto chart. He then distributes a two-page handout to each participant. Your handout explains how to construct a cumulative table from a frequency table, while Joan's handout explains how to draw the Pareto curve on top of a bar graph. Vince reassures you by explaining that different participants have different handouts and asks everyone to work through the handout independently. Your handout assumes that you have already tabulated the raw data (and you don't know how to do it) and explains how to add different frequencies to keep a running total. You read the handout and complete a couple of practical exercises.

Vince now organizes you and the other participants into teams of five. Different members of your team have mastered the five different steps in the construction of a Pareto chart. Vince gives the teams unorganized data about customer complaints related to nine different products and asks the participants to construct a Pareto chart. You don't know how to begin, but your teammate Ann claims that she has mastered the first step. She proceeds to arrange the number of complaints into a table, explaining what

she is doing. When she completes the activity, you realize that you can apply your step to the table and create a column of cumulative frequencies. You explain what you are doing as you compute the cumulative frequencies. When you are done, Shane uses the table to construct a bar graph, which is apparently the next step in the activity. Eventually, your team completes the Pareto chart with everyone contributing. After you finish the first exercise, Vince gives another set of data for the second exercise, urging all team members to learn from each other. You are glad that you paid attention to the different steps because the next activity turns out to be an individual contest to see who can construct a new Pareto chart the fastest. You come in second in this contest.

In this textra game, EACH TEACH, different people learn different steps from a handout and work in team teaching and learning from each other.

More Textra Games

Here are condensed instructions for conducting three other textra games:

LEARNING TEAM. Divide the reading assignment into convenient sections and prepare a set of short-answer questions for each section. Organize the participants into teams and ask them to study the first section of the handout. Encourage team members to coach each other and get ready for a quiz game. Assign all participants to different contest groups so that each group has a representative from each team. Use the short-answer questions and conduct a quiz game among the contestants in each group. At the end of the contest, send the players back to their original teams to combine the points earned by each member. Repeat the procedure of cooperative learning and competitive contests with each section of the handout. The team with the most combined points wins the game.

MINING THE LIBRARY. Collect several books on the same topic. Ask participants to select and read one of the books, looking for immediately applicable techniques. After a suitable pause (or during the next meeting), ask each participant to find a partner and share the practical technique. Now ask each pair to review the techniques, select the more practical of the two, and share it with another pair of participants. Finally, ask each team of four to select the more practical of the two techniques and present it to the entire group.

RIPOFF. This is a textra game for exploring the broad cultural aspects of a country. Obtain copies of English-language news magazines (or newspapers) from the target country. Separate them into individual pages and distribute two or three pages to each participant. Ask participants to review the pages and write down salient cultural characteristics reflected in the news items, articles, and advertisements. Participants should write these characteristics on index cards, one item per card. After a suitable pause, collect the cards from all participants. Organize the participants into teams

and give each team equal-sized piles of cards. Now ask the teams to organize the cards into suitable clusters and identify the most salient cultural characteristics of the country. Compare the lists of characteristics generated by different teams.

Advantages and Cautions

You can plug in existing handouts and reprints to create an instant training game. Textra games combine the effective organization and independent study of written materials with the peer support and team learning of games. Different types of textra games can be used for achieving different types of instructional objectives. Don't use these games to compensate for sloppy writing and don't write review questions that emphasize recall of meaningless facts.

Ready-to-Use Textra Game
TIME TRAVEL: The Framegame

TIME TRAVEL is a textra game into which you can easily plug new content. TIME TRAVEL is best-suited for achieving training objectives that require participants to adapt and apply basic rules and principles. You can do this simply by changing the handouts while keeping the rules of the game the same. CREATIVITY PRINCIPLES, the sample TIME TRAVEL game described below, uses four short handouts exploring the principles of creative thinking. You can substitute other short handouts and create your own game.

Generic Rules

Here are the generic rules for this framegame:

- PREVIEW the principle by skimming through the handout. Then read the handout for details.

- PERSONALIZE the principle by selecting a project and applying the principle to this project.

- PROJECT into the future by visualizing what will happen five years from now as a result of the project to which you applied the principle.

- PLOT a short story that incorporates your future projection.

- PRESENT your short story to a partner. Listen to your partner's story.

- REPEAT your story to another participant who has worked with a different principle. Listen to this participant's story.

CREATIVITY PRINCIPLES

Purpose

To learn, adapt, and apply basic principles of creative thinking.

Participants

Any number can play. The best game involves twelve to forty participants.

Time

30 to 45 minutes. The exact time requirement depends on the number of handouts and the amount of time allotted to each round.

Supplies

- A set of short handouts dealing with four basic creative-thinking principles. These are reproduced at the end of this chapter and should be cut into four half-page handout masters. Reproduce copies of each handout on different colored paper.
- A timer and a whistle to help you stick to the schedule.

Flow

Distribute the handouts. Give one handout to each person, making sure that approximately equal numbers of copies of each handout are distributed.

Ask the participants to read the handouts. Give these instructions to the participants, using your own words: "Before you begin reading, think of a couple of questions to which you want to find the answers. Then, skim through the handout to get the main points. Then read for details. Underline key words and prepare an outline of the main points." Announce a 5-minute time limit and blow the whistle at the end of 5 minutes.

Ask the participants to apply what they read to a personal project. Give these instructions to the participants, using your own words: "Select a project that you are currently working on. Decide how to apply the ideas from the handout to this project. Explore how to modify these ideas to fit your goals, needs, and constraints." As before, announce a 5-minute time limit and blow the whistle at the end of 5 minutes.

Invite the participants to project themselves into the future. Give these instructions to the participants, using your own words: "Imagine that five years have passed. You have successfully completed the project with significant positive results. Imagine specific details of the impact of the project on different aspects of your life. Connect the main ideas from

Design Your Own Games and Activities

the handout to your fame and fortune five years from now." Announce a time limit of 3 minutes and blow the whistle at the end of 3 minutes.

Invite the participants to create the plot of a short story. Give these instructions, using your own words: "This story should incorporate your five-year projection that you undertook in the previous activity. The theme of the story should be about how the ideas in the handout changed your life. Come up with a plot that begins with an initial problem, proceeds through a project that incorporates ideas from the handout, details the ups and downs of this project, and dramatically ends with the successful conclusion. Make sure that it is a positive story in which you live happily ever after. Don't curb your imagination, and remember to keep linking your story back to the ideas from the handout." As before, announce a time limit of 5 minutes and blow the whistle at the end of 5 minutes.

Ask the participants to present their stories to their partners. Give these instructions, using your own words: "Find a partner who has a handout of a different color. Imagine that you accidentally meet each other after five years. You are comparing notes about the consequences of reading the handout. Take turns telling the story that you created earlier. When you are the storyteller, be enthusiastic and embellish your success. When you are the listener, congratulate your partner on his or her success." Suggest a 2-minute storytelling period for each partner. At the end of the first 2 minutes, blow the whistle and ask the partners to switch the roles of storyteller and listener. After another 2 minutes, blow the whistle again and announce the end of the storytelling period.

Ask the participants to find a new partner and repeat the process. Suggest that participants find new partners with handouts of colors different from their previous partners. Encourage the partners to embellish their success stories with more imaginary details. Remind the listeners to exaggerate their pleasure at their partner's success. Impose a 2-minute time limit for each story.

Conclude the activity. Repeat the storytelling sessions to suit the available time. Ask the participants to nominate the best storyteller for handouts of each different color and have these storytellers present their latest version to the entire group. Remind the participants that they have an opportunity for making the story come true by applying the principles from the handouts. Distribute additional copies of the handouts so that all participants have copies of all four handouts.

Design Your Own TIME TRAVEL Game

As a framegame, TIME TRAVEL is best-suited for achieving training objectives that require participants to adapt and apply basic principles.

Here are samples of suitable content for this framegame:

- Criteria for customer satisfaction
- Formulas for financial security
- Leadership behaviors
- Marketing principles
- Problem-solving techniques
- Rules for cross-cultural communication
- Team-building principles
- Time-management techniques

Use this framegame to explore several related principles rather than dealing with a single principle. The sample game described previously deals with four different principles of creative thinking.

For an effective game, use three to seven principles. If you have more than seven principles, choose six or seven of the most important ones. If necessary, play the game twice with different sets of principles.

Prepare brief handouts describing each rule. CREATIVITY PRINCIPLES uses half-page handouts. Since we want to encourage the participants to come up with personalized adaptations of these principles to their own situations, avoid the temptation to provide too many details. Do not exceed a one-page limit.

You can write your own handouts or copy materials from books (making sure to conscientiously follow all copyright requirements). Many books contain several short discussions of rules related to personal and professional development.

Walk on Both Feet!	Put Yourself Under the Gun!
Different ways of thinking have their own extremes. Thinking at the extremes is dangerous, but thinking in the middle is mediocre. To produce exciting but balanced ideas, alternate between the extremes.	Totally free thinking does not produce useful ideas. The right amount of constraints increases the usefulness and productivity of creative ideas. If there are not enough external constraints, impose them yourself.

Different ways of thinking have their own extremes. Thinking at the extremes is dangerous, but thinking in the middle is mediocre. To produce exciting but balanced ideas, alternate between the extremes.

Creative thinking is not a single type of thinking, but rather a combination of different types. At one extreme, you have to generate lots and lots of ideas. This is *divergent* thinking. At the other extreme, you have to filter down these ideas into a few useful ones. This is *convergent* thinking. Convergent thinking is the opposite of divergent thinking.

But thinking at one of the extremes can be dangerous because we end up with biased ideas. At the same time, middle-of-the-road thinking can be mediocre thinking. In the creative process, we arrive at balanced thinking by oscillating between the two extremes.

Here are some extreme positions along different dimensions of thinking:

Rational thinking involves logical and systematic thinking. You base your thoughts on verified facts. You derive your ideas using a logical process. *Intuitive* thinking involves going beyond the data and coming up with ideas that are not directly based on the verifiable facts. You base your thoughts on imagination and fantasy. You trust your instincts about the validity of your ideas.

Adaptive thinking involves accepting and working within a given set of assumptions and constraints. You come up with efficient strategies for achieving a specified set of goals while operating by an existing set of rules. *Innovative* thinking involves challenging existing assumptions and constraints. You come up with breakthrough strategies by doing different things to reach different (but worthwhile) goals and by rejecting the existing set of rules.

Analyzing involves breaking down larger objects or events into increasingly smaller ones. *Synthesizing* involves combining smaller objects or events into larger ones.

The important principle in creative thinking is to remain flexible and become fluent in all types of thinking. You should think along different dimensions and in opposing ways. Your mind should be able to hold different thoughts (even contradictory thoughts) at the same time.

Totally free thinking does not produce useful ideas. The right amount of constraints increases the usefulness and productivity of creative ideas. If there are not enough external constraints, impose them yourself.

Creative thinking is not always wild, imaginative, out-of-box thinking. There are times you should get inside the box and think in a disciplined fashion under real-world constraints.

Given total freedom, we prefer divergent, analytical, intuitive, innovative, and lateral thinking modes. We need some constraints to force us into the opposite modes of thinking to achieve a balance.

Deadlines have a powerful effect in concentrating your attention, pumping more adrenaline into your system, and making you more productive.

Necessity is the mother of invention and external constraints impose necessity. Here are a few examples of realistic constraints:

- Cramped space
- Discerning customer
- Divergent opinions
- Enforced procedures
- Finicky sponsor
- Fixed budget
- Impatient buyers
- Insufficient data
- Limited number of pages
- Minimal personnel
- Moving targets
- Tight deadline
- Tough standards

Set up your own constraints similar to those listed above. Commit yourself to these constraints, believing that they are real life-or-death issues. This should straighten up your priorities, focus your mind, and force you to work at higher levels of efficiency.

Distill Crude Ideas!	Cultivate Multiple Personalities!
There are no useless or stupid ideas. Use even the "worst" idea as the starting point for generating new practical ideas. In solving a problem or planning to profit from an opportunity, you tend to classify your ideas into "good" and "bad" categories. Then you select the good ideas and discard the bad ones. Sometimes you do this consciously, and sometimes unconsciously. A paradox in creative thinking is that most "good" ideas are actually bad ones and "bad" ideas contain the best ones. This is because "good" ideas typically match your conventional notions and make you feel comfortable. Implementing these ideas can only strengthen the traditional approach. In contrast, because "bad" ideas make you uncomfortable, by definition, they suggest unconventional approaches. Work on these ideas to come up with breakthrough strategies. An effective technique in creative thinking is to treat "bad" ideas as starting points for generating good ones. Use them to provoke you into thinking along different lines. Free associate with these ideas until you come up with more that are unconventional and yet practical. Here's an example of an apparently stupid idea for satisfying the customers in your restaurant: Turn off the lights. Using this stupid idea as a starting point, we can come up with these other ideas: • Use candles instead of fluorescent light. • Provide an optimum level of privacy to permit couples to indulge in romantic behavior without embarrassment. • Darkness accentuates the other senses. Appeal to the other senses by perfuming the air, providing soft chairs, serving spicy food, and piping in soft music. • Waiters and patrons stumble in darkness. Lay out the room and the furniture in an obstacle-free fashion. • Turning the lights off surprises people. Provide pleasant surprises to your patrons such as having the waiters tip the customers (with gift certificates for a free dinner). • Turning the lights off may frighten some customers. Make a list of things that may frighten customers and remove them.	Look at a situation from diverse points of view to come up with creative ideas. If you don't have access to a diverse team, simply play different roles yourself. Diverse teams produce powerful, creative ideas because their members look at a problem (or an opportunity) from different vantage points. However, such teams present logistic problems in getting organized. We can benefit from diversity without the hassle of organizing a cross-cultural or cross-functional team simply through creative role playing. This strategy involves assuming different personalities and thinking from different points of view. Edward de Bono, a prolific writer on creativity, has developed a technique called *six thinking hats* in which people put on one of six different hats and use a thinking mode associated with that hat. For example, a white hat is associated with objective thinking while a red hat is associated with emotional thinking. You can increase your creativity by assuming different personalities and perspectives and training yourself to think in that role. You can change from one role to another to increase the number of ideas and their quality. Here are some dimensions along which you may assume appropriate roles: • Age (examples: *7-year-old boy and 80-year-old woman*) • Culture and ethnicity (examples: *African* and *Australian*) • Customer type (examples: *longstanding loyal customer* and *new customer*) • Gender (examples: *male* and *female*) • Personality (examples: *introvert* and *extrovert*) • Political preference (examples: *liberal* and *conservative*) • Primary value (examples: *economy* and *quality*) • Profession (examples: *accountant* and *artist*) • Reaction to change (examples: *innovator* and *resister*) • Social class (examples: *rich* and *poor*) • Time perspective (examples: *focused on long-term results* and *impatient for immediate results*)

6 Item Processing

Item processing is a special type of textra game in which individuals and teams generate, organize, and sequence ideas, facts, questions, complaints, or suggestions. As a result of the activity, participants create organized lists of items. More importantly, this activity enables participants to construct meaningful categories and sequences from isolated items. This results in deeper understanding and easier recall of the content.

TENSES

You and other members of your team are attending a training session called Achieving Your Vision. You have no clue about the content of the session, and your confusion is further increased when Patti, the facilitator, begins an activity called TENSES.

Patti gives everyone a piece of paper with ten lines. She says, "Think about the work-related activities that you did yesterday. Write down ten of these activities, using short words or phrases like attend staff meeting or submit reimbursement form." You begin your list with "Attend my performance review meeting" because that was the most memorable thing that happened yesterday. You add more items like "Lunch meeting with John."

When everyone is ready, Patti continues: "I want you to classify each activity according to whether it was in the past, present, or future tense. Let me explain: For example, if I had lunch with a client to apologize for failing

to meet a deadline, it was about the past. If I had a lunch to discuss our plan for the next quarter, it was about the future. And if I had a lunch with a client just because I enjoy talking with her, it was about the present. Once you have decided on the tense, give it a '1' if it is about the past, give it a '5' if it is about the present, and a '9' if it is about the future. Of course, you may not be able to categorize an activity exclusively in one of these three time frames. So use any number between 1 and 3 to refer to the past, between 4 and 6 to refer to the present, and between 7 and 9 to refer to the future."

You return to your list and begin with the performance review. It was supposed to be about future goals, but your manager and you spent most of the time attacking and defending your past behavior. So you give it a "2." You continue with each of the other activities in your list.

Patti announces the next step: She wants you to add up the numbers and divide the total by 10. When you do so, you find that your average is 3.1. Patti explains that the number indicates in which of the three tenses—past, present, or future—you primarily work. You are irritated because you always wanted to be a futuristic person, but the average seems to indicate that you live in the past.

Before you can go back and change the original numbers, Patti wants you to identify the three most important activities on your list. The numbers associated with these activities range from 6 to 8. So most of your important activities are future-oriented. Next Patti asks you to identify the three most time-consuming activities. You discover that you spend most of your time in the past. Patti now asks you to identify the three most enjoyable activities in your list. They turn out to be present- and future-related activities.

Patti announces that she is going to move on to a team activity. You are frightened about divulging your secret thoughts to other people. Fortunately, however, Patti wants the team to identify and process team activities during the last month.

Uses and Limitations

When I design training materials, I wade through a lot of facts, concepts, numbers, strategies, principles, steps, and other types of "items." I analyze, compare, organize, and sequence these items and convert them into neat little handouts, diagrams, and bullet charts. In this process, I learn a lot about the training topic. And my participants receive logically structured, tightly edited, easy-to-understand pieces of text.

Recently, however, I have started giving participants the original, disorganized collection of items and have them go through the training design process that I have been using. In some cases, I even ask my participants to generate original sets of items and then process them. The results have been impressive. Participants like the activity and learn more from it (as measured by having them present the content and discuss its

application to the workplace). In hindsight, the reason is obvious. As they struggle to make sense of the bits of information, participants construct their own structure and organize their own meaning. The final organization of the content belongs to them. They own the content!

Item processing has some limitations. It requires more time than the time needed to "cover" the same content using a set of bullet-point slides. *Suggestion: Don't use this approach with unimportant content.*

Participants want the "correct answer" because they are not confident about the way they organized the content. *Suggestions: Give your version of the final product after they have constructed their version. Discuss discrepancies between your version and their version.*

Participants don't have the experience and expertise to generate their own content. *Suggestion: Limit this strategy to topics about which participants have enough background.*

Participants may be unaware of critical situations and ignore items related to them. *Suggestion: Add expert-generated items with participant-generated items before they begin processing.*

Used appropriately, the item processing strategy can produce impressive learning outcomes. Its effectiveness is just another example of the power of changing the role of learners to be temporary designers.

Types of Item Processing Activities

You can design and use a wide variety of item processing activities. Here are some of the variable factors:

Types of Item. The key component of any item processing activity is a set of items. These items may contain different forms, presented in different formats, and come from different sources.

Item Content. The items in the TENSES game described above were work activities. In other activities, the items may take a variety of forms, such as rules of thumb, customer needs, team values, market characteristics, controversial statements, consumer complaints, technical standards, cultural patterns, organizational policies, and critical data.

Item Format. The items in the TENSES game were written on a piece of paper. The items in your activity may be written on separate cards, printed in a handout, listed on a poster, displayed on computer screen, or transmitted as an e-mail message.

Item Source. The items in the TENSES game came from participants themselves. Other sources of items include experts, stakeholders, and customers. The items may be generated just for the activity through an interview or a questionnaire or they may be borrowed from such existing sources as books, manuals, and company records.

Types of Processing. Another important factor in these activities is the nature of processing. In the TENSES game, participants classified the

items into three main categories (past, present, and future) and several subcategories. Here are other approaches:

- *Organizing.* Participants cluster the items in different ways.
- *Tabling.* Participants create a suitable table and place the items in appropriate boxes.
- *Evaluating.* Participants evaluate the items by rating them or ranking them into categories ranging from the best to the worst.
- *Sequencing.* Participants arrange the items in a sequenced list in order of priority, importance, cost, or benefit.

Interactions. Another important factor in an item processing activity is the nature of interaction among participants. In the early part of the TENSES game, participants worked independently. In the second part of the game, they moved into an interactive team-based procedure. Depending on the type of items and your purpose, you may use individual processing, processing with a partner, and teamwork. You may also combine these types of interactions.

Ready-to-Use Item Processing Activity
SILENT MOVIES

Those of you who work in the area of quality management or creative problem solving will recognize SILENT MOVIES as an affinity diagramming activity in which participants sort, classify, and organize different items on cards. In addition to organized brainstormed data, affinity diagramming enables participants to learn more about a topic, its elements, and interrelationships.

The version of SILENT MOVIES described below deals with training design guidelines. You can conduct SILENT MOVIES with a similar set of items accumulated over a period of time or generated through just-in-time brainstorming.

Participants

Any number. Best for ten to thirty.

Time

30 to 60 minutes, depending on the number of items.

Materials

- Sets of items written individually on cards, one set for each team. (Copy the content items from Training Design: Faster, Cheaper, and Better on page 67.)

- Handout, SILENT MOVIES Instructions (page 66), one copy for each participant
- Blank index cards
- Paper clips

Flow

Organize teams. Divide the participants into at least two teams, each with at least three members.

Brief participants. Distribute copies of the instruction sheet to all participants. Ask them to read the instructions individually. After a suitable pause, clarify the instructions as needed.

Distribute the items. Give one complete set of item cards to each team. Briefly explain the nature of the items.

Coordinate the activity. Ask teams to begin their task and organize the item cards. Announce a suitable time limit. Move among the team observing the activities. Keep track of the time.

Conclude the activity. Blow the whistle at the end of the time limit. Ask teams to arrange their item cards and headings on the table and invite participants to review other teams' products.

Debrief the activity. Discuss the similarities and differences among different teams' arrangements of the same content items. Also ask participants to reflect back on the activity and share their insights about the topic.

SILENT MOVIES Instructions

- Take ten cards from the pile and spread them on the table, written side up.
- Stand around the table and silently read the ideas on the cards.
- Sort the cards silently and independently, using the guidelines below.
- Review other participants' actions. Move cards from one location to another to improve the arrangement.
- However, do not talk to the other team members.
- When you have sorted the initial set of ten cards, spread the other cards, written side up. Repeat the same procedure.

Guidelines

Duplicate Idea

If two cards contain exactly the same idea (but are worded differently), combine them into a single item by attaching them with a paper clip.

> *Review what someone else has done similarly and use the ideas. Look at similar courses and borrow the design.*

Similar Idea

If two cards contain similar ideas (but not exactly the same ones), place them near each other.

> *Collect and store templates for different types of training materials and use them when appropriate. Look at similar courses and borrow the design.*

More than One Idea

If a single card contains more than one idea (written as one or more sentences), divide them into two cards by copying one of the ideas on a blank card and crossing it out from the other card.

> *Make a videotape of a master performer doing the job, show this model to learners, and coach them in how an idea is divided into these two cards. Show a videotape model to learners and coach them in how to perform the task.*

Different Idea

If a card contains an idea that is different from the previous ones, place it away from the other cards.

> *Use the Internet for research if an idea is different from any of the earlier ones so it will be set aside from the other cards.*

What to Do After All Cards Have Been Sorted Out

- You may begin talking to each other. Briefly discuss the arrangement with the other team members. Make suitable changes and improvements.
- Review the cards in each cluster. Come up with a suitable heading for the cluster. Write this on a card and place it on top of the cluster.
- Count the total number of clusters.
- If you have fewer than five clusters, perhaps it is too few. Review the cluster with the most cards and divide them into two different clusters. Write new heading cards for these clusters.
- If you have more than nine clusters, you have too many. Review the clusters with the fewest cards and combine them into a single cluster.
- Review the cards in each cluster and arrange them in some logical order.

Design Your Own Games and Activities

Training Design:
Faster, Cheaper, and Better

Content for item cards:

1. Focus on activities and exercises. Relate existing documentation to these exercises instead of creating new training materials.
2. Don't bother with needs analysis. Assume that training is the appropriate answer.
3. Brainstorm with end users to find their wish lists of the perfect product.
4. Don't bring different subject-matter experts into the same room. Interact with them through e-mail messages.
5. Start with the end goal in mind and work backward.
6. Before beginning, ask yourself what you want the learners to be able to do after training.
7. Design your assessment at the same time as creating your objectives.
8. Limit input to the fewest subject-matter experts necessary to accomplish the training objective.
9. Start each design with this idea in mind: "Learning is the creating of meaning–not the consumption of knowledge."
10. Know your audience!
11. Focus on what the trainee needs to learn.
12. Figure out what you need your learners to know. Prioritize the outcomes.
13. Review other participants' actions. Move cards from one location to another to improve the arrangement. However, do not talk to the other team members.
14. Don't "design" it; just deliver it using whatever materials you currently have access to.
15. Write the Facilitator Guide first. Then prepare other materials needed to teach the course.
16. Don't reinvent the wheel.
17. Use question cards explaining what will be taught. Have the students take the materials; use cards as an example of how the information will be used.
18. Keep it simple and to the point.
19. Avoid working with (or working in) committees.
20. Make an outline, but work backward from the result to content.
21. Combine design and evaluation.
22. Involve discussion and brainstorming (learning from each other) as the core training methodology.
23. Form a team of subject-matter experts, designers, writers, word processors, graphic artists, and programmers at the beginning of the project. Make sure that everyone is involved from the start.
24. Encourage the subject-matter expert and the learner to talk and listen to each other.
25. Let the designer control the instructional design process.
26. Hire an expert performer to be the instructional designer. Have this person design and develop the training course.

(Continued)

27. Interact with your learners throughout the design phase.
28. Have the subject-matter expert look at the outline before beginning to design the training.
29. Identify the needs. Contact similar organizations that may have training already in place. Modify the design.
30. Have the subject-matter experts facilitate a training session. Document what they do during the class and use this as the outline for the new course.
31. Combine the analysis and design phases. They tend to blur together anyhow.
32. Set up an opportunity for learners to practice using the skill to be learned.
33. Reuse what works as a template.
34. Have subject-matter experts design the course using design templates.
35. Keep instructional methods highly interactive and activity-based.
36. Be very focused on the performance problem.
37. Stay focused on the original request. Don't "branch out" from the request when you conduct the analysis.
38. Ask the clients what they want and brainstorm the design immediately.
39. Automate the process. Use computers in all stages.
40. Use a team to share ideas and perform different tasks associated with instructional design.
41. Key in on a main concept, simplify it, break it down, and deliver it logically.
42. Look at similar courses and borrow the design.
43. Involve subject-matter experts and learners together in brainstorming sessions.
44. Eliminate the instructional designer from the process.
45. Use a timetable to keep developers on track.
46. Create objectives as you go. Create the design without creating the entire architecture.
47. Identify activities that embody the content.
48. Know your subject matter. Start the training session and invite learners to ask questions. Respond to these questions. Fill in additional information as needed.
49. Design with the end in mind.
50. Utilize ideas from a smaller group of the total audience regarding what the training should look like.
51. Get learners to make up case studies and scenarios for each other to practice.
52. Determine up-front with the client what results are required.
53. Videotape a subject-matter expert. Use it as the core of the training package.
54. Observe a subject-matter expert coaching a learner. Use this process as the basis for your training course.
55. Ask the instructional developer to teach the course.
56. Make the students design the course.
57. Consult with subject-matter experts.
58. Keep the training material simple and specific to the training objectives.
59. Create reusable knowledge objects that can contain information and interactivity. Use these objects for multiple purposes.

Design Your Own Games and Activities

60. Develop content as you implement the training program. First, write a skeleton of content by classifying the training objective. Hit main issues for instructor to cover with a couple of practice examples. Then implement the course and flesh it out.
61. Prepare an outline of entire course first.
62. Let people create their own learning designs with templates. Upload them on the web.
63. Get input from your customers throughout.
64. Trim "fat" out of your design. Only teach the most relevant material.
65. Talk to the manager who ordered the training material. Then talk to two or three future users of it.
66. Observe your students in their work setting.
67. Design instruction on a topic that interests you.
68. Talk directly to the target audience.
69. Start with a rough draft version of the training program. Try it out with the first group and make suitable changes.
70. Have subject-matter experts write about the most important skill to be learned.
71. Break instruction down into simple, concise concepts.
72. Focus on the performance needed. Begin at the end and work backward.
73. Use a monster search engine to quickly filter ideas.
74. Get to the point right away. Teach what specifically needs to be learned.
75. Develop a rapid prototype. Test and refine this prototype.
76. Complete the design using the same team of people.
77. Clearly define the objectives and outcomes.
78. Reduce the number of people involved in the process.
79. Focus on what you want the learner to be able to do differently.
80. Clearly find out who you are writing for.
81. Write fast.
82. Have subject-matter experts create the learning objectives based on a predetermined formula.
83. Ask a subject-matter expert to build the course. Use this version for the basic content and add suitable activities.
84. Combine steps in the design process.
85. Determine the single most important objective of the proposed course. Focus on it.
86. Identify resources to assist in developing objectives, such as subject-matter experts, target audience, written materials, policies, observations on the job, and feedback.
87. Write the test questions first and get agreement from a subject-matter expert. Then teach the answers to the test.
88. Understand the objective.
89. Shorten whatever you plan to present. Plan time for Q&A and brainstorming.
90. Reduce the number of objectives.
91. Have faith in your gut feeling for what is needed.

(*Continued*)

92. Write test questions at the same time as you write objectives.
93. Leverage as much information as you can from other similar reliable sources.
94. Skip the task analysis step. Begin with the design and do the necessary analysis just in time.
95. Create design templates, using an authoring system for computer-based instruction.
96. Ask the learners what they need to know.
97. Determine what you want to say and say it. Then ask students to say it back.
98. Gather a couple of key ideas from a subject-matter expert and build a course around these concepts.
99. Have the learners design the specification for the training content. Also have the learner write parts of the training content.
100. Ask the learners to "perform" as part of training. Then they "know" they can do it, because they have done it.
101. Work with the end users. Get their input.
102. Make it personal: Involve the participants physically, mentally, and emotionally.
103. Have a few representative learners write down what they want to learn and how they want to learn it.
104. Quickly jot down major ideas, outline these ideas, and fill in details.
105. Make training activity-based, not presentation-based. Presentations should exist only to support activities.
106. Facilitate on-the-job learning. Avoid training.
107. Eliminate the middle man. Link up the subject-matter expert with learners.
108. Find out the problems your users are calling for help with and put them in your instructional materials.
109. Break down the knowledge and skills into small nuggets to be maximally flexible in the final training presentation.
110. Storyboard the process.
111. Ask learners to write down a brief, specific example of an effective, proven method for performing a task.
112. Begin with the end in mind.
113. Involve the learners in the design process continuously, not just at the end.
114. Don't wait for needs assessment to be completely documented before moving on to other activities.
115. Combine task analysis with objective writing and evaluation strategies.
116. "Steal" similar materials from other related courses.
117. Cut out layers of bureaucracy and regulatory requirements.
118. Start with the end in mind.
119. Prioritize the tasks and work on need-to-know materials before nice-to-know materials.
120. Create a template and have a subject-matter expert fill in the blanks.
121. Immediately interview and involve a subject-matter expert.
122. Begin with a specific end result.

123. Briefly discuss the arrangement with other team members. Make suitable changes and improvements.
124. Define your target audience. Based on the definition of the audience (with a small group), determine what tasks they need to perform.
125. Hit each step in the systematic approach to instructional design very briefly. For example, just interview one learner and make that your complete learner analysis.
126. Ask all subject-matter experts to re-evaluate procedures and eliminate unnecessary steps. Then teach a more efficient procedure.
127. Picture the desired end product and work backward to the beginning step.
128. Copy and steal everything.
129. Make an outline and develop the course from this outline. Make changes in the outline where needed.
130. Start with each objective and create an engaging exercise that targets that objective.
131. Get all team members involved from the beginning. Don't add new players to the team later.
132. Combine the analysis and design phases. Several other phases could be combined also.
133. Use your test questions to measure the achievement of the training objectives. If the questions make no sense, neither do the objectives.
134. Modify another training product.
135. Spend time at the beginning of the project to clearly define the instructional objectives, desired results, and audience.

7 Video Vitamins

Video Vitamins are special types of framegames that enhance the instructional value of training videos. In a typical video vitamin, participants watch a videotape and then play one or more games that help them review, reflect on, and apply the new values, concepts, and skills.

KEY POINTS

Bill is facilitating a video vitamin activity called KEY POINTS with a group that includes you. The activity is designed around a training video, Team Building: What Makes a Good Team Player. This 19-minute video, produced by CRM Films, features a boat-building scenario in which the team's progress is stalled largely due to style differences among its members. Host Glenn Parker describes how the problem is created by different team-member styles (contributor, collaborator, communicator, and challenger) and explains how each different style actually adds value to the team. The story has a happy ending when the team converts its member-style differences into valuable assets.

Before showing the video, Bill asks participants to note key points as they watch the video by taking notes on a sheet of paper throughout the video session. When the video ends, Bill asks participants to organize themselves into teams of five. There are six teams in the room and your team includes Alan, Barbara, Chuck, and Debra. Bill now asks each team to come up with a consensus list of the top ten key points from the video. Before you get started, however, Bill outlines a special scoring system: Each item in each team's list will receive a specific number of points that equals

the number of teams with the same (or similar) point. For example, if all six teams listed the key point, "Challengers prevent the team from taking unnecessary risks," then each team gets 6 points for that item. However, if only one team came up with the key point, "The label for all team-member styles begin with the letter C," then that team gets a single point for the item. Bill encourages all teams to think in terms of what the other teams would identify as key points.

You find the scoring system slightly confusing, but Barbara assures you that she can explain it later. So your team members go through individual notes and record a dozen key points on a flip chart. After 5 minutes, Bill announces a 1-minute warning. You remove two of the key points from your list to come up with the top ten.

Bill asks teams to take turns reading one key point at a time. After the first item is read, Bill asks how many other teams have the same or similar key point. Since your team has the same key point (stated in slightly different words), you raise your hand. All teams receive 6 points for this popular key point because it is on every team's list. Bill repeats the procedure and awards different numbers of points for different items depending on the number of teams choosing it. At the end of the session, your team has a total of 17 points, which turns out to be the second highest score.

During debriefing, Bill asks participants if they can guess the primary team-member style of the other members in their team. You are sure that Barbara is a communicator and you are surprised when Chuck classifies you as a challenger.

Uses and Limitations

Videos are second only to lecture presentations as a popular training method. Hundreds of training videos are commercially available. In addition, trainers use excerpts from popular movies to illustrate such concepts as leadership, communication, teamwork, and sexual harassment. Corporate training departments produce their own videos, ranging from the CEO explaining the mission of the organization to a focus group discussing customer expectations.

The major advantage of video is the standardization of the training content. The major disadvantage is that most video-based training tends to be passive. This is where video vitamins enhance the instructional value with focused activities, just like interactive lectures enhance presentations and read.me games enhance handouts.

Here are some suggestions for increasing the instructional effectiveness of video vitamins:

- Select the most appropriate game structure to suit the training topic and participant characteristics.

- Before showing the video, brief participants about what they should watch out for.

- After showing the video, get into the video vitamin without unnecessary explanations.

- If the video vitamin involves role playing, be sure to debrief participants. Give some time for everyone to come out of role before the debriefing discussion.

Here are some caveats about the use of video vitamins:

- Don't use videos just because they are available and interesting. Make sure that the video has relevance to the training objective.

- Don't use a lengthy video in its entirety. Show just the relevant segments.

- Don't make the video vitamin too complex or lengthy.

Types and Examples

Bill Matthews provides a convenient classification system for video vitamins, depending on the type of video that is used:

> *Story line* videos tell a story. This type includes several training videos and all of commercial videos. *Case study* videos are similar to story line videos. However, the stories they tell are real events from the workplace or authentic reconstructions. *Talking-head* videos present a lot of information about a specific topic. Sometimes they tend to be a "data-dump."

Video vitamins that work best with story line videos involve rewriting the story, anticipating the ending, or stepping into the role of different characters. Here are two examples of this type of video vitamin from Bill Matthews:

IN THE END. Before showing the video, ask participants to pretend to be scriptwriters and to pay particular attention to the story line. Stop the tape at a suitable point and ask teams to create their own versions of how the story ends. After a suitable pause, ask each team to present a synopsis of the rest of the action. Roll tape to show the actual ending. Identify the winning team that created the ending closest to the actual ending. Debrief by comparing alternative endings.

RASHOMON. The frame for this activity is based on Akira Kurosawa's 1951 classic Japanese movie, *Rashomon*, in which the same incident is recollected in distinctively different ways by the four major characters (a samurai, his wife, a bandit, and a woodcutter). At the beginning of this video vitamin, assign different key roles from the video's story line to each participant. Ask participants to watch the story from the assigned point of view. After the video, assemble participants into same-role teams and have them reconstruct the story from that character's point of view. After a suitable pause, ask teams to present the different versions. Debrief by focusing on cultural and individual differences.

KEY POINTS, the video vitamin described earlier, works effectively with a case-study video. Here's another video vitamin from Bill Matthews for use with case studies:

A SIMPLE TWIST OF FATE. This video vitamin is for the "what-if" phase in debriefing. Brief participants to pay particular attention to various factors that influence the results in the case study. After the video, ask participants to speculate on the consequences of one of these factors being different (example: *team members are from different national backgrounds*). Pause for a suitable time and have participants share their speculations with a partner. Repeat the process by changing other factors, one at a time. Finally, debrief by focusing on factors that influence the outcomes in participants' workplace.

If we consider talking-head videos as packaged lectures, we may use interactive lecture formats.

QUIZ INTERLUDE. Ask participants to take notes as they watch the video. Pause the tape after 7 to 10 minutes and ask teams to come up with three closed questions and one open question based on the content from the video. After a 3-minute pause, invite a randomly selected team to ask a closed question and to select a member of another team to respond. Award two points for a correct answer. Invite another team to ask its open question. Give all teams 30 seconds to prepare a response. Ask the questioning team to select a team and invite its spokesperson to give the response. Now ask another team for an alternate response. The questioning team decides which response is better and awards points to the team that provided it. Repeat the same process after playing each of the subsequent segments of the video.

Ready-to-Use Video Vitamin
BOOSTERS AND BASHERS

Here is a preview of the game: During the first phase, participants anonymously reveal their attitude toward the content of the video program. During the second phase, they make exaggerated presentations about the advantages and disadvantages associated with the content of the video program. During the third phase, they brainstorm strategies for enhancing the advantages and reducing the disadvantages.

Purpose

To objectively evaluate the concept or technique presented in a video program and to discover ways of enhancing its advantages and reducing its disadvantages.

Participants

Three or more, divided into groups of three participants. Best game is played with fifteen to thirty participants.

Time

30 minutes to 1 hour.

Materials

- Copies of the Instruction Sheets from the end of this chapter (one copy for each participant)
- A transparency of the Reaction Rating Scale (end of this chapter)
- Worksheet for Computing the Average Rating (end of chapter)
- Blank sheets of paper

Flow
Phase 1. Attitude Check

Brief the players. Explain that the first phase of the game explores participant reactions to the content of the video program. You will be collecting anonymous initial reactions from everyone to get the game started.

Label the content. Identify the main message presented in the video program. This could be a strategy, concept, technique, process, or value. Come up with a suitable label for this content (example: *leadership, celebrating diversity, the Internet, empowerment, or customer satisfaction*).

Collect reaction data. Project the 9-point Reaction Rating Scale on the screen or copy it on a sheet of flip-chart paper. Ask each participant to select a number between 1 and 9 (both numbers inclusive) to indicate his or her current reaction to the content of the video program. Instruct participants to write this number of a small piece of paper, fold it, and give it to you.

Ask for predictions. After a suitable pause, collect all pieces of paper with the reaction ratings. Invite participants to look around the room and try to guess other people's attitudes along the 9-point scale. Ask them to make a prediction of the average rating of all participants, correct to two decimal places.

Assign individual work. After another suitable pause, ask each participant to prepare a two-column table and list the advantages along one column and the disadvantages along the other. Encourage participants to take this task seriously because it will help them during the next phase of the game.

Identify the winning predictor. While participants are working on their assignment, use the Worksheet for Computing the Average Rating to tabulate the reaction ratings and compute the average. When ready, identify the participant who made the closest prediction by revealing the average gradually, building up the suspense. For example, if the average is 6.42, ask participants who made a prediction between 3 and 9 to stand up. Then ask participants with a prediction between 5 and 8 to remain standing. Continue with increasingly closer ranges such as 5.5 to 7.5, 6 to 7, 6.25 to 6.75, and 6.4 to 6.5. Award the Outstanding Psychic title to the person who made the closest prediction.

Phase 2. Structured Dialogues

Brief the players. Explain that this phase of the game will require participants to play the roles of enthusiastic boosters and cynical bashers of the video content. The goal of this phase is to help everyone evaluate the video content with realistic enthusiasm and healthy skepticism.

Form triads. Ask participants to organize themselves into groups of three. Instruct members of each triad to stand at some convenient space, a little bit away from the others.

Assign roles. Identify the tallest member in each triad. She will be the first Listener. The person to her right will be the Booster, and the person to her left will be the Basher.

Explain the procedure. Explain that this phase of the game will be played in three rounds, with each member of the triad assuming a different role in each round. During a round, the Booster and the Basher will take turns trying to persuade the Listener to acquire an extremely positive or an extremely negative attitude toward the content of the video program. In this fast-paced activity, participants will have to think rapidly on their feet because they will have only 45 seconds to make their impassioned presentations.

Preview the steps. Distribute copies of the three Instructions sheets and explain that each sheet corresponds to one of the three roles. Ask each participant to follow along the instructions for his or her role as you present the steps. Explain what different people do during the question, answer, presentation, and scoring steps.

Conduct the first round. Check to see if the Listener in each triad has a watch to time the 45-second presentations. Begin the activity by asking the Listener to randomly select one of the other two triad members. This person immediately asks a single question and the listener gives a brief answer.

Design Your Own Games and Activities

Then the speaker extols the virtues of the content of the video program (if she is a Booster) or exaggerates the negative aspects (if she is a Basher). The Listener listens carefully and calls time after 45 seconds. The other member of the triad now repeats the procedure of asking a question, listening to the answer, and making the 45-second presentation. Finally, the Listener secretly distributes 7 points between the Booster and the Basher.

Continue the activity. Walk among different triads, listening to the presentations. Remind participants that the Listener in each round becomes the Booster during the next round. Help participants change their roles and continue the activity.

Determine the winner. At the end of three rounds, ask all three triad members to open the point distribution sheets they received. Instruct participants to add up the points and to identify the high scorer in each triad. Also identify the person with the highest score among all triads and award him or her the title, Best Speaker from Both Sides of the Mouth.

Phase 3. Action Planning

Brief the players. Explain that the purpose of the third phase is to share the insights and information gained during the earlier rounds. There will not be any winners during this round, but all participants will benefit from it.

Combine the triads. Reorganize participants into teams of five. Encourage each team to include members from as many different teams as possible.

Assign team task. Remind participants of the two-column table (of the advantages and disadvantages) that they constructed during the first phase. Ask teams to construct a similar table by combining what individual members learned during earlier phases of the game. Announce a suitable time limit.

Construct a common table. At the end of the time limit, draw a two-column table on a sheet of flip-chart paper. Invite teams to take turns calling out an advantage or a disadvantage related to the content of the video program. Record these items in the appropriate column of the table.

Discuss implementation ideas. Ask participants to review the two-column table. Invite them to come up with strategies for maximizing the advantages and minimizing the disadvantages. Discuss these ideas and come up with an action plan for implementing them in the participants' organization.

Reproduced from *Design Your Own Games and Activities* by Sivasailam (Thiagi) Thiagarajan with Raja Thiagarajan with permission of the publisher. Copyright © 2003 by John Wiley & Sons, Inc.

Instructions to the Listener

In the Beginning
Find two other participants and form a triad. Stand at a convenient location facing the other two members of your triad.

You Are the Listener
During the first round, you will be the Listener if you are the tallest member of the triad. During the other two rounds, the person who was the Booster during the previous round will become the Listener. Whenever you are a Listener, stand between the other two members of your triad.

Listen to the First Presentation
During each round, the person standing to the left of the Listener is the Booster and the other person is the Basher. As the Listener, you randomly point to either the Booster or the Basher. This person asks you a single question (that will help her determine how to persuade you). Give a brief answer. Immediately after your response, the person who asked the question should begin talking, boosting or bashing the message presented in the video. Note the time, listen to the presentation, and cut it off after 45 seconds by saying, "Time's up!"

Listen to the Second Presentation
After the first presentation, point to the other triad member. This person will repeat the earlier procedure of asking a question, listening to your answer, and presenting her message for 45 seconds.

Score the Presentations
As soon as the second person stops talking, quickly decide how to distribute 7 points between the Booster and the Basher to reflect the relative merit of their presentations. Don't let your personal attitude toward the message on the videotape bias your judgment. Secretly write the points you want to award on two small pieces of paper, fold them, and give them to the Booster and the Basher. Make sure that they do not open the point-distribution sheets until later.

Get Ready for the Next Round
During the next round, you will play the role of the Booster. The Basher in the previous round will become the Listener. Think of a useful question to ask while waiting for the Listener to randomly select between you and the Basher.

Instructions to the Booster

In the Beginning
Find two other participants and form a triad. Stand at a convenient location facing the other two members of your triad.

You Are the Booster
During each round, one of the triad members will play the role of the Listener. If you are standing to the left of the Listener, you will assume the role of the Booster. Your task is to persuade the Listener to feel positive toward the message presented in the video. (The other member of your triad, the Basher, will be trying to make the Listener feel negative.) You have to think fast on your feet since you have no time to prepare the message and only 45 seconds to present it. However, you will have a chance to ask the Listener a single question to determine how to position your message.

Wait for Your Turn
The Listener will select you or the Basher to go first. If the Basher goes first, carefully listen to her message, mentally preparing suitable counter-arguments to present during your turn. Also think of a simple open-ended question that will elicit useful information about how to persuade the Listener to your way of thinking.

Ask Your Question
Use a simple open-ended question that probes the Listener's values and beliefs about the content presented in the video. Listen carefully to the response.

Make Your Presentation
Immediately launch into your presentation, linking your statements to the Listener's response. Emphasize the benefits and advantages of the concepts and processes presented in the video. If you had heard the Basher's presentation earlier, try to remove or reduce its impact through logical counter-arguments. Remember that you have only 45 seconds. Be selective about the points that you want to make—instead of trying to speak fast.

Receive Your Score
As soon as both you and the Basher have made your presentations, the Listener will distribute 7 points between the two of you to reflect the relative merit of the presentations. The Listener will give you a folded piece of paper with the number of points awarded to you. Do not open this piece of paper until everyone has played all three roles.

Get Ready for the Next Round
During the next round, you will play the role of the Basher. (The Basher in the previous round will become the Listener.) Think of a useful question to ask while waiting for the new Listener to randomly select between you and the Booster.

Instructions to the Basher

In the Beginning Find two other participants and form a triad. Stand at a convenient location facing the other two members of your triad.

You Are the Basher During each round, one of the triad members will play the role of the Listener. If you are standing to the right of the Listener, you will assume the role of the Basher. Your task is to persuade the Listener to feel highly negative toward the message presented in the video. (The other member of your triad, the Booster, will be trying to make the Listener feel highly positive.) You have to think fast on your feet since you have no time to prepare the message and only 45 seconds to present it. However, you will have a chance to ask the Listener a single question to determine how to position your message.

Wait for Your Turn The Listener will select you or the Booster to go first. If the Booster goes first, carefully listen to her message, mentally preparing suitable counter-arguments to present during your turn later. Also think of a simple open-ended question that will elicit useful information about how to persuade the Listener to your way of thinking.

Ask Your Question Use a simple open-ended question that probes the Listener's values and beliefs about the content presented in the video. Listen carefully to the response.

Make Your Presentation Immediately launch into your presentation, linking your statements to the Listener's response. Emphasize the detriments of the concepts and processes presented in the video. If you had heard the Booster's presentation earlier, try to remove or reduce its impact through logical counter-arguments. Remember that you have only 45 seconds. Be selective about the points that you want to make—instead of trying to speak fast.

Receive Your Score As soon as both you and the Booster have made your presentations, the Listener will distribute 7 points between the two of you to reflect the relative merit of the presentations. The Listener will give you a folded piece of paper with the number of points awarded to you. Do not open this piece of paper until everyone has played all three roles.

Get Ready for the Next Round During the next round, you will play the role of the Listener. Fortunately, you don't have to spend time preparing for this role.

Reaction Rating Scale

What is your initial reaction to the content of the video program? Indicate your reaction by selecting one of the numbers in this 9-point scale:

1 = extremely negative

2 = very negative

3 = negative

4 = slightly negative

5 = neutral

6 = slightly positive

7 = positive

8 = very positive

9 = extremely positive

Worksheet for Computing the Average Rating

Rating	Number of Participants	Rating x Number of Participants
1		
2		
3		
4		
5		
6		
7		
8		
9		
Totals		

Average rating = Total of the third column/Total of the second column

Video Vitamins

8 Debriefing Games

Debriefing Games are interactive strategies that are used for encouraging reflection and dialogue about an earlier activity or event. These games require processing of a common experience to extract key learning points from it. They generally encourage participants to identify and express emotions, recall events and decisions, share lessons learned, relate insights to other real-world events, speculate on how things could have been different, and plan for future action.

MOOD CHECK

You are one of the thirty employees attending a discussion session today. You work for a pharmaceutical company that recently merged with another European company. You notice that about half of the participants are from the other company. You are still feeling somewhat sore about the suddenness of the merger and you don't know how to interact with the "others."

Lori, your facilitator, briefly welcomes all of you and asks everyone to spend a few minutes thinking back on the merger. This doesn't sound like an auspicious beginning, but you keep your mouth shut and let your mind wander. After a couple of minutes, Lori distributes a one-page handout that contains these sixteen different adjectives: angry, betrayed, challenged, confused, cooperative, dynamic, enthusiastic, excited, expanding, global, growing, indifferent, optimistic, powerful, uncertain, and uninformed. She asks everyone to review these adjectives and circle the three that best describe their current feelings toward the merger. You scan the list and

impulsively circle "betrayed" and "uninformed." It requires a few minutes of reflection before you grudgingly circle the word "global."

After a suitable pause, Lori collects the handouts from everyone (without looking at the circles) and replaces them with unmarked copies. She now asks you and the others to make a prediction of the top three adjectives selected by all the participants in the room by placing the numbers 1, 2, and 3 in front of the appropriate words. You figure out that most of your co-workers would have circled words similar to the ones that you circled, but you are not sure about the "others." Maybe they feel positive and excited about the whole deal. While you are pondering this dilemma, you notice that Lori is busy with the marked lists and a calculator.

After a couple of minutes, Lori checks to see that everyone has made a prediction. Because she wants to maintain confidentiality of participant responses, she explains that she would not ask anyone to publicly reveal which words he or she selected. Instead, she goes through the list, one word at a time, specifying how many people circled that word. Lori builds up the suspense by pausing after reading the word and before announcing the number of people who circled it. "Betrayed" turns out to be the word with the highest number of circles—28! What surprises you is the fact that many of the "others" are obviously feeling the same way that you and your colleagues do.

Shortly after announcing the results, Lori conducts a discussion about the causes of different negative feelings and how the new organization—and its individual employees—can reduce these feelings and can replace them with other more positive ones.

Advantages and Limitations

Debriefing games have several benefits. We have repeatedly established the case for debriefing. While experience may be the best teacher, raw experience alone does not automatically guarantee that people learn from it. People learn from experience only when they reflect on it, gain valuable insights, and share these insights with each other.

A major challenge in conducting a debriefing discussion is how to channel the energy and enthusiasm of the group so none of its valuable insights are lost in the chaos and confusion of everyone wanting to talk about everything at the same time. Debriefing games add control and order to the discussion without killing its spontaneity. These games prevent the few vociferous speakers from dominating the conversation with shallow thoughts.

Debriefing games have their limitations. For one thing, the time requirement is hard to predict because a lot depends on the chemistry among the participants. Therefore, these games are hard to schedule. Unless you and your participants are flexible, you may not have enough time to explore different avenues of discussion. Worse yet, the group may continue beating a dead horse in an attempt to fill the allotted time.

It is also important to realize that debriefing in general, and the debriefing game in particular, is not a license to practice amateur psychotherapy. As a facilitator, it is important that you seek additional professional help before attempting to conduct a debriefing game following a traumatic event.

Types of Debriefing Games

A convenient method for classifying debriefing games is to relate the purpose of the game to one or more of the phases in the debriefing procedure. Here are the six phases in my debriefing procedure:

1. *How do you feel?* Invites participants to get strong feelings and emotions off their chests. Make it easier for them to objectively analyze the experience during the later phases.

2. *What happened?* Collect data about what happened during the earlier experience. Encourage participants to compare and contrast individual recollections.

3. *What did you learn?* Encourage the participants to generate and test different principles. Ask participants to come up with key learning points and discuss them.

4. *How does this relate to the real world?* Discuss the relevance of the experiential activity to participants' real-world experiences.

5. *What if?* Encourage participants to apply their insights to new contexts. Use alternative scenarios to speculate on how people's behaviors would change.

6. *What next?* Ask participants to undertake action planning. Invite them to apply their insights from the experiential activity to the real world.

MOOD CHECK, the debriefing game described earlier, is an example that belongs to the first ("How do you feel?") phase. The next section contains examples of debriefing games related to other phases.

More Examples of Debriefing Games

GROUP GROPE. The debriefing version of this popular game is best suited for use in Phase 3 ("What did you learn?") of the debriefing model. Ask participants to reflect on their common experience and individually come up with four different answers to the question, "What did you learn from this experience?" Hand out four blank index cards to each participant for writing each answer on a different card. After a couple of minutes, collect the cards, mix them well, and redistribute four random cards to each participant. Instruct participants to review the responses on the cards and exchange cards with each other to make their sets better reflect their personal insights. Any participant may exchange any number of cards with any other participant, and every participant must exchange at least one

card. Later, direct participants to compare their cards and form teams with people with similar cards. There is no limit to the number of participants who may team up, but a team may keep no more than three cards from its combined collection. At the end of this process, ask each team to read the responses from the three cards selected by its members.

DEBATES. This game is designed for use with Phase 3 ("What did you learn?") of the debriefing model. It encourages participants to check general principles against data and logic. This game is an effective follow-up to the previous GROUP GROPE game. Prior to conducting the game, come up with a set of principles based on the lessons learned from the earlier experience. (Example: *People are excited about new ideas while they attend a conference but they implement very few of these ideas back in their workplace*). At the beginning of the game, present each principle and briefly explain it. Divide participants into twice as many teams as there are principles. (Example: *If you have explained four principles, organize eight teams.*) Assign two teams to each principle. Between the two teams, identify one as the supporter and the other as the attacker. Give sufficient time for each team to reflect on their previous common experience and other similar experiences, and come up with arguments to support or attack the principle assigned to it. Later, select a team at random and give it 2 minutes to present its case. Then ask the opposing team to present its case. Repeat the process with other teams and other principles.

IFFY ENVELOPES. This version of the ENVELOPES game is best suited for Phase 5 ("What if?") of the debriefing model. Before the game, prepare four or five what-if questions. (Example: *What if professional conferences were conducted on the Internet?*) Write each of these questions on the face of a blank envelope. Divide participants into teams of one to seven members. Distribute a different what-if envelope to each team. Ask its members to brainstorm suitable responses to the question and write them on an index card. At the end of the time limit, ask teams to put the index card inside the envelope and pass the envelope (with the index card inside) to the next team. Each team now reads the new what-if question and (without looking at the card inside the envelope) comes up with its own responses within the next 2 minutes. Repeat the procedure until each what-if envelope contains three sets of responses. After the envelopes have been rotated one more time, ask each team to open the envelope and review the response cards. Instruct each team to identify the top three best responses (which may be on the same or different cards) and report them to the entire group.

RAPID SURVEY. This game can be used to collect information related to all phases of the debriefing model. Divide participants into six teams. Assign questions related to a different phase of the debriefing model to different teams. Ask the teams to assemble in convenient corners and spend 3 minutes designing a strategy for collecting responses from all participants (including its own members) to the team's question. After 3 minutes, announce the

beginning of the survey period. Ask teams to collect responses to its question using the strategy designed earlier. After 3 minutes of data collection, ask teams to retire to their corners and analyze the data. Each team produces a summary of its results on a sheet of flip-chart paper. Finally, conduct a show-and-tell period during which each team makes a 1-minute presentation of its findings.

Ready-to-Use Debriefing Game
THIRTY-FIVE

In this activity, participants reflect on an earlier experience and identify important lessons they learned. They write one of these lessons as a brief item. The winner in this activity is not the best player, but the best item.

Participants

Any number. The best activity involves 10 to 100.

Time

15 to 30 minutes

Materials

- Index cards
- Whistle

Flow

Brief participants. Recall an earlier experience. Ask each participant to write an item on an index card that captures an important lesson learned from this experience. Instruct participants to keep the item short, specific, clear, and legible. Ask for an example to illustrate the item. Announce a suitable time limit.

Let go. After 3 minutes, blow the whistle and give instructions for getting ready for the next steps. Ask each participant to review his or her idea and silently gloat about its elegance and power. Then ask participants to emotionally detach themselves from their guideline and get ready to launch it into the world.

Switch items. Ask participants to turn their cards down to hide the item. When you blow the whistle, participants are to stand up, walk around, and exchange the cards with each other. Participants should not read the items on the cards they receive but should immediately exchange the cards with someone else. They should continue doing this until you blow the whistle again.

Reproduced from *Design Your Own Games and Activities* by Sivasailam (Thiagi) Thiagarajan with Raja Thiagarajan with permission of the publisher. Copyright © 2003 by John Wiley & Sons, Inc.

Find a partner. Blow the whistle to begin the exchange process. After about 20 seconds, blow the whistle again to stop the process. Ask participants to stop moving and to pair up with any other nearby participant.

Compare and score. Ask each pair of participants to review the two items on the two cards they have. They should distribute 7 points between these two items (no fractions or negative numbers) to reflect their relative merit. Participants should write these numbers on the backs of the cards.

Conduct the second round. After a suitable pause for scoring, blow the whistle again and ask participants to repeat the process of moving around and exchanging cards. When you blow the whistle again after 20 seconds or so, participants stop moving, find a partner, compare the two items on their cards, and distribute 7 points. The new score points should be written below the previous ones.

Conduct three more rounds. Tell participants that you will be conducting three more rounds of the activity. Suggest to participants that they should maintain high levels of objectivity by disregarding earlier numbers and by keeping a poker face when they have to comparatively evaluate the item they themselves wrote.

Count down to the winning items. At the end of the fifth round, ask participants to return to their seats with the cards they currently have. Ask them to add the five score points and write the total. After a suitable pause, count down from thirty-five. When a participant hears the total on the card, he or she should stand up and read the item on the card. Continue this process until you have identified the top five or ten items.

Discuss the items. Briefly comment on the top items and invite participants to make their comments.

Follow up. Thank participants for generating the items and evaluating them. Tell them that you will type up a complete set of items and distribute them either through regular mail or e-mail. (Be sure to follow up on this promise!)

Design Your Own Games and Activities

9 Card Games

Cards contain items that are associated with different categories from a classification system (example: *four types of learners*) or a process (example: *six steps in the creative problem solving process*). Along with the item, each card contains an identification number. Several different *card games* can be played with a deck of classification cards by treating each category as a suit and the last digit of each number as the value of the card.

INTELLIGENT CARDS

You are attending a training session on multiple intelligences. Sonia is your facilitator. She makes a brief presentation about seven types of intelligence. To help you better understand this classification system, Sonia invites you to play a card game that requires you to read items associated with different intelligences and correctly classify each of them. She gives you a sample card that contains an item about one type of intelligence along with an identification number. Sonia explains that the game you are about to play is similar to the children's game of *Crazy Eights*. Not having played any card games in your deprived childhood, you wait for additional instructions.

You play the game with four other participants. One person shuffles the deck of game cards and deals eight cards to each player, one card at a time. The object of the game is to get rid of the eight cards in your hand. The dealer places the rest of the deck (called the *stock*) face down, turns the top card face up, and places it by the side of the stock. This card is the first one in the discard pile; players take turns discarding a card from their hand on

top of this card. The card that you discard must meet one of these criteria: The item on the card should relate to the same type of intelligence as the top card on the discard pile. Or the last digit of the number on the card should match the last digit of the number on the top card.

You make your first discard without having to think too hard because the number on your card is 18 and the number on the top discard is 78. The card you discard contains an item associated with *musical intelligence.* The next player discards another card that contains an item associated with the same type of intelligence. While the others are playing their cards, you study the cards in your hand and arrange them according to different types of intelligence. When it is your turn again, you have no problem matching a card with *intrapersonal intelligence.* Patti, the next player, does not have any card that can be discarded. She has to take cards from the top of the stock, one card at a time, until she finds another card that belongs to *intrapersonal intelligence* (or a card with the same last digit). Patti adds the cards she picked up (without showing them to anyone) to her hand. Later during the game, Marla explains that if your card matches both the type of intelligence and the last digit of the number, you get to discard any other card from your hand. Marla's bonus discard belongs to *logical intelligence.* Patti discards a card claiming that it also belongs to *logical intelligence.* Chuck challenges her, arguing that the card does not belong to logical intelligence. You check a reference table (which lists the card numbers and the type of intelligence associated with each) and discover that Chuck is right and Patti is wrong. Patti has to take back her card and take another card from Chuck's hand.

Later in the game, Chuck wins the game by being the first player to get rid of all his cards. However, the game continues with the remaining players. You end up being the second player to get rid of all your cards.

Classification Cards

Classification card games use a deck of sixty to one hundred twenty cards. All cards are related to a process or a classification system. Ideally, the process should have four to seven steps, or the classification system should have four to seven categories. Each card contains an item that is associated with a specific step or category. The item in the cards could take a variety of forms, including definitions, key features, activities, strategies, tactics, guidelines, data, outputs, symbols, criteria, regulations, advice, facts, examples, problems, and quotes. Sometimes, the same card may belong to more than one step or category. For example, the advice, "Conduct an employee survey" could belong to either the *needs assessment* step or the *evaluation* step of the instructional-development process. Similarly the statement "Traditionally emphasized in formal education" may belong to either category of *linguistic* or *logical* intelligence in our game. The total cards are randomly arranged and each card is given a sequential number for cross-reference. A reference table lists the number of each card and the correct category associated with the item on that card.

Uses and Limitations

Classification card games are appropriate for the mastery of concept frameworks or systematic processes. Rather than passively listening to a lecture, reading a handout, or watching a demonstration, playing one of these card games requires participants to make several rapid decisions accurately. The card game format provides repeated practice until participants reach a high degree of fluency in recalling, differentiating, and applying various steps and concepts. On the negative side, the excitement of winning the card game may overpower the instructional value of making critical decisions. This may result in the players memorizing the correct classification associated with specific items rather than making fine discriminations based on understanding and analyzing the item on the card. This problem can be reduced to some extent by using a large number of game cards.

More Examples

AUDITORY SLAPJACK. This card game provides an effective introduction to any classification system. Here's how this game is played with cards from Glenn Parker's *Team Players* system, which categorizes members of a team into four types: goal-directed *collaborators*, issue-oriented *challengers*, task-oriented *contributors*, and process-oriented *communicators*. Players seat themselves at a table, around a spoon. One of the players takes the top card from the deck and reads the item aloud. The first player to grab the spoon gets to announce the type of team player associated with the item. Other players check the response against the type given in the reference card. If correct, the player takes a poker chip from a bowl. If incorrect, the player returns a poker chip to the bowl. The game continues with different players taking turns to pick a card and read the item.

LEARNING STYLES POKER. The *Building Excellence* card deck features items associated with individual learning styles. These items are divided into six categories: *environmental, emotional, perceptual, physiological, sociological,* and *psychological*. The poker game requires players to assemble a set of six cards with these relative ranks based on the similarity of learning style categories among the cards: one pair, two pairs, three of a kind, full house (three of a kind and a pair), unique (each card of a different category), three pairs, four of a kind, two triplets, five of a kind, and six of a kind. In the basic game, each player receives eight cards. Each player reviews the cards and gives two cards to the player on the right and two to the player on the left. The players then discard two of their cards, keeping a hand of six. They reveal any three cards face up and begin betting as in a regular poker game. After the first round of betting, they reveal two more cards and conduct another round of betting. Eventually, the player with the highest-ranked set of six cards wins the game.

COACHING ROUNDS. This solitaire game uses cards with items associated with five steps of Andrew Kimball's coaching procedure. Five piles of six

cards are dealt face down. These piles are labeled with the five steps of *connecting, observing, assessing, coaching,* and *honing.* The player takes the top card of any pile and turns it face up. She classifies the item on that card and places it at the bottom of the pile with the appropriate label. She then turns over the top card of that pile, classifies it, and places it at the bottom of the appropriate pile. This process is repeated until one of the piles has all cards turned face up. The player's score equals the total number of cards turned face up.

Ready-to-Use Classification Card Game
TEN TRICKS

More than three decades ago, B. W. Tuckman pointed out that all teams go through four stages of *forming, storming, norming,* and *performing* in their development. This powerful model has practical implications for building, maintaining, facilitating, and leading high-performance teams.

TEN TRICKS is a game with classification cards that is designed to help people master Tuckman's model. It uses a deck of fifty-two cards, each with a statement associated with different stages in the team-development process. This addictive game begins with a brief presentation of the team-development process and gives players numerous chances to review different elements associated with each stage of the process.

Purpose

To rapidly recognize the behaviors, attitudes, thoughts, perceptions, expectations, problems, and strategies associated with the four stages of team development.

Participants

Two to five. Best with four players.

Time

10 to 15 minutes. The game may be replayed several times to determine the winner of a match.

Supplies

- A deck of Team Development (TD) Cards. This deck contains eighty cards, listed in the handout on page 96 at the end of this chapter.
- One copy of the Four Stages of Team Development handout on page 96 for each participant.

Design Your Own Games and Activities

- Copies of the Team Development Classification Table to be used for settling disputes during the game. The table lists each card number and the correct team-development stage (or stages) associated with it. A copy of this table is on page 98.
- Copies of the What Card Is That? handout that explains how to determine the number and stage of a TD card.
- Copies of How to Play TEN TRICKS on page 100.
- Copies of the How's Tricks? handout at the end of the chapter.

Flow

Assemble play groups. Organize participants into groups of three to six. Seat each group around a table and give out one deck of TD cards per group. Also distribute a copy of the Classification Table, asking participants to place it with the printed side down.

Introduce the four stages. Distribute copies of the handout, Four Stages of Team Development. Make a brief presentation, using examples that are relevant to participants

Brief the players. Acknowledge that most participants may not have a complete grasp of the four stages in team development. Explain that you are going to play a card game that will help them become more fluent with these stages.

Introduce the TD cards. Ask each player to pick up a TD card from the deck at the table. Ask a player to read the statement on the card and invite everyone to identify the team-development stage associated with the statement. Announce the correct stage. Demonstrate how to verify the stage by using the Classification Table. Emphasize that the Classification Table should be used only when there is a dispute about which stage a card belongs to.

Explain the value and the stage of each card. Use the information from the handout, What Card Is That? Give some practice in determining the value of several TD cards.

Explain the rules. Distribute copies of the handouts, How to Play Ten Tricks and How's Tricks. Walk the participants through the rules.

Monitor the game. Ask the players at each table to select the first dealer and begin the game. Walk around the room, clarifying rules and settling disputes among players as needed.

Conclude the game. Stop the game when a player wins the match. Alternatively, stop the game after an appropriate time limit and announce that the players with the highest scores win.

Four Stages of Team Development

In 1965, B. W. Tuckman, who had been studying the behavior of small groups, published a model that suggests that all teams go through four distinct stages in their development:

Forming   The first stage in a team's development is forming. During this stage, the team members are unsure about what they are doing. Their focus is on understanding the team's goal and their role. They worry about whether the other team members will accept them. Team members frequently look for clarification from their leader.

Storming   The second stage in a team's development is storming. During this stage, the team members try to get organized. This stage is marked by conflict among the members and between the members and the leader. Through this conflict, the team attempts to define itself.

Norming   The third stage in a team's development is norming. This stage follows storming, after the team members have succeeded in resolving their conflicts. They now feel more secure with one another and with their leader. They effectively negotiate the structure of the team and the division of labor.

Performing   The fourth stage in a team's development is performing. During this stage the team members behave in a mature fashion and focus on accomplishing their goals. This stage is marked by direct, two-way communication among the team members.

Team Development Cards

Here are the numbers and statements for each of the eighty cards. You can type these numbers and statements on rectangular boxes using your favorite word processor. Then, photocopy them on card stock and cut them into game cards.

1. All members participate in all team activities.
2. Disagreements become more civilized and less divisive.
3. Feeling of us-them increases.
4. Ground rules become second nature to team members.
5. If there is a formal leader, team members tend to obey him or her.
6. Leadership is shared among different members.
7. Cautious
8. Leadership role is rotated among appropriate members.
9. Members are anxious and suspicious of the task ahead.
10. Challenging
11. Members are more committed to their subgroups than to the team as a whole.
12. Members are more friendly toward each other.
13. Members are not committed to the group's goal.
14. Collaborating
15. Conversation is polite and tentative.
16. Each team member decides what his or her role should be.
17. Everyone begins to experience success.

18. Members are not fully committed to the team goal.
19. Members are proud to be chosen for the team.
20. Members are relieved that things are progressing smoothly.
21. Everyone is wondering, "Why are we here?"
22. Members are satisfied about the team's progress.
23. Members argue with each other—even when they agree on the basic issues.
24. Everyone wants to have his or her say.
25. Facilitator encourages team members to critique their behaviors.
26. Members attempt to figure out their roles and functions.
27. Members begin to enjoy team activities.
28. Facilitator encourages team members to discuss their negative feelings.
29. Facilitator helps team members uncover and discuss hidden agendas.
30. Members challenge, evaluate, and destroy ideas.
31. Members choose sides.
32. Members compete with each other.
33. Facilitator points out violations of ground rules and helps team members revise the ground rules, if appropriate.
34. Facilitator uses an icebreaker to help team members get acquainted with each other.
35. Members deal with each other with greater confidence.
36. Members develop great loyalty to the team.
37. Members don't have enough information to trust each other.
38. Members feel comfortable about their roles on the team.
39. Members feel confident about disagreeing with each other.
40. Team members decide on the appropriate level of risk taking.
41. Members feel empowered. They take initiative without checking with the leader.
42. Members feel excitement, anticipation, and optimism.

43. Members form subgroups that get into conflicts.
44. Members freely ask questions and express their frustrations.
45. Members have a better idea of whom to trust and whom to distrust.
46. Members have a realistic sense of trust based on their experiences with each other.
47. Members have clear understanding of one another's strengths and weaknesses.
48. Members take a "wait-and-see" approach.
49. Members tend to avoid the tasks and argue about ground rules.
50. Members tend to be polite to each other.
51. Members tend to become complacent.
52. Members understand the team processes.
53. Members' feelings and attitudes keep fluctuating.
54. Most conversations are to and from the team leader.
55. Most discussions are about getting the task done.
56. Most discussions are shallow.
57. No ground rules established. Members depend on their previous team experiences to decide how to behave.
58. Regular team meetings are replaced by a variety of as-needed communications.
59. Several conflicts develop.
60. Some members become bored with the routine and begin looking for new challenges.
61. Some members demonstrate passive resistance.
62. Team members decide who should do what.
63. Some members dominate team discussions.
64. Some members still dominate team discussions.
65. Team members depend on the facilitator to explain what is going on.
66. Team members experience this stage after storming and before performing.

(Continued)

Team Development Classification Table

F: Forming • **S:** Storming • **N:** Norming • **P:** Performing

Card Number	Stage	Card Number	Stage	Card Number	Stage	Card Number	Stage
1	P	21	F	41	P	61	S
2	N	22	P	42	F	62	N
3	N	23	S	43	S, N	63	F, S
4	P	24	S	44	S	64	S
5	F	25	N	45	N	65	F
6	P	26	N	46	N, P	66	N
7	F	27	P	47	P	67	F
8	P	28	S	48	F	68	P
9	F	29	N	49	S	69	P
10	S	30	S	50	F	70	P
11	S	31	S	51	P	71	P
12	N, P	32	S	52	P	72	F
13	F	33	N	53	S	73	N
14	P	34	F	54	F	74	P
15	F	35	N	55	P	75	N
16	N	36	N, P	56	F	76	P
17	P	37	F	57	F	77	N
18	F	38	N, P	58	P	78	P
19	F	39	N, P	59	S	79	F
20	N	40	N	60	P	80	N, P

What Card Is That?

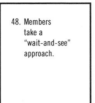

Every playing card has a value and a suit. This card, for example, is the *7 of diamonds.* The value is 7 and the suit is diamond.

> 48. Members take a "wait-and-see" approach.

Every TD card has a *value* and a *stage*. This TD card, for example, is the *8 of forming.*

The value of the TD card is indicated by the last digit of the number on the card. The value of this card is *8*, which is the last digit of its number, 48.

The stage of the TD card is indicated by the statement on the card. This card is a *forming* card because the statement belongs to the forming stage.

It is easy to determine the value of a TD card: Just ignore the first digit of the card. So 12, 22, 32, 42, 52, 62, 72, 82, and 92 all have the same value of 2. Values run from 0 (the lowest) to 9 (the highest).

It takes some effort to determine the stage of a TD card. Read the statement on the card, analyze it, and classify it correctly.

Some TD cards may belong to more than one stage. When you play one of these cards, you choose the stage to which it belongs.

How to Play TEN TRICKS

Deal
Give ten cards to each player. Place the rest of the deck aside. (These cards are not used during the game.)

Bidding
Arrange the ten cards in your hand into different stages and review them. Bid the total number of tricks that you plan to take.

Object of the Game
The object of the game is not to win as many tricks as possible, but to win the exact number of tricks that you bid. In some cases you may have to deliberately lose tricks. Although each player plays for himself or herself, players usually team up with others to force a player to win a trick and exceed his or her bid.

First Trick
The person seated to the left of the dealer leads a card, announcing its value and stage. Other players take turns to play a card to the trick. Players should play a card of the same stage if they are able to do so. If they don't have a card of the stage, they may discard any other card.

Subsequent Tricks
The winner of a trick leads a card for the next trick. Game continues as before.

Tied Tricks
If two high cards of the same value are played to a trick, the first player who played one of these cards wins the trick.

> Example: Carol plays a 5 of norming. David plays 6 of norming (card 26), Andy plays another 6 of norming (card 36), and Beth plays a 0 of norming. This trick has two high cards of the same value (6). David wins it because he played his card first.

End
Game ends when all ten tricks have been played out.

Scoring
You earn 100 points for winning the exact number of tricks that you bid. If you exceed or fall below your bid, you lose 20 points for each trick over or under.

Match
Record each player's score. Collect all the cards, shuffle them, and deal another round for a fresh game. Continue playing until someone accumulates 250 points and wins the match.

How's Tricks?

If you play any card game that involves taking tricks (such as Bridge, Whist, Euchre, or Hearts), you will have no difficulty in learning how to play Ten Tricks. Even if you don't play any card games, you can master it quickly.

In card players' terminology, to lead a card is to play the first card. One player begins the first round (called the first trick) by leading any card from his or her hand. Other players take turns to play a card of the same category. If you don't have a card of the same category, you may play a card that belongs to any other category. After everyone has played a card, the person who played the highest card of the original category wins the trick. (In case of a tie, the person who played a card first wins.) This player collects all the cards in a neat pile and places them aside. The player who won the trick leads the next hand.

> Here's an example: Andy leads card 27, which belongs to the performing stage. The value of the card is 7. Beth has two cards that belongs to the performing stage: 8 and 41. Since she wants to win the trick, she plays the 8 (which has a higher value than the other card in her hand and the card led by Andy). Carol, who is the next player, also has two cards belonging to performing stage: 52 and 76. Since both of them are lower in value than Beth's card, Carol knows that she cannot win the trick. Therefore she plays the 52, the lower-valued card. David, the last player, has no card that belong to the performing stage. So he discards a card of the lowest value, 40, which belongs to the norming stage.

Beth wins this trick and leads 29 to begin the next trick.

10 Board Games

Board Games borrow structures and play materials from popular recreational games to create highly motivating training events. Board games typically use game cards and dice to encourage individuals and teams to demonstrate their mastery of concepts, principles, skills, and problem-solving strategies.

A wall painting in a pyramid on the tomb of Hesy of the Third Dynasty, completed around 2650 B.C., is one of the earliest records of an educational board game. The painting shows Senat, a board game in which players move their pieces from a beginning space depicting death toward the final space depicting the House of Revival. Ancient Egyptians probably learned about the Netherworld by playing this board game.

Board games such as Monopoly, Scrabble, Dungeons and Dragons, and Trivial Pursuit are primary artifacts associated with American popular culture.

THIRTY STEPS

You are attending a workshop on creative problem solving. You have received a brief introduction to the six steps of the creativity process. You are now ready to play a board game called THIRTY STEPS to explore details of each step.

You and three other players sit in front of a game board that has thirty spaces from START to FINISH. Each player selects a playing piece and parks it on the START space.

One of the players shuffles a deck of game cards and deals ten cards to each player. Each card has an item (strategy, tactic, behavior, thought, or

outcome) associated with one of the six steps of the creativity process. During the first round, you study your ten cards and pick out those that belong to the first step of the creativity process. When it is your turn, you read your selected cards, one card at a time. If nobody objects, you throw a die after reading each card and move your piece forward on the game board.

If somebody objects, talk it over with the objector. If neither of you can persuade the other, check with a table called the Feedback Card for the official answer. If you are right, the objector moves back two spaces and you throw the die and move forward. If you are wrong, you move back two spaces and the objector throws the die and moves forward.

After you have presented all your selected cards that belong to the first step of the creativity process, the next player does the same thing. You follow the same procedure until everyone has presented all cards belonging to the first step. You continue the game by identifying cards associated with each step of the creativity process. During some rounds, you may receive a CHANCE card that instructs you to move forward extra spaces, or move backward, or trade places with someone else's piece.

You win the game by being the first player to reach the FINISH space on the game board. Alternatively, the game may be played with a time limit. In this case, the player who is the farthest ahead on the game board wins the game.

More Examples of Board Games for Training

THIRTY STEPS. This is a race-and-chase board game. Here are brief descriptions of three other board games.

PARCHEESI WITH QUESTION CARDS. This is another race game modified for instructional purposes. Here's what the board looks like:

Each player has two pieces that begin at the player's home base. There are three decks of question cards; the first deck has 1-point questions, the second deck has 2-point questions, and the last deck has 3-point questions. When it is your turn, you announce whether you want to answer one card or two. You then draw one or two cards from your choice of decks. If you answer your question cards correctly, you move one of your pieces forward that many spaces. If you take two cards, you must answer both questions correctly in order to move at all during this turn. If you land on a square that contains another player's piece, you knock that piece back to the start (unless it is a sanctuary square, which can be shared by any number of opposing pieces). The first player to take both his or her pieces all the way around the board and back to the home base wins the game.

PRODUCTS. This is an example of a cyclical board game that simulates real-world cycles. The game board looks like a Monopoly board. You begin the game with a pawn and a certain amount of play money. You decide how to invest some or all of your money. You then throw the dice and move your

Design Your Own Games and Activities

piece forward. Follow the instructions on the space where you land. You may be asked to pick a CHANCE card and pay (or receive) different amounts of money depending on your initial investments. Other spaces may give you a chance to invest more money. You play the game for a specific number of rounds. You win if you end up with the most money at the end of the game.

FOUR IN A ROW. This is played on a 5 × 5 board with labeled rows and columns. Each square has one of five colors. The game is played by two to four players. When it is your turn, the player seated to your right picks up a game card and reads the question on the card. You have 15 seconds to answer the question. If your answer is correct, you can place one of your chips in a square belonging to the column, row, or color specified on the game card. The first player to get four squares in a line (or four squares of the same color) wins the game.

Ready-to-Use Board Game
EMPTY OR FULL?

Are you an optimist or a pessimist? It doesn't really matter which you are, because people of either personality type can be effective, successful, rich, and famous. In fact, you need the ability to think both optimistically and pessimistically to become more creative and adaptive. Here's a game that stretches your ability to use both views and become a flexible thinker.

Purpose

To think creatively by making optimistic and pessimistic statements about any situation.

Object

To move two playing pieces from opposite corners to the center of the game board, shown here.

Time

30 to 45 minutes (See Variations for adjusting the time requirement.)

Participants

Three (See Variations for suggestions for handling larger groups.)

Materials

- Reproduce the game board at the end of this chapter. For the best result, make a poster-sized enlargement of the game board.

- Three pairs of poker chips or pawns of different colors. In an emergency, you can use three pairs of pennies, nickels, and dimes.

- A standard, six-sided die.

- List of suggested "trigger words." Prepare a list of about ten words or phrases about which players can make optimistic or pessimistic statements. Distribute one copy for each player. For this game, almost any word should work.

  Example: Economy, Health, Broccoli, Environment, Politics, Meteors, Hawaii, Downsizing, Basketball, and Sexual Harassment.

Flow

Brief the participants. Begin with a mini-lecture and a discussion of these topics: optimism and pessimism, the advantages and disadvantages of either viewpoint, the need for a balanced view, personal preferences, and the need to practice thinking from the other point of view. Alternatively, you can conduct the game first and then debrief the players to elicit these learning points.

Demonstrate how to make statements. Explain that the game requires participants to play the role of a cockeyed optimist and a gloomy pessimist with equal ease. Read the first suggested trigger word and invite a participant to make an optimistic statement about it. Ask other participants to produce more optimistic statements. Now ask another participant to make a pessimistic statement about the same trigger word. Invite other participants to concoct more pessimistic statements. Explain that during the play of the game, players will be required to make statements of either type.

Set up the game board. Identify the unnumbered circle at the top-left corner of the game board as the starting point for pessimists. The circle at the bottom-right corner is the starting point for optimists. Ask each player to select a color and place one piece of this color on each of the two starting points. At the beginning of play, each circle will have three different pieces, one from each player.

Select one person to be the first emcee. Explain that the players will take turns being the emcee for each round of play. Ask players to select the tallest person to be the first emcee.

Ask the emcee to announce a trigger word. Distribute copies of the suggested trigger words. Explain that the list contains words or phrases. Players will make an optimistic or pessimistic statement about each word or phrase. The emcee can select one of these words or phrases or come up with an original word or phrase. Ask the emcee to announce the trigger word for the first round.

Design Your Own Games and Activities

Ask players to make statements. Ask the other two players to prepare a brief statement (of not more than 15 seconds duration) about the trigger word. The player may select either an optimistic or a pessimistic viewpoint. The statement should reflect an extreme example of the player's viewpoint. When ready, the player raises his or her hand. When both players are ready, the emcee points to one of the players. This player makes the statement. Immediately after this, the other player presents his or her statement.

Ask the emcee to award points. The emcee evaluates each statement independent of the other. He or she awards 0 to 3 points according to this scoring system:

0   If the emcee cannot decide whether the statement is optimistic or pessimistic

1   If the statement is *mildly* optimistic or *mildly* pessimistic

2   If the statement is *moderately* optimistic or *moderately* pessimistic

3   If the statement is *extremely* optimistic or *extremely* pessimistic

Ask players to move their pieces. Each of the other two players moves the appropriate piece (depending on whether the statement was optimistic or pessimistic) the number of spaces equal to the number of points awarded by the emcee.

Continue the game. Ask the player seated to the left of the previous emcee to act as the next emcee. Repeat the game the same way as in the previous round. Continue playing the game in this fashion with different players taking turns to be the emcee.

Introduce the equalizer move. After the third round (when every player has had one turn at being the emcee), ask the new emcee to throw a die before announcing the trigger word. If the die turns up 1, 2, 3, or 4, the round proceeds as usual. If the die turns up 5 or 6, the players should do the following:

- *If a player's pieces are at different numbered circles in the two paths,* move the piece that is closer to the center backwards until it is as far away as the other piece. (For example, if one piece is at the 7 circle, and the other is at the 10 circle, move the 10 piece back to its 7 circle.)

- *If a player's pieces are at the same numbered circles in the two paths,* move both pieces two spaces toward the center of the game board.

After moving all players' pieces, the game continues as usual with the emcee announcing a new trigger word.

   The emcee should throw the die (and make the equalizer move if it is 5 or 6) at the beginning of each subsequent round.

Conclude the game. The game ends when one player reaches the center circle with both pieces. This player wins the game. The winner now becomes the "permanent" emcee while the other two players continue the game to determine the second-place winner.

Debrief the players. To gain the maximum value from EMPTY OR FULL, invite the players to discuss their experiences. Here are some suggested questions to prompt this discussion:

- Which type of statement was difficult for you to make during the game? Is this true of your life in general?

- Which type of statement did you dislike more? How did you feel while making these statements? Why do you think you felt that way?

- In general, are you an optimist or a pessimist? How difficult is it for you to take the opposite viewpoint?

- How did you feel when you had to think of statements from a viewpoint that was against your natural inclination?

- Can you make an optimistic statement about pessimists? A pessimistic statement about optimists?

- What is the relationship between your public behavior of making statements and your private behavior of thinking? Do you think that making several statements of one viewpoint will make it easier for you think in that viewpoint?

- Did you find yourself coming up with faster and more extreme statements during the later rounds of the game?

- What tips do you have for someone who wants to think more optimistically? More pessimistically?

- Are there some topics about which you cannot assume an optimistic viewpoint? A pessimistic viewpoint? Why do you feel that way?

- This game rewards you for being extreme. Does this type of extreme thinking have value in real life?

- Which do you prefer: thinking optimistically, thinking pessimistically, thinking both ways, thinking neutrally? Under what conditions will each of these types of thinking be of value?

Variations

More people? With fewer than ten people, divide the group into three teams of approximately equal size and conduct the game as a team activity. With larger groups, play several games simultaneously.

Not enough time? Play the game for a specific time period (such as 15 minutes). At the end of this time, equalize each player's pieces. The player whose pieces are closest to the center wins the game.

Design Your Own Games and Activities

POLARITY

EMPTY OR FULL, the board game described on the previous pages is based on a generic game called POLARITY, a *framegame*, which means it is deliberately designed to permit loading different instructional content into the same generic board game format. You can use this framegame to instantly design your own training activity.

Here is the principle behind POLARITY: Thinking involves different approaches and effective thinking requires the ability to use many different approaches. Flexible thinkers are both rational and intuitive, impulsive and reflective, liberal and conservative, and academic and practical. The best way to acquire flexible thinking is to practice thinking aloud from various viewpoints.

POLARITY is designed to help players acquire the ability to think flexibly and communicate adaptively. EMPTY OR FULL (described above) requires players to produce optimistic and pessimistic statements. It forces players to practice thinking and speaking from their weaker viewpoint and expands their thinking tool kit.

Generic Rules for POLARITY

Here are the generic rules for POLARITY:

- Identify two opposite thinking styles or viewpoints. Prepare a set of trigger words (or phrases, questions, or situations) about which players can make opposing statements.

- Explain the two opposing viewpoints. Demonstrate how to make statements that reflect the opposite extremes. Present a trigger word and invite players to contribute statements from both extremes.

- Select one player to be the first emcee. Ask this emcee to announce a trigger word.

- Ask the other two players to make an extreme statement about the trigger word from either viewpoint.

- Ask the emcee to award 0 to 3 points to reflect the extreme nature of the statement.

- Ask players to move their pieces one space per point toward the center of the board.

- Continue the game with different players taking turns being the emcee.

- After the third round, introduce the equalizer move: Throw a die and if it lands on a 5 or a 6 ask each player to follow these instructions (Skip to the next step if the die turns up 1, 2, 3, or 4.):

  "If your pieces are at different distances from the center, move the piece that is closer to the center backwards until it is as far away as

the other piece. *If your pieces are at the same distance from the center*, move both pieces two spaces toward the center of the game board. The player whose pieces reach the center circle first wins the game.

Compare these generic rules with the specific rules for EMPTY OR FULL on page 109. You can also learn more details about each step from EMPTY OR FULL.

Empty or Full? Game Board

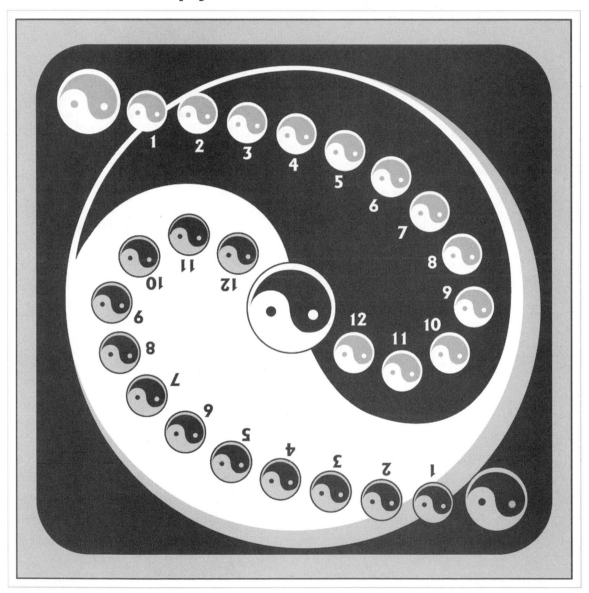

11 Matrix Games

Matrix games require participants to occupy boxes in a grid by demonstrating a specific skill or knowledge. The first participant to occupy a given number of boxes in a straight line (horizontally, vertically, or diagonally) wins the game. The matrixes provide a structure for matching or classifying individual items or organizing and comparing a set of items.

There is apparently an ancient and universal human need to line things up. From the primeval game of Nine Men's Morris through medieval versions of tic-tac-toe to the relative modern creation of bingo, several games share the concept of moving three counters or marking five boxes to form a horizontal, vertical, or diagonal straight line.

READING FOR BINGO

You are participating in READING FOR BINGO, a game conducted by a corporate trainer named Joan. You are a salesperson and the game is used as a part of a one-day workshop on a new software program released by the company. As a pre-workshop reading, you receive a copy of a brochure that outlines the features, benefits, and competitive advantages of the new product. You are about to discard the brochure when you see a note from Joan. The note instructs you to not only read the brochure but also to prepare ten review questions about the content and bring them to the workshop. The note threatens you with public humiliation if you do not take the assignment seriously and promises significant rewards if you do. So you read the brochure and write ten questions.

At the workshop, Joan collects your question cards and gives you a bingo card. It is a 5×5 matrix with the numbers 1 to 25 arranged in a random order. Each participant has a bingo card with a different arrangement of the same numbers. After getting everyone's attention, Joan shuffles the question cards she collected from everyone and picks up the top card. She announces that it is Question 1 and reads it aloud. She asks everyone to write the answer on a piece of paper. After a suitable pause, Joan announces the correct answer and asks each participant to check a neighbor's answer. Your answer is correct and you get to mark Box 1 in the bingo card. Joan now picks up the next card and throws it away, claiming that the question is too similar to the first one. She declares the question on the next card to be Question 2 and reads it. You go through the same steps as before. Joan now proclaims that the first participant to mark five boxes in a straight line on the bingo card will win a valuable prize. The game proceeds as before. Question 3 is easy because it is from a card that you wrote. A few rounds later, Mike yells, "Bingo" and waves his card with five marked boxes in the same column. Joan congratulates him, gives him a sports shirt with the company logo, and asks him to continue playing. By the time the game ends, you have completed a painless review of the major benefits and features of the new software program.

Critical Features of Matrix Games

Matrix games are played on a grid with three to five boxes along each side. In the basic matrix game, each participant works independently on a separate card. All cards have the same items (such as the numbers 1 through 25 in the sample game), but arranged in different order. The facilitator presents a "stimulus" and participants mark the box on the matrix card that has a matching item.

Winning a matrix game involves different combinations of three factors: chance, spatial intelligence, and mastery of the training content. Chance is reflected in the way the items are arranged on a particular card. Spatial intelligence helps you choose which box to mark in matrix games that let you choose among alternative boxes. (The sample game, READING FOR BINGO, did not give participants this choice.) Finally, mastery of the training content helps you win boxes. In READING FOR BINGO, participants who studied the brochure carefully had better chances of winning the game.

Advantages and Limitations

Matrix games are easy to develop and easy to use. Participants rapidly master the simple rules of the game. The games are also very flexible, permitting you to load them with new content and use them repeatedly. The games have a nice balance between chance and skill. Slower learners do not lose hope during the early stages of the game because of the chance element. You can use the matrix format to develop a variety of games to suit different types of training content.

Matrix games have limitations. Because they resemble bingo games, participants may think that they are games of pure chance. Matrix games usually tend to be used with verbal content, encouraging participants to memorize factual information. A critical requirement for an interesting matrix game is to ensure that no two cards are identical. Ordinarily, this would require tediously typing each card individually. However, this problem is solved with the Zingo software program (Thiagarajan, 1999) that enables you to print tens of thousands of different matrix cards from a single set of items.

Types of Matrix Games

There are many alternative ways to design matrix games. READING FOR BINGO involved a 5×5 grid. You can use grids of different sizes. A large number of participants played READING FOR BINGO independently, each person working on a separate card. You can play the games with smaller groups or teams, with players collaborating or competing with each other. In READING FOR BINGO, the items in the matrix were independent of each other. In your game, you can create matrixes of specific types.

Here are some examples of different types of matrix games:

SEVEN INTELLIGENCES is a classification-type matrix game. This game deals with a classification system of seven different types of intelligence such as logical intelligence, musical intelligence, visual intelligence, and verbal intelligence. The 5×5 matrix card has the names of the seven intelligences, each name randomly repeated on three or more boxes. The facilitator describes a statement (example: *You can hum a tune after hearing the song only once*) and participants decide which primary intelligence is involved in the performance (example: *musical intelligence*). Each participant plays with an individual card and chooses which of the boxes with the appropriate intelligence to mark.

Matrix-2 games involve a two-dimensional table. For example, the matrix card in a game called TEAMS has a table with four columns and four rows. The columns represent the four stages in the development of a team (as defined by Bruce Tuckman [1994]) and the rows represent four types of team members (as defined by Glenn Parker [1996]). TEAMS is played by three participants on the same card. The players take turns acting as the judge. One participant selects a box and he and the other participant write a statement identifying a desirable behavior of the specific type of team member at a specific stage of team development. (Example: *At the perform-ing stage, the challenger confronts the team with evidence of its stagnation.*) The judge reviews the two statements and selects the better one. The player who wrote this statement puts his or her initials in the box. The game continues with participants taking turns to act as the judge. At the end of the game, when all boxes are filled, the person with initials in the most boxes wins the game.

Matrix-1 games are similar to matrix-2 games, except that the same set of headings is associated with both the columns and the rows of the table. In a game called ETHNICITY, the columns are labeled with five different ethnic groups in the workplace. The same labels are also applied to the five rows. As a result, the boxes in one of the diagonals have the same column and row labels. To win a box along this diagonal, the two competing participants write statements that identify the most salient characteristic of this ethnic group. To win a box above the diagonal, participants write statements about the most important similarity between the two ethnic groups. Finally, to win a box below the diagonal, participants write statements about the most significant difference between the two ethnic groups.

Ready-to-Use Matrix Game
APPLES AND ORANGES

You are frequently admonished not to compare apples with oranges because they don't share identical characteristics. In real life, however, you are often forced to compare apples and oranges, such as when you decide what fruit to take with you when you visit your niece who is recovering from a tonsillectomy. You may actually end up comparing apples, oranges, coloring books, balloons, and video game cartridges—and end up taking a gallon of Ben & Jerry's ice cream.

Comparisons among very unrelated alternatives is a fact of life in the workplace. Here are some examples:

- You are about to run out of funds. How do you reduce costs: downsize the team, ask everyone take a pay cut, ask for additional funds, take a loan, or reduce your goals?

- You can hire only one consultant to help you establish the corporate policy on sexual harassment. Who should you hire: lawyer, communication specialist, human performance technologist, political consultant, or cultural anthropologist?

- You are hired to attract more subscribers to a newsletter. What would you do: reduce the subscription rate, conduct a direct-mail campaign, send out free copies, offer attractive incentives, collect credible endorsements, or conduct a sweepstakes?

APPLES AND ORANGES enables participants to systematically and objectively select the best item among several alternatives that do not share common features. While the game requires participation from all players, it has an interesting twist. At the end of the game you do not identify the winning player, but the winning idea.

Purpose

To identify and discuss the costs and potential benefits of alternative solutions and to select the best solution.

Participants

Three to ten.

Time

30 minutes to 2 hours. Exact time requirement depends on the number of alternatives, number of participants, diversity among participants, number of people affected by the decision, and the potential impact of making a wrong decision.

Materials

- Handout, Costs and Benefits (one copy for each participant)
- Overview and Rational sheets for participants
- Handout similar to the sample Comparison Matrix (one copy for each participant)
- Flip chart
- Felt-tipped markers

Flow
Phase 1

Get ready. Get yourself ready by becoming familiar with the principles and procedures associated with APPLES AND ORANGES. Begin the game by briefing the participants.

Do your homework. Read the Costs and Benefits handout (page 122 at the end of this chapter). Think of specific alternatives your participants are going to choose among. Figure out various costs and benefits associated with each alternative. Then read the Overview and Rationale sheet to understand how the game is played and why it is played that way. Finally, review the specific steps described below along with excerpts (in sans serif typeface) from a game that we played recently.

Draw a comparison matrix. See the sample Comparison Matrix on page 124, which shows a comparison matrix for five alternatives. Draw your matrix on the flip chart. The number of rows and columns in the matrix should equal the number of alternatives. For example, if you have only three alternatives to choose from, you will use a 3 x 3 matrix. Label the columns

and the rows with the same set of letters (A, B, C, and so on). Label each box inside the matrix with two letters, the first one identifying the column and the second one identifying the row. Leave the boxes along the diagonal that has the same row and column labels (A-A, B-B, and so on) blank. The boxes above this diagonal are used for comparison of costs; the boxes below the diagonal for comparison of benefits. During the game, you will circle the letter identifying the lower-cost or the higher-benefit alternative.

Brief the Players. Explain why you are making a choice and what items you are choosing among. Reduce the alternatives to a small number (between three and six). List the alternatives on a flip chart, labeling them A, B, C, and so on. Briefly describe the key features of each alternative, for example:

> A committee has come up with several ideas for solving the parking problem in your downtown office. You have reduced these ideas to five alternatives and listed them on a flip chart:
>
> - Build a multilevel parking lot
> - Encourage employees to carpool
> - Schedule staggered working hours
> - Run a corporate shuttle bus service
> - Support telecommuting

Phase 2

Compare costs. Work on the top half of the comparison table to arrange alternatives in order of their relative costs.

Identify cost factors. Briefly explain different types of costs such as development cost, purchase cost, installation cost, maintenance cost, and upgrade cost. Give examples of costs associated with money, time, personnel, and psychological factors. Ask participants to specify the types of costs associated with different alternatives.

> Using Alternative A (building a multilevel parking lot), you would present these sample costs:
>
> - Development cost: cost of building the parking lot
> - Purchase cost: price of parking meters
> - Installation cost: cost of setting up parking meters
> - Maintenance costs: cleaning the parking lot and collecting money from the meters
> - Upgrade cost: replacing parking meters with new models that accept credit cards

Design Your Own Games and Activities

You also point out that all these costs incorporate time, money, and people. As a sample psychological (emotional) cost, you point out that many employees may be upset by the possibilities of cutting down beautiful trees to build an ugly parking lot.

Relate costs to different items. Ask participants to discuss the types of costs associated with each alternative and whether each of these costs is low, medium, or high.

In discussing telecommuting as an alternative, participants identify a high psychological cost associated with employees missing opportunities for socializing with their co-workers around water coolers. Also telecommuting at home may make it easier for some employees to procrastinate and to experience additional stress with tight deadlines.

Compare costs of paired alternatives. Display the comparison matrix on the flip chart. Point out that the boxes along one of the diagonals are blank. Explain that the boxes above this diagonal are for cost comparisons. Each box contains two alternatives and every alternative is paired with every other alternative. Draw an enlarged copy of the matrix on the flip chart. Identify the box labeled B-A and ask participants to discuss the relative costs of the two alternatives.

Participants compare the costs of building a multilevel parking lot with the costs of encouraging car pooling.

Select the lower-cost alternative. Ask participants to select the lower-cost alternative. If there is disagreement, encourage participants to talk to each other until they reach consensus. Circle the appropriate letter in the box to indicate the lower-cost alternative.

Participants quickly decide that encouraging car pooling is definitely less costly than building a multilevel parking lot. So you circle letter "B" in this box.

Repeat the process. Point randomly to another box above the diagonal. Invite participants to discuss the relative costs of the two items listed in the box. After a suitable pause, ask participants to circle the letter identifying the lower-cost alternative. Repeat this process until you have circled a letter in each of the boxes above the diagonal.

You point to the box labeled E-C. Participants conduct a heated discussion to compare costs of scheduling staggered working hours and supporting telecommuting. The discussion takes a longer time because most of the costs (such as the feeling of resentment among people who are assigned to the late-night shift) appear to be indirect

and intangible. Finally, participants conclude that support of telecommuting is less costly than staggered schedules and circle the letter "E." They repeat this process with each of the other eight boxes above the diagonal.

Arrange alternatives according to their costs. Count the number of times each letter is circled. The alternative associated with the most frequently circled letter is the lowest-cost item. Beginning with this alternative, arrange all alternatives from the lowest cost to the highest cost. In the case of two letters being circled the same number of times, invite participants to discuss the situation and arrive at a consensus choice of the lower-cost alternative.

Here are the results at the end of cost-comparisons among alternative solutions to the parking-lot problem: B-4, C-3, E-2, D-1, and A-0.

Phase 3

Compare potential benefits. Use a method similar to the one used in the previous phase to arrange alternatives in order of their relative benefits.

Explain the rationale. Point out to participants that just because they have identified the costs of different alternatives, it does not mean they can choose the lowest-cost alternative as the best one. It is possible that the cheapest alternative does not offer any significant benefits. So it is important to also compare the potential benefits of different alternatives.

Identify benefit factors. Briefly explain different types of potential benefits such as immediate profits, future profits, cost savings, time savings, and employee satisfaction. Give examples of benefits associated with money, time, personnel, and personnel factors. Ask participants to specify the types of benefits associated with different alternatives.

Using Alternative A (building a multilevel parking lot), you present these sample benefits:

- Future profits: you can charge a modest parking fee
- Cost saving: you save costs associated with employees arriving late
- Time saving: employees don't have to waste time looking for a place to park
- Employee satisfaction: employees are happy about the corporation improving their work conditions

Relate benefits to different items. Ask participants to discuss the types of potential benefits associated with each alternative and whether each of these benefits is low, medium, or high.

In discussing telecommuting as an alternative, participants identify a high psychological benefit because they feel more empowered and

Design Your Own Games and Activities

that the corporation trusts them to make appropriate decisions. They also identify enormous time saving because employees do not have to commute to work every day.

Compare potential benefits of paired alternatives. Direct participants' attention to the comparison matrix on the flip chart. Explain that the boxes below the blank diagonal are for benefit comparisons. Each box contains two alternatives, and every alternative is paired with every other alternative. Point to the box labeled A-B and ask participants to discuss the relative benefits of the two alternatives.

Participants compare the potential benefits of encouraging car pooling with the potential benefits of building a multilevel parking lot.

Select the higher-benefit alternative. Ask participants to select the higher-benefit alternative. If there is disagreement, encourage participants to talk to each other until they reach consensus. Circle the appropriate letter in the box to indicate the higher-benefit alternative.

After some interesting debate, participants decide that building a multilevel parking lot is potentially more beneficial than encouraging car pooling. They believe that most employees will be reluctant to give up their "transportation freedom" and so attempts at car pooling will not be effective. So you circle letter "A" in this box.

Repeat the process. Point randomly to another box below the diagonal. Invite participants to discuss the relative benefits of the two items listed in the box. After a suitable pause, invite participants to circle the letter identifying the higher-benefit alternative. Repeat this process until you have circled a letter in each of the boxes below the diagonal.

You point to the box labeled C-E. Participants discuss the potential benefits of telecommuting with staggered working hours. They quickly decide that telecommuting has higher potential benefits, particularly in terms of employee satisfaction. They circle the letter "E." They repeat this process with each of the other eight boxes above the diagonal.

Arrange alternatives according to their potential benefits. Count the number of times each letter is circled. The alternative associated with the most frequently circled letter is the highest-benefit item. Beginning with this alternative, arrange all alternatives from the highest benefit to the lowest benefit. In case of two letters being circled the same number of times, invite participants to discuss the situation and arrive at a consensus choice of the higher-benefit alternative.

Here are the results at the end of benefit-comparisons among alternative solutions to the parking-lot problem: A-4, D-3, E-2, B-1, and C-2.

Phase 4

Make the final choice. Select the best alternative by reviewing and discussing cost and benefit comparisons.

Choose the best alternative. Compare the lowest-cost and the highest-benefit alternatives identified during the past two phases of the game. If they are the same, then this alternative is obviously the best one (because it provides the most benefits at the least cost).

Unfortunately, the sample game does not provide such clear results. Actually, the lowest-cost alternative (carpooling) offers the lowest benefits. Similarly, the highest benefit alternative (multilevel parking lot) costs the most!

Discuss and decide. If the lowest-cost and the highest-benefit alternatives are different from one another, invite participants to discuss the situation and to reach consensus on the most suitable alternative. If appropriate, invite participants to brainstorm new alternatives or to combine some of the existing alternatives.

After a thoughtful discussion, participants decide that encouraging telecommuting is the best overall strategy for reducing the parking lot problem. They also decide to combine this strategy with that of voluntary car pooling.

Phase 5

Debrief participants. To obtain the maximum long-term benefits from APPLES AND ORANGES, invite participants to discuss their experiences. Here are some suggested questions to prompt this discussion:

- What would have been your choice if we had not gone through this comparison procedure?

- Are you comfortable with the final choice? If not, what are the reasons for your discomfort?

- If we invited all participants to secretly vote for their personal choice now, do you believe that the results would be the same?

- Did the game permit you to give your input and express your opinions?

- What are the advantages of using this game? What are its disadvantages?

- What are some situations in which you would not use this game? Why not?

- Can you use this game for the selection of a political candidate? What modifications would you make to the game?

- How would you modify this game for use in making personal decisions?
- How would you modify this game for use with a large group?
- How would you modify this game to speed it up?

Variations

Here are some options you can employ to customize this game.

Not enough time? Reduce the number of alternatives. Prepare a short list of specific cost and benefit factors. Make a single pass through the boxes above the diagonal and compare both costs and benefits. Alternatively, ask one team to work on cost comparisons while another team works on benefit comparisons.

Ample time? Increase the number of alternatives. Conduct the game in three installments: cost comparison, benefits comparison, and final choice. Separate each installment by a few days, during which time teams interview people and collect objective data.

Too many participants? Create a "graffiti wall" with a large-size version of the comparison matrix. Invite individual participants to write cost and benefit comparison statements on sticky note paper and attach them to appropriate boxes. Later, ask participants to review these notes and independently vote for the best alternative.

Too few alternatives? Don't use this procedure unless you have at least three alternatives.

Too many alternatives? With more than six alternatives, comparisons become cumbersome. Identify the top three to six alternatives. Use a multiple voting procedure to accomplish this. List the alternatives on a flip chart and give three sticky colored dots to each participant. Invite participants to vote their preferences by placing the colored dots next to selected alternatives. A participant may place several dots next to the same alternative to indicate the intensity of his or her preference. Count the numbers of colored dots to identify the top alternatives.

Reproduced from *Design Your Own Games and Activities* by Sivasailam (Thiagi) Thiagarajan with Raja Thiagarajan with permission of the publisher. Copyright © 2003 by John Wiley & Sons, Inc.

Cost and Benefits

Every solution or strategy has different costs and benefits associated with it. The process of comparing costs and benefits of alternative solutions is called a cost-benefit analysis. The best solution is the one that has low costs and high benefits.

This game involves a cost-benefit analysis. To help you make the best use of the game, here are some background facts about costs and benefits:

Costs The price of implementing a solution is its cost. There are different types of costs, and you may classify them according to whether you incur them before (*developmental* costs), during (*installation* costs), or after (*maintenance* costs) you implement the solution.

Not all costs involve money. You can classify additional types of costs into such categories as time, effort, personnel, supplies, learning, morale, discomfort, and lost opportunities.

You can also classify costs into *direct* and *indirect* categories. For example, the cost of conducting a training workshop is a direct cost. The working time lost by the employees attending the workshop is an indirect cost.

Benefits Benefits are positive outcomes of implementing a solution. You can classify benefits into *immediate* profits and *future* profits. Reduced cost is another type of financial benefit.

In addition to financial benefits, you have additional benefits that can be classified as time saving, effort saving, improved effectiveness, workforce reduction, increased competencies, improved morale, improvement in other psychological factors, and increased opportunities.

Reproduced from *Design Your Own Games and Activities* by Sivasailam (Thiagi) Thiagarajan with Raja Thiagarajan with permission of the publisher. Copyright © 2003 by John Wiley & Sons, Inc.

Overview and Rationale

During the game, we pair up each alternative with every other alternative. In each pair, we compare the costs associated with the two alternatives and identify the lower-cost alternative. Later, we repeat the same process to identify the higher-benefit alternative in every pair. Finally, we select the best alternative that offers high benefits at low cost.

Why do we separate cost comparisons from benefit comparisons? This separation permits us to avoid what psychologists call the "halo" effect, which tempts us to ignore (or reduce) the costs associated with high-benefit alternatives.

Why do we compare only two items at a time? Our brains find it easier to review just two sets of information rather than manage larger amounts.

Why make other comparisons if we find out that alternative A is less costly than all other alternatives? This conclusion does not help us figure out whether alternative B is less costly than C, and so on. We need this type of information to arrange all alternatives in order of their costs and, later, in order of their potential benefits. This will permit us to select the "best" alternative, which may turn out to be the third costliest one with the second highest benefits.

When is this game inappropriate? If you have a fairly simple choice involving just two or three alternatives, by all means go ahead and make your decision without the cost-benefit analysis. Also, if you are under a tight deadline, make your decision quickly. For example, don't waste your time with this game to choose the best way to escape a burning building.

Why involve other people when you can make the choice yourself? It is possible that you may miss some critical information. Other people may have different perspectives that will prevent costly mistakes.

Why waste time with all these elaborate discussions? Part of the reason is to give ownership of the solution to the people who will be involved in its implementation. Discussions during the game enable us to bring out all hopes and anxieties, misgivings and expectations. This enables us to improve the solution and to implement it more efficiently.

Reproduced from *Design Your Own Games and Activities* by Sivasailam (Thiagi) Thiagarajan with Raja Thiagarajan with permission of the publisher. Copyright © 2003 by John Wiley & Sons, Inc.

Comparison Matrix

	A	B	C	D	E
A		B A	C A	D A	E A
B	A B		C B	D B	E B
C	A C	B C		D C	E C
D	A D	B D	C D		E D
E	A E	B E	C E	D E	

Design Your Own Games and Activities

12 Paper-and-Pencil Games

Paper-and-pencil games require players to make their moves by writing or drawing something on paper. A typical game may involve players working on a small piece of paper (example: *writing a key word on a tiny Post-it Note*) or a large sheet of paper (example: *drawing a mural of the organization's vision on three yards of butcher paper*). Paper-and-pencil games may incorporate elements of role play, simulation, or quiz contest.

HELP-DESK DIALOGUE

You are a help-desk employee (HDE) participating in an in-house training workshop. Diane is your facilitator. She divides participants into pairs and you are teamed with Joan.

Diane explains that you will be participating in a different kind of role play. For one thing, instead of talking, you will write your statement. You will also write your thoughts (internal dialogue). You will participate in two role plays at the same time, playing the role of an HDE in one and a customer in the other.

Diane gives everyone a small, wire-bound notebook. She explains that you will write your statements on the front of the page and write your thoughts on the back. Following Diane's directions, you put yourself in the role of a customer with a computer problem. You open your notebook to the first page and write down what you say when your telephone call to the help desk is answered.

You exchange notebooks with Joan. You now play the role of a help desk employee and respond to Joan's statement. You read this customer's

statement and, on the back of the page, write your thoughts about the statement. Then on the next page (a front page), you write what you would tell the customer. Diane suggests that you may find it easier to write your response first and then figure out what thoughts led you to this response.

After writing your response, you and Joan exchange the notebooks again. You return to the role of the customer and read the HDE's response to your earlier statement. Diane tells you not to read any of the back-page thoughts. On the back of the current page, you write your thoughts about the HDE's response. On the following page you write what you say next.

The role play continues in this fashion with you alternating between the customer's role and the HDE's role. You are creating two independent telephone dialogues. In your notebook, you are always the customer. In Joan's notebook, you are always the HDE. Initially, you hurry up to write your responses to Joan's statements. Later, you begin monitoring and recording your thoughts before responding. This is an insight that you share with the others during Diane's debriefing.

Advantages and Limitations

The major advantage of paper-and-pencil games is that they can be played anywhere at any time. Usually, you don't require special supplies and materials. This type of game produces a permanent record of the players' actions. For training purposes, participants can analyze these records and discuss their insights. Paper-and-pencil games have limitations also. Not everyone has sufficient language skills to enjoy playing these games. And if you make the games nonverbal by asking participants to draw something, people usually complain that they don't have the artistic abilities or the graphic skills required for playing the game. Recently, I came across another interesting limitation: Some participants are paranoid about committing themselves to paper. They worry that what they write (or draw) may be used against them at a later time. In general, however, most participants enjoy paper-and-pencil games.

Types of Paper-and-Pencil Games

Paper-and-pencil games come in a variety of forms. Some are serious, while others are lighthearted. Some involve two players, while others accommodate larger groups. Here are four major categories of these games, classified according to their purpose:

Role plays. Some paper-and-pencil games use a written version of a role play. HELP-DESK DIALOGUE, described above, belongs to this category.

Review games. Some paper-and-pencil games use a quiz contest approach to encourage participants to review what they have learned. Here's a brief description of a lighthearted example called Q&A&Q.

This game is for four or more players. Each player writes a question at the bottom portion of a piece of paper and gives it to the next player. All

players now write the answer to the question on the piece of paper they received. They write this answer above the question and fold the bottom part of the paper so that the question is hidden but the answer is visible. Each player once again passes the piece of paper to the next player. Players now study the answer and write a question that would have elicited the answer. They write the question above the answer and fold the paper so that the answer is hidden but the most recent question is visible. This process is repeated for several rounds. Finally, everyone opens the papers and reads all the questions and answers.

The results are always amusing. Here's an example from the game we played at the end of a training session on teamwork:

> Question 1: How many stages of team development does Tuckman's model specify? Answer 1: Four.
> Question 2: What is the minimum number of members required for an effective team? Answer 2: Five.
> Question 3: How many minutes should a team spend in brainstorming solutions to a simple problem? Answer 3: 10.
> Question 4: What is the maximum number of members for an effective team? Answer 4: Seven.
> Question 5: How many lines of text should the team facilitator record on a single sheet of flip-chart paper to permit maximum readability? Answer 5: 10.

Puzzle games. These are usually two-person games in which players try to stump each other with puzzles they have created. We recently played a version of the perennial classic HANGMAN in a change-management workshop. Here's how the game works: We pair off participants. The first player thinks of a word or a phrase that identifies a characteristic of an effective change agent and draws blank lines for each letter in this word or phrase. This player also draws the picture of gallows and a noose. The second player guesses a letter that might be in the word. If correct, the first player writes this letter on the appropriate blank spaces. If the guess is incorrect, the first player draws a head under the noose. As the game proceeds, the first player adds different body parts (two arms, two legs, and the trunk) to the unhappy victim at the gallows. The second player wins if she or he correctly guesses the word or phrase before the hanging body is completed.

Simulation games. You can incorporate a paper-and-pencil game in a simulation game. Here's an example: WIGGLES is a game that uses a page of dotted squiggly lines. In the basic game, players take turns to mark a line segment. Whenever a player marks a segment that encloses an area, that area belongs to him or her. The game ends when all line segments are marked. The player who occupies the most enclosed areas wins the game. A leadership simulation incorporates WIGGLES and explores the tradeoff between control and empowerment. This game involves five players, one of

whom is the leader. During his or her turn, each player can mark three different line segments. However, the leader may specify which line segments should be marked by each player. The players' goal is to occupy the most number of enclosed areas and get the highest individual score. The leader's goal is to minimize the difference between the highest and lowest player scores. These potentially conflicting goals create an interesting challenge to the leader.

Ready-to-Use Paper-and-Pencil Game
ONE-ON-ONE

Here is a paper-and-pencil game that explores our assumptions about competition and collaboration. It is a metaphorical simulation that incorporates a word game.

Purpose

- To explore factors that facilitate competition or collaboration between two people.
- To help the participants to identify their assumptions about interacting with someone else.

Time

45 minutes (25 minutes for the activity and 20 minutes for debriefing).

Participants

Two to two hundred (or more), playing in pairs.

Materials

- Play Grid. Reproduce the grid on page 132. This is an 8 x 8 grid, divided into quadrants. The top right and the bottom left quadrants have thicker borders.
- Enlarged Play Grid. Prepare a transparency of the Play Grid or copy it on a sheet of flip-chart paper.
- Instructions sheet. Reproduce the instructions on pages 133–134. These instructions explain how to play a word game on the Play Grid.
- Additional Instructions sheet. The instructions on these cards specify three more rules, including the rule about winning the game. There are actually eight versions, each with two identical rules and one rule (about winning) that is different. Make copies of the Additional Instructions sheet on page 135 and cut along the dotted lines. (During play randomly give one card to each participant.)

Design Your Own Games and Activities

Room Setup

This activity involves a two-person game. Arrange pairs of chairs facing each other, with a writing surface in the middle.

Preparation

Master the word game. Read the instructions for playing the game. Reproduce the Play Grid and play several rounds of the game with a co-facilitator or friend. Familiarize yourself with the scoring system. Play the game several times, using different sets of additional instructions.

Flow

Brief the players. Distribute copies of the Play Grid and the Instructions sheet. Invite a participant to play the game with you, using the transparency or the enlarged Play Grid on the flip chart. Demonstrate how to play the game, making frequent references to the Instructions sheet.

Conduct the practice round. Ask participants to pair up. Instruct members of each pair to sit across from each other and place a copy of the Play Grid between them. Invite participants to begin playing the game. Walk among the participants and provide necessary clarification of the rules. If any participant wants to know how to win the game, urge him or her to continue playing the practice game and explain that you will reveal a few additional rules shortly.

Begin the "real" rounds. Conclude the practice round after about 2 minutes of play. Answer any questions about the play of the game.

Distribute copies of Additional Instructions. Do not publicize the fact that different players have different rules for winning the game.

Monitor the play of the game. Blow a whistle to announce the start of the game. Start a timer. Walk among the participants, reminding them not to talk.

Conclude the game. Blow the whistle at the end of 10 minutes. Ask participants to remain silent for 1 more minute. Ask each participant to write down a number from 1 to 5 to indicate the level of competition or cooperation during the play of the game, using this scale:

    1 = extremely cooperative
    2 = cooperative
    3 = both cooperative and competitive
    4 = competitive
    5 = extremely competitive

Identify the winners. Ask the winners to stand up. There would be some confusion and surprise because both members of several pairs may stand

up since each of them won according to the rule on his or her Additional Instructions. Reveal that there were different definitions of winning. Invite participants to read alternative rules about winning the game.

Debrief the players. To obtain the maximum learning value from ONE-ON-ONE, invite players to discuss their experiences. Remember that the purpose of this game is to explore factors that influence competition and collaboration. Choose and use appropriate questions from the following sets:

How do you feel?

- How do you feel about the game?

- Earlier groups of players reported feelings of confusion, frustration, delight, and surprise during the play of this activity. What are some possible causes of each of these feelings?

- How do you feel about the other player?

- How do you feel about the fact that different players had different rules for winning? Why do you feel that way?

- How did you feel about the gag order?

What happened?

- What interesting things happened during the play of this game?

- What happened during the beginning of the game? What happened later?

- What was the most important moment during the play of the game? What happened at that moment?

- Did the other player surprise you with any of his or her behavior during the game?

- How did you keep track of the scores? How did you react to the differences between your score and the other player's score?

What did you learn?

- This game is about competition and collaboration. What were some important learning points from the game?

- How did you rate the level of competition and collaboration in the game? What factors contributed to this rating?

- Here are some insights reported by earlier groups of players. Does your experience support each of these principles?

  Most people assume that games are competitive.

  Actions speak louder than words. Even though you did not talk, your moves in the game clearly indicated whether you were trying to compete or collaborate.

Design Your Own Games and Activities

It is difficult to collaborate with someone when only one of you can achieve the goal.

Sometimes it is possible to have complementary goals that permit both players to win according to different rules.

How does this relate?

- What real-world processes does this activity relate to?
- How do the alternative goals reflect different agenda among team members?
- When you are working with a partner, how do you define winning?

What if?

- What if everybody played by the same rule? How would that have changed your behavior during the game?
- What if you can write only vowels and the other player can write only consonants?
- What if you had a 2-minute time limit?
- What if you were permitted to write two letters during each turn?
- What if the winners received a cash prize?
- What if three players played the game with a single common quadrant?
- What if you played on a larger grid?
- What if you were permitted to talk to each other—but did not know that the rules for winning were different?
- What if your territory was larger than the other player's territory?

What next?

- How would you behave differently if you were to play this game again?
- What advice would you give to a friend who is about to play ONE-ON-ONE for the first time?
- How would you modify the game to encourage a high level of collaboration? High level of competition?
- Considering what you have learned from this game, would you behave differently toward your real-world partners?

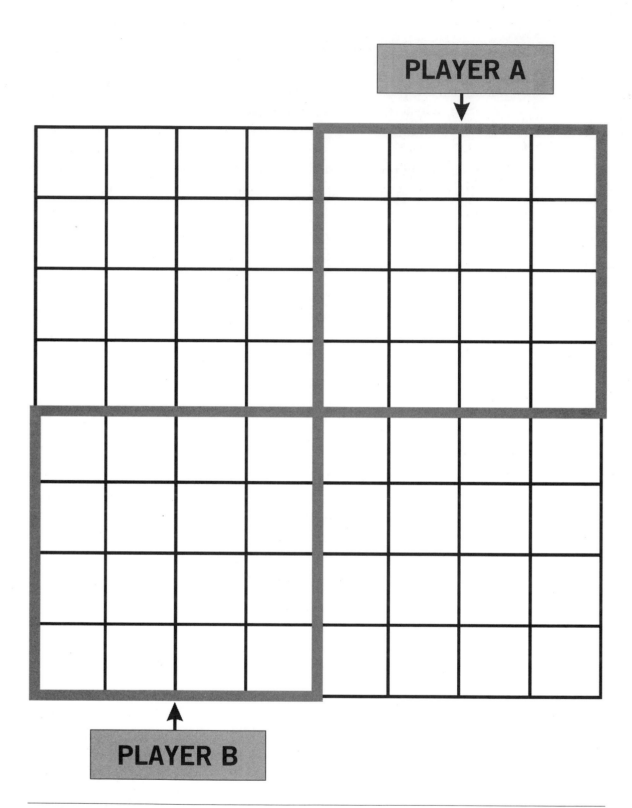

PLAYER A

PLAYER B

Instructions

Choose Quadrants   Decide who will be Player A and who will be Player B. The grid has a quadrant for Player A and another for Player B. The other two quadrants belong to both players. Identify your quadrant.

Begin the Game   If you are Player A, begin the game by writing any letter in any space in the grid. You can write this letter in your quadrant, in Player B's quadrant, or in one of the common quadrants.

Continue the Game   Take turns writing a letter in any space.

Create Words   You earn points whenever a set of adjacent letters spell out a word (of two or more letters) that can be read from left to right or top to bottom. The word should appear in any standard dictionary and should not be a proper noun, a hyphenated expression, or a foreign word.

Calculate Points   Each letter in the new word is worth a point. This point does not belong to the player who created the word, but to the player (or players) in whose quadrant the letter is found. Letters in the common quadrant provide points for both players.

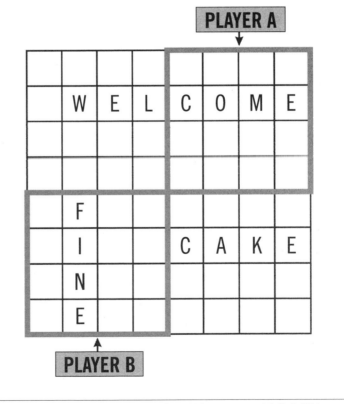

(Continued)

Examples:

You are Player A and you wrote the final E to spell the word WELCOME. Your score is 7 (because three letters are in your quadrant and four letters are in a common quadrant). Player B's score is 4 (because four letters are in a common quadrant).

You are Player B and you wrote the final E to spell the word FINE. You score 4 points for the four letters in your quadrant. The other player scores nothing because none of the letters are in Player A's quadrant or in a common quadrant.

You are Player A and you wrote the final E and to spell the word CAKE. Both you and Player B score 4 points because all four letters are in a common quadrant.

Modify Words
Any new word that results from modifications of a previous word is scored again.

Players take turn spelling new words by adding a letter to the front or back of the previous words: AN, RAN, RANK, PRANK, PRANKS. After each turn, the new word is scored.

Help or Block
You can use a letter to help the other player (example: *write an E after AM to create AME, which the other player can convert into GAME or NAME*) or to block the other player (example: *write a Q at the end of WELCO to create WELCOQ, which cannot be converted into any word*).

Continue Playing
Take turns writing letters. Whenever a new word is created, calculate the points for yourself and for the other player. Keep track of the score.

Design Your Own Games and Activities

Additional Instructions

Observe the time limit. The game is played for 10 minutes.
Obey the gag order. Do not talk to each other during the play of the game.
Win the game. The game ends when all spaces in the grid are filled with letters or when the time limit is up. You win if you score *more* points than the other player.

Observe the time limit. The game is played for 10 minutes.
Obey the gag order. Do not talk to each other during the play of the game.
Win the game. The game ends when all spaces in the grid are filled with letters or when the time limit is up. You win if you score more points than the other player and if your combined total score is more than 80 points.

Observe the time limit. The game is played for 10 minutes.
Obey the gag order. Do not talk to each other during the play of the game.
Win the game. The game ends when all spaces in the grid are filled with letters or when the time limit is up. You win if you score at least 10 more points than the other player.

Observe the time limit. The game is played for 10 minutes.
Obey the gag order. Do not talk to each other during the play of the game.
Win the game. The game ends when all spaces in the grid are filled with letters or when the time limit is up. Both of you win if the difference between your score and the other player's score is less than 3.

Observe the time limit. The game is played for 10 minutes.
Obey the gag order. Do not talk to each other during the play of the game.
Win the game. The game ends when all spaces in the grid are filled with letters or when the time limit is up. Both of you win if your combined total score is more than 80 points. Otherwise, both of you lose.

Observe the time limit. The game is played for 10 minutes.
Obey the gag order. Do not talk to each other during the play of the game.
Win the game. The game ends when all spaces in the grid are filled with letters or when the time limit is up. You win if you score *fewer* points than the other player.

Observe the time limit. The game is played for 10 minutes.
Obey the gag order. Do not talk to each other during the play of the game.
Win the game. The game ends when all spaces in the grid are filled with letters or when the time limit is up. You win if you score more points than the other player—but not more than 3 points.

Observe the time limit. The game is played for 10 minutes.
Obey the gag order. Do not talk to each other during the play of the game.
Win the game. The game ends when all spaces in the grid are filled with letters or when the time limit is up. You win if you score at least 10 points fewer than the other player.

13 Instructional Puzzles

*A puzzle **is a baffling** problem that requires concentrated study and ingenious thought to arrive at a solution. Solving a puzzle frequently requires intuition; and the solution is usually preceded by sudden illumination. Puzzles are similar to games in their ability to engage people on the task. However, while a game may produce different outcomes, puzzles result in a single solution. Most puzzles serve a recreational purpose; *instructional puzzles* help the solver achieve some training objectives.

CONSULTANTS

You are a manager in a software engineering company. John, a facilitator from the performance improvement division, is conducting a workshop on organizational learning. He kicks off the training session with a game called CONSULTANTS. In this game, you and twenty other participants are given a puzzle sheet with fifty triplets. John explains that each triplet is a set of three words linked by a common fourth word that is not given. When the same linking word is placed before or after each of the three words in the triplet, you create well-known compound words or phrases. To illustrate the puzzle-solving procedure, John presents this triplet on a flip chart:

B E L T—H O L E—P I T C H

You look at the first word and think of belt buckle and sunbelt. But neither buckle nor sun could be the link word. While you are pondering the connections among the three words, Sandy blurts out, "Black" and explains that this linking word creates BLACK BELT, BLACK HOLE, and PITCH BLACK.

John now gives everyone $500 in play money. He identifies five participants as consultants. John gives each consultant a list of a few link words. He informs them that anyone can hire a consultant for $10 and collect any of the following four pieces of information: whether the linking word appears before or after each of the three words, the number of letters in the linking word, the first letter of the linking word, and the last letter of the linking word. John announces that the first person to solve all fifty triplets will receive a $1,000 prize (unfortunately, only in play money). You proceed to solve a few of the triplets easily. You figure out that the linking word for BOMB—FATHER—LINE is TIME. After solving twelve triplets, you run out of steam. So you locate a consultant and pay her $20 to find out that the linking word for DIP—SOUP—STEAMED has nine letters and begins with the letter "V." You immediately figure out that the word is "VEGETABLE." While you are debating whether to spend more money for additional clues, John stops the game. He identifies five participants who have solved the most triplets at this time and makes them additional consultants. He also changes the fee structure. Each consultant can now negotiate how much to charge for different clues and can even sell the complete solution. As one of these new consultants, you look around for potential clients. You offer to give George the linking word for Triplet 27 for $100, but you are undercut by Gail who sells the solution for a mere $50. After three more minutes of play, John introduces another change: Participants can now exchange solutions with each other. The game ends when Sandy solves all of the fifty triplets. John conducts a debriefing to drive home the point that a lot of expertise is available among the employees in your organization. By sharing the knowledge and skills, the company can save the money paid to outside consultants.

Benefits and Uses

The major advantage of using instructional puzzles is their ability to keep participants working on a task with great concentration. Here are different ways in which instructional puzzles can be used.

Simulation games. CONSULTANTS is an example of a simulation game that incorporates a puzzle. In this game, the triplet puzzle is used to represent problem-solving and knowledge-management tasks. You can embed a variety of puzzles in simulation games that explore teamwork and interpersonal skills.

Preview. Distribute an instructional puzzle to your participants a few days before the training session. Use the puzzle as a pretest or as a teaser. Assure participants that they will be able to solve the entire puzzle at the end of the training session.

Reward for punctuality. Rather than punishing people for coming ahead of time, distribute copies of an instructional puzzle. Encourage participants to get a head start on solving the puzzle. Later, resume the session after each

coffee break by giving additional clues to encourage participants to return on time.

Brain energizers. Between one training unit and the next, instead of taking a stretch break, have participants solve an instructional puzzle. After a suitable pause announce the solution.

Post-test. Give the final test in the form of a crossword puzzle. Wait for the players to solve the puzzle and then give them the solution for a self-check.

Follow-up. A week after a training session, send a follow-up puzzle to participants. Incorporate major learning points in the puzzle. A few days later, send everyone a postcard with the solution.

Interactive lectures. Distribute a crossword puzzle at the beginning of your presentation and encourage participants to solve as much of it as possible. Interrupt your presentation every 10 minutes for a puzzle-solving break that requires participants to recall and use content from your presentation. Continue this procedure until participants have completely solved the puzzle at the end of your presentation.

Review. Near the end of your session, ask teams to design their own puzzles related to the training content. Later, ask teams to exchange the puzzles they created and solve them.

Limitations

A few warnings about the use of instructional puzzles:

Frustration. Some participants may be so frustrated by the puzzle that they may give up. Maintain an optimum level of difficulty by providing appropriate hints to participants.

Embarrassment. Some participant may suffer from anxiety attacks because of previous experiences with puzzles. Avoid forcing people to confess their inability to solve the puzzle. Encourage participants to work with a partner or as a team to reduce personal embarrassment.

Unfamiliarity. Different groups have their own favorite puzzle format. It is possible that some participants may not be familiar with the type of puzzle that you are using. Provide participants with a job aid for solving the puzzle. Walk them through the first few steps of the solving procedure.

Irrelevance. You may have a really intriguing puzzle that has nothing to do with your instructional objective. The impact of this type of puzzle will be to distract participants from your learning point. Be sure that the puzzle incorporates relevant content or simulates a relevant process.

Types of Puzzle

We can divide instructional puzzles into three types on the basis of the types of solution: *words*, *messages*, and *other*. The first two types provide

frames for easily loading instructional content. The last type is particularly suited for incorporation into simulation games. Here are brief descriptions of samples from these three types:

Word Puzzles

Crossword puzzle. Most participants are familiar with this popular puzzle format. With inexpensive software programs, you can easily create this type of puzzle on any instructional topic. (See page 145 for a sample crossword puzzle from a training workshop on conflict management.)

MATCHLESS ITEMS. The puzzle maker takes eight sets of three related pieces of information (examples: *model numbers*, *prices*, and *key benefits*) and randomly places them in a twenty-five-box grid. The last box contains another related piece of information that is not associated with any of the sets. Your task is to find the odd piece of information. (See page 146 for a sample matchless items puzzle from a training workshop on Asian countries.)

Sentence Puzzles

CHUNKS. The puzzle maker cuts a message into three-character chunks (including punctuation marks and spaces between the words) and places these chunks in a random order. Your task is to rearrange the chunks to form the original sentence. (See page 147 for a sample chunks puzzle on conflict management.)

LETTER DROP puzzles. The puzzle maker places letters from a message in a scrambled order in different columns. Your task is to move each letter to an appropriate box in a grid to spell out the original message. (See page 148 for a sample letter drop puzzle on change management.)

Other Types

SCRAMBLED GRAPHIC. The puzzle maker converts a technical diagram into several square tiles of identical size. Your task is to rearrange the tiles to reveal the original diagram.

Topological puzzles. The puzzle maker links pieces of string, wire, and wood into interlocked forms. Your task is to unlink different sections of the puzzle.

Ready-to-Use Instructional Puzzle Activity
CRYPTIC STRATEGIES

In the knowledge economy, people will invest time and money to collect, create, organize, and package bits of information. This game requires teams to solve a set of cryptograms to simulate economies related to information processing.

Purpose

- To explore the relationships among time, money, and information.
- To explore how teams make decisions that involve potential risks.

Time

45 minutes

Participants

Minimum: two; maximum: thirty; ideal: ten to thirty.

Materials

- How to Decode Cryptograms handout for each participant (page 149)
- Eight Cryptograms handout for each team (page 150)
- How to Play CRYPTIC STRATEGIES for each participant (page 154)
- Check Register for each team (page 155)
- Decoding Key (for use by the facilitator, page 156)
- Timer

Flow

Organize participants. With fewer than six participants, conduct this game as a contest among individuals. With six or more participants, divide them into three or more teams with two to six members each. It does not matter if some teams have an extra member.

Distribute materials. Give a copy of How to Decode Cryptograms to each participant and a copy of Eight Cryptograms to each team. Explain that the teams should decode all eight cryptograms. Point out that each cryptogram uses a different code.

Explain rules of the game. Distribute a copy of the handout, How to Play CRYPTIC STRATEGIES to each participant. Walk participants through the set of instructions for playing the game.

Explain how financial transactions will be handled. Distribute copies of the Check Register to each team. Instead of using play money, each team will use a simulated check register with an opening balance of $20,000. The check register has columns for time, activity, charge to team, payment to team, and balance. Whenever a team buys information, the appropriate cost will be entered as a "charge to team" and the amount will be subtracted from the current balance. Whenever the team decodes a cryptogram, the appropriate amount will be entered under "payment to team" and added to the current balance.

Begin the game. Remind participants of the 20-minute time limit and start the timer.

Sell information. Whenever any team wants to know the correct equivalent for one or more letters in a cryptogram, charge the required fee first. Since the code is different from one cryptogram to another, double-check the specific cryptogram for which they need the information. Secretly check with your Decoding Key and supply the appropriate information.

Pay for decoded messages. If a team has decoded a cryptogram, secretly check it against your list of decoded messages. If the team's message is correct, add $2,000 to the team's balance.

Collect money for minutes spent. If a team has decoded all eight messages, check the timer for the number of minutes it spent on the decoding task. Charge $1,000 for each minute it spent on the decoding task.

Conclude the game. Announce the end of the game if all teams have decoded all eight cryptograms or if the play time of 20 minutes has expired. Charge the necessary amount to each team for the number of minutes it spent on the decoding task.

Identify the winning team. Ask the teams to count the total amount of money they have. Identify the team with the most money and congratulate its members for winning the game.

Debrief the participants. Invite the participants to reflect on the game and share insights. Use the six sets of suggested questions below. Remember that these questions are not meant to be used in a linear fashion. Encourage spontaneous comments and let the discussion flow naturally. Fall back on the prepared questions during periods of silence or hesitation.

How do you feel?

- How do you feel about the game in general?
- Earlier participants reported feelings of frustration, elation, boredom, and accomplishment during the play of the game. What are some possible causes of each of these feelings?
- How do you feel about other members of your team? About members of other teams?
- Did some members of your team have a special talent for decoding cryptograms? How do you feel about them?
- How did you feel when you decoded the first cryptogram?
- Did your team win the game? If so, how do you feel about it? If your team did not win the game, how do you feel about the winning team?

What happened?

- What interesting things happened during the play of the game?

- What happened at the beginning of the game? What happened later?

- Did your team discuss a general strategy before decoding cryptograms or did you begin decoding without an overall plan?

- What was the most important moment during the play of the game? What happened at that moment?

- How did you distribute different tasks among members of your team? Did someone assume the leadership role?

- Did all members of your team work on decoding the same cryptogram or did different members work on different cryptograms?

- How did you decide whether to buy information—and when to buy it? What factors did you take into consideration in making these decisions?

What did you learn?

- This game is about knowledge management, problem solving, and teamwork. What were some important learning points from the game?

- Here are some insights reported by earlier groups of players. Does your experience support each of these principles?

    It takes time to get a team organized and to involve everyone in the decision-making process.

    Some tasks are better performed by a team, while others are more suited for individual work.

    Different team members have different work-style preferences: Some people work systematically while others work intuitively. Some people take time to plan while others jump into action. Some people focus on getting the team organized while others are eager to get the job done.

    It takes money to make money.

    Sometimes it is difficult to decide who contributed the most to the success of a team.

    The presence of other teams increases the motivation level among team members.

    Most decisions involve tradeoffs among time, money, and information.

    Decoding one cryptogram makes it easier to decode other cryptograms—even though each cryptogram uses a different code.

How does this relate?

- What real-world processes does this activity relate to?
- What are the real-world analogues of the 20-minute time limit and the $20,000 budget?
- What are the similarities between the teamwork in the game and teamwork in your organization?
- In what ways do the activities in the game reflect activities in your workplace? In what ways do they differ from each other?
- How do the principles discussed earlier relate to your organization?

What if?

- What if you had to decode the cryptograms without being able to buy any information? How would that have changed your behavior during the game?
- What if you had twenty different cryptograms to decode?
- What if you had a 5-minute time limit?
- What if you had only $3,000 in your budget?
- What if we used real money (although in smaller amounts) instead of play money?
- What if we did not give you copies of the handout on how to decode cryptograms?
- What if your team had many more members? What if your team had far fewer members? What if this game were played as an individual contest?

What next?

- How would you behave differently if you were to play this game again?
- How would you organize your team the next time you play this game?
- How would you modify the game to encourage collaboration among different teams?
- Considering what you have learned from this game, how would you behave differently in real-world team projects?

Design Your Own Games and Activities

Conflict Management Crossword Puzzle

Across

1. Unable to work together
6. Items presented for acceptance or rejection
7. Answer to a problem
9. Ability to make judgments without discrimination
11. Refusal to accept facts
12. Clash between two groups or individuals
14. Necessities
17. Objective
18. Accommodation by both sides
19. Emotion aroused by a real or supposed wrong
22. Judgments reached after consideration
25. Mutual need
27. Agreement by (almost) everyone involved
28. Unlike logical thinking, this is always present in a conflict

Down

1. Important item to be settled
2. Be compatible with
3. Deliberately running away from a conflict
4. Should be replaced by the word "and"
5. Fair or same
8. Unequal treatment
9. People hate losing this
10. Perception of one's worth (hyphenated)
13. Declarations of intention to do something unpleasant
15. Disgrace from losing a conflict
16. Type of story that is hard to come by during a conflict
18. Closed meeting to discuss tactics
20. Esteem toward the other person
21. Activities expected or assigned to a person
23. Thoughts
24. What conflicting parties should do with the final decision
26. Not win, not lose

Matchless Items Puzzle

Asian Nations

Match each Asian nation with its capital and language. Find the single items that cannot be matched.

New Delhi	Kabul	Maldivian Divehi	Colombo	Khmer
Yangon	Kuala Lumpur	Timphu	Male	Dzongkha
Maldives	Dari	Hindi	Mandarin	Cambodia
Phnom Penh	Bahasa Melayu	Sinhala	Burmese	Bhutan
Afghanistan	India	Sri Lanka	Malaysia	Myanmar

Chunks Puzzle: Conflict Management

We took a sentence and cut it up into three-character chunks (including the spaces and punctuation marks). We arranged these chunks in an alphabetical order.

Solve the puzzle by rearranging the chunks to form a sentence.

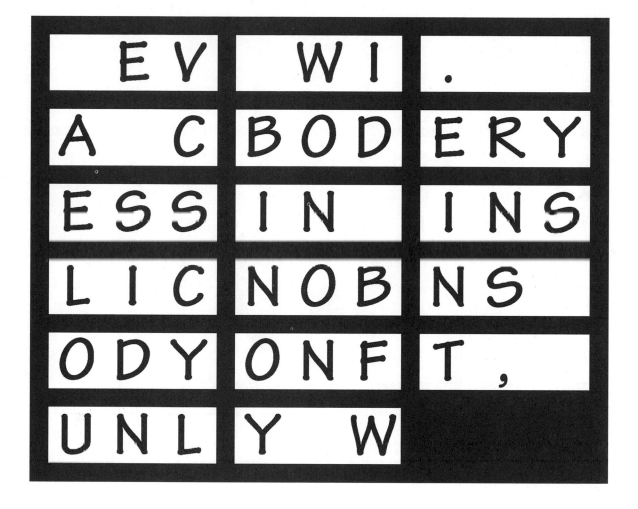

EV	WI	.
A C	BOD	ERY
ESS	IN	INS
LIC	NOB	NS
ODY	ONF	T,
UNL	Y W	

Letter Drop Puzzle: Victor Hugo on Change

To solve this puzzle, move each letter to one of the empty boxes below it. (Don't put any letters in the black boxes.) If you place all the letters in the correct boxes, you will spell out a message, reading from left to right and top to bottom.

All punctuation has been placed in appropriate boxes. Black boxes mark the spaces between words in the message.

Important note: A word does not end at the end of a line unless there is a black box there.

```
C  H        E     A                 A  E  E
I  I  A  A  C  E     E  O  E  O      H  K  I  G  E
N  N  N  C  G  L  E  P  O     T  R      O  O  N  N  I
R  O  T  N  I  P  E  Y  S  U  R      R  O  O  R  P  O
Y  S  U  R  K  T  L  Y  V  U  S  C  Y  P  U  T  S  P
```

Design Your Own Games and Activities

How to Decode Cryptograms

In a cryptogram, each letter in a message is replaced by another letter of the alphabet. For example, LET THE GAMES BEGIN may become this cryptogram: YZF FOZ JUKZH CZJVQ. In the cryptogram Y replaces L, Z replaces E, F replaces T, and so on. Notice that the same letter substitutions are used throughout this cryptogram: Every E in the sentence is replaced by a Z, and every T is replaced by an F.

Here are some hints for decoding a cryptogram:

Letter Frequency	The most commonly used letters of the English language are e, t, a, i, o, n, s, h, and r. The letters that are most commonly found at the beginning of words are t, a, o, d, and w. The letters that are most commonly found at the end of words are e, s, d, and t.
Word Frequency	One-letter words are either a or I. The most common two-letter words are to, of, in, it, is, as, at, be, we, he, so, on, an, or, do, if, up, by, and my. The most common three-letter words are the, and, are, for, not, but, had, has, was, all, any, one, man, out, you, his, her, and can. The most common four-letter words are that, with, have, this, will, your, from, they, want, been, good, much, some, and very.
Word Endings	The most common word endings are -ed, -ing, -ion, -ist, -ous, -ent, -able, -ment, -tion, -ight, and -ance.
Doubled Letters	The most frequent double-letter combinations are ee, ll, ss, oo, tt, ff, rr, nn, pp, and cc. The double letters that occur most commonly at the end of words are ee, ll, ss, and ff.
Punctuation	A comma is often followed by but, and, or who. It is usually preceded by however. A question often begins with why, how, who, was, did, what, where, or which. Two words that often precede quotation marks are said and says. Two letters that usually follow an apostrophe are t and s.

Reproduced from *Design Your Own Games and Activities* by Sivasailam (Thiagi) Thiagarajan with Raja Thiagarajan with permission of the publisher. Copyright © 2003 by John Wiley & Sons, Inc.

Eight Cryptograms

CRYPTOGRAM #1

C N A   V R   W H G Y R V W D H S H Y L :

Q N W L G D G Q N Y L Z   C H N W Y   L V

W H Q H N L   F H P N O G V W Z   L P N L   N W H

W H A N W K H K .

CRYPTOGRAM #2

U Y V   R E   Q C R Z D R I Y U   U Q Y P I D I L :

Q K Q I Z O   Z J Y Z   Y P Q   Y B B R C T Y I D Q X

A M   D I Z Q I O Q   Q C R Z D R I O   P Q O S U Z

D I U R I L - U Y O Z D I L   U Q Y P I D I L .

CRYPTOGRAM #3

```
D O L     B W     O M J R T P     D P O Q S R S C :
```

```
O M J R T P     Q P F E B S X R S C     E Q B X H M P F
```

```
I B Q P     P W W P M J R T P     D P O Q S R S C
```

```
J G O S     E O F F R T P     D R F J P S R S C     B Q
```

```
Q P O X R S C .
```

CRYPTOGRAM #4

```
Z V O     E L     N Q V P R K P T     V M H
```

```
L T T H G V P S :     Z T V Q M T Q C     P V M M E R
```

```
W V L R I Q     C S K J J C     N K R I F R
```

```
Q T N T V R T H     N Q V P R K P T     V M H
```

```
L T T H G V P S .
```

CRYPTOGRAM #5

C L V   B P   E S I A J B M T   I N E I S J I D G I :
☐☐☐   ☐☐   ☐☐☐☐☐☐☐☐   ☐☐☐☐☐☐☐☐☐☐ :

D I V   C I L S D J D W   T Q B M C F   Z I
☐☐☐   ☐☐☐☐☐☐☐☐   ☐☐☐☐☐☐   ☐☐

C J D U I F   H B   (L D F   Z M J C F   B D)
☐☐☐☐☐☐   ☐☐   (☐☐☐   ☐☐☐☐☐   ☐☐)

H Q I   I N E I S J I D G I   B P   H Q I
☐☐☐   ☐☐☐☐☐☐☐☐☐☐   ☐☐   ☐☐☐

C I L S D I S .
☐☐☐☐☐☐☐ .

CRYPTOGRAM #6

M W P   G C   K A X K F K X V W M
☐☐☐   ☐☐   ☐☐☐☐☐☐☐☐☐☐

X K C C J B J A L J D :   X K C C J B J A E
☐☐☐☐☐☐☐☐☐☐☐ :   ☐☐☐☐☐☐☐☐☐

I J G I M J   M J W B A   K A   X K C C J B J A E
☐☐☐☐☐☐   ☐☐☐☐☐   ☐☐   ☐☐☐☐☐☐☐☐☐

P W Q D .
☐☐☐☐ .

Design Your Own Games and Activities

CRYPTOGRAM #7

Y M T · S L · I G Y G W M B R G : · G L L G R C V W G

Y G M I B V B E · V D · I G Y G W M B C · C S · C P G

Y G M I B I ' D · Y V L G · M B K · T S I J .

CRYPTOGRAM #8

G R M · K P · B K H S F Y T H B C : · R V Y G D

G I R F H T F I · T T C Y L F I · R G L S H A T H D

R Y K H S · D F R L H L H S · K Q W T B D L Z T I ,

B K H D T H D , · R B D L Z L D L T I , · R H V

D I I D · I D T A I ,

How to Play CRYPTIC STRATEGIES

What Do You Have?
- A play period of 20 minutes
- A budget of $20,000
- A set of seven cryptograms (each with a different code)
- Instructions for decoding cryptograms

What Do You Do?
- Working with other team members, decode the cryptograms.

How Do You Win?
- Your team wins if it has the most money at the end of the game.

How Do You Make Money?
- You receive $2,000 for decoding any one of the cryptograms. You get increasing payments for decoding additional cryptograms: second cryptogram, $2,500; third cryptogram, $3,000; and each of the subsequent cryptograms, $3,500.

How Do You Spend Money?
- At the end of the game, we charge you $1,000 for each minute you spent in decoding the cryptograms. The faster you decode all seven cryptograms, the less money you spend.
- You can also buy information to help decode the cryptograms. Your facilitator will sell you the correct letter that corresponds to any code letter. Since each cryptogram uses a different code, specify the cryptogram for which you want to buy the appropriate information. Then specify any code letter in that cryptogram. Remember that the information about the code letter is true only for the specified cryptogram.
- The cost of information progressively increases as you ask for more information about each cryptogram. Here's how much each code letter (for the same cryptogram) will cost:
  - First code letter: $200
  - Second code letter: $400
  - Third code letter: $800
  - Fourth (and each of the subsequent) code letter: $1,000
- For example, if you want the information about one letter each for five different cryptograms, it will cost you $1,000. If you want information about five code letters in the same cryptogram, it will cost you $3,400.
- You may purchase information about code letters any time during the play period, but only if you have the necessary funds. You have to pay in advance for the information.

Design Your Own Games and Activities

Check Register

Time	Activity	Charge to Team	Payment to Team	Balance
	Opening Balance			$20,000.00

Decoding Key (for facilitator's eyes only)

Cryptogram 1   A = W, B = K, C = L, D = C, E = G, F = B, G = I, H = E, I = U, J = Z, K = D, L = T, M = Q, N = A, O = V, P = H, Q = P, R = F, S = M, T = Y, U = X, V = O, W = R, X = J, Y = N, Z = S

Decoded message: Law of reinforcement: Participants learn to repeat behaviors that are rewarded.

Cryptogram 2   A = B, B = C, C = M, D = I, E = F, F = J, G = Z, H = X, I = N, J = H, K = V, L = G, M = Y, N = Q, O = S, P = R, Q = E, R = O, S = U, T = P, U = L, V = W, W = K, X = D, Y = A, Z = T

Decoded message: Law of emotional learning: Events that are accompanied by intense emotions result in long-lasting learning.

Cryptogram 3   A = Z, B = O, C = G, D = O, E = P, F = S, G = H, H = U, I = M, J = T, K = B, L = W, M = C, N = K, O = , P = E, Q = R, R = I, S = N, T = V, U = Y, V = Q, W = F, X = D, Y = J, Z = X

Decoded message: Law of active learning: Active responding produces more effective learning than passive listening or reading.

Cryptogram 4   A = X, B = V, C = S, D = Q, E = O, F = J, G = B, H = D, I = H, J = Z, K = I, L = F, M = N, N = P, O = W, P = C, Q = R, R = T, S = K, T = E, U = Y, V = A, W = M, X = G, Y = U, Z = L

Decoded message: Law of practice and feedback: Learners cannot master skills without repeated practice and feedback.

Cryptogram 5   A = V, B = O, C = L, D = N, E = P, F = D, G = C, H = T, I = E, J = I, K = J, L = A, M = U, N = X, O = Y, P = F, Q = H, R = Z, S = R, T = S, U = K, V = W, W = G, X = M, Y = Q, Z = B

Decoded message: Law of previous experience: New learning should be linked to (and build on) the experience of the learner.

Cryptogram 6   A = N, B = R, C = F, D = S, E = T, F = V, G = O, H = G, I = P, J = E, K = I, L = C, M = L, N = Z, O = M, P = W, Q = Y, R = J, S = Q, T = B, U = K, V = U, W = A, X = D, Y = X, Z = H

Decoded message: Law of individual differences: Different people learn in different ways.

Cryptogram 7   A = M, B = N, C = T, D = S, E = G, F = J, G = E, H = B, I = R, J = K, K = D, L = F, M = A, N = Y, O = X, P = H, Q = Z, R = C, S = O, T = W, U = P, V = I, W = V, X = U, Y = L, Z = Q

Decoded message: Law of relevance: Effective learning is relevant to the learner's life and work.

Cryptogram 8   A = M, B = C, C = Y, D = T, E = Q, F = R, G = L, H = N, J = H, K = O, L = I, M = W, N = Z, O = P, P = F, Q = B, R = A, S = G, T = E, U = X, V = D, W = J, X = K, Y = U, Z = V

Decoded message: Law of congruency: Adult learners require alignment among training objectives, content, activities, and test items.

14 Audio Games

Audio games are training activities that primarily depend on recorded audio messages (such as audiotape, MP3, digital recording, or computer recording) to provide the training content, structure the training activity, and collect players' responses. Most audio games use few or no visuals.

THE CADUCEUS CRISIS

You and ten other executives working for an HMO have been invited for a change-management briefing. Your group is divided into two subgroups of five and seated around a round table. One of your colleagues turns on an audio player. The narrator explains that you are about to participate in an audio-controlled case entitled The Caduceus Crisis by Dr. Diane Dormant.

The narrator welcomes everyone and sets up the activity:

> "As the story opens, we are in the corporate headquarters of Caduceus Corporation, a nationwide hospital management corporation. J. Parer, executive vice president, is presiding over a meeting. You'll have no difficulty in recognizing Parer, who is the tallest person around the table. Let me pause briefly while Parer says 'Hello' to all of you.
>
> "Seated to Parer's right are the two systems designers from corporate headquarters, Rodriguez and Spock. Will these two people please identify themselves?"

Because of your location to the left of Steve, the tallest person (and, therefore, the person playing the role of Parer), you are cast in the role of

King. The audiotape goes on to provide additional details about each role. Then the tape continues:

> "Recently, Caduceus Corporation has shifted over to a new database system. Because of complaints from hospital personnel, J. Parer, the executive vice president of Caduceus, has called the meeting today to gather information about problems related to the implementation of the new database system."

Taking the cue from the tape, Steve, in the role of Parer, calls the meeting to order. You participate in an interesting discussion of the costs, benefits, obstacles, and support for the new system. You stick to your role of being somewhat skeptical, while some others exhibit positive perspectives.

After about 15 minutes, the narrator comes back to suggest that you wrap up your discussion in the next minute or so. A minute later, the narrator provides details about what happened since this meeting. The story line takes you to another meeting, this time among system designers, to discuss the implementation problems from the designers' perspective. You get to play a different role (as D. Jacobs, an optimistic systems designer) during the 20 minutes of the second meeting. The same procedure is used during the third meeting, which takes place at the Houston regional office, where you play the role of the controller from a large local hospital and discuss implementation problems from the end-users' perspective.

At the conclusion of the third meeting, the audiotape invites everyone to take a break. When you return, the narrator takes you through a debriefing discussion with a series of provocative questions. During this debriefing, your group identifies the key point that during times of change, different stakeholders perceive different realities and all stakeholders should be involved in designing the implementation plan.

Advantages and Limitations

The CADUCEUS CRISIS illustrates some of the advantages and limitations of the audio games strategy. Here are the advantages of audio games:

Audio games take care of the mechanics of facilitation. The audio recording enables a group to participate in the activity without the need for an external facilitator. In the CADUCEUS CRISIS, the recording provides all background information, gives instructions to participants at each phase of the activity, keeps track of the time, and coordinates the debriefing.

Audio games provide replicable experiences. The two subgroups in the sample play of CADUCEUS CRISIS went through the same activity. If this audio game is used with other groups, the same activity will be replicated each time.

Audio games can be played when participants' eyes and hands are occupied otherwise. We frequently play audio games while driving long distances (making sure that the driver does not get distracted). Single-player audio

games can be played by individuals who are engaged in some repetitive activity such as jogging.

Audio games are ideally suited for certain types of training objectives. Although this was not a factor in the CADUCEUS CRISIS, it is obvious that audio games are most suited for achieving objectives related to conversation and listening skills.

Here are some limitations of audio games:

Audio games cannot be played any time, anywhere. Although audio playback equipment is readily available, we still have to make sure that the audio recording can be played back at a suitable volume and quality.

Audio games require self-management by participants. In the CADUCEUS CRISIS, there is nothing to prevent participants from turning off the tape recording and continuing the discussion past the assigned time. In the absence of a facilitator in audio games, it is important that participants monitor and manage their own activities.

More Examples

The CADUCEUS CRISIS is an example of an auto-facilitated audio game. In this type of game, there is no need for an external facilitator to conduct the game since all aspects of the game are incorporated in the audio recording. Here are brief descriptions and examples of four other types of audio games:

Guided visualization. In this type of audio game, the audio recording leads individual players through a visualization activity. In REINCARNATION, the recording asks you to mentally list five major achievements, beginning with the current year and working back to early childhood. After a suitable pause, the recording asks you to participate in a science fiction scenario, where you are born in an alternate universe. Everything else on this planet is exactly the same as on Earth, except your gender is the opposite: If you are a man, you will be a woman, and vice versa. The audio recording now asks you to speculate how the types, priorities, costs, and benefits of your life achievements would be different.

Recorded responses. In this type of audio game, participants record their responses on audiotape. In HALF TIME, participant teams record a summary (of the key learning points of a lesson) that lasts exactly 60 seconds. After listening to summaries from different teams, participants re-record the summary to last exactly 30 seconds. During the third and final round, teams reduce the summaries to 15 seconds.

Jolt. It is possible to conduct a brief audio game that helps participants to gain valuable insights. In a jolt called AUDIO MEMORY, the recording recites the names and positions of the top ten playing cards from a shuffled deck (example: *one, six of diamonds; two, five of clubs*). After a pause, the

audiotape asks for the names of playing cards associated with a position (or the position of a specific playing card). After a few rounds of play, smarter participants figure out the strategy of forming an informal team and dividing the task among its members so each member merely remembers the names and positions of just two cards in the ten-card sequence.

Framegame. Some audio games provide a template for plugging in different instructional content. In PAIRED LEARNING, participants are divided into two groups. Group A participants are sent outside the room while group B participants listen to a recorded lecture for 5 minutes, without taking any notes. Group A participants now return and pair up with a Group B informant, who recalls and presents the content from the recorded lecture. After 5 minutes, Group B members respond to a series of recall questions presented by the audiotape recording. Each individual participant's score belongs not only to him or her, but also to the informant. Now members of Group A are sent outside, while the next 5 minutes of the lecture are played to members of Group B, who become the informants during the next round of the game.

Ready-to-Use Audio Game
INSERT AND DELETE

Audio games primarily depend on recorded messages (such as audiotape, MP3, digital recording, or computer recording) to provide the training content and to structure the training activity. INSERT AND DELETE is an example of an audio game that depends exclusively on an audio recording. You don't conduct this game in the traditional sense because it runs on "auto pilot": One of the participants turns on an audio player in the beginning and all participants simply follow the recorded instructions.

Purpose

- To explore characteristics of effective facilitators.
- To improve listening skills.

Participants

Any number

Time

30 to 45 minutes

Supplies

- Audio recording
- Audio player

Design Your Own Games and Activities

Preparation

Record the audio script. Use the script that begins below. If possible, use more than one person to record this script. Use one person to provide all instructions and the other person to present the lists of definitions.

Record the sound of a bell, whistle, or an electronic beep whenever the <TONE> sign appears in the script. (The headings in the following script are for your information only. Do NOT include them as a part of the audio recording.)

Set up the room. In front of the room, place an audio player with the recording ready to play. Make sure that this audio player has a loud enough speaker and has a PAUSE button. If the game is to be played without a facilitator, leave this printed piece of initial instruction in some prominent place:

"Please press the <PLAY> button when all participants are present. Thanks!"

Script for the Audio Game

Introduction

Greetings!

Are you ready to play a game?

The basis of this game is a survey in which we asked a group of participants and facilitators to identify critical characteristics of effective facilitators. I am going to present this list to you. Please listen carcfully because your score in this game depends on your ability to listen—and to recall what you heard.

Please put away your pencils, pens, and all other writing instruments. Don't take any notes during this activity because we are attempting to make you better listeners.

If you are ready, let me present the list of characteristics of effective facilitators. I shall introduce each characteristic in this list with this tone.

<Tone>

List of Characteristics

Confidence is one of the characteristics of effective facilitators. These facilitators have a lot of confidence in their ability to work with a team.

<Tone>

Effective facilitators are *active listeners*. They listen carefully to team members and make use of the information.

(Continued)

<Tone>

Expertise in facilitation techniques is another characteristic of effective facilitators. These facilitators are very skillful in selecting and using different techniques to help teams share information and make decisions.

<Tone>

Flexibility is another characteristic of effective facilitators. They use a variety of techniques to suit different types of teams, different purposes, and different amounts of available times.

<Tone>

Enthusiasm is another characteristic of effective facilitators. These facilitators express their personal excitement and high levels of motivation.

<Tone>

Integrity is another characteristic of effective facilitators. These facilitators are honest in all their dealings.

<Tone>

Effective facilitators have a high level of *self-awareness*. They know their strengths and weaknesses and personal biases and preferences.

This concludes my initial presentation of some of the characteristics of effective facilitators. I have a few more items in this list, but before I continue with the presentation, I am going to test your recall of this list.

Round 1

I am going to present the list of characteristics of effective facilitators again. Listen carefully, because I am going to insert an additional item in the list.

Please don't take any notes and don't talk to anyone else while I am talking.

<Tone>

Confidence is one of the characteristics of effective facilitators. These facilitators have a lot of confidence in their ability to work with a team.

<Tone>

Effective facilitators are *active listeners*. They listen carefully to team members and make use of the information.

<Tone>

Expertise in facilitation techniques is another characteristic of effective facilitators. These facilitators are very skillful in selecting and using different techniques to help teams share information and make decisions.

Design Your Own Games and Activities

<Tone>

Flexibility is another characteristic of effective facilitators. They use a variety of techniques to suit different types of teams, different purposes, and different amounts of available times.

<Tone>

Effective facilitators are *creative*. They come up with new and innovative approaches to help team members achieve their goals.

<Tone>

Enthusiasm is another characteristic of effective facilitators. These facilitators express their personal excitement and high levels of motivation.

<Tone>

Integrity is another characteristic of effective facilitators. These facilitators are honest in all their dealings.

<Tone>

Effective facilitators have a high level of *self-awareness*. They know their strengths and weaknesses and personal biases and preferences.

Team Formation

We are now going to test your ability to identify the extra item inserted in the list.

But before we do that, please organize yourself into teams of four or five members.

Somebody press the PAUSE button on the audio player. When you have organized your teams, press PAUSE again so I can continue to facilitate this game.

Test 1

Thank you.

Talk with other members of your team and identify the item that was inserted during the preceding presentation.

Somebody press the PAUSE button on the audio player. When all teams have identified the extra item, please press PAUSE again so I can continue with the game.

(Continued)

Results 1

Thank you again.

You probably did not have any problems recognizing this as the inserted item:

<Tone>

Effective facilitators are *creative*. They come up with new and innovative approaches to help team members achieve their goals.

If you recalled "creativity" as the inserted item, give your team 1 point.

Round 2

Are you ready for the next round of the game? This time I am going to do two different things: First, I am going to present the previous list, but in a different sequence. Second, I am going to insert *two* more items somewhere in the list.

So listen carefully. As before, please don't take any written notes. And please don't talk to anyone until I have completed my presentation.

Here's the list—in a different sequence and with two new items:

<Tone>

Effective facilitators are *active listeners*. They listen carefully to what team members say and make use of the information.

<Tone>

Confidence is one of the characteristics of effective facilitators. These facilitators have a lot of confidence in their ability to work with a team.

<Tone>

Open-mindedness is another characteristic of effective facilitators. These facilitators set aside their personal preferences and actively listen to all team members.

<Tone>

Expertise in facilitation techniques is another characteristic of effective facilitators. These facilitators are very skillful in selecting and using different techniques to help teams share information and make decisions.

<Tone>

Enthusiasm is another characteristic of effective facilitators. These facilitators express their personal excitement and high levels of motivation.

Design Your Own Games and Activities

<Tone>

Flexibility is another characteristic of effective facilitators. They use a variety of techniques to suit different types of teams, different purposes, and different amounts of available times.

<Tone>

Effective facilitators are *creative*. They come up with new and innovative approaches to help team members achieve their goals.

<Tone>

Effective facilitators are *inclusive*. They increase the diversity of the team and encourage team members to express different points of view.

<Tone>

Effective facilitators have a high level of *self-awareness*. They know their strengths and weaknesses and personal biases and preferences.

<Tone>

Integrity is another characteristic of effective facilitators. These facilitators are honest in all their dealings.

Test 2

Talk with other members of your team and identify the two items that were inserted during this presentation.

Somebody press the PAUSE button on the audio player. When all teams have identified the two extra items, please press PAUSE again so I can continue with the game.

Results 2

Thank you.

Here are the two extra items that were inserted during the previous presentation.

<Tone>

Open-mindedness is another characteristic of effective facilitators. These facilitators set aside their personal preferences and biases and actively listen to all team members.

<Tone>

Effective facilitators are *inclusive*. They increase the diversity of the team and encourage team members to express different points of view.

Give your team 1 point each if you recognized "open-mindedness" and "inclusiveness" as the inserted items.

(*Continued*)

Round 3

Are you now ready for the next round? If you are anxious about the increasing length of the list, I have some good news. During this round, I will not add any extra items. Instead, I am going to delete two items from the list. Your task is to identify and recall these two items. I am also going to make another change: Instead of presenting a lengthy description of the characteristic, I am just going to use a single word or phrase.

Listen carefully. Please don't take any notes. And please don't talk to anyone until I have completed my presentation.

Here's the list—in a different sequence, in a shortened form, and with two items *missing*:

<Tone>

Integrity

<Tone>

Expertise in facilitation techniques

<Tone>

Active listening

<Tone>

Creativity

<Tone>

Enthusiasm

<Tone>

Open-mindedness

<Tone>

Inclusiveness

<Tone>

Self-awareness

Test 3

Talk with other members of your team and identify the two items that were deleted during the previous presentation.

Somebody press the PAUSE button on the audio player. When all teams have identified the two deleted items, please press PAUSE again so I can continue with the game.

Design Your Own Games and Activities

Results 3

Thank you.

Here are the two items that were deleted during the previous presentation.

<Tone>

Confidence

<Tone>

Flexibility

Give your team 1 point each if you recognized these deleted items.

Round 4

Good news: This is the last round! During this round, I am going to leave out two items. Your task is to identify these items. To make your task a little more challenging, I am also going to change the words used to identify different characteristics.

Listen carefully. Please don't take any notes. And please don't talk to anyone until I have completed my presentation.

Here's the list—in a different sequence, with revised wording, and with two items missing:

<Tone>

Empathic listening

<Tone>

Encouraging diversity

<Tone>

Honesty

<Tone>

Innovation

<Tone>

Open-mindedness

<Tone>

Self-understanding

(Continued)

Test 4

Talk with other members of your team and identify the two items that were left out during the previous presentation.

Somebody press the PAUSE button on the audio player. When all teams have identified the two missing items, please press PAUSE again so I can continue with the game.

Results 4

Thank you.

Here are the two items that were left out during the previous presentation.

<Tone>

Expertise in the use of facilitation techniques

<Tone>

Enthusiasm

Give your team 1 point each if you recognized these items.

Conclusion

What's your team's total score? The maximum score is seven.

Congratulations on your teamwork. And congratulations on mastering the top ten characteristics of effective facilitators.

Now you know what to do when you are facilitating your own team!

15 Telephone Games

Telephone games involve the play of interactive training games by using telephones and answering machines. Most of these games incorporate elements of role play and virtual teamwork.

HELP!

You and fourteen other new call-center employees have just completed a workshop on how to provide technical assistance to users of a software program. The workshop is structured around a checklist dealing with the six areas of customer focus (indicating a genuine interest in serving the customer), product knowledge (accurate information on the use of the software program), listening skills (identifying the needs of the customer), language skills (communicating technical information using plain language), coaching skills (helping the customer apply new techniques), and telephone skills (using different functions in the telephone). At the end of the workshop, Larry, the facilitator, gives each participant extra copies of the checklist along with the names and telephone numbers of two other participants.

During the next three days, you play HELP! according to Larry's instructions:

- You call one of the two participants assigned to you and play the role of a customer with a specific technical problem (that you make up).

- You spend 5 to 10 minutes interacting with the other participant (who plays the role of a help-line consultant) and follow her instructions.

- Immediately after the session, you rate the performance of your telephone consultant using a five-point scale on each of the six checklist items.

- You leave a message on Larry's answering machine identifying yourself, the participant you interacted with along with your ratings, and a few specific details about each item. You repeat the same process with the other participant assigned to you.

- In the meantime, you receive telephone calls from two other participants in which you play the role of a technical consultant, making sure that your telephone consultation will receive high ratings on the checklist. You recognize one of these role players, but you follow Larry's instructions and maintain your role all the time.

A couple of days after the game, Larry calls you and asks you to guess your strong and weak areas during your role play as the telephone consultant. In the course of this conversation, Larry gives you feedback from your two "customers" and helps you work out an action plan for improving your skills.

Uses and Limitations

The global reach of telephones is increasing and the cost of telephone calls is decreasing with technological breakthroughs such as satellite transmission, fiberoptics, cell phones, pagers, speaker phones, videophones, conference calls, airfones, Internet telephony, sophisticated answering machines, unified messaging, and speech recognition. It is no surprise that a significant amount of business—both local and global—is conducted over the telephone. However, training applications of telephone technology are mostly ignored. Ironically, even training on telephone skills is delivered through videotapes and classrooms.

The types of telephone games explored below can be conducted with the use of commonly available equipment found in every office and home. These games are particularly effective with such business topics as telemarketing, help lines, order taking, advisory services, and market surveys. In general, however, you can modify any face-to-face game for delivery over telephone lines.

A few words of caution about conducting telephone games: Make sure that you have participants' permission before you (or the other players) begin calling them. Don't fall into the type of disrepute associated with telemarketers through disruptive and rude behaviors. Encourage individual participants to work out suitable schedules.

More Examples

HELP! the game in which you participated vicariously, is an example of the role play type of telephone game. Here are examples of other types of telephone games:

AUDIO ONLY. This is an example of the serial type of telephone game in which the first player calls the second, the second player calls the third, and so on. Very often, call center people have to use spoken words to deal with visuals, as in this piece of dialogue I overheard recently: "Do you see an icon near the top left side of the screen that looks like a triangle with a dot in the center? Double click on that icon. Do you see a dialogue box with a blinking cursor? Great. Now type. . . ." The object of this game is to effectively receive and send information over the telephone. The game is loosely based on the children's game of TELEPHONE, except players use real telephones. To begin the game, the facilitator sends a postcard to the first player with an abstract line drawing consisting of overlapping rectangles, circles, triangles, and other geometric figures. This player now calls the second player and describes the drawing so that player can sketch a replica. The game continues with the second player repeating the process with a third one, using his or her version of the drawing. After completing the task, each player mails the drawing, along with his or her name, to the facilitator. At the end of the game, the facilitator compares each drawing with the preceding one and awards a score to reflect how effectively the message was received. The facilitator then compares the drawing with the succeeding one and awards another score to reflect how effectively the message was delivered.

LUCKY CALLER. This is an example of the parallel type of telephone game in which players call each other in any order. The object of this game is for participants to master factual information. Here's a sample version of this game that deals with technical terms related to telephony. At the beginning of the game, the facilitator calls one player at a time and distributes twenty technical terms and their definitions at the rate of two per player. (Example: *A bridge is an automatic device that answers calls from different sites and mixes them for teleconferencing.*) Players now call each other individually and exchange the terms and definitions. Whenever a player feels ready, he or she calls the facilitator, who asks questions about seven random technical terms from the list of twenty. If any of the answers is incorrect, the player has to call back later and take the test again (which may involve other items from the list). The first player to correctly answer all seven questions wins a prize. However, the game continues with all players calling in to pass the seven-question test. The seventh player to answer all the questions correctly gets a special prize for being the lucky caller.

ALL OR NOTHING. This is an example of a cash game played over the telephone. The object of the game is to explore such factors as communication, trust building, and personal sacrifice. At the beginning of the game, participants are asked to call a telephone number and listen to a message. The message tells players that they can ask for $10 or no money within a five-day period. Up to five players will receive $10 payments, but only if

80 percent of the players call in and indicate their choice and no more than five players ask for the $10 amount. Players are encouraged to call other players and plan a joint strategy. When ready, players individually call the facilitator and give the choice between $10 or no money. After recording the choice, the facilitator debriefs the player by asking questions about how he or she made the decision, how this decision is similar to other decisions made by team members, and what would have been the decision if the payment amount were $100. At the end of the game, the facilitator leaves another telephone message with the results of the game and a summary of players' responses to the debriefing question.

GLOBAL REACH. The object of this game is to familiarize participants with international telephone procedures. The facilitator calls two players, appoints them as the leaders of different teams, and gives each of them the telephone numbers of three to five team members. Each team is then given the name of a city in another country. The challenge for the team is to conduct a telephone interview with a citizen of the other country who is a member of his or her own profession. For example, if participants are accountants, they may be asked to locate and interview an accountant in Yangoon in Myanmar. Team members interact only through telephone calls to plan their strategy and to implement it. When the task is complete, the team leader gives a summary of the interview responses to the facilitator. In addition, members of both teams debrief each other and jointly produce a list of guidelines for making international telephone calls.

Ready-to-Use Telephone Game
CONFERENCE CALL

A significant number of virtual teams conduct group discussions among their geographically dispersed members through telephone conference calls. Here's an activity that uses conference calls to learn how to make better use of conference calls.

Purpose

To explore and apply appropriate guidelines for effectively participating in group discussions conducted through telephone conference calls.

Participants

Five to eight

Time

30 minutes to 1 hour

Materials

- Copies of five sets of guidelines for each participant

  How to Ensure Proper Telephone Etiquette

  How to Handle Participants Who Don't Talk Enough

  How to Handle Participant Who Talk Too Much

  How to Handle Impatient Participants Who Keep Trying to Shorten the Discussion

  How to Handle Wandering Participants Who Waste Time with Tangential Discussion and Excessive Analysis

- Copies of the Conference Call Rating Scale
- Copies of the Debriefing Questions handout

Flow
Preparation

Prepare yourself to conduct the activity. Familiarize yourself with the process and the content. Read through the flow of the activity and review the sets of guidelines.

Assign roles and responsibilities to participants. Individually call each participant and assign a role corresponding to each of the five sets of the guidelines. Assign the role of an observer to the sixth participant. If you have more than six participants, assign some roles to more than one participant. If you have fewer than six participants, assume one of the roles (but not the role of the observer) yourself. If necessary, assign more than one role to some participants.

Send guidelines to participants. Fax the appropriate set of guidelines to each participant or send it as an e-mail note. Do this immediately after assigning roles to different participants.

Set up the conference call. Select a work-related topic for discussion by team members during the conference call. Prepare an agenda and select a suitable time for the conference call. Make sure that participants in different time zones will not be forced to stay up late or wake up early. Send instructions for taking part in the conference call to all participants.

Begin the Activity

Brief participants. Explain that the activity has two purposes: It is an actual team meeting to discuss an important work-related topic. It is also an opportunity to learn about telephone skills that contribute to conducting effective conference calls.

Explain the roles. Explain that different participants are given different guidelines for ensuring effective behaviors during a conference call. Each participant should subtly attempt to implement these guidelines during the conference call—while paying attention to the discussion and participating in it.

Introduce the observer. Explain that this participant will be monitoring the discussion and will not take part in it.

Discuss the topic. Introduce the discussion topic. Invite participants to discuss it. Play a low-key facilitative role, letting the discussion take its natural course.

Conduct Mid-Course Debriefing

Stop the discussion. After about 10 minutes, get all participants' attention. Explain that you are going to place the discussion on hold while you debrief the conference call.

Identify the first criterion. Ask participants to rate how everyone observed telephone courtesy that is appropriate to conference calls. Instruct participants to use a five-point rating scale in which 1 is poor performance and 5 is excellent performance.

Ask for everyone's ratings. Check with each participant for his or her rating of the overall telephone courtesy demonstrated by members of the group. Discuss the range of ratings and the average. Invite participants to share the reasoning behind their ratings.

Ask for the observer's rating. Now ask the observer to share his or her rating on telephone courtesy along with some sample behaviors. Briefly discuss this information.

Share guidelines. Invite participants to guess who was entrusted with the set of guidelines in this area. Identify the participant with this role. Ask this person to share the guidelines on his or her list. Invite other participants to briefly discuss these guidelines and to add other appropriate items to the list.

Repeat the procedure. Explore the area of "equal distribution of air time," using the same procedure of asking for everyone's ratings, asking for the observer's ratings, and discussing them. Then explain that two participants were entrusted with guidelines in this area: one with guidelines for handling participants who talk too much and the other with guidelines for handling people who don't talk enough. Invite everyone to guess who these participants could be, then share the guidelines, discuss them, and add other appropriate guidelines.

Repeat the procedure. Explore the area of "appropriate pace of discussion." Explain that two participants were entrusted with guidelines in this area: one with guidelines for handling impatient participants and the other with

Design Your Own Games and Activities

guidelines for handling wandering participants. Invite everyone to guess who these participants could be, then share the guidelines, discuss them, and add other appropriate guidelines.

Brief participants again. Invite everyone to return to their discussion of the original work-related topic. In the ensuing discussion, suggest that all participants monitor their own behavior and the behavior of others to ensure proper telephone etiquette, equal distribution of "air time," and appropriate pace of discussion.

Continue the discussion. Play a low-key facilitative role as before. Conclude the discussion at an appropriate juncture, making sure to reserve about 10 minutes for the final debriefing.

Conduct the Final Debriefing

Rate the discussion along all three areas. Ask all participants, including the observer, for ratings on the same five-point scales used earlier. Discuss whether these ratings have improved or deteriorated. Ask for suggestions on how the ratings can be improved further.

Discuss other debriefing questions. Ask participants to refer to the handout with the list of debriefing questions. Select and suitable questions from this list and conduct discussions.

Follow up. Thank everyone for their enthusiastic and mindful participation. Make arrangements to send a fax or an e-mail with copies of the sets of guidelines. Also schedule the next conference call and specify what additional behaviors would be explored during that call.

How to Ensure Proper Telephone Etiquette

- Make sure that you know which number to call and how to join the conference call.
- Call the conference number a few minutes before the scheduled time.
- Do not use a speaker phone (unless it is specially designed to work as a conference phone).
- Treat the conference call as if it were a face-to-face meeting. Avoid interruptions.
- Avoid distracting noises such as clicking a pen or tapping on the desk.
- Avoid distractions. Don't try to write a report or proofread a letter while participating in the conference call.
- Always identify yourself before making a comment.
- Put your telephone on "mute" while listening to others. This cuts out distracting noises from your location. But don't forget to release the mute button before speaking!

How to Handle Participants
Who Don't Talk Enough

- Direct questions to silent participants. Ask open-ended questions, but make sure that they can be answered easily.

- Ask the silent participant to comment on (or to summarize) someone else's statement.

- Ask everyone to take turns talking for 30 seconds.

- Ask questions related to the silent participant's area of interest and expertise.

- Reinforce (in a sincere fashion) any comment from the taciturn participant.

- Assign the role of "encourager" to one of the participants. The encourager's responsibility is to identify and draw out reluctant participants.

How to Handle Participants
Who Talk Too Much

- Call on other participants to respond or comment on the topic.

- Suggest that all participants should take turns speaking on the topic.

- Limit each participant to 30 seconds.

- Interrupt the participant with a question directed toward someone else.

- Acknowledge the participant's comment and involve others: "That was an interesting comment, Diane. I wonder how Joe feels about it?"

- Gently explain to the excessive talker that it is important to hear from everyone.

- Assign the role of "equalizer" to one of the participants. The equalizer's responsibility is to ensure equal "air time" for all participants.

How to Handle Impatient Participants Who Keep Trying to Shorten the Discussion

- Stress the importance of the topic and the need for a thorough discussion.
- Before the conference call, talk individually to different participants about the importance of getting everyone's input and ownership.
- Use a structured approach for taking turns in discussing the topic.
- Before the conference call, get agreement on how much time should be spent on discussing each topic.
- Ask the impatient participant for his or her views on the topic and alternative suggestions for the next step.
- Channel the impatient participant's energy into interviewing each of the other participants and summarizing their comments.

How to Handle Wandering Participants Who Waste Time with Tangential Discussion and Excessive Analysis

- Before the conference call, get agreement on how much time should be spent on discussing each topic.
- Before the conference call, talk individually to different participants about the importance of staying on the topic and keeping the discussions focused.
- Redirect the wandering participant to the topic by asking relevant questions.
- Ask specific questions of other participants.
- Tell the wandering participant that his or her comments are tangential and suggest that they may be discussed during another conference call.
- Differentiate between broad decision making and detailed action planning. Suggest that detailed planning can be undertaken later by one or two of the participants.
- Ask the wandering participant to prepare a detailed analysis and fax it later to all participants.

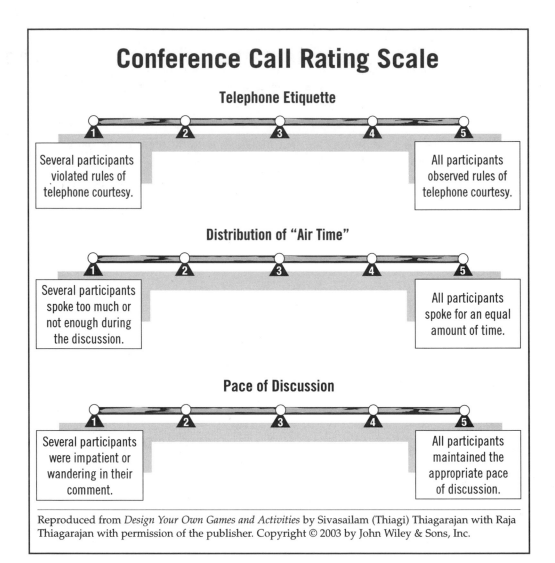

Conference Call Rating Scale

Telephone Etiquette

1   2   3   4   5

Several participants violated rules of telephone courtesy.	All participants observed rules of telephone courtesy.

Distribution of "Air Time"

1   2   3   4   5

Several participants spoke too much or not enough during the discussion.	All participants spoke for an equal amount of time.

Pace of Discussion

1   2   3   4   5

Several participants were impatient or wandering in their comment.	All participants maintained the appropriate pace of discussion.

Debriefing Questions

1. Did you pay more attention to your behavior during the second part of the discussion? If so, how did this fact affect your participation in the discussion?

2. Which was easier: Finding lapses in your own behavior or lapses in other participants' behaviors.

3. Which of the five sets of guidelines was violated most often? Why do you think this happened?

4. Should we develop sets of guidelines for other aspects of conference calls? What should be the areas for these guidelines?

5. Which of these arrangements is the best one:

   • One person monitors all participants' behaviors

   • All participants monitor everyone's behaviors.

   • Each participant monitors the behavior of another participant assigned to him or her.

   • Participants monitor their own behavior.

16   Game Shows

A game show is a contest modeled after a popular TV programs. The format involves a contest among a few selected participants, watched by spectators ("studio audience"). The training version of the game show features questions from specific instructional content.

PM CHAMPIONSHIP

You have been through three hectic days of a workshop on project management. At 4 p.m. on Friday, Alexa, your instructor, is getting ready to play a videotape as the final review. You groan inwardly because you are sure that it is going to be a talking-head presentation reciting a lot of technical stuff. So you are pleasantly surprised when the videotape turns out to be in the format of a popular TV game show.

The show begins with three contestants (Ann, Bob, and Carl) being introduced. They stand behind their podiums, each holding a buzzer. The personal scoreboard on each podium displays a zero. With applause in the background, Alexa struts on screen as the game host. The screen now displays a 6 × 5 grid with a total of thirty tiles. The six columns are labeled with project-management categories: scope, time management, budgeting, quality control, communication, and risk management. The tiles in each column are marked with point values for questions in five levels of difficulty: 100, 200, 300, 400, and 500. Ann, the first contestant, asks for a 100-point question on budgeting. A question pops on the screen and Alexa reads it aloud: "What is the name of the cost-estimating technique that uses the actual cost of a previous, similar project?" Bob is the first contestant to

press the buzzer and he gets to answer the question: "Analogous estimating." Alexa announces that the answer is correct and Bob's scoreboard now displays 100 points. Bob now selects the next question by specifying the category and the point value.

The game proceeds with contestants pressing their buzzers and giving answers. If the answer is correct, the contestant earns the appropriate point value and his or her scoreboard displays the new total. If the answer is incorrect or if the contestant hesitates too long, the point value is subtracted from the contestant's score. As the game progresses, you and your fellow participants get excited and begin yelling out the answers before the TV contestants.

At the end of the first round, the three contestants have very close scores: 2,000, 2,200, and 1,900. The second round of the game is conducted in exactly the same way except the point values are doubled (from 200 to 1,000) and a different set of question categories is used: activity duration estimating, project plan development, activity sequencing, schedule development, risk quantification, and procurement planning. At the end of the second round, Carl leads with a total score of 8,300. Bob's score is 5,200, and Ann (who gave a series of impulsive incorrect answers) trails with a score of 3,400.

The final round of the contest involves a single question from a new category (Life Cycle of a Project). Before the question is revealed, the three contestants secretly bet points from their current totals. After Alexa reveals the question and reads it, contestants have 30 seconds to write their answers. All three contestants answer the question correctly. Both Ann and Bob have bet all their points and they end up with 6,800 and 10,400 respectively. Carl has bet 2,101 points and he ends up with a total of 10,401 and wins the contest by a single point!

As the game show ends, you realize that the questions and answers have provided a painless review of the workshop content.

Game Shows and Training

Most U.S.-based readers would have recognized this sample activity as an adaptation of the popular television game show, "Jeopardy." There are two major differences between the TV show and the sample presented above: In the TV show, the host displays and reads "answers" and the contestants respond in the form of questions. The TV show rewards the winner with an actual cash prize (while the other two contestants are consoled with "valuable gifts").

Although my friend Marc Prensky (2000) points out (in his book, *Digital Game-Based Learning*) that Jeopardy is the greatest hidden tool in corporate training, it is surprising that the game show format has not become more popular in the interactive training field. This is particularly surprising, especially since TV game shows play such an important role in the U.S. pop culture. These game shows are exported to different parts of the world, just as some of the most current U.S. game shows have been imported from other countries.

Types of Game Shows

The majority of TV game shows involve questions and answers. In general, game shows require each contestant to provide a more acceptable answer than the others. The type of answer in game shows falls into the following three categories:

Faster, correct answer. Game shows of this type require the winning contestant to be the first to respond with the correct answer. Examples of this type include "Jeopardy" and "Win Ben Stein's Money." The correctness of the answer is determined by checking with subject-matter experts. For training purposes, this format is especially useful with technical content.

More popular answer. Game shows of this type require contestants to guess the most frequently given answers to open-ended questions. Examples of this type include "Family Feud" and "Card Sharks." The winning answer is predetermined by polling a group of (usually one hundred) people. For training purposes, this format is especially useful in such areas as sales and customer services (example: "What are the most frequent complaints from our customers?")

Matching answer. Game shows of this type require contestants to guess the response of another person. Examples of this type include "Newlywed Game" and "3's a Crowd." The acceptability of the answer is determined by its match to a previous response given by another player. For training purposes, this format is especially useful in such areas as active listening and diversity training.

Uses and Limitations

Game shows can be used in the training environment in several different ways, particularly to provide practice and review. Here are some examples:

Videotaped show. The sample game show is an example of this approach. A videotape recording contains a game show that features questions to systematically review the main learning points. The facilitator plays the videotape and encourages participants to watch the show and vicariously participate in it.

Live show. In this approach, the facilitator stages the game show with contestants selected from the participants. To increase instructional effectiveness, the facilitator may organize participants into teams and provide appropriate time for each team to prepare for the contest. Each team may select a representative to be the contestant or—to increase the suspense—the facilitator may randomly select a member to represent each team. To increase the level of accountability for personal learning, the facilitator may also use different contestants from each team during the different parts of the game show.

Broadcast show. With satellite technology, we may provide distributed learning opportunities by broadcasting the game show originating from one location to other training locations within the organization.

Generating questions. We can leverage the motivational impact of the game show format by asking teams of participants to write questions for use in the contest. This preparatory activity will probably produce more learning outcomes than the actual game show itself. We can also use participants as the hosts and judges in the game show.

As a training tool, the game show format suffers from a few limitations. Here are some examples:

Show me the money! Cash prizes and personal tortures associated with contestants' decisions about how much money to risk adds a major dramatic element to TV game shows. It's unlikely that training budgets will permit such generous cash awards. So we have to strengthen other elements of the game show to increase its interest level.

Celebrity hosts. The success of a TV game show depends on the personality of the host who conducts the game. Most game show hosts have acquired celebrity status. Conducting a successful game show requires more skills to be added to those of facilitating a training activity.

Spectator sports? It is easy for viewers of a game show to decline into a passive couch-potato mode in search of flaccid entertainment. To prevent this, we have to use appropriate strategies to encourage and facilitate active participation by the audience.

Ready-to-Use Game Show
COOPETITION

COOPETITION attempts to combine the interest value of a TV game show with instructional value of a training game. It borrows features from popular game shows and adds a few innovative features:

- COOPETITION combines elements of cooperation and competition. In the first part, contestants cooperate with each other to increase the amount of prize money. During the second part, contestants compete one-on-one against each other to be the sole winner of the prize money. During the third part, contestants cooperatively contribute to the next treasure chest and compete with each to other to win the prize money.

- COOPETITION uses three types of questions and judging strategies. The first part involves closed questions, with the facilitator deciding whether the answer is correct or not. The second part involves open questions with a panel of judges selecting the better answer between the responses from two different contestants. The third part involves a creative task with members of the audience choosing the best product.

Purpose

COOPETITION is a framegame that is designed to review the training content taught earlier. It can also be used as a self-contained training game in which participants spend an hour or so in studying (independently, or with a partner, or as a part of a learning team) handouts and other reading materials.

Participants

COOPETITION works best with twenty or more participants. Five contestants and five judges are selected from the group. You may use a ten-item test and select the first five contestants who answered all items correctly to be the contestants. It is best to select the judges randomly. The rest of the group acts as the "studio audience."

Time

In the tradition of TV game shows, COOPETITION lasts for exactly 30 minutes, including three "commercial breaks" of 2 minutes each.

Equipment and Setup

Here's the ideal setup with electronic gadgets. Those with less generous budgets can improvise by using tables, stools, bells, and whistles.

The stage. A raised stage is placed in front of the room with podiums for the contestants and the facilitator, along with two soundproof booths.

Contestant podiums. During the first part of the show, each contestant stands behind an individual podium.

Soundproof booths. During the second part of the show, pairs of contestants are seated in soundproof booths. Both contestants can hear the facilitator. The contestants cannot hear each other, but everyone can hear them.

Sheets of paper and felt-tipped pens. During the third part of the show, contestants work behind their podiums to develop a creative product.

Facilitator's station. The facilitator stands behind a podium with question cards neatly arranged for reference, but hidden from the others.

Timer. A countdown timer is located at the facilitator's podium.

Common display. A large electronic scoreboard is suspended above the contestants' podiums with space for display of dollar amounts.

Judges' chamber. The five judges are seated in the first row of the audience. Each judge has an electronic audience response device for use during the second part of the show.

Audience location. Members of the audience are seated in front of the stage. Each of these participants has an electronic response device for using during the last part of the show.

Questions

One of the key requirements for COOPETITION is a set of questions for use by the facilitator. This game show requires three sets of questions, corresponding to the three parts of the activity. Here are brief explanations and examples of these types. (The examples are from a training session on breast cancer.)

Closed questions. These questions have a short, single, correct answer. You will need eighty to one hundred questions for use during the first part of the game. The list of questions should also contain the correct answers (including acceptable alternatives) to simplify the facilitator's task. Here are some examples:

- What is the five-year survival rate after treatment for localized breast cancer? (96.3 percent)
- Where are lymph nodes usually removed by the surgeon to see if the cancer has spread? (from the underarm)
- What drug is usually used in hormone therapy for breast cancer? (tamoxifen)

Open questions. These questions permit a variety of acceptable answers. You will need another set of eighty to one hundred questions for use during the second part of the game. Here are some examples:

- Immediately after the diagnosis of breast cancer, many women are haunted by the questions, "What could I have done to prevent it?" "Why did I get it?" and "Why me?" How would you answer these questions?
- Give a simple explanation of how radiation works in the standard treatment for breast cancer.
- What are two important factors to be taken into consideration by the breast cancer patient in selecting a doctor?

Creative task. You will need a single question that requires a creative response for use during the third part of the question. Here are some examples:

- Design a logo for a breast-cancer support group.
- Come up with a slogan that emphasizes the importance of regular mammograms.
- Suggest a name for a website with authoritative information about breast cancer.

Cash prizes. The game show as described below uses cash prizes. Although it is definitely not the same, I usually conduct the game with play money.

Flow

Preliminaries (2 minutes)

Assign roles. Announce the names of the five contestants and have them come up to the stage and stand behind a podium. Announce the names of the five judges and ask them to sit at their reserved seats in the middle of the front row. Chat with the judges so they can briefly introduce themselves to the audience. Repeat the same procedure with the contestants.

Preview the show. Explain that the game involves a cooperative part during which contestants accumulate prize money. During the second part, contestants go one-on-one with each other, trying to outlast the opponents and collect the prize money. During the third round, contestants compete with each other to develop a product that would be voted as the most creative one and win another bundle of prize money.

Part 1 (10 minutes)

Preview this part. Announce that this part will last for 10 minutes, during which time contestants cooperate with each other to accumulate a lot of cash in the prize bundle. They do this by taking turns to answer questions related to the training topic. Correct answers add more money to the prize bundle, while incorrect answers reduce the amount. However, if a contestant gives an incorrect answer, any other contestants can correct it.

Explain the rules. Present the following information in your own words:

- The facilitator will read the question.

- The selected contestant should answer the question immediately. If the contestant hesitates for more than 10 seconds, it is treated as an incorrect answer.

- At the beginning of this part, the amount of money in the prize bundle is 0. Every time a correct answer is given, this amount increases by $10.

- If the answer is incorrect (and if none of the other contestants correct it), the prize bundle is reduced by $10.

- If the selected contestant does not answer, or if the answer appears to be incorrect, any other participant may correct it by giving an alternative answer within 10 more seconds.

- If the second answer is correct (even if the first answer is incorrect), the prize bundle is increased by $10. If the second answer is incorrect (even if the first answer is correct), the prize money is reduced by $10.

- No contestant can correct other contestants' answers more than five times during this part of the game.

Start the timer. Set the timer for 10 minutes and press the button to begin the countdown.

Begin the activity. Display zero amount on the scoreboard. Read the first question. Wait for the answer—and any correction. Increase or decrease the prize bundle depending on whether the answer is correct or incorrect. Update the common scoreboard to indicate the amount of money currently in the prize bundle.

Repeat the process. Read the questions one at a time. Select the next player to answer. Process the answer (and any correction) as before.

Double the increment. When the prize money reaches $200, explain that all future answers will be worth $20. Correct answers will add $20 to the prize bundle, and incorrect answers will subtract $20.

Conclude the first part. When the timer beeps to indicate the end of the 10-minute period, announce the conclusion of the first part. Point to the dollar amount on display and explain that this prize bundle will be won by a single contestant during the second part.

First "Commercial Break" (2 minutes)

Announce a "commercial break." Explain that you will be presenting an important public service announcement for the next 2 minutes. Present a brief mini-lecture related to the training topic.

Part 2 (10 minutes)

Preview this part. Explain that pairs of contestants will independently respond to an open-ended question and the judges will select the better of the two answers. The winner in a best-of-three series will continue, while the loser is replaced by the next contestant. When this part of the game ends, the surviving contestant will win all the money in the prize bundle.

Set up the first round. Randomly select a contestant and seat her in the soundproof booth marked "A." Place the next contestant in the other soundproof booth marked "B."

Brief the judges. Explain that you will ask an open-ended question of the contestant in Booth A. After she gives her response, you will ask the same question of the contestant in Booth B. After this person gives her answer, each judge will immediately select "A" or "B" in the response device to identify the better answer. The contestant who received the most votes wins the first question. The process will be repeated and the contestant who wins the best-of-three rounds stays in the booth while the other contestant is replaced.

Start the timer. Set the timer for 10 minutes and press the button to begin the countdown.

Design Your Own Games and Activities

Start the activity. Turn off the sound in Booth B, read an open-ended question to the contestant in Booth A, and ask for an immediate answer. After listening to the answer, ask the same question of the person in Booth B. After listening to this answer, check the judges' choices and to find out who received the most votes.

Announce the results. Identify the contestant who won the first round.

Repeat the process. This time, read the question to the contestant in Booth B and get her answer. Then ask the contestant in Booth A to give the answer. As before, check the judges' votes and identify the winner of the second round.

Repeat if necessary. If the same person won the first two rounds, there is no need to conduct another round. If there is a tie, conduct the third round as before.

Replace the losing contestant. Send the contestant who lost back to her podium and ask the next contestant to take her place.

Continue the activity. Keep replacing losing contestants with the next contestant. During later rounds of this part, each contestant will make several appearances.

Conclude the session. When the timer goes off, announce that the next contest will be the last one. Whoever wins this best-of-three set wins the prize bundle.

Award prize money. Display the amount on the individual scoreboard in front of the winner's podium. Announce that each of the other contestants will receive $100 as a consolation prize. Display these amounts in each contestant's individual scoreboard.

Second "Commercial Break" (2 minutes)

Conduct the second "commercial break." Present a mini-lecture on the training topic, summarizing the key learning points.

Part 3 (4 minutes)

Preview this round. Explain that all contestants will invest some amount from the money they currently have. The final part will involve a contest among all five contestants, and the winner will receive twice the total amount invested by all five contestants.

Explain the investment procedure. Each contestant will write the investment amount secretly. Contestants may invest any amount up to the total amount they currently have ($100 for four contestants and a larger amount for the winner of the second part.) The total investment should be at least $317. If the investment falls below that amount, there will not a final part to the game show.

Ask for investment amounts. Ask each contestant to write her name and the investment amount on a piece of paper. Announce a 30-second time limit for this decision.

Reveal the investment amounts. Pick up the pieces of paper, mix them up, and read each investment amount without identifying the name of the contestant. As you read each investment amount, display the running total on the common scoreboard.

Decide on the next step. If the total investment is below $317 (an unlikely event), announce the end of the game show. If it is $317 or more, proceed to the next part.

Announce the creativity contest. Read instructions for the final task. (This will involve the production of a graphic, symbol, slogan, jingle, or label related to some key element of the training topic.) Tell the contestants to use the felt pens and sheets of paper to create this product within the next 2 minutes.

Present the next "commercial" message. Set the timer for 2 minutes. While the contestants are busy with the task, make your final call-to-action presentation related to the training topic.

Display the products. At the end of 2 minutes, collect the products from the contestants (without letting anyone see who produced which product). Mix these sheets of paper and display them, one at a time, pausing for about 15 seconds each.

Poll the audience. Ask audience members (and the judges) to pick up their response devices. Explain that you will display the products again in the same order, identifying each product with the letters A to E. Ask each participant to choose one of the five products and press the corresponding letter in the response device as soon as you have completed your display.

Announce the winner. Display the products and check the results of the audience poll. Begin with the product that received the least number of votes and proceed toward the one that received the most votes. Hold up the product and announce the number of votes it received. After displaying the winning product, ask for the creator of this product to identify him- or herself. Award this person twice the amount invested earlier by the five contestants.

Conclusion

Upgrade the scores. Subtract the amounts invested earlier by each contestant. Then add double the amount of the total investment to the winner of the creativity contest.

Announce the end of the session. Thank the audience, the judges, and the contestants. Congratulate everyone for their increased mastery of the training objectives.

17   E-Mail Games

In e-mail games, the facilitator and players communicate to each other by sending electronic notes. Unlike fancier web-based or real-time games that involve sophisticated graphics and simultaneous play in chat rooms, e-mail games are limited to low technology and text messages. Most e-mail games are divided into several rounds spread over a period of days or weeks. In addition to training, these games can be used for encouraging participation in a variety of activities.

DEPOLARIZER

The company that has employed you for the last eleven years has been recently acquired by a larger company. Most of the top management is enthusiastic about this acquisition, but they are not sure about how regular employees are reacting. They asked HR to take the pulse of all employees, and the person in charge decided to play an e-mail game called DEPOLARIZER. You are a lucky member of a group of twenty employees who participate in the game.

During the first round of the game, Leslie, the facilitator, sends out an e-mail note asking you to indicate your reaction to being sold to a larger company on a nine-point scale. On this scale, 1 is extremely pessimistic, 2 is very pessimistic, 3 is pessimistic, 4 is slightly pessimistic, 5 is neutral, 6 is slightly optimistic, 7 is optimistic, 8 is very optimistic, and 9 is extremely optimistic. Leslie's note also invites you to add a short statement explaining your position on the rating scale. You respond with a 3 and this explanation: "Most employees were not consulted during the negotiations. We are unsure

about what decisions were made about the fate of current employees and we are skeptical of top management's intentions."

Leslie's second note thanks you for your participation in the first round and asks you to predict the average reaction of the twenty players on the nine-point scale, correct to the second decimal place. Once again, you are invited to add a note of explanation to your choice. After some thought, you predict 3.01 and explain that most regular employees probably feel the same way that you do.

Leslie's third note reports that the actual average reaction was 2.55 and identifies John as the "psychic winner" for predicting an average reaction of 2.50. You are somewhat surprised by the level of pessimism among the players. Leslie's note continues, requesting you to write a list of reasons to be pessimistic or optimistic about the situation. Before you list these reasons, however, you have to assume a role. If your last name begins with the letters A through L, you pretend to be an extremely pessimistic person (with a 1 on the reaction scale); if your last name begins with the letters M through Z, you pretend to be an extremely optimistic person (with a 9 on the reaction scale). Your list should contain at least three reasons. Since your last name begins with a T, you set aside your personal pessimism and list eight reasons to be positive, including this: "As a bigger player in the industry, we should be able to find a larger, global market for our company's products." After writing your list, you notice that you are beginning to feel a bit more bullish about your future.

Leslie's fourth note is a lengthy one. It contains a list of fifty-seven reasons, alternating between pessimistic and optimistic. Intrigued, you read through the list, trying to locate the ones that you contributed. In the process, you are impressed by some of the other reasons. You now have a broader feel for the future impact of the current situation. At the end of the note, Leslie asks you to select your current position on the nine-point scale, based on your review of the list of positive and negative reasons. You decide to move slightly away from your previous pessimistic stance to a position of 4.

In the next few notes, Leslie conducts the prediction activity again. In the last note, Leslie reports that the average value has shifted slightly to 3.08 and the range of personal reactions has moved away from the extremes. Leslie thanks you for providing valuable data about employee reactions to the current situation. Two weeks later you receive an internal memorandum to all employees from the company president with a frank discussion of the pessimistic factors and reassurance that top management will do their utmost to reduce any negative impact on the current employees. You are glad that the data collected during the play of the game is being put to some good use.

Uses and Limitations

E-mail games permit interaction among participants from around the world. Geographically dispersed players can arrange their participation to suit

Design Your Own Games and Activities

their personal schedules. With the Internet and intranets, we can achieve this powerful any-time, any-place advantage at little or no cost. However, e-mail games have critical limitations: To permit widespread participation, you have to allot several days for each round. These generous deadlines may encourage players to procrastinate and miss the deadline. In addition, players with overflowing mailboxes may accidentally or intentionally ignore the e-mail notes about the game.

More Examples

1001 FACTOIDS. This e-mail game encourages players to collect, distribute, and review factual information related to any job-relevant topic (such as Singapore, where your corporation is planning to establish a local plant). During the first round, players are given the topic (Singapore) and twenty factoids (brief statements of facts) related to it, organized under ten to twenty categories (such as geography, history, current events, cultural values, politics, famous people, ethnic groups, business practices, law, and taboos). The e-mail note also identifies different sources of information about the topic. Players are invited to contribute up to five new factoids every day before 4 p.m. at the facilitator's location. The facilitator reviews these contributions, awards 1 point for each contribution, updates a Hall of Fame list with the names of the players with the top five scores, and updates the list of factoids by adding edited items. The game continues day after day with the players contributing not more than five factoids that are not currently on the updated list. The game is designed to last until players have identified 1001 factoids about the topic. A variation of this game, called 1001 TIPS, invites players to contribute up to five tips a day for achieving a specific goal (example: *having fun in the office*).

CROSS SCORE. This game requires participants to come up with short, creative answers to an open-ended question (examples: *"What is the single most important characteristic of a typical customer?"* or *"What business are we really in?"*). Before kicking off the game, the facilitator organizes players into two groups of five to fifteen players and explains that members of each group will independently judge the responses of the members in the other group. During the first round, each player receives the open-ended question and a list of e-mail addresses of the members of the judging group. Each player writes a short, creative answer to the question and sends it as an e-mail note to each member of the judging group. Immediately after the deadline, each player looks at all the answers from the other team, selects the best answer, and e-mails it to the facilitator. During the next round, the facilitator gives 1 point for each time an answer is selected as the best one and anonymously lists all of the answers and the scores awarded to each. Usually, the game is repeated once a week with a new open-ended question each week.

TEAMWORK. This game is designed for virtual teams working over the Internet. The game uses an interesting scoring system that rewards individual contributions to the team's output. At the beginning of the game,

players are divided into three to five teams, each with five to seven members. During the first round, players are given a common planning task (example: *prepare a marketing plan for the new software program*) and a list of criteria. Virtual teams organize themselves in any fashion, interact through e-mail notes, and complete the task. During the second round, a panel of experts evaluates the plans from different teams and distributes 100 points among these plans to reflect their relative rating on the list of criteria. The experts also provide a brief critique of each plan. While the experts are completing their evaluation, the facilitator asks each player to send in a secret code name and a confidential recommendation for dividing the team's score points among the other members of his or her team. The recommended percentage should be based on each player's evaluation of different team members' contributions to the team's plan. The facilitator computes average percentages for each player of each team. During the third round, the facilitator publishes each team's plan, the expert critique of the plan, the scores awarded to each plan, and a list of code names and individual scores (computed as the appropriate percentage of the team's score).

Ready-to-Use E-Mail Game
C3PO

We have played this e-mail game with players from around the world several times during the past few months. C3PO helps us collect ideas related to different challenges, including improving member services in a professional organization and increasing people-to-people interaction in Internet training.

Purpose

To generate—and share—ideas about how to handle a challenge.

Sample Challenges

- How to reduce disruptive behaviors during team meetings
- How to delight our customers
- How to persuade top management to increase our budget allocation
- How to transform our instructors into facilitators
- How to attract more subscribers to the newsletter

Time

Four days to four weeks. The game is best conducted during a four-day period.

Players

Any number can play, but this activity works best with ten to thirty players.

Requirements

You and the players should have access to e-mail and know how to use it.

Overview

The game consists of three rounds. In the first round, the facilitator presents a challenge and announces a deadline. Each player sends an e-mail with three ideas for handling the challenge. The facilitator records the ideas from all players, removes duplicates, and prepares a common pool of ten to fifteen ideas.

In the second round, the facilitator posts the pool of ideas. Each player votes for three ideas that he or she finds personally most appealing. The facilitator tabulates the votes from all players and arranges the ideas in a "popularity list."

In the third round, the facilitator presents the common pool of ideas and asks each player to predict which three ideas would have received the highest number of personal votes. The facilitator scores each prediction based on the actual number of votes the three ideas received. The player with the highest total score wins the game.

Preparation

Identify the players. Decide whether participation in the game should be voluntary or required. To simplify sending your e-mail messages, use an existing listserv or create a mailing list.

Specify the challenge. Write a thought-provoking how-to question. Provide enough detail to make the challenge clear, but leave it sufficiently open-ended to encourage alternative ideas.

Prepare a schedule. The game involves three rounds. Depending on the number of players, their geographic dispersion, and complexity of the challenge, you may allow up to one week for each round of the game. In estimating the time requirement, be sure to include enough time for processing responses from players.

Conducting Round 1

Send out an e-mail message. Present an overview and instructions for Round 1 inviting players to send three ideas for handling the challenge. Use the appropriate template from page 195 at the end of this chapter. In this template, replace the underlined words, phrases, and sentences with your own content.

Process inputs from Round 1. Cut and paste all the ideas submitted by the players. Cluster the ideas into suitable categories. Select a set of ten to fifteen non-redundant ideas. (If you have many more, randomly select ten to fifteen ideas. With more than fifteen ideas, players will have difficulty making decisions during the next round.)

Create a pool of ideas. Edit the selected ideas as needed. Arrange them in a random order. Number the ideas in this list.

Conducting Round 2

Send an e-mail message. Present instructions for Round 2, inviting players to choose the top three ideas that personally appeal to them the most. Also present your pool of selected ideas. Use the appropriate template from page 196 at the end of the chapter, replacing the underlined words with your own content.

Create a spreadsheet. Place idea numbers from the pool as column headings. Enter the data. Type the name of each player and assign 1 point in the column that corresponds to each of the ideas selected by that player. Find the total number of "votes" for each idea.

Create the popularity list. Arrange the ideas from the one receiving the most votes to the one receiving the least.

Conducting Round 3

Send an e-mail message. Present instructions for Round 3, inviting players to submit their predictions for the top three ideas. Also present the same pool of ideas presented in the preceding round. Use the appropriate template from page 197, replacing the underlined words with suitable content.

Compute the score for each player's predictions. Use this procedure: (1) Multiply the number of votes received by the idea predicted to be the first choice by 3; (2) Multiply the number of votes received by the idea predicted to be the second choice by 2; (3) Multiply the number of votes received by the idea predicted to be the third choice by 1; (4) Add these three numbers together. This is the score for this player's prediction.

Announce the Results

Send the final e-mail message. Use the appropriate template from page 198, replacing the underlined words with your own content. Include the popularity list (created at the end of Round 2) in this e-mail message.

Debrief the players. Include a list of open questions that invite players to review different ideas and select and implement a few of them.

Design Your Own Games and Activities

C3PO: ROUND 1

WHAT IS THIS? This is an introduction to an e-mail game called C3PO. The name of the game stands for Challenge, Pooling, Polling, Prediction, and Outcome, which are the five components of the game.

The basic flow of the game consists of three rounds during which you and the other players generate ideas, vote for your personal top three ideas, and predict the group's top three ideas.

WHAT IS THE CHALLENGE? Here's my challenge for you: <u>How could we increase people-to-people interaction in Internet training</u>?

WHAT DO YOU DO? Prepare a list of suitable ideas. Select your three best ideas and send them to <u>thiagi@thiagi.com</u>. Please identify the subject as "C3PO-Round 1" (without quotes).

Send your three ideas before <u>11:59 p.m., Wednesday, April 28, 1999</u>.

WHAT WILL I DO? I will process the ideas and conduct the next round of the game soon after.

THANKS! Thanks for everyone who is planning to participate.

C3PO: ROUND 2

WHAT IS THIS? This is the second round of the e-mail game called C3PO. You can join this game right now—even if you did not participate in the first round.

WHAT HAPPENED DURING ROUND 1? During the first round, I presented this challenge to the players: <u>How do we increase people-to-people interaction in Internet training</u>?

Each player responded with three ideas. I recorded the ideas, removed duplicates, and prepared a common pool of <u>fifteen</u> ideas, editing the ideas slightly.

THANK YOU. I want to thank all the enthusiastic players who contributed <u>sixty-one</u> exciting ideas during the first round of the game.

WHAT DO YOU DO IN ROUND 2? Review the common pool of <u>fifteen</u> ideas (listed below) for <u>increasing people-to-people interaction in Internet training</u>.

Vote for the three ideas that are most personally appealing to you.

Send me an e-mail note, identifying the idea that you personally find to be the most appealing. Then tell me which idea is the second most appealing. Finally, tell me which idea is the third most appealing.

You don't have to retype the ideas. Just give me their identification numbers from the list.

If you'd like, add a comment at the end of your e-mail message explaining why you chose those three ideas and passed up the others.

E-MAIL DETAILS. Please send your e-mail note directly to me at <u>thiagi@thiagi.com</u>. Please identify the subject as "C3PO-Round 2" (without quotes).

Send your email response before <u>11:59 p.m., Saturday, May 29, 1999</u>.

WHAT WILL I DO? I will give 3 points for your top idea, 2 points for the second idea, and 1 point for your third idea. I will do the same for the votes from all other players. Using these scores, I will arrange the ideas into a popularity list. I will conduct the third round of the game soon after.

REMEMBER, you can join the game even if you did not participate in Round 1.

COMMON POOL OF IDEAS. <List the pool of ideas here.>

C3PO: ROUND 3

WHAT'S THIS? This is the third round of the email game called C3PO. You can join this game right now—even if you did not participate in the first two rounds.

WHAT HAPPENED IN THE FIRST TWO ROUNDS? During the first round, I presented this challenge: How do we increase people-to-people interaction in Internet training?

Each player emailed three ideas. I recorded the ideas, removed duplicates, and prepared a common pool of fifteen ideas, editing the ideas slightly.

During the second round, I invited players to review this pool of fifteen ideas and to select the three most appealing ones. I received the choices from twenty players and arranged the ideas in order of their popularity.

WHAT DO YOU DO IN ROUND 3? I am not going to show you this popularity list. Instead, I want you to predict the top three items on this list. Please review the common pool of fifteen ideas given below and predict which ones are the top three in the popularity list. I will compare your prediction with the actual popularity list. You win the game if you make the most accurate prediction.

Send me an e-mail note with the identification numbers of your predicted top three ideas. (You do not have to retype the ideas themselves.) List the numbers in order of their popularity, with the most popular item on top. This is all I need, but feel free to add comments, including justifications for your predictions.

E-MAIL DETAILS. Please send your e-mail predictions directly to me at thiagi@thiagi.com. Identify the subject as "C3PO-Round 3" (without quotes).

Send your predictions before 11:59 p.m., Tuesday, June 1, 1999.

WHAT WILL I DO? I will announce the exciting final results soon after.

THANKS! Thank you for your participation.

COMMON POOL OF IDEAS. <Attach the pool of ideas here.>

C3PO: OUTCOMES

THE RESULTS ARE IN. And the winner is <u>Rachel Paterson of the Royal National Institute for the Blind, somewhere in the United Kingdom.</u> Congratulations, Rachel!
<u>Rachel received a perfect score of 93.</u>

<u>Closely following Rachel was Michelle Wolfe, who scored 92 and missed the perfect score by just one point</u>!

<u>The other scores ranged from 20 to 85.</u>

ANOTHER WAY TO WIN. There is another way to score your performance in this game. Since the popularity list is based on what you (and the other players) contributed during the first round, you can award yourself points for the original contribution. For each of your original ideas, give yourself points equal to the number of votes it received. If your score is above <u>30, you are an expert; between 10 and 30, you are good; between 5 and 10, you are fair; and between 0 and 5, you will benefit by reading other people's ideas.</u>

See whether you can retrieve your original list of three ideas and score yourself.

GRATUITOUS SUGGESTION. The list below contains several practical ideas. Take another look at the ideas, select the few that appeal to you the most, and implement them in the near future.

THANKS! Congratulations to the winners and a hearty thank you to all players.

POPULARITY LIST. <Present the popularity list here.>

---

18 Improv Games

Improv games are activities adapted from improvisational theater, where the actors do not use a script but create the dialogue and action as they perform. When used as an interactive training technique, improv games facilitate the mastery of skills related to such areas as creativity, collaboration, communication, and change.

COMPANY PICNIC

At the recent annual conference of the North American Simulation Gaming Association (NASAGA), Alain Rostain conducted an excellent session on improv games. This is what I experienced in that session:

Alain announced a role-playing game called COMPANY PICNIC. He handed me and each of the thirty other participants a large playing card. He asked us to place the cards on our foreheads, facing out, so that everyone could see the card except the person who received the card. Nobody was permitted to look at his or her own card until the very end of the game.

Here's how Alain set up the game: "You all work for Widgets Incorporated and have gathered for a summer picnic in celebration of a very successful first half of the year. For about 5 minutes, you interact with as many people as you can. Treat each person as if his or her status in the company corresponds to the card on the forehead (2 is low, Ace is high). For example, a 2 might work in the mailroom, an Ace could be the CEO, and a 10 might be a vice president. Your objective is to subtly give others clues to the cards that they hold, while assessing the clues others are giving you about your card. You don't get to tell the others about their cards. You don't

get to say things that you would not normally say. So 'Go get my car' or 'Throw this away for me' are not subtle enough to say to a 2. But a brief hello with little eye contact might be."

During the role-play, I had fun snubbing the little people and fawning on the Queens and Kings. Most people were nice to me, and I decided that I was a 9 or a 10.

When the time is up, Alain asked everyone to form one line from lowest (2) to highest (A), depending on where we thought we fell in status. We did this without looking at our cards and without telling others if they were out of place. Once a single-file line was formed, participants checked their cards to see how they did.

It turned out that my card was a Jack. We all realized that everyone has a lot of expertise in what Alain called "status skills." As he debriefed the activity, participants shared the clues that helped them figure out where they were on the status line. I noticed that a few participants were way out of position and wondered why. We talked through possible explanations. The debriefing evolved into a rich discussion about status, its use as a communication tool, and its role in the workplace.

What Is an Improv Game?

In improvisational theater (which is not stand-up comedy), teams of actors create and perform scenes on the fly, often based on suggestions from the audience. They do this without any preplanning. Some of the scenes that are created are extraordinary and move the audience to tears and laughter, and some scenes never get off the ground. That is the nature and risk of making it up on the spot.

Over the years, improv trainers have developed hundreds of exercises to help actors collaborate better, take more risks, improve their listening skills, and act more spontaneously and creatively. Many of these games are in the public domain. Improvisers play some of these games over and over again to warm up before performances. When adapted to the workplace and debriefed appropriately, these games make powerful interactive training tools. Unlike some simulation games, improv games can be replayed several times to deepen the learning. In improv games, there is no right answer, but only practice and refinement of key skills.

Types of Improv Games

Alain classifies improv games into three groups, depending on when they are most useful during a training session:

- *Openers* are used at the beginning of a session to quickly get participants working comfortably together.

- *Energizers* are used in the middle of a session to provide a quick pick-me-up.

- *Closers* are used at the end of a session to send participants off on a high note.

Alain also uses another classification scheme based on the purpose of the improv game:

- Creativity juicers are used before or during brainstorming to help participants flex their spontaneity muscles, overcome their fear of making mistakes, and release their full creative potential.
- Team-building interventions are used to build collaboration and team spirit and open the door to a candid exchange of thoughts and perceptions.
- Training tools are used for building interpersonal skills in such areas as communication, listening, presentation, change management, and facilitation.

The key to using any type of improv game successfully lies in setting up the right context and conducting the right level of debriefing. As a creativity trainer, Alain has taken thousands of people, from engineers, salespeople, and accountants to tax partners, executive managers, and CEOs, through improv games with effective results.

More Examples

Here are three more improv games that I enjoy playing and conducting:

HELP DESK. This is an improv game that I use in technical training. Three improvisers are seated at a "help desk" in front of the room. The first improviser asks the audience for a technical problem. Then he or she picks up an imaginary telephone, responds to an imaginary caller, and conducts a discussion about solving the technical problem. Once this conversation is established, the second improviser asks the audience for another technical difficulty and repeats the process of establishing a telephone conversation with another imaginary caller. After a while, the third improviser does the same. Once all three conversations are in full swing, improvisers take turns trading the focus of the scene among themselves by suitably changing the volume, intensity, rapidity, amount, and nature of the telephone conversation.

THE PERFECT FOLLOWER. This is an improv game that I use in leadership training. One improviser plays the role of a leader and the other a follower. The two conduct a discussion related to project planning. If the follower's behavior is not satisfactory, the leader claps his or her hands and explains the reason for dissatisfaction (examples: *too obsequious, too assertive,* or *does not listen actively*). The offending follower is immediately replaced by another participant, who tries to do better and last longer. The leader may fire the followers for any reason whatsoever and is allowed to act in an inconsistent fashion.

HALF LIFE. This is an improv game that I use to improve communication skills. The first improviser makes a 1-minute presentation explaining a critical concept related to the instructional topic. The second improviser

summarizes this presentation in 30 seconds. The third improviser summarizes the previous summary in 15 seconds. The fourth improviser does a 7-second summary. No summary may introduce new topics or facts not mentioned in the preceding presentation. After the fourth improviser, the cycle is repeated with a 1-minute presentation on a different topic by the next improviser.

Ready-to-Use Improv Game
QUICK DRAW

This is one of our favorite games for illustrating collaborative creativity. It is simple, fun, and effective. It has never failed to prove that we can unleash much more creativity by working together than by working alone. It is also a wonderful activity to set up a brainstorming session and to illustrate basic principles of idea generation.

QUICK DRAW (our name for this activity) and many other improv-based exercises are in the public domain. Our thanks to the hundreds, even thousands, of people who have contributed to this rich set of experiential activities.

Purpose

To explore the power of playfulness and collaborative creativity.

Time

10 minutes for the activity and 10 minutes for debriefing.

Participants

At least four. We have conducted this activity with hundreds of participants in a single session.

Materials

- Felt-tipped pens of different colors, one pen per participant
- Blank paper
- Flip chart
- Two flip-chart markers
- Summary of the QUICK DRAW Instructions, printed on a flip-chart sheet (see page 206)
- Sample QUICK DRAW sheet (page 207)

Design Your Own Games and Activities

Flow

Pair up. Pair the participants up. If you have an odd number of participants, join the group to complete the last pair. Have each pair find a space to sit next to each other with a joint writing surface.

Hand out paper and pens. Make sure each player has a colored pen and each pair has at least three sheets of blank paper. Don't use light-colored pens such as yellow or beige.

Brief the participants. Display the summary of instructions on the flip chart. Tell the participants that they will be working in pairs. Give these instructions, using your own words:

> "You and your partner will be drawing a picture, one line or feature at a time. One player starts by placing two small circles on a page to represent eyes. Players then alternate adding a line or feature, working as quickly as possible. When a player hesitates, the drawing is done. The players then title the drawing one letter at a time, again alternating with each letter and ending when one player hesitates. You may laugh, but you must not talk. We will collect the drawings and create a gallery in the back of the room."

Demonstrate the procedure. If you have an assistant, demonstrate the procedure in the front of the room on the flip chart. If you don't have an assistant, select a participant to demonstrate the procedure with you. Work with whatever the two of you generate spontaneously. If you hesitate, stop in the same way that you want participants to stop. Point out that the title doesn't have to make sense or spell real words, although it might. If you don't have an assistant, and if you feel comfortable trying this, take one pen in each hand and demonstrate the procedure as if you were two players.

Launch the activity. Have the participants begin the activity. If you are free to do so, move around the room, coaching pairs on the side, collecting completed drawings, and laying them out in a circle in the back of the room.

Coach on the side. Remind participants to follow these important instructions:

* Start with two small circles or dots.
* Stop when you hesitate.
* Take turns to create the title.
* The title is finished when you hesitate.
* Do at least three different drawings—with titles.
* Don't talk!

Form a circle and observe. As some pairs complete their third drawing, ask them to go to the back of the room and look at the exhibits. Let participants take their time looking at all drawings.

Debrief the participants. Tell the participants that you would like to conduct a debriefing discussion to reflect on the activity and share insights. Use the six sets of suggested questions below. Remember that these questions are not meant to be used in a mechanical fashion. Encourage spontaneous comments and let the discussion meander along its natural flow. Fall back on the prepared set of questions during periods of silence and redundancy.

Debriefing Questions

How do you feel?

- How do you feel about the activity?
- Earlier groups of participants reported feelings of discomfort, playfulness, surprise, and confusion during this activity. What are some possible causes of each of these feelings?
- How did you feel at the beginning of the activity? Near the end of the activity? Why did your feelings change?
- How do you feel about your drawings? How do you feel about the drawings created by other pairs?
- How do you feel about your partners? Did your feelings change during the activity?
- How do you feel about the pairs who finished early? The pairs who finished late?
- How do you feel about your creative ability? About your ability to collaborate with a partner?

What happened?

- What interesting things happened during the activity?
- What happened during the beginning of the activity when you started working on the first drawing?
- What happened while you were waiting for your turn?
- What happened when you hesitated for the first time?
- What happened when you began titling the picture?
- How did your behavior change between the first and the third drawing?
- What happened when you finished the third picture?
- What happened when you saw the other people's drawings?
- When did you feel frustrated? Elated? Afraid? On a roll?
- What worked for you? What got in the way?

Design Your Own Games and Activities

What did you learn?

- What was the most important learning point from this activity for you?
- What insights did you get about creativity? Playfulness? Spontaneity? Working with a partner?
- Here are some insights reported by earlier groups of participants. Does your experience support each of these principles?

  You are more creative when working with another person than when working by yourself.

  It is easier for you to take risks when you are working with someone else.

  With a little practice, you can feel comfortable in throwing yourself into the unknown experiences.

  Neither of the partners can dominate the activity or control the other person.

  A spirit of playfulness contributes to creativity.

  Working silently forces you to focus on the task.

  It is impossible to predict the outcome of a collaborative activity, but it is always a pleasant surprise.

  Since we could not hesitate, we could not censor our spontaneous ideas.

  I am not totally responsible for the quality of the drawing. This takes a lot of pressure off of me.

  Partners built off of each other's ideas.

  We have to accept and incorporate everything, even our mistakes.

  Not knowing exactly where we are going makes the activity more playful.

  We have to stay in the present when we cannot plan our next move.

How does this relate?

- What real-world processes does this activity relate to?
- How does the collaboration in this activity relate to collaboration in your workplace?
- How does this activity relate to brainstorming?

What if?

- What if you worked in triads (three-member teams) instead of pairs? How would that have changed the activity and its outcomes?
- What if you worked by yourself?
- What if you were appointed as the leader of your partnership?

- What if you were permitted to talk during the activity?
- What if you did not have to begin with two circles for eyes?
- What if you had to switch partners at the end of each drawing?
- What if you were asked to choose the best drawing at the end of the activity?
- What if a panel of judges chose the best drawing at the end of the activity?
- What if a group of children participated in this activity?
- What if you could work after any hesitation until you decided to stop?
- What if you had to work on each drawing for 3 minutes?

What next?

- What advice would you give a participant who is about to play QUICK DRAW for the first time?
- How would you behave differently if we were to conduct this activity all over again?
- How would you change your participation in brainstorming sessions, based on what you learned from this activity?
- Considering what you have learned from this activity, would you behave differently in your workplace? In what way?

QUICK DRAW Instructions

1. Work with your partner.
2. Place two small circles to represent eyes.
3. Take turns adding one line or feature.
4. There are no rights or wrongs; anything you do is fine.
5. Work as quickly as possible.
6. Stop drawing when either one of you hesitates.
7. Add a title, one letter at a time.
8. Alternate with each letter.
9. There are no rights or wrongs; any letter you add is fine.
10. Work as quickly as possible.
11. Laugh if you feel like it.
12. Don't talk—even if you feel like it.

Design Your Own Games and Activities

Sample QUICK DRAW

19 Openers

Openers (also known as icebreakers) are activities for jump-starting a training session. An effective opener helps participants achieve a combination of objectives, including previewing the workshop, getting acquainted with fellow participants, working collaboratively with others, establishing ground rules, sharing a common experience, sharing current knowledge, and getting energized.

DESIGNER TAGS

You are attending a three-day strategic planning session. This is the first day, and you pick up your name tag (with just your name) and grab a doughnut. At exactly 8:30 a.m., the workshop facilitator, Ethan, welcomes everyone. He points out that participants are chosen from different departments to encourage cross-functional cooperation.

To help you get better acquainted with other participants, Ethan is going to conduct an opening activity called DESIGNER TAGS. He asks everyone to secretly look at the back of his or her name tag and read the name of another participant who is a "mystery client." You check your name tag and find the name, Lynne. Ethan explains that you will have five 2-minute periods to pair up with another participant and to share information about yourself and your job. One of the people whom you talk to during these five rounds should be your mystery client. However, you should not let the other person find this out. Slightly confused, you talk to Karen during the first round. She seems to know how to play the game and bombards you with questions

about your family, your hobbies, and your job. You ask similar questions and listen to Karen's answers. Just when you are about to run out of conversational topics, Ethan blows a whistle, announces the end of the first round, and asks everyone to switch partners. You meet Roy from the accounting department and hold an interesting conversation. During the third round, you get to talk to your mystery client, Lynne, who is from the marketing department. You collect all sorts of intriguing information about Lynne, without making it obvious that her name is on the back of your name tag.

Two rounds later, Ethan gives everyone a blank name tag card and felt-tipped pen. He asks each participant to create a name tag for the mystery client by drawing pictures on the card, leaving enough space for the participant's name. You are not good at drawing pictures but you manage to sketch two identical babies because you remember Lynne telling you proudly that she is the mother of twin girls. You decorate the rest of the name tag with colorful balloons and stars. After about 3 minutes, Ethan asks everyone to stop their artwork, write the name of the mystery client on the back of the card in small letters, and place the card on a large table with the picture side up. He now invites everyone to identify their own specially designed name tag, pick it up, and verify the name on the back. You pick up a garishly illustrated name tag with a dagger dripping blood since you have confessed your addiction to murder mysteries to several people during the earlier rounds. You confirm your guess by turning the card over and finding your name there. Ethan now asks everyone to write their names on the decorated side of the name tag and replace your earlier bland tag with this one. As a final activity, he asks everyone to explain what the pictures signify and to guess who drew the picture. You make two incorrect guesses before you identify Roy as your name tag designer.

During the 20 minutes of the activity, you had lots of fun and learned interesting things about other participants.

Using Openers

Most trainers start their sessions with an icebreaker or opener. When effectively used, an opener can grab participants' attention and get them ready for collaborative learning. Openers can provide useful orientation to the instructional topic, training format, and fellow participants.

A few words of caution about the potential abuse of icebreakers and openers: Some trainers begin their sessions with a fun activity, totally ignoring the purpose of the opener. Participants complain because these trivial exercises waste everyone's time. To avoid this complaint, design or adapt the opener to relate to the training topic. Keep the activity brief and explain why you are conducting it. If you are working with a group of participants who already know each other, don't waste time on "getting acquainted" activities. If you are planning to use games and exercises throughout the session, skip the opener and begin with one of the other activities.

Types of Openers

Different types of openers help you achieve different purposes. Some openers act as icebreakers that help participants learn about each other. DESIGNER TAGS, the opener described above, primarily serves this purpose.

Here are examples of three other types of openers:

Establishing ground rules.   Openers can help you establish ground rules for the training session. Here's an opener called DEMANDS that requires a playful spirit. Ask participants to think of unpleasant experiences with previous training sessions. Give each participant a sheet of flip-chart paper and a felt-tipped marker and ask him or her to write one demand of you, the trainer. Give some examples like "Frequent breaks" and "Straight answers to questions." After a suitable pause, ask participants to hold up their demand signs and silently walk around the room. Invite participants to read other people's demands without making any comments. After a few minutes, ask participants to pair up with someone, read and discuss the two demands, and jointly decide which one to keep and which one to discard. After a suitable pause, ask both partners to hold the selected demand sign by the opposite corners and silently walk around the room studying the other demand signs. After a few minutes, ask participant pairs to team up into groups of four or six and select one of the demands. Continue this activity to reduce the demands to a final set of three or four. Tape these demands to the wall and solemnly agree that you will meet them. Invite participants to give you immediate feedback during the session if you violate any of the demands. Now hold up three or four of your "counter-demands" (that you had prepared earlier) with statements such as "Return from breaks on time" and "Turn off your cell phones and beepers." Invite participants to help you by accepting and implementing these guidelines.

Encouraging positive self-disclosure.   MISSING ACHIEVEMENT is an opener that encourages participants to talk positively about themselves. Before your training session, get ready for the game by asking each participant to identify a personal achievement that he or she is very proud of. Make a list of participants' names and achievements. Select any thirteen participants. Prepare a 5×5 bingo card with the name of each participant in a box and the achievement in another box. Since you have room for only twenty-five of the twenty-six items (thirteen names and thirteen achievements), you will have to leave out one of the achievements. At the beginning of the session, ask participants to mingle and talk about their achievements. Recommend that participants ask open-ended questions and respond without any false modesty. Announce a 7-minute time limit. At the end of this time, give the bingo cards to participants and explain that their task is to identify the name on the card that cannot be matched to an achievement. Ask participants to whisper the answer to you. Permit participants to mingle some more and continue their conversations. Stop the game after a half-dozen people have identified the correct name. Conclude the opener by reading everyone's name and achievement—including those

that were left off of the bingo card. Congratulate participants on their achievements and explain how proud you feel to be working with such an accomplished group.

Working collaboratively with others. My friend Kevin Eikenberry (past president of the North American Simulation and Gaming Association) designed an opener called PIECES. To get ready for this activity, buy children's jigsaw puzzles with fifty to one hundred pieces. You need a different puzzle for each team of four to six participants. Let us assume that you have five teams of six members each. Take four pieces from the first puzzle and mix one of them with the pieces from each of the other puzzles. Repeat the procedure so that each puzzle set misses four of its pieces and includes one piece from each of the other puzzles. Distribute the pieces from the first set into six envelopes (one envelope for each team member) and label the envelopes "Team A." Prepare similar envelopes for the members of the other teams, labeling them Team B, etc. Begin the activity by randomly distributing the envelopes to participants. Ask them to find other members of their team, sit at a table, and assemble the picture. Sooner or later, participants will notice that they are missing some critical pieces and holding some useless ones. If they complain to you, just shrug your shoulders and suggest that the pieces probably got mixed up. Eventually, participants will work with the other teams to complete the task. When all pictures are correctly assembled, congratulate the teams and conduct a quick debriefing. Explain that you will be using several team activities throughout the session. From this opening activity, participants should remember that they have important pieces to contribute, not only to their own team but also to the other teams.

Ready-to-Use Opener
ROBOT

ROBOT is an excellent icebreaker for a training session on change because both its content and process are related to the topic. In one sense, you don't have to conduct this activity; it runs on autopilot. When participants arrive, you are not even in the room. They find a message instructing someone to press the PLAY button on a VCR. A robot appears on TV and facilitates the activity. Don't worry about being replaced by automation, though. Near the end of the session, the robot hands over the control to you.

Purpose

- To explore words and concepts associated with change.
- To experience reactions to situations in which actual events do not match your expectations.

Participants

Any number

Time

20 to 30 minutes

Materials

- ROBOT videotape (see Script for the Videotape on page 215)
- Word association cards prepared from the suggested list on page 219
- VCR
- TV monitor
- Flip charts
- Felt-tipped markers
- Index cards
- Cardboard container

Preparation

We have reduced your responsibilities during the activity—and increased your responsibilities before the activity. Prior to the play of ROBOT, you need to take care of three things:

Produce the videotape. Don't get carried away. You are not producing a *Star Wars* sequel. Make a simple home movie in which you (or one of your talented friends) play the role of a ROBOT. For example, my friend Chris put a grocery bag over my head (with two holes for my eyes) and seated me on a low stool in front of our heat pump. The cables and hoses from the heat pump appeared to be attached to my head and shoulders. Chris recorded my monologue on a cheap hand-held video camera. I mimicked a synthesized computer voice (which my unkind friends claimed to be easier to understand than my usual accent). You will find the script (and a few directions) for this videotape on pages 215 through 219.

Prepare word association cards. You need a set of 20–30 index cards, each with a different word associated with change. You will find a suggested list of words on page 219. Feel free to delete, modify, and add your own words that are associated with change.

Set up the room. At the back of the room, set up a table with a large cardboard box. Throw the prepared word association index cards inside the box. Place a sign that says "Interchange Peripheral" on this table.

At the back of the room, find convenient wall space for taping flip-chart posters. Tape a sign that says "Graphics Display Area" to the wall.

In front of the room, place a VCR and a TV monitor. Insert your ROBOT videotape and make sure it is rewound to the correct starting point. Also

make sure that the VCR clock is set to the correct time. Place the remote control for the VCR near the monitor. Set up a flip chart with this message: "Please press PLAY on the VCR at exactly 8:33 a.m."

Flow

Hide outside the room. The first part of this opener is conducted by a robot appearing on a videotape. Your main task during this part is to stay out of sight. You may stand outside the closed doors of the room.

Let the robot do its thing. This is what happens inside the room:

- Participants write four words associated with change, each word on an index card.

- Participants exchange their four cards for three cards written by other people.

- Teams of participants at each table select three cards with words that are most strongly associated with change.

- Participants create and display posters that reflect the three words associated with change.

Enter the room. Make your dramatic entrance when you hear the sound of applause. Begin the poster-reading activity. Thank participants for cooperating with your friend, the robot. Explain that you are going to use the posters in a quick activity.

Ask participants to guess the words. Invite them to look at the first poster and call out words that are reflected by the graphics. Ask the members of the team that created the poster not to give any clues or feedback. After a suitable period of time, ask the team members to read the words on the three selected cards.

Repeat the process. Ask participants to guess the words embedded in the other posters. Conclude the session when you have processed all posters.

Debrief the activity. Write the words embedded in the posters on a sheet of flip-chart paper. Ask participants to review the cards that were not selected. List these words on the flip chart also. Use this list as the basis for the following discussions:

- Can we classify the words on this list into positive, negative, and neutral categories? Which category contains the most words?

- Try to recall the four words that you wrote. Which category—positive, negative, or neutral—did most of these words fall into?

- Which types of people are likely to feel positive about change? Which types are likely to feel negative? Which types are likely to feel neutral?

- Is it possible for all people to feel positive about a change? What type of change would it be?
- Which word on the list is found most frequently on the cards?
- Which word on the list surprises you the most as being associated with change?
- After all the work you did with these words associated with change, which word is currently the one word that you most strongly associate with change?

Continue with these types of general questions:

- What were your expectations about how today's session would begin? How different was the actual opening activity from these expectations? What was your initial reaction to these differences?
- Some groups of participants refuse to participate in this activity. Why did you not exhibit this type of resistance?
- As the robot explained at the beginning of the activity, it makes logical sense not to have an "expert" trainer talking about change. In spite of that, several participants resist this activity. Why do you think this happens?
- The robot presented you with a structured activity. How would you have felt if the robot gave you no instructions, asked you to figure out how you wanted to conduct the session—and disappeared? What would you have done in such a situation?

Script for the Videotape

Instructions

1. The script involves only one character, the robot. If you are playing the robot, don't memorize the lines; just present the content in your own words.
2. Ask an off-camera person to sound a bell or blow a whistle whenever the <TONE> sign appears in this script.
3. You need a count-down timer to indicate the remaining time allotted to different activities. Set up the timer whenever the <TIMER> sign appears in this script. Ask the cameraperson to zoom in close on the timer and fill the screen with the image of time being counted down.
4. Boxed words that appear in this script are captions to be shown on screen. Write the boxed words on pieces of card stock. Ask the cameraperson to shoot these captions at appropriate junctures in the script.

(Continued)

Greetings, participants!

Thank you very much for activating me.

Random Opening and Beginning Operations Transmitter.

My name is ROBOT—which stands for Random Opening and Beginning Operations Transmitter. I will be facilitating an opening activity during the next 20 minutes.

You may be surprised to see a robot instead of a human facilitator. But when you think about it, it makes a lot of sense. Today's topic is CHANGE and you are all experts in this topic. You have been subjected to change and you have tried to change other people. Change is affecting your personal and professional life every day. With this rich storehouse of personal experience, you don't need an external expert to bore you with theoretical frameworks and academic models.

I am here to empower you to take charge of your own learning. I will provide you with a structured activity that permits you to share concepts, principles, procedures, and strategies based on your own personal experience with change.

Ground Rules

Before we begin, may I suggest a few ground rules?

<TONE>

This tone signals that I am about to make an important announcement. Whenever you hear this tone, please stop whatever you are doing and ask others to stop whatever they are doing. Then please listen to my announcement.

You will be working on several timed activities. During the activity you will see a count-down timer on the TV screen. Keep an eye on the timer. If it looks like you are going to finish the activity ahead of time, slow down and shift to a more reflective mode. On the other hand, if it feels like you are going to run out of time, hurry up. Sometimes, you may have to shift to a new activity, even if you have not finished your current activity.

Activity 1: Word

Let's get started on the first activity. This is an independent activity, which means that you do not talk to each other.

On your table, you will see several input forms that you call index cards. Each one of you, please take four of these cards.

Change

- This workshop is about change. When you hear the word change, what other words, ideas, concepts, or issues pop into your mind?
- Your task is to write down different words associated with CHANGE. Please write a single word on each of your four cards. Obviously, there are no correct or incorrect answers. Write down whatever words come to your mind.
- Remember: one word per card.
- You have 52 seconds to complete the task. Please begin now.

Activity 2: Card

<TONE>

Thank you for looking up at the sound of the tone.

Here's your next activity. This is also an independent activity.

Please go to the back of this room, where you will see a rectangular table with a container labeled "Interchange Peripheral."

Pick up three index cards from inside the container. Then drop your four word-association cards into the container. Remember to pick up three cards first before dropping your four cards. This way you don't end up with your own cards.

Once you have picked up three cards, review the words on them. Arrange the cards according to the strength of the association between the word on the card and the word change. Whichever card has the word most strongly associated with change should be placed on top of your pile. Place the card with the next strongest association below this card.

You have 2 minutes to complete this task. Please do not interact with each other.

<TIMER: COUNTING DOWN FROM 2 MINUTES>

Activity 3: Team Up

<TONE>

Some of you may not have cards with words strongly associated with change. But don't worry because you can strengthen your hand through teamwork.

During the next activity all participants at each table will form a team. If you don't like the other people at your table . . . tough!

(Continued)

As a team, show your cards to each other. Review everyone's cards and jointly select the three cards with words that have the strongest association to change. Remember that everyone should participate in this selection process.

You have 3 minutes for this activity. Please begin now.

<TIMER: COUNTING DOWN FROM 3 MINUTES>

Activity 4: Graphics

<TONE>

Ready or not, here we go to the next team activity.

Please retrieve a graphic interface tablet sheet—I think you call them flip-chart paper—from the back of the room.

The task for your team is to create a graphical poster on one page of the flip-chart paper. The poster should visually represent the three selected words most strongly associated with change.

Here's a major restriction: You should not use any alphanumeric characters in your graphic poster. In other words, do not use ASCII characters 60 to 276. These characters are letters, numbers, and symbols that are usually found on a typical computer keyboard.

You have 3 minutes to complete this task. Please begin now.

<TIMER: COUNTING DOWN FROM 3 MINUTES>

Activity 5: Display

<TONE>

Please stop your graphical rendering.

Congratulations on your brilliant poster.

Will the members of each team take your poster to the back of the room? Locate the section marked as the "Graphic Display Area." Mount your poster on the wall, using single-sided adhesive strips quaintly called "masking tape."

Please press the PAUSE button on the VCR. After you have completed the activity, please remember to reactivate me by pressing the PAUSE button again.

Conclusion

Thank you for reactivating me.

Your displays look great!

During my recent hibernation, I reviewed the behavioral data from your previous activities. Based on my meta-analysis of these data, I have concluded that the time has come for me to hand you over to my android counterpart. This new facilitator will coordinate the rest of the session.

Before I disappear into cyberspace, I would like to thank all of you for your enthusiastic participation. You made my task easy and pleasant. For your collaborative effort, you deserve a big round of applause. Please give yourselves a hand.

Suggested List of Words for Word Association Cards

Agent	Opportunity
Coins	Pain
Conspiracy	Productivity
Constant	Progress
Downsizing	Rapid
E-commerce	Re-engineering
Evolution	Resistance
Expansion	Revolution
Globalization	Stress
Grassroots	Technology
Innovation	Tension
Marketplace	Top-down

20 Closers

Closers are activities that help you wind down a training session. An effective closer helps participants achieve a combination of objectives, including summarizing the content, reviewing major learning points, testing for mastery, providing feedback, planning for application activities, and celebrating the completion of the session.

DOUBLE NEGATIVE

You are participating in a workshop on financial planning that is drawing to a conclusion. Larry, the facilitator, announces a final brainstorming activity. He asks each participant to write down several ideas for ensuring that none of the new skills learned in the workshop will ever be implemented in the workplace. At first, you think that you misheard what Larry said, but he repeats the same sentence. Intrigued by the task, you write down "Burn the workshop manual" as the first idea on the list. After some more thinking, you come up with several other ideas. As you are writing down the sixth idea, Larry interrupts to invite everyone to call out their ideas. Different participants respond enthusiastically, and Larry records ten ideas on a flip chart.

Larry confesses that his actual goal is to come up with ideas that ensure transfer and application of all new skills. He is impressed with the list of ingenious ideas for achieving the opposite of his goal. He now invites everyone to take each idea and flip it over 180 degrees to transform it into a positive action. As an example, he points to one of your ideas (about burning the workshop manual) and asks for help in reversing it into a

positive suggestion. Someone suggests storing the manual inside a fireproof safe. Larry smiles and asks for other variations on the same theme. Someone else suggests keeping the workshop manual on the desk and referring to it every day. Later in this discussion, you offer an alternative to another original negative idea about single-handedly trying to transform the organization. You suggest that a positive alternative is to focus on changing each person's individual behavior in some small way. Susan suggests another alternative from the same original idea: Work with a few friends to organize a financial planning team.

After listing several more positive suggestions for applying the new skills to the workplace, Larry asks each participant to select three guidelines for personally ensuring maximum transfer of skills from the workshop. He distributes index cards and asks everyone to write three positive ideas that are most personally useful. As you write three practical ideas on your index card, Larry suggests keeping the card in your pocket as a handy reminder of what you could do.

Using Closers

Most facilitators begin their interactive sessions with icebreakers, but only a few wind down their sessions with suitable closers. However, it is obvious that you need a strong, memorable activity to help participants review and summarize the session, to celebrate its conclusion, to provide feedback to each other, and to plan for the implementation of the new principles and procedures. One of the reasons for this lack of use of closers is the tendency for other training activities to take up more time than originally scheduled. This results in dropping the closer, since it apparently does not add any new content. Also, near the conclusion of the training session, most participants are impatient to rush home, and the closer frustrates their plans for an early departure.

Precautions

Ending a training session without a closer is like conducting an intense experiential activity without debriefing. Without the closer, the training session loses its impact. Therefore, it is important to set aside sufficient time for the closer activity and to establish ground rules about everyone mindfully participating in the activity.

Near the end of a training session, you may be interested in either a systematic review or an action-planning activity. However, at this time, your participants are likely to be suffering from cognitive overload and in a right-brain state of mind characterized by an inability to function in a linear fashion and to focus. Therefore, your closers need to be playful and open-ended.

Your closers usually serve two types of purposes: those related to training objectives and those related to social functions such as celebrating, leave-taking, and networking. Often these two purposes are inconsistent

with each other and you have to maintain a balance between them. Sometimes you may have to use two short closers instead of a long one to achieve your goals.

Types of Closers

Different types of closers help you achieve different purposes. For example, DOUBLE NEGATIVE, the closer described above, is particularly useful for action planning and for applying new skills to the workplace.

Here are some other examples of closers for different purposes:

Reviewing major learning points. HIGHLIGHTS is a closer that helps participants think back on the training session and identify critical elements. To conduct this activity, ask all participants to find a quiet corner and review their notes. Invite them to recall events during the training session and identify the critical ones. Ask them to create a storyboard that captures the key activities and learning points associated with each. Explain that a storyboard is a series of rough sketches, each approximately 3 inches by 5 inches, that capture key ideas. Pause for at least 5 minutes while participants complete this activity. Later, organize everyone in groups of four to seven. Within each group, ask participants to take turns presenting their storyboard sketches, describe what they consider to be the major points, and why they think so. After everyone has completed his or her turn, ask each group to identify the most frequently mentioned learning points.

Testing for mastery. QUESTION CARDS is an ingenious closer that helps you administer a test without increasing participants' anxiety level. To conduct this activity, prepare a set of cards with review questions on one side and the correct answer on the other side. At the beginning of the activity, distribute ten blank cards to each participant and ask everyone to independently prepare ten question cards, referring to their handouts and notes, if necessary. After a suitable pause, collect all the question cards, mix them with your question cards, and shuffle them thoroughly.

Organize participants into groups of four to seven and give a packet of question cards to each group. Ask the groups to place the cards, question side up, in the middle of the table. Select one player in each group to be first. This player should read the question on the top card, without removing it from the pile. Within ten seconds, the player should come up with an answer. If this answer appears to be incorrect, any other player may yell out, "Challenge!" Turn the question card over to reveal the correct answer. If the original player's answer is correct he or she receives 1 point. If the player's answer is incorrect and if nobody challenged, no points are awarded. If the player's answer is incorrect and if there was a challenge, the challenger gets 2 points. It is now the turn of the next player to read the question on the next card. Repeat the procedure for a suitable period of time. When time is up, the player with the most points wins the game.

Celebrating the completion of the session. CERTIFICATES is a closer that helps you to conclude a multi-day training session on an upbeat note. Although CERTIFICATES is a closer, you have to set up the activity during the first hour of the first day of the training session. At this time, give each participant a large envelope with a blank certificate (adorned with impressive borders, scrolls, and seals), color pens, stickers, and an index card with the name of a "target" participant. Make sure that no participant gets an envelope with his or her own name as the target. Ask participants to keep the name of the target participant a secret—and surreptitiously observe this participant throughout the training session. Explain that each participant is to prepare a certificate of completion for his or her target with specific details of this participant's unique characteristics, contributions, and behavior patterns. Participants should work on the certificates during their spare time and be ready to present them at the closing ceremony.

Before the closing ceremony, announce a 5-minute final preparation time for putting finishing touches on the certificate. After these 5 minutes, begin the closing ceremony by outlining the procedure: You will randomly select a participant to be the first presenter. This person will come to the front of the room and briefly describe the unique characteristics and contributions of his or her target, without naming the person. After intriguing the other participants for a few minutes, the presenter will identify the target—who comes to the front of the room amidst applause from all participants. After receiving the certificate, the target becomes the next presenter and repeats the ceremonial procedure. After briefing participants, coordinate the ceremony, maintaining a fast pace and good-natured fun.

Ready-to-Use Closer
TRIPLE FEEDBACK

Closers help you wind down a training session. Different types of closers encourage participants to summarize the content, review major learning points, test for mastery, provide feedback, plan for application activities, and celebrate the completion of the session.

TRIPLE FEEDBACK is a closer that focuses on reviewing key ideas and providing feedback. It begins with participant teams producing a poster that summarizes major points from the training session. Participants then evaluate the posters and give feedback to each other. They do this both individually and in teams. The activity involves a wide variety of evaluation and feedback strategies, but it has a flexible format that can expand or shrink to fit the available time.

Time

This closer consists of an initial session followed by two separate evaluation and feedback sessions. Each session lasts for 15 minutes. If you are conducting a multi-day workshop and if you have about an hour, we recommend that you conduct all three sessions in the suggested sequence. If your time is limited, you can compress the time requirement by dropping one or more sessions to suit your constraints or special needs. If you want to focus on evaluation and feedback skills, you can expand the activity with longer debriefing discussions.

Participants

Twelve or more, divided into four or five teams of three or more members. Works best with twenty to thirty participants, divided into teams of five.

Session 1. Preview Posters

Purpose

To review and summarize the key ideas from the training session.

Time

15 minutes

Materials

- Handout of Preview Poster Instructions (see page 230) for each participant
- Flip charts, one for each team
- Set of felt-tipped markers of different colors, one for each team
- Timer
- Whistle

Flow

Organize teams. If participants have been working in teams during earlier sessions, keep the teams intact. Otherwise, organize participants into four or five teams, each with at least two members. It does not matter if some teams have an extra member.

Brief participants. Distribute copies of the Preview Poster Instructions. Ask participants to review these instructions. Answer any questions.

Start the activity. Send each team to different corners of the room where the flip charts are located. Remind participants to turn the flip charts around so that members of other teams cannot see their posters. Start the timer and ask teams to get started.

Monitor the activity. Walk around the room observing the teams in action. Speed up slower teams by announcing how much time is remaining.

Conclude the activity. Give a 1-minute warning. Blow the whistle at the end of 10 minutes. Ask participants to leave their flip charts and gather in the middle of the room.

Begin the next session. Start this session away from the flip charts.

Session 2. Poker Chips and Paper Cups
Purpose

- To provide evaluation feedback to team members and other teams.
- To explore the differences between individual and team evaluation, process and product evaluation, and inclusive and exclusive evaluation.

Time

15 minutes

Materials

- Handout titled Process Evaluation Instructions (see page 230) for each participant
- Handout titled Product Evaluation Instructions (see page 231) for each participant
- Paper cups, one for each participant and an extra one for each team
- Poker chips, thirteen for each participant and an extra set of thirteen for each team
- Timer
- Whistle

Flow

Brief participants for process evaluation. Distribute copies of the Process Evaluation Instructions. Ask participants to review the instructions. Answer any questions.

Start the activity. Distribute individual paper cups and thirteen poker chips to each participant. Ask participants to write their names on the paper cups and place them on the table. Tell participants that they have 2 minutes to reflect on their earlier activity and decide how to distribute the poker chips among the other members of their team. Remind participants that they should not drop any of their poker chips into their own paper cups. Start the timer.

Set up the posters. Tear posters from the flip charts and tape them to the wall in random order (so no one can determine which team created which poster). Place an empty paper cup below each poster.

Design Your Own Games and Activities

Conclude the process-evaluation activity. At the end of 2 minutes, blow the whistle and announce the end of process evaluation. Ask each participant to pick up her or his paper cup and count the poker chips. This number indicates how the members of the team evaluated each person's relative contribution to creating the poster. Thirteen poker chips indicate an average level of contribution.

Brief participants for the product-evaluation activity. Distribute copies of the Product Evaluation Instructions. Ask participants to review the instructions. Answer any questions.

Start the product-evaluation activity. Give thirteen poker chips to each team. Ask team members to study each poster and jointly decide how to distribute the poker chips to reflect the relative merit of each poster. Remind participants that they should include their team's poster in this relative evaluation process (and try to remain objective). Start the timer and announce that they have to complete the evaluation and drop their poker chips in appropriate paper cups within the next 5 minutes.

Conclude the activity. Give a 1-minute warning. Blow the whistle at the end of 10 minutes. Ask each team to count the number of poker chips in their paper cup. If there are more than thirteen poker chips in their paper cup, their poster is rated to be above average. Fewer than thirteen poker chips indicates that the poster is rated to be below average.

Debrief the session. To help participants get the maximum learning out of this activity and to ensure reflection and sharing of insights, conduct a debriefing session. Use the six-phase debriefing model (with these key questions: How do you feel? What happened? What did you learn? How does this relate to your workplace? What if . . . ? What next?). Include these specific questions to emphasize concepts related to evaluation and feedback:

- Evaluating your team members' contribution focused on the *process*. Evaluating the relative merits of different posters focused on the *product*.

- What are the differences between process and product evaluation? Which one is more important? What are the advantages and disadvantages of each of these two types of evaluation? When would you conduct process evaluation and when would you conduct product evaluation?

- When you evaluated the contributions of your team members, you worked as an individual. Later, when you evaluated team posters, you worked as a team.

- What are the differences between *individual* evaluation and *team* evaluation? Which one is easier? Which one is more objective? What are the advantages and disadvantages of each of these two types of

evaluation? When would you conduct individual evaluation and when would you conduct team evaluation?

- When you evaluated your teammates, you did not include yourself as one of the people to be evaluated. This is *exclusive* evaluation. When you evaluated the posters, you included your team's poster among the items to be evaluated. This is *inclusive* evaluation.

- What are the differences between exclusive and inclusive evaluation? Which one is easier? Which one is more objective? What are the advantages and disadvantages of each of these two types of evaluation? When would you conduct exclusive evaluation and when would you conduct inclusive evaluation?

Session 3. Good News, Bad News

Purpose

- To provide positive and negative evaluation feedback on posters created by other teams.

- To explore the differences between affirmative and critical feedback, anonymous and open feedback, quantitative and qualitative feedback.

Time

15 minutes

Materials

- Affirmative Evaluation Instructions (see page 231) for each participant
- Critical Evaluation Instructions (see page 232) for each participant
- Index cards
- Timer
- Whistle

Flow

Number the posters. Post a sticky note paper on each poster and number the poster. On the blank side of an index card, write the numbers of each poster. Give one index card to each team, making sure that no team gets a card with the number of the poster it created. Ask the teams to keep the numbers on their index cards hidden from the other teams.

Brief participants for affirmative evaluation. Distribute copies of Affirmative Evaluation Instructions. Ask participants to review the instructions. Answer any questions.

Conduct the affirmative-evaluation activity. Ask members of each team to conduct an affirmative evaluation of the poster of the number written on

Design Your Own Games and Activities

their index card. Each team has 3 minutes to discuss the merits of the poster and write down at least three and not more than six positive feedback comments on the card. Start the timer.

Conclude the affirmative-evaluation activity. At the end of 3 minutes, blow the whistle and announce the end of evaluation. Collect the card (with positive feedback comments) from each team.

Brief participants for critical evaluation. Distribute copies of Critical Evaluation Instructions. Ask participants to review the instructions. Answer any questions.

Conduct the critical-evaluation activity. Give each team another index card with a poster number, making sure that no team receives the number of the poster it created or the number of the poster it affirmatively evaluated during the preceding round. Ask team members to critically discuss the poster and write down at least three and not more than six negative feedback comments on the card within the next 3 minutes. Start the timer.

Conclude the critical-evaluation activity. At the end of 3 minutes, blow the whistle and announce the end of the evaluation period. Collect the card (with negative feedback comments) from each team.

Distribute feedback comments. Give the appropriate positive and negative feedback cards to each team. Ask team members to review and discuss the comments among themselves. Announce a 3-minute time limit for this activity. Start the timer and stop the session at the end of 3 minutes.

Debrief the session. Conduct a debriefing session as before. Include these specific questions to emphasize concepts related to evaluation and feedback:

- During *affirmative* evaluation you focused on the positive aspects of the posters. During *critical* evaluation, you focused on the negative aspects.

- What are the differences between affirmative and critical feedback? Which one is easier to conduct? Which type of feedback was easier for you to accept? Which type of feedback was more useful? What are the advantages and disadvantages of each of these two types of evaluation? When would you conduct affirmative evaluation and when would you conduct critical evaluation?

- Throughout this activity, you gave your feedback anonymously. In your workplace you have to give feedback openly. What are the differences between *anonymous* and *open* feedback? Which type of feedback is easier for you to give? Which type of feedback is easier to give openly: positive or critical? Which type of feedback is easier to receive? Which type of feedback is more useful? What are the advantages and disadvantages of each of these types of feedback?

- During the previous session, your poster received *quantitative* feedback (specific number of poker chips without any comments). During this session, your poster received *qualitative* feedback (positive and negative comments without any scores).

- What are the differences between quantitative and qualitative feedback? Which type of feedback is easier for you to give? Which type of feedback is easier to receive? Which type of feedback is more useful? What are the advantages and disadvantages of each of these two types of feedback?

Preview Poster Instructions

Task	Create a poster that summarizes the key points covered in this training session.
Audience	The poster should be designed for participants attending future sessions of this training program.
Intended Use	• The poster will be placed on the walls of this room during future training sessions. • The poster has to be self-contained. No one will explain its purpose or content. • The purpose of the poster is to provide a preview of the training contents.
Content	• The poster should summarize key points covered in this training session. • The poster may contain text, symbols, and pictures.
Constraints	• Your poster is limited to one sheet of flip-chart paper. • You can only use the colored felt-tipped markers supplied to you. • You cannot paste or attach anything to the poster.
Process	• All members of the team should jointly produce a single poster. • You may refer to the workshop handouts and your notes.
Time Limit	10 minutes

Process Evaluation Instructions

Task Evaluate the relative contributions of other members of your team.

Time Limit 2 minutes

Steps
1. **Collect your supplies.** Get a paper cup and thirteen poker chips from the facilitator.
2. **Personalize your cup.** Write your name on the paper cup and place it on the table.
3. **Do a comparative evaluation.** Think back on how your team designed and produced your poster in the previous session. Recall how different members of your team participated in this activity.
4. **Distribute poker chips.** Decide how you want to distribute the thirteen poker chips among all other members of your team in such a way that the number of poker chips given to each person reflects his or her relative contribution to the production of the poster. Remember these constraints:
   - You have to distribute all thirteen poker chips.
   - You may not give yourself any of the poker chips.
   - You have to give more poker chips to team members who contributed more to the production of the poster.
5. **Drop poker chips in paper cups.** Secretly drop the appropriate number of poker chips into each paper cup with a team member's name.

Product Evaluation Instructions

Task Evaluate the relative merits of the Preview Posters.

Time Limit 5 minutes

Steps
1. **Collect your supplies.** Send a representative from your team to get thirteen poker chips from the facilitator.
2. **Do a comparative evaluation.** Silently study the posters from all teams (including your own). Move to a convenient location and discuss the relative merits of the posters with other members of your team.
3. **Distribute poker chips.** Decide how you want to distribute the thirteen poker chips among the different posters in such a way that the number of poker chips given to each poster reflects its relative merit, in comparison with the other posters. You may use any criteria for evaluating the posters. Remember these constraints:
   - You have to distribute all thirteen poker chips.
   - You should include your poster in the evaluation process (but you should compare it with the other posters in an objective fashion).
   - You have to give more poker chips to the poster that is better than the others.
4. **Drop poker chips in paper cups.** Secretly drop the appropriate number of poker chips into the paper cups placed below each poster.

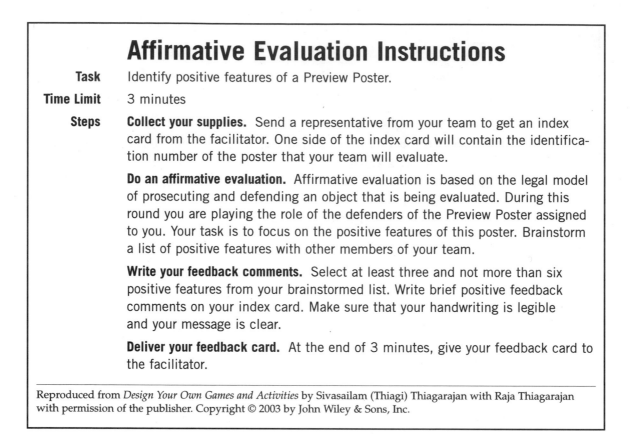

Affirmative Evaluation Instructions

Task Identify positive features of a Preview Poster.

Time Limit 3 minutes

Steps **Collect your supplies.** Send a representative from your team to get an index card from the facilitator. One side of the index card will contain the identification number of the poster that your team will evaluate.

Do an affirmative evaluation. Affirmative evaluation is based on the legal model of prosecuting and defending an object that is being evaluated. During this round you are playing the role of the defenders of the Preview Poster assigned to you. Your task is to focus on the positive features of this poster. Brainstorm a list of positive features with other members of your team.

Write your feedback comments. Select at least three and not more than six positive features from your brainstormed list. Write brief positive feedback comments on your index card. Make sure that your handwriting is legible and your message is clear.

Deliver your feedback card. At the end of 3 minutes, give your feedback card to the facilitator.

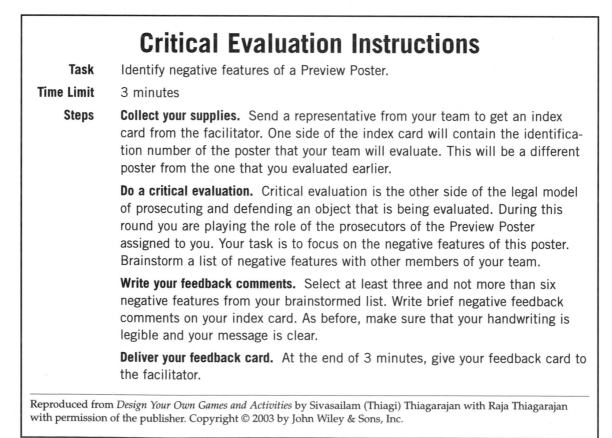

Critical Evaluation Instructions

Task Identify negative features of a Preview Poster.

Time Limit 3 minutes

Steps **Collect your supplies.** Send a representative from your team to get an index card from the facilitator. One side of the index card will contain the identification number of the poster that your team will evaluate. This will be a different poster from the one that you evaluated earlier.

Do a critical evaluation. Critical evaluation is the other side of the legal model of prosecuting and defending an object that is being evaluated. During this round you are playing the role of the prosecutors of the Preview Poster assigned to you. Your task is to focus on the negative features of this poster. Brainstorm a list of negative features with other members of your team.

Write your feedback comments. Select at least three and not more than six negative features from your brainstormed list. Write brief negative feedback comments on your index card. As before, make sure that your handwriting is legible and your message is clear.

Deliver your feedback card. At the end of 3 minutes, give your feedback card to the facilitator.

Part 2

Simulation Games

21 Introduction to Simulation Games

What is a simulation? Technically speaking, it is the representation of the objects, characteristics, behaviors, and relationships of one system through the use of another system. For example, a model of an office building uses pieces of wood and paint to represent a concrete structure and the landscape surrounding it. Similarly, a computer program uses algebraic equations and graphs to simulate the flow of air traffic at O'Hare airport.

What is a game? It is an activity with four critical features: *conflict* (obstacles that prevent the achievement of a goal), *control* (rules that deal with different aspects of play), *closure* (a special rule that indicates how the game comes to an end), and *contrivance* (inefficiency built into play of the game).

Combining these two definitions, we can specify that *simulation games contain play objects, goals, rules, and roles that reflect real-world objects and processes.* When used for training purposes, a simulation game enables participants to experience an "almost" real experience, discover underlying principles, and practice appropriate skills.

SIMCITY® 2000

Last week, you signed up to become a volunteer member of the mayor's advisory committee. Today is the first meeting of this committee. Your friendly facilitator divides the group into five teams and provides access to SIMCITY® 2000, a computer simulation game designed by Maxis to explore different aspects of planning and running a city. Your facilitator invites you to play with the simulation game any way your team wants to, but warns

that next Friday a panel of experts will inspect different cities administered by different teams. The team with the best city (as judged by several quality-of-life criteria) will win the game.

It takes you some time to figure out how to play this game, but fortunately one of the younger members in your team is familiar with computer games. Through trial and error, you learn how to put the simulation on "pause" while you set up residential, commercial, and industrial zones and connect them with roads. You then experiment with different menus, tools, and windows. When your team decides to build a power plant, you have a choice among coal, oil, gas, wind, solar, hydroelectric, and nuclear plants. Team members argue with each other and eventually decide on a nuclear plant. You now release the simulation from "pause" and find out that you have the choice of four different growth speeds for the city. You select a medium speed and watch houses, factories, and shopping malls popping up on the map. A newspaper appears on the screen with national and local news. You have access to the budget window, where you specify property tax rate and allocate funds to police, fire, health and welfare, education, and transit. While you are doing all these things, an "engine" in the background computes changes in your city (in terms of such factors as traffic, land value, pollution, and unemployment). Whenever you choose, you may go to a graph window and see how your city is changing over time. Another window permits you to implement such items as sales tax, an anti-drug campaign, a homeless shelter, and a public smoking ban. Your choices produce different effects on the population of the city, crime rate, pollution, and so on. At one juncture, you realize that you have not planned for adequate water supply nor budgeted funds for water towers, treatment plants, pumps, and pipes. So you float a bond to raise enough money. Through careful governance, you maintain a healthy growth rate. You must be doing something right because the software program announces a surprise reward and erects a statue in honor of your team in the middle of the downtown area.

Advantages of Simulation Games

Your vicarious experience with SIMCITY® illustrates the power of simulation games as a training strategy:

- Because a simulation game is very close to on-the-job training, it ensures effective transfer and application of what you learn in the game to the real world. Your team's decisions and actions in SIMCITY® are very similar to the decisions and actions of a real-world city council.

- Simulation games provide immediate and realistic feedback. In SIMCITY®, you see the impact of your decisions and actions on several critical factors related to the development of the city. You can get this feedback immediately in the form of graphs and charts.

- Simulation games reduce the risk to the players. Any inappropriate decisions made during the play of SIMCITY® do not result in immediate

impeachment and imprisonment. Nor does the increased pollution and crime rate affect real people.

- Simulation games provide opportunities for repeated practice. If you are not doing a good job as the mayor in SIMCITY®, you can close down the game and start again. You can discover important urban government principles through trial-and-error experimentation.

Types of Simulations

SIMCITY® is an excellent example of a *computer simulation game*. This type of simulation game is a software package that presents a scenario, requires participants to make decisions and implement them, performs complex computations to determine the impact of these decisions on various parameters, presents the results, and modifies the scenario. Most computer simulations use multimedia presentations with colorful graphics and sound effects.

There are several other types of simulation games based on the purpose, process, and types of objects used. Here are brief descriptions of some of the base types:

High-Fidelity Simulations

High-fidelity simulations incorporate objects and processes that are as close to reality as possible. These simulations reflect a large number of real-world factors and complex relationships among them. They are specially useful for training participants to implement exact procedures. Table 21.1 shows some different types of high-fidelity simulations.

Action Learning. This type of simulation game brings participants as close to the real world as possible. In this technique, a team conducts a critical project and then reflects on its experience in order to learn new principles and procedures. In a typical action-learning project, a team of employees solves a real, complex, strategic problem that is affecting the organization. In the process of solving the problem, team members develop their skills and knowledge and gain insights through continuously reflecting on behaviors related to problem definition, idea generation, solution implementation, and results evaluation.

Reflective Teamwork Activities (RTAs). These are briefer versions of action learning. In this technique, the team is given a task and is asked to objectively examine the process it used to complete the task. For example, in an RTA called STAGES, participants discuss different stages in the development of a team and then reflect how, in the process of their discussion, they went through the same stages that they discussed.

The Case Method. This method involves a written account of a situation surrounding an organizational problem. Participants work individually and in teams to analyze, discuss, and recommend appropriate solutions and to critique each other's work. In some cases, the facilitator may recount the

Table 21.1 Types of High-Fidelity Simulations

Simulation	Key Feature	Ready-to-Use Activity	Page
Action Learning	Real, complex, strategic projects	CALL TO ACTION	247
Reflective Teamwork Activity	Work on a task and reflect on the process	MULTIPLE FEEDBACK	258
The Case Method	Analyze a case and decide on suitable action	TROUBLED TEAM	270
Training Device	Physical objects that simulate real-world objects and processes	TEAM MAZE	298
Production Simulation	Design and development of a product	BULLET SLIDES	288
Procedural Simulation	Dress rehearsals for real-world events		
Troubleshooting Simulation	Systematic analysis of problems to find root causes		
Disaster Simulation	Handling natural or organizational disasters		

actual decisions implemented in the real-world situation on which the case was based.

Training Devices. These are physical objects used by an interacting group of participants to learn complex technical procedures or to explore interpersonal principles. Some of these devices are specially created for technical training (example: *flight simulators*), while some are created for some other purpose (example: *Hula Hoops*) but used for training.

Production Simulations. These simulations involve the design and development of a product. Different teams compete with each other to create the best product. The activity begins with teams receiving specifications for the final product, along with an evaluation checklist. Teams also have access to training sessions, job aids, reference materials, sample products, and expert consultants. Final products from different teams are evaluated by outside experts, end users, and peers on a variety of relevant dimensions.

Procedural Simulations. These simulations are dress rehearsals of real-world events, as in the case of conducting a raid to rescue hostages, evacuating a building during a fire, or being subjected to a surprise inspection by auditors from the funding agency. By working through these simulations, participants get ready for real-world events.

Troubleshooting Simulations. Another type of simulation requires participants to systematically find the causes of problems and to fix the problems. These simulations use realistic simulators (as in the case of debugging faulty machinery) or computer printouts of output data (as in the case of slowing down the loss of market share).

Disaster Simulations. Here participants are required to cope with natural or organizational disasters, such as an earthquake or downsizing. By dealing with simulated disasters, participants learn to make rapid collaborative decisions in complex and changing situations.

Low-Fidelity Simulations

Low-fidelity simulations are based on simplified models of reality that incorporate only a few selected factors from the real world. These simulations are especially useful for encouraging participants to discover principles. Some different types of low-fidelity simulations are shown in Table 21.2.

Metaphorical Simulation Games. MSGs reflect real-world processes in an abstract, simplified fashion. MSGs are particularly useful to teach principles related to planning, generating ideas, testing alternatives, making decisions, utilizing resources, and working under time pressure.

Interactive Stories. These are fictional narratives that involve participants in a variety of activities. In one type of interactive story, the facilitator presents a story and discusses its significance in a debriefing discussion.

Table 21.2. Types of Low-Fidelity Simulations

Simulation	Key Feature	Ready-to-Use Activity	Page
Metaphorical Simulation Game	Abstract reflections of real-world processes	PUZZLE PIECES	312
Interactive Story	Storytelling that involves participants	A DEATH IN MY FAMILY	321
Role Playing	Participants taking on characteristics and attitudes	GUT TALK	335
Cash Game	Use financial outcomes to explore interpersonal principles	CHANGE MANAGEMENT	346
PC Simulation	Using playing cards to create micro-worlds	CARD SETS	353
Jolt	Brief experiential activities to provide wake-up calls	TRIPLE JOLT	365

In another type, the facilitator pauses at critical junctures in the middle of a story and invites listeners to play the role of a character and make appropriate decisions. In still another type, participants themselves create and share stories that illustrate key concepts, principles, or procedures.

Role Playing.   Role plays involve participants taking on characteristics, personalities, and attitudes in order to achieve a variety of training and performance-improvement outcomes. Participants act out their roles in a spontaneous and realistic manner under imaginary conditions imposed through a scenario.

Cash Games.   This type of game involves actual monetary transactions to explore interpersonal skills (such as negotiation) and concepts (such as cooperation). The cash used in these games effectively simulates real-world events and elicits natural behaviors and emotions in participants.

PC Simulations.   This type of simulation uses playing cards to reflect real-world objects and processes. The rules of PC simulations typically encourage participants to discover principles of interpersonal interaction and inductive thinking.

Jolts.   Jolts are interactive experiential activities that lull participants into behaving in a comfortable way and then suddenly deliver a powerful wakeup call. Jolts force participants to re-examine their assumptions and revise their habitual practices. A typical jolt lasts for a few minutes but provides enough insight for a lengthy debriefing.

The Importance of Debriefing

Simulation games provide participants with valuable experience in realistic settings. However, such experience does not guarantee that participants will learn from it. This is because people learn from experience only when they reflect on it, gain valuable insights, and share these insights with each other.

Debriefing is the process of facilitating participants to help them reflect on their experience, gain valuable insights, and share them with each other. This technique is particularly important in dealing with complex simulations. In these situations, debriefing helps participants to recall large-scale simulations, analyze the elements, derive cause-effect relationships, and decide the best course of future action. Debriefing is also useful when a simulation game elicits emotional involvement. Participants feeling intense emotions—whether positive or negative—find it difficult to focus on logical relationships and principles. In highly emotional situations, most participants make mindless assumptions and jump to unwarranted conclusions. Used appropriately, debriefing can support simulation games by adding a rational component. Finally, debriefing is useful in deriving insights from abstract simulations (such as metaphorical simulation games and jolts). The debriefing discussion enables participants to match the

Design Your Own Games and Activities

metaphor with real-world analogues and prepare action plans for the immediate application of new insights.

The chapters that follow provide explanations and examples of different types of simulations. A common element that is integrated with different simulations is the emphasis on debriefing. Unfortunately, many commercially available simulation games ignore debriefing or add a list of discussion questions as an afterthought. We cannot overemphasize the importance of paying attention to debriefing before, during, and after the design of your simulation game.

Remember, the simulation game is just an excuse for conducting the debriefing discussion.

22 Action Learning

Action learning involves a team that conducts a critical and strategic project and then reflects on it to learn new things. In a typical action-learning project, a team of employees solves a real, complex, strategic problem that is affecting the organization. In the process of solving the problem, team members develop their skills, knowledge, and insights through continuously reflecting on behaviors related to problem definition, idea generation, solution implementation, and results evaluation.

PROJECT NET GAIN

You are a trainer working for a U.S. software design company that is about to merge with an Australian corporation. The U.S. company markets its services all over North America and Europe. The Australian counterpart covers emerging markets in Asia. The top management of both corporations has given you three months and a "reasonable" budget to conduct an action-learning project for designing and implementing an Internet and intranet communication system for the employees, suppliers, and customers. Your mission is to take care of both the technical and the human side of the new communication system.

You organize your action-learning team from a group of six people from different departments, selecting three people from each of the merging corporations. You also include a representative from your major supplier and another representative from the Australian company's major customer. The eight members of your action-learning team work in three locations—San Jose, California; Adelaide, South Australia; and Singapore.

You spend the first couple of days of your team meetings orienting the members to the philosophy and principles of action learning. You then plunge the team into specifying requirements for the communication network, identifying important criteria such as ease of access, reliability, and security. Your team then divides itself into two subgroups to focus on the technical aspects and the interpersonal aspects of the project. Both groups meet every other day, and you debrief everyone about what is happening and what insights may be gained from the experience. You encourage the subgroups to challenge one another and to offer ideas for integrating the two components of the project. Because of the tight deadline, the group hires and manages technical specialists to install the system. You try out the system with a small pilot group and make suitable modifications based on their feedback. You develop reference manuals and online performance support systems to train employees to use the new system.

By the time the final details of the merger are worked out, your new communication network is ready to roll. Your action-learning team has proactively solved technical and interpersonal problems. Equally importantly, you and your team members have grown a lot, both personally and professionally.

What Is Action Learning?

The term "action learning" is frequently used to refer to a variety of interactive training activities. However, we are using the term to refer to a specific methodology that has been around for more than sixty years.

Here is a brief historical note about the origin and spread of action learning: In 1912, the British commissioner who investigated the sinking of the Titanic was appalled by the behavior of planners and builders who did not raise any issues about the safety of the ship for fear of appearing stupid in front of experts. He shared this piece of information with his son, Reg Revans, who later worked as a physicist at the Cavendish Laboratory in an entirely different mode of collegial interaction where scientists questioned each other, raised disturbing issues, and collaboratively solved problems and created new knowledge. In 1945, when Revans became the director of education and training for the National Coal Board in the United Kingdom, he used his experiences to create problem-solving teams of four or five managers who periodically acted as consultants to each other. These groups successfully solved problems and learned from the process. Revans labeled the approach *action learning* and applied it to solve problems and develop people in different organizations. However, action learning was mostly neglected by trainers and consultants until the 1970s when it began rapidly spreading to different industries in different countries.

Here are three key factors related to the action-learning process:

Task. A challenging problem lies at the heart of all action-learning projects. This challenge should involve a real organizational task—not a simulated task contrived for learning purposes. The task should have strategic, long-term consequences for the entire organization and not for just one department. It should not be a task that could be accomplished by the application of some standard operating procedure, but should require the creation and application of new approaches.

Team. Action learning is undertaken by teams of four to eight people who are as different from each other as possible to ensure maximum learning. The members of this team should be drawn from different departments, should represent different cultural backgrounds, and should reflect individual differences in personality, thinking, and learning styles.

Thoughtful action. Effective action-learning projects should balance teamwork and team learning. This requires setting aside enough time and other resources so that team members can accomplish the task, reflect on the process, gain new principles and insights, and share with one another.

Why Use Action Learning?

The combination of doing and thinking in action-learning projects results in several unique benefits:

Ownership. Because the team comes up with a plan and immediately implements it, team members take greater ownership of the project than any top-down project that is imposed on them.

Creativity. Diversity among members of the action-learning team ensures different points of view. Also, teams are more willing than individuals to take greater risks. These factors result in ideas that are more creative than those generated by individuals or by members of a homogeneous committee.

Communication. Cross-functional action-learning teams increase and improve communication among employees from different branches, departments, and functional groups. By empowering an action-learning team to make decisions and to take appropriate actions, we are forcing—and rewarding—its members to talk with each other with a focus on the total organization rather than on a specific department.

Personal growth. Action learning transforms both the organization and the individuals. On the personal side, people learn new skills and knowledge related to their jobs. They particularly gain interpersonal skills related to leadership, teamwork, diversity, and decision making. Team members also benefit from a big-picture view of the organization and learn how their

personal efforts can contribute to—and benefit from—the effort of teams, departments, the organization, and the community that surrounds the organization.

Application. In contrast to classroom learning or web-based training, action-learning projects produce skills and knowledge that are immediately transferable to the workplace. The action-learning process contains all the advantages of on-the-job training (OJT). In most cases, the advantages go beyond those of OJT because action learning involves taking on more important strategic challenges that confront entire organization as a total system.

Types of Action Learning

Action learning involves the three critical elements of task, team, and thinking. It uses the action steps of selecting a challenge, organizing a team, collecting information, analyzing the problem, generating ideas, evaluating alternatives, selecting the solution set, and implementing it. Each of these action steps is accompanied by the learning steps of reflection, generalization, and application.

While all action-learning projects involve these critical elements and steps, they may vary along other dimensions:

Teams. In the project-based approach, an action-learning team is organized to complete a specific task. When the team accomplishes this task (and has learned from the process), it is disbanded. In a team-based approach, an action-learning team works on different projects—sometimes simultaneously, sometimes one after another. In this approach, members of the team take turns presenting problems that they are facing. When one person presents his or her problem, the other members act as consultants. An action-learning team of this type continues functioning for an indefinite period of time, taking on different tasks.

Commitment. Some action-learning projects are of short duration (a few weeks), while others are longer (a few years). Sometimes, employees are assigned to an action-learning team on a part-time basis while they continue with their normal work responsibilities. At other times, the employee is deputed to participate in an action-learning team on a full-time basis. Obviously, long-term action-learning projects with full-time members are more likely to result in effective action and effective learning.

Interaction. Members of action-learning teams typically hold several face-to-face meetings. With the recent advent of the Internet, websites, chat rooms, forums, and e-mail, virtual action-learning teams are springing into action with their members located around the globe.

Learning. In the emergent-topics approach, action-learning teams analyze their actions without using any pre-selected category systems. This results

in somewhat unpredictable (but relevant) learning outcomes. In the targeted topics approach, the task for the action-learning team is deliberately selected to provide opportunities for exploring some specific topic. This action-learning approach is specially suited for learning about such topics as change management, problem solving, team building, leadership, communication skills, and personal mastery.

Ready-to-Use Action Learning Activity
CALL TO ACTION

Action learning requires a team to simultaneously solve a real, complex, strategic problem and to learn from the process by continuously reflecting on its behavior. Here is an activity that involves a project to implement action learning in an organization.

Purpose

- To organize and facilitate an action-learning team.
- To plan and implement an action-learning project and to learn from the activity.

Time

1 hour for the initial session. Schedule and time requirements for other sessions will be decided by participants.

Participants

Four to eight, drawn from different divisions of an organization.

Materials

- Action Learning: What Is It and How We Can Benefit from It (See suggestions below on how to write this one-page handout)
- Planning Checklist (see page 250)
- Debriefing Checklist (see page 251)
- Roles and Functions in an Action-Learning Team (see page 252)
- Discussion Questions (see page 253)
- How Things Can Go Wrong (see page 254)

Preparation

Plan the project. This activity involves organizing and facilitating an action-learning team that includes you and three to seven other members from different departments in your organization. This team will act as a continuing action-learning group, taking on different projects and learning from each

of them. The first project will involve the task of planning and implementing an action-learning program in your organization. Analyze the needs, goals, and activities of this project within your organizational context.

Write a description. Prepare a one-page description of action learning and how this technique can benefit the organization and its individual employees. Borrow the content from the description of action learning at the beginning of this chapter, but provide specific ideas and details related to your organization.

Entice a sponsor. To ensure organization-wide application and sustained implementation of the action-learning program, enroll the support of a top manager in your organization. Explain your vision for the program to this sponsor and obtain commitment for needed resources, including released time for team members. Also obtain an enthusiastic statement in support of the program from your sponsor.

Recruit team members. Select a group of three to seven managers for the action-learning team. Make sure that these team members will share your belief in the program and commit time, energy, and other resources to support it.

Schedule the first session. Work out a convenient location and time for the initial meeting. Send a memo with a tentative agenda and a one-page description of action learning.

Conduct the First Session

Welcome team members. Briefly thank everyone for joining the team. Share your enthusiasm and excitement about the project. Ask each team member to introduce himself or herself.

Brief team members. Quickly review highlights of the action-learning technique and its potential benefits. Explain that this team will be a continuous action-learning team, taking on projects of interest to different members. Explain that you would like the first project to be yours because it will give the team an opportunity to explore the technique of action learning.

Confirm the agenda. Ask team members to review the agenda and suggest suitable changes. Jointly decide on the amount of time to spend on this meeting.

Modify and use the Planning Checklist. Explain that you would like to use a structured approach for the team's planning activities. Distribute copies of the Planning Checklist. Invite team members to review the checklist and suggest suitable revisions.

Establish goals and plan of action. Immediately use the checklist to plan the activities for the rest of the session. Facilitate the discussion to decide

what goals are to be achieved during this initial meeting and how the team should work together.

Modify and use the Debriefing Checklist. Since reflection and learning are critical elements of the project, explain that you would like to use a structured approach for debriefing the team from time to time—and especially at the close of the day's session. Distribute copies of the Debriefing Checklist and explain its use. Invite team members to review the checklist and suggest suitable revisions. Use the checklist immediately to debrief the team about the activities so far.

Distribute other handouts. Give each team member copies of Roles and Functions in an Action-Learning Team, Discussion Questions, and How Things Can Go Wrong. Briefly explain the purpose and content of each handout.

Ask for volunteer facilitators. Explain that you would prefer not to play the dual roles of project owner and facilitator. Invite any other member of the team to take over the facilitation task. Alternatively, suggest that team members can take turns facilitating the rest of the meeting.

Conclude the session. Set aside the final 10 minutes for planning the activities for the next session and for final debriefing. Encourage other team members to facilitate these activities. Strongly suggest the use of the steps in the Planning Checklist and the Debriefing Checklist.

Conduct Subsequent Sessions

Follow up. After the first session, remind team members of action items through memos, e-mail messages, and telephone calls. A few days before the next meeting, send a reminder and a tentative agenda.

Reuse the two checklists. During the second meeting (and all subsequent meetings), use the Planning Checklist and the Debriefing Checklist to structure team discussions.

Use a systematic process. During the action-learning project use the following steps, which are similar to those included in the Planning Checklist: specify goals, collect relevant information, generate alternative ideas, evaluate the costs and benefits associated with each idea, select the best ideas, integrate these ideas into an action plan, and implement the plan.

Maintain a balance between action and learning. Remember the dual goals of action and learning. Encourage team members to reflect on their actions, gain useful insights, and share them with each other.

Progress to other projects. Establish a specific end date for the first project. Celebrate its conclusion. Build on the momentum and utilize the team's increased skills and knowledge by starting another project to help some other team member.

Planning Checklist

Use the following six items to structure any planning activity. Your plan could be related to the entire project (of several months' duration) or a brief activity (of a few minutes' duration). Use the checklist in a flexible manner. Feel free to rearrange the items into a different order, to skip some items, and to revisit previous items.

1. *Specify project goals.* Examine why each goal is important. If appropriate, shift to higher-level goals.

2. *Discuss relevant information.* Share different facts and perceptions associated with project goals. Encourage alternate points of views.

3. *Specify the gap.* Determine the difference between the current state and the ideal state implied in the project goals.

4. *Generate ideas.* Use different techniques to come up with strategies for achieving the project goals.

5. *Evaluate ideas.* Filter the ideas by comparing the costs and benefits associated with each. Select the best set of ideas.

6. *Integrate ideas.* Combine the selected ideas into an action plan.

Debriefing Checklist

Use the following six sets of questions to structure the debriefing activity to help team members to reflect on their experiences, discover useful insights, and share them with each other. You may use the checklist to reflect on the entire project, a complete meeting session, or a small incident. Use the checklist in a flexible manner. Encourage spontaneous comments related to any of the checklist items at any time. If the conversation degenerates into a tangential discussion, return to specific questions on the checklist.

1. How do you feel? What is your reaction to the activity or the incident? Why do you feel that way? Why do you think others feel differently?

2. What happened during the activity or the incident? What are the differences in our recollections? What were the critical incidents? What were the causes? What were the consequences?

3. What did you learn? What insights did you gain? What are some general principles that you discovered? What new skills and knowledge did you acquire?

4. How does this relate to other aspects of our work life? In what ways is our behavior similar to or different from our typical behaviors?

5. What if some of the factors were different? What if we had more members in the team? What if we had fewer members? What if we had more time to discuss the issues? What if we had less time?

6. What next? How can we use our insights and increased knowledge in our future sessions? How can we use them in our workplace?

Reproduced from *Design Your Own Games and Activities* by Sivasailam (Thiagi) Thiagarajan with Raja Thiagarajan with permission of the publisher. Copyright © 2003 by John Wiley & Sons, Inc.

Roles and Functions in an Action-Learning Team

Project Owner

- Explain the problem or the opportunity.
- Specify project goals.
- Ask for useful input and feedback.
- Provide background information.

Facilitator

- Coordinate group discussions.

Coordinator

- Schedule team meetings.
- Arrange for meeting rooms, equipment, and supplies.

Record Keeper

- Capture key points from team discussions.
- Create action plans.
- Distribute discussion summaries and action plans to all team members.

Discussion Questions

1. What is the primary goal for our project? Why is this an important goal?

2. How would we know that we have achieved our goal? How should we evaluate the success of our project? What products should we deliver at the end of this project?

3. What obstacles may prevent us from reaching our goals?

4. What are our action goals? What are our learning goals?

5. What is the goal for this session? How does it relate to the project goal?

6. What should be the size of the project team?

7. Who should be the members of the project team? Should we invite other people to join the team?

8. Should we use external facilitators to help our team?

9. What are the important roles and functions of team members?

10. What resources do we need to achieve the project goals?

11. How long should this project last?

12. What types of information do we need? What are different sources of information? How should we collect relevant information from different sources?

13. What things can go wrong with the project? What are the causes for potential failure? How can we remove them or reduce their impact?

14. How frequently should the project team meet? How long should each meeting last?

15. What should be ground rules for project team meetings?

16. What is the best way to schedule meetings to ensure that everyone can participate?

17. How should we bring about the action-learning methodology to the rest of the organization?

18. What types of organizational goals are suitable for action learning?

19. What is the relationship between action learning and various change efforts in our organization?

20. What is the relationship between action learning and training and development efforts in our organization?

21. How can we maintain an appropriate balance between—

    • Teamwork and individual work?
    • Meetings and other modes of communication?
    • Project work and regular work?
    • Action and learning?
    • Completing this project and getting ready for future projects?
    • Individual reflection and team discussion?

How Things Can Go Wrong

Although action learning is a simple concept, it demands attention to several details in order to derive maximum benefits. Here are six things that can go wrong in an action-learning project, along with guidelines for preventing these problems:

1. *Lack of personal commitment.* Sometimes, team members may treat their action-learning activities as extra workload on top of their regular job assignments. When there is a conflict of interest, they may neglect or postpone the action-learning activity in preference to other work-place demands. This problem is especially associated with projects to which busy employees are assigned on a part-time basis. To avoid this type of problem, recruit highly motivated employees, relieve them of other job responsibilities, and reward them with suitable incentives.

2. *Lack of organizational commitment.* Successful action-learning projects require top-management champions who provide the necessary budget and time. Lack of management support frequently results in lack of personal commitment. Unless the team is provided with the resources and authority for collecting information, making major decisions, and implementing changes, they are unlikely to undertake serious actions and achieve significant learning. To avoid this type of problem, do not launch an action-learning project without committing the necessary resources.

3. *Internal resistance.* Traditional training departments feel threatened by action-learning projects because they do not fit in their competency areas related to classroom teaching or multimedia materials. Similarly, people who thrive on the power structures of isolated departments frequently resent cross-functional action-learning teams invading their decision-making territory. To avoid this type of problem, work on changing the organizational culture toward accepting new learning and performance paradigms before launching an action-learning project.

4. *Poor choice of team members.* An action-learning team of just two or three members does not have any checks and balances that ensure careful consideration of different factors. On the other hand, a team with ten or more members does not provide sufficient airtime to individual members. Team members who are too similar to each other may not explore alternative approaches and benefit from healthy difference of opinions. On the other hand, team members who are hostile toward each other may waste too much time fighting diversity battles rather than making decisions and learning from their actions. To avoid problems with team membership, pay careful attention to the number and nature of team members and ensure optimum diversity among professional backgrounds, departmental affiliations, cultural variables, and individual preferences.

5. *Imbalance between action and learning.* A team that focuses its attention exclusively on undertaking rapid and drastic action without reflecting on its causes and consequences will not learn anything significant in the process. On the other hand, a team that spends too much time collecting data, debating issues, constructing theoretical rationale, and identifying multiple criteria before taking action and reflecting on what they did and why they did it will probably paralyze itself into academic learning without useful action. To avoid this type of problem, devote equal time, resources, and attention to the two elements of action learning.

6. *Inefficient facilitation.* A facilitator with a traditional attitude toward training and a set of old-fashioned instructional skills may sabotage the effects of an action-learning project by imposing his or her own opinions and lecturing on the content. To avoid this type of problem, appoint an external facilitator who has the maturity and methodology to manage the action-learning process by guiding the team through making its own decisions and creating its own content.

Design Your Own Games and Activities

23 Reflective Teamwork Activities

Most interactive experiential activities use a process to explore some content. In a *reflective teamwork activity* (RTA), the process and the content merge with each other. For example, in an RTA, participants may discuss different stages in the development of a team and then reflect how, in the process of their discussion, they went through the same stages that they discussed.

ET—EFFECTIVE TEAMS

You have been assigned to a newly formed customer-relations team and Mark, the facilitator, conducts a game. He invites you and the other participants to write down four characteristics of effective teams, each on a separate index card. Mark collects all the cards, adds some cards with statements that he had written earlier, shuffles the cards thoroughly, and gives each participant three cards. You study the statements on the cards and arrange them in order of how strongly you agree with each statement. During the next round, you exchange cards with other participants, trying to collect cards with statements that are more agreeable to you. During the next round, you form a team with three other participants. All four members of your team combine your cards and jointly select the three cards with statements that everyone agrees with. As a team, you prepare a poster using only pictures (no text) to convey the essence of the three selected statements about effective teams. When this task is completed, teams take turns presenting their posters and justifying their choices.

After the activity is completed, Mark facilitates a reflective debriefing period: He invites all team members to compare their teamwork (during the collaborative selection of the three cards and the creation of the poster) with the characteristics of effective teams depicted in the posters. The ensuing discussion results in reflection and sharing of insights.

Advantages and Uses of RTAs

In a reflective teamwork activity, participants work as a team on an actual task, rather than playing a role or working on a simulated task. After completing the task, team members reflect on their behaviors and explore principles and procedures related to relevant aspects of teamwork.

Reflective teamwork activities are especially useful with intact teams whose members have been working (or who plan to work) with each other on an actual project. In this context, the RTA brings members of the team closer together and provides them with a common language to discuss their past experiences and future plans.

More Examples of RTAs

P-MAX: PARTICIPATION TO THE MAXIMUM. This reflective teamwork activity focuses on increasing and improving the participation of all members in a team project. You can conduct P-MAX in 30 to 60 minutes with ten to forty participants who are organized into an even number of teams. Pair up teams so that the two teams in each pair can take turns observing one another. Let us assume that one such pair consists of the Red Team and the Blue Team. During the first round, ask members of the Red Team to draw on the flip chart a colorful picture that depicts the organization's vision. Announce a 5-minute time limit. Ask members of the Blue Team to observe the Red Team's performance, taking special note of behaviors and interactions that encourage or discourage team members' participation. During the second round, ask members of the Blue Team to analyze their observational data and prepare a checklist of do's and don'ts to encourage maximum participation of all members. While this is happening, ask the Red Team to observe the Blue Team's activity, making note of behaviors that elicit or inhibit enthusiastic participation. During the third round, pair up members of the Red and Blue teams. Invite each pair to hold a debriefing conversation reflecting on their experiences and observations on the two different projects (drawing a picture and preparing a participation checklist). Instruct each pair to come up with three recommendations for improving the frequency and quality of team members' participation.

SWITCH. This reflective teamwork activity explores the challenges associated with losing and gaining team members in the midst of a long-term project. You can conduct SWITCH in about 30 to 60 minutes with ten to forty participants who are organized into teams of four to seven members. Begin by asking all teams to conduct a brainstorming discussion

Design Your Own Games and Activities

for 10 minutes. Assign this "losing" topic to one half of the teams: "How can we handle losing some members of our team in the midst of a long-term project?" To the other half of the teams, assign this "gaining" topic: "How can we handle the addition of new members to our team in the midst of a long-term project?" After about 5 minutes of the brainstorming activity, randomly select one or two people from the teams working on the "losing" topic and send them to join the teams working on the "gaining" topic. Ask the reorganized teams to continue their brainstorming activity for 4 more minutes. At the end of this time, blow a whistle and announce the end of the activity. Conduct a debriefing session by inviting participants to reflect on their previous teamwork experience. Use these questions to identify suitable strategies for working efficiently when the team is disrupted by the removal or addition of members:

- What are the major problems associated with losing team members? Gaining team members?

- What strategies could we use to reduce the disruption when some team members are removed? When some new members are added to the team?

- What actually happened when your team lost one or more of its members in the midst of the brainstorming activity? Gained one or more new members?

- How did you feel when you were removed from your team in the midst of the brainstorming activity? When you were added to another team in the midst of their activity?

CELEBRATE. This RTA involves the development of two ceremonies for celebrating the completion of a team project—and uses one of them to celebrate the completion of the RTA. You can conduct CELEBRATE in 30 to 60 minutes with any number of participants, divided into teams of four to seven members. Each team plays this game independently. To start the game, tell the team members that they comprise a special task force established to develop two generic ceremonies to celebrate the completion of a project. The first ceremony is to be a grand one (for the completion of a major project) and it may involve a $500 budget, a week of preparation, and several hours of celebration. The second ceremony is to be a modest one (for the completion of a smaller task) with no special budget or preparation time and involving no more than 10 minutes of celebration. Announce a 20-minute time limit for the activity. Suggest that team members take turns describing their ideas and that all members select the best ideas and combine them into the two ceremonies. After 15 minutes, announce the time and suggest that the team use the remaining time to get closure on the second ceremony. At the end of the assigned time, congratulate the team and ask them to implement the plan for the brief ceremony to celebrate the successful completion of the activity. After the team finishes its celebration, conduct a reflective debriefing session, discussing how practicable their plans for the brief ceremony were.

TEAM PROFILE. This RTA is a special type of icebreaker that helps team members to collect and share important information about themselves. You can conduct TEAM PROFILE in 30 to 60 minutes with at least six participants. Begin the activity by dividing the team into three subteams of two or more people. Explain that each subteam will be collecting, analyzing, and reporting information about the characteristics and preferences of team members. Assign the following three topics to the three subteams: *members' experiences, expertise,* and *expectations.* Ask the three subteams to spend 5 minutes planning the questions and procedures they would use to collect information. Then ask each subteam to spend the next 10 minutes interviewing members of the other subteams to collect appropriate data. After this, ask subteams to analyze and organize the information. Finally, ask each subteam to make a 2-minute presentation summarizing their major findings. Follow with a reflective debriefing to discuss whether the team members' behaviors were aligned with their expectations and whether the team fully utilized each member's experiences and expertise.

Ready-to-Use Reflective Teamwork Activity
MULTIPLE FEEDBACK

In a reflective teamwork activity (RTA), the content and the process merge with each other. For example, participants may discuss different stages in the development of a team and then reflect how, in the process of their discussion, they actually went through the same stages that they discussed. Here is an RTA related to giving one-on-one feedback.

Here is a preview of this activity: Participants practice giving feedback in a series of role plays that involve simulated scenarios. Following each role play, participants are asked to give suitable suggestions to the primary role players. Later, the facilitator points out that these "suggestions" are actually feedback statements and debriefs participants about their ability to apply the same guidelines for effective feedback under different situations.

Purpose

To give effective feedback in a face-to-face situation.

Participants

Five or more. With ten or more, organize participants into approximately equal-sized groups of five to nine.

Time

30 to 60 minutes. Exact time requirement depends on the number of participants in each group.

Materials

- Copies of the How to Give Effective Feedback checklist (page 265)
- Clipboards
- Blank sheets of paper
- Timer
- Whistle

Flow

Distribute copies of the checklist. Give each participant a copy of the How to Give Effective Feedback checklist. Explain that the ten items on the checklist specify the training objectives and content. Invite participants to skim through the content of the checklist.

Brief participants. Explain the increasing importance of giving face-to-face feedback to individuals in the workplace. Relate this skill to teamwork, performance improvement, coaching, and performance review. Discuss the checklist items by explaining and providing additional examples. Invite participants to give their own examples.

Specify a scenario for the first round. Work with participants to come up with a scenario for the first round of role playing. Specify a situation that requires face-to-face feedback (example: *not writing your section of a report on time*) and provide details about the feedback giver (example: *team leader*) and the feedback receiver (example: *team member who interviewed customers*). Work out only the minimum information required so that there is plenty of room for interpretation and improvisation by the role players.

Organize groups and assign roles. If you have ten or more participants, divide them into approximately equal-sized groups of five to nine. Within each group, assign these roles:

- Feedback Giver (FG)
- Feedback Receiver (FR)
- FG's Coach
- FR's Coach
- One or More Observers (The number of observers depends on the number of participants in the group: a group of five has a single observer, while a group of nine has five observers.)

Provide time for planning and preparation. Announce a 3-minute preparation time. During this period, the FG and her coach work out specific plans for giving feedback based on an analysis of the situation and the FG's identification of checklist items to focus on. Similarly, FR and

her coach plan how to react to the feedback in a realistic (but sufficiently challenging) manner. Observers meet and divide up the items in the checklist among themselves.

Organize the space for role play. At the end of 3 minutes, ask groups to set up the role-play stage: Place two chairs facing each other for the FG and the FR. Arrange chairs for the observers. Ask the FG's coach to stand behind the FR, holding a clipboard and blank sheets of paper. Position the FR's coach behind the FG with similar supplies. Explain that, during the role play, the coaches can hold up suitable prompts to their players (examples: *Ask for permission to give feedback. Get more insistent about explaining that it was not your fault.*) without distracting the other role player.

Conduct the role play. When all participants in each group have taken their positions, announce that the role play will last for 3 minutes. Start the timer and ask players to begin. Move around the groups and observe the activity without interfering.

Provide suggestions for improvement. Blow a whistle at the end of 3 minutes to conclude the role play. Explain that the focus in this training activity is on giving feedback. Ask all members of the group to think back on the role play and come up with one suggestion for the FG on how to improve her performance. After a suitable pause, ask group members to give their suggestions in this order: observers, FR's coach, FG's coach, and FR. Then ask the FG to come up with a suggestion for improving her own performance. Finally, provide some general suggestions based on your observations.

Reassign roles. Explain that you are going to repeat the role-play activity to provide opportunities for other participants to practice giving feedback. Ask participants to change their roles in this fashion to get ready for the next round of role play:

- FR becomes FG's coach
- FG's coach becomes an observer
- One of the observers becomes FR's coach
- FR's coach becomes FG
- FG becomes FR

Repeat the procedure. Work with participants to come up with another scenario for the second round of role play. Provide 3 minutes of planning time. Conduct the role play for 3 minutes. Invite all participants to provide performance-improvement suggestions to the FG.

Conduct reflective debriefing. After the second round, invite participants to think of how many people acted as FGs during the preceding two rounds.

Playfully point out that every participant had two opportunities to act as an FG, because they all had to provide real-life feedback when they were making suggestions to the designated FG during each round. Pause briefly for this fact to sink in. Invite participants in each group to reflect how their suggestions for improvement to the FG implemented or violated the checklist items. Through appropriate questioning, help participants realize that they frequently and automatically provide feedback to each other.

Continue with the activity.   After spending sufficient time on the reflective debriefing, continue with the role plays using the previous procedure. Remind participants to provide suggestions to the FG in a mindful mode, incorporating all the checklist items.

Conduct final debriefing.   When everyone has had an opportunity to play the role of the Feedback Giver, conduct a final debriefing discussion. Use the suggested list of questions below.

Suggested Debriefing Questions

While debriefing, remember that the purpose of this reflective teamwork activity is to explore factors that influence the effectiveness of feedback. Encourage a free-flowing discussion among the participants and return to these questions when the conversation slows down.

How do you feel?

- How did you feel about giving feedback to someone in the role-play situation?
- How did you feel about receiving feedback from someone in the role-play situation?
- How did you feel when the facilitator pointed out the similarity between making suggestions (to the feedback giver in the role play) and giving feedback during the role play?
- How did you feel about giving real-life feedback (in the form of suggestions) to the role player at the end of each round?
- How did you feel about receiving real-life feedback from everyone else at the end of the round when you played the role of the feedback giver?
- Which checklist item made you feel most uncomfortable? Why?

What happened?

- If you were a feedback giver, how did you go about performing in the role play?
- If you were a feedback receiver, how did you go about performing in the role play?
- If you were a coach, how did you help the feedback giver?

- If you were a coach, how did you help the feedback receiver?
- If you were an observer, what interesting things did you observe?
- After a round of role play, how did you go about making suggestions to the feedback giver?
- How did your behavior change after the facilitator pointed out the similarity between making suggestions and giving feedback?

What did you learn?

- Which checklist item is the most important? Why do you think it is the most important? Would other people also consider it to be the most important?
- Which checklist item is the most difficult for you to implement? Why do you think it is the most difficult? Would other people also consider it to be the most difficult?
- Which checklist item is most frequently violated in your workplace? What are the reasons for this?
- Should we eliminate any of the checklist items? If so, which one? Why?
- If you were asked to combine two of the checklist items into one, which ones would you combine?
- Should we add more items to this checklist? If so, what items do you suggest?
- If you were asked to divide one of the checklist items into two, which one would you divide? What exactly would the new items say?

How does this relate?

- Thinking back on a typical day in your workplace, how many times do you give feedback? How many times do you receive feedback?
- How mindful are you in giving feedback to others in your workplace? What types of feedback require you to think and plan ahead? What types of feedback do you automatically give?
- Do you have any interesting examples of how one of the checklist items was implemented or violated in your workplace recently?

What if?

- What if the feedback receiver acted very defensively and began attacking you?
- What if you did not have a coach?
- What if everyone was invited to give feedback according to his or her natural inclinations instead of following the guidelines in a checklist?
- What if the facilitator never pointed out the similarity between giving feedback and making suggestions?

What next?

- How would you apply your insights and skills from this activity to the way you give feedback in your workplace?

- Which checklist item should you personally focus on? How do you plan to improve your ability to implement this checklist item?

Using MULTIPLE FEEDBACK as a Framegame

Framegames are templates for the instant creation of training games. The structure of a framegame is specially designed to permit easy replacement of old content with new.

MULTIPLE FEEDBACK is a framegame. The steps in its flow can be used with any interpersonal skill that involves one-on-one interaction. For example, we have used this framegame to teach participants how to receive and use feedback from others. This version of the game, called LISTEN AND LEARN, makes an excellent follow-up to MULTIPLE FEEDBACK.

LISTEN AND LEARN uses a checklist with ten guidelines. These guidelines deal with such areas as avoiding defensiveness, asking for clarification, establishing mutual goals, requesting appropriate support, and planning the first step. The scenarios used in this game are similar to those used in MULTIPLE FEEDBACK, except the focus is on the receiver of feedback instead of the giver. The steps in playing LISTEN AND LEARN are exactly the same as in MULTIPLE FEEDBACK.

Here are a dozen other interpersonal skills that we have plugged into the MULTIPLE FEEDBACK framegame:

- Coaching

- Delegating

- Negotiation

- Telemarketing

- Asking for a raise

- Interviewing for a job

- Handling help-desk calls

- Collaborating with a partner

- Making assertive statements

- Dealing with customer objections

- Working with a Japanese colleague

- Saying "No" to unreasonable requests

Try creating your own game on some interpersonal skills using MULTIPLE FEEDBACK as the basic frame.

Ready-to-Use Scenarios

We recommend that you create just-in-time scenarios for MULTIPLE FEEDBACK role plays by working with suggestions from participants. This approach gives partial ownership of the game to participants and ensures that the scenarios are job-relevant. Sometimes, however, time constraints may preclude this approach. If you don't have enough time, choose, use, or adapt from the ten different scenarios shown in Table 23.1.

Table 23.1. Scenarios for Role Plays

Feedback Giver	Feedback Receiver	Situation
Co-Worker 1	Co-Worker 2	Your co-worker does not complete his share of a joint assignment.
Manager	Employee	Your employee does not meet deadlines for monthly reports.
Employee	Manager	Your manager does not give you enough time to complete your monthly reports.
Team Leader	Team Member	The team member criticizes other people's ideas during initial phases of brainstorming.
Manager	Employee	Your employee states her performance goals in vague, unmeasurable terms.
Client	Graphic Designer	The preliminary design for your brochure is too unconventional for your target audience.
Writer	Typesetter	Your typesetter has left out three paragraphs of the original material.
Manager	Receptionist	Your receptionist makes personal telephone calls and ignores the waiting visitors.
Co-Worker 1	Co-Worker 2	Your co-worker tells off-color jokes that offend you.
Coach	Employee	Your employee blames everyone else for the delay in completing an assigned task.

How to Give Effective Feedback

1. **Focus on helping the other person, not on expressing your feelings.**
   DO think: "How can I help Alan to improve his brainstorming skills?"
   DON'T think: "I'm irritated with Alan criticizing my ideas. Maybe I should give him some feedback about how disappointed I am."

2. **Give feedback on what happened recently, not on what happened in the past.**
   DO say: "John, when you interrupted Marie just now, . . ."
   DON'T say: "John, ever since you joined the team five years ago, . . ."

3. **Give feedback with permission; don't impose it on others.**
   DO say: "Diane, may I give you some feedback about the way you prepared the action plan?"
   DON'T say: "Diane, let me tell you how to improve your action plan."

4. **Give specific information, not general comments.**
   DO say: "The logo that you designed does not include our focus on web-based training."
   DON'T say: "You designed a stupid logo."

5. **Describe; don't infer or evaluate.**
   DO say: "You arrived 7 minutes late to the meeting."
   DON'T say: "You are a lazy person, probably due to your parents pampering you as a child."

6. **Balance positive and negative information; don't nag.**
   DO say: "Your report is on time, and it contains some typos."
   DON'T say: "You misspelled 'access' on the first page, your margins are all long, you did not include the copyright line, your graph does not have captions, and . . ."

7. **Focus on modifiable behavior, not on things outside the person's control.**
   DO say: "Why don't you just say, 'Thank you' when someone compliments you?"
   DON'T say: "Why don't you stop blushing every time somebody compliments you?"

8. **Give information that you own, not hearsay information from others.**
   DO say: "You keep interrupting me."
   DON'T say: "Patti says that you frequently interrupt her."

9. **Offer suggestions; don't impose requirements.**
   DO say: "Perhaps you may want to use a flip chart."
   DON'T say: "I want you to prepare some flip-chart pages before the meeting."

10. **Discuss the other person's understanding; don't stop with a monologue.**
    DO say: "Can you tell me what you heard me say about documenting your travel expenses?"
    DON'T say: "Thanks for listening to my suggestions. See you after your trip."

Reproduced from *Design Your Own Games and Activities* by Sivasailam (Thiagi) Thiagarajan with Raja Thiagarajan with permission of the publisher. Copyright © 2003 by John Wiley & Sons, Inc.

24 The Case Method

The case method combines analysis with action. It requires participants to analyze a record of a realistic and complex situation (called a "case") from multiple viewpoints and to identify alternative actions. Participants then discuss their analyses, assumptions, and recommendations to deepen their understanding of the technical content surrounding the case and the interactive process of open-minded inquiry.

RECALLED

You and a few other trainers are about to conduct a series of technical training sessions in Malaysia. You are now being briefed about your first international assignment. Your facilitator gives you a three-page case and asks you to spend 15 minutes analyzing the content.

The case is about Harriet, a technical trainer sent to help her counterparts in a software engineering corporation in South India. Harriet convinces the local trainers to replace traditional lectures with interactive presentations. The local trainers accept the idea and create outlines for interactive lectures. Then one day, Mr. Kumar, the grandfather of the founder of the corporation, visits the training group. During a rambling speech, he says that trainers should always be respected and obeyed as gurus. Much to Harriet's dismay, most local trainers agree with the old man. To prevent major damage, Harriet interrupts the old man and explains that recent findings in cognitive sciences have demonstrated the benefits of encouraging students to challenge trainers' statements. Mr. Kumar ignores Harriet and extols humility as

the most important requirement for effective learning. In spite of Harriet's protests, several participants rush to agree with Mr. Kumar's philosophy. After Mr. Kumar leaves, Harriet confronts the team about their unwillingness to challenge inaccurate and outmoded paradigms. Participants now agree that Harriet's views are accurate and useful. However, soon after this incident, Harriet's company abruptly recalls her to its California headquarters and replaces her with another trainer.

Your first task is to read the case, analyze it, identify key issues, write down significant points, and get ready for a discussion. It is obvious to you that the Indians in the story don't like female trainers. You try to keep an open mind, however, and come up with other ideas about Harriet's problems. After 15 minutes, your facilitator starts a discussion by inviting Ethan to present his analysis of the case. He then asks for someone else to present an alternative analysis. This is followed by heated discussion about the key issues that contributed to Harriet's abrupt removal. You express your opinion that Harriet's gender was the cause of the problem. Another participant argues that gender is not the major issue, but that being disrespectful to an elder is. Several participants suggest other issues, such as the incompatibility of interactive training with local cultural values and general resistance to change. Your facilitator does not make any substantive comments, but prevents the discussion from coming to a premature conclusion. So many issues have been raised that when the discussion ends, you feel frustrated at not being able to nail down the correct solution. Your facilitator suggests that there is no single answer and that everyone will experience a similar sense of frustration in his or her field assignment.

Uses and Limitations of the Case Method

The primary advantage of the case method is its real-world relevance: Participants frequently complain about major differences between solving problems in the training session and solving problems in the real world. Problems that are tackled during training come in neat little packages. They lend themselves to logical analysis and suggest a correct solution. In contrast, most real-world problems are messy. They do not have a single cause that can be easily identified and effectively removed. The case method involves problems that are much more reflective of real-world situations. They have multiple causes and lend themselves to alternative solutions. As a result, participants who are trained with case materials are not disillusioned when they apply their skills to real-world problems. During training, they observe other participants floundering with the multiple realities of an ambiguous problem. This experience increases their ability to tolerate ambiguity.

The case method has other advantages:

- It helps participants acquire skills related to analysis, critical thinking, and decision making. Case materials present the problem in a larger context and encourage participants to apply their skills in a variety of situations.

Design Your Own Games and Activities

- It helps participants learn how to process large amounts of information. In dealing with cases, participants learn to separate facts from inferences, organize facts, look at situations from a broader perspective, and explore alternative ideas and solutions.

- It helps participants master interpersonal skills required for building on other people's perceptions and ideas and influencing others to accept and act on their own analyses. The discussion of the case strengthens participants' ability to work as a team to analyze and solve problems.

The case method has some disadvantages:

- Not all participants benefit from the case method. Those who have been conditioned to expect a single answer are frustrated by the multiple realities approach of the case method.

- Not all facilitators can effectively conduct a case session. This method requires high levels of competency related to both the technical content and to the interactive process. The case facilitator has to maintain a delicate balance between guiding the discussion and driving it.

Types of Case Method Activities

The core of the case method is the case. A well-organized case begins with an overview of the critical content. The main part of the case is usually presented in the form of a narrative story with a set of key characters, their roles, and their relationships. Depending on the nature of the case, this narrative may include dialogue and action, along with qualitative details about assumptions and perceptions and quantitative data about schedules and finances. Most cases focus on a single central issue or main question. A case may also include background information to provide a specific context for the activities and issues. Some cases may contain supporting documents, such as tables, charts, and technical reports. Some cases may be accompanied by facilitator notes with suggested questions and anticipated issues for the main discussion and sample analyses and expert comments for a follow-up discussion.

The specific materials and methods used in a case session may take a variety of forms. Here are some examples:

Source.   There are several different bases for developing a case. RECALLED, the case presented earlier, is a composite narrative based on the cross-cultural experiences of several professional workers on overseas assignments. Most authors use a combination of their own experiences and reports from their friends to create realistic cases. In general, it is not a good idea to use a single local incident (such as an incident of workplace violence) to develop a case for training purposes because participants' prior knowledge may interfere with an open-minded analysis. Some authors begin with a standard procedure or a conceptual model and create a fictional case to illustrate it. This approach usually results in cases that have a contrived feeling to them.

Purpose. Most cases require participants to both analyze a situation and plan suitable action. However, a specific case may emphasize one purpose over the other. For example, RECALLED focuses more on what-went-wrong analysis than on the what-should-we-do planning.

Length and complexity. RECALLED is presented through two pages of text. Other case materials may range from short vignettes of one hundred words to lengthy descriptions (with several technical attachments) of one hundred pages. The complexity of a case is not related to its length. Although RECALLED is presented as a short document, it contains so many issues associated with cultural, national, ethnic, gender, and age differences that it may justifiably require several hours (or even several days) for comprehensive analysis and discussion.

Presentation media. RECALLED was presented as printed text. Cases can be presented through a variety of other media. Here are some examples:

- *Video.* A videotape recording may present realistic details of a case. For example, a case dealing with an accident investigation may use a videotape. Participants may be permitted (and encouraged) to replay the tape to review details. Usually, video presentations focus on critical incidents and use text materials to provide background information.

- *Computer.* CD-ROMs or websites may present cases that contain several layers and levels of detail. For example, a case involving commercial real-estate marketing may use a combination of computer and Internet presentations that allow participants to selectively review such details as market trends, competitive pressures, credit ratings, and economic conditions.

- *Live presentations.* In this approach, several people play the roles of stakeholders and present facts, perceptions, and opinions related to a key issue. For example, a case dealing with sexual harassment may be presented by the accusers, the accused, the investigators, and the arbitrator. Participants may be permitted to ask questions of different presenters. Such live presentations may be supported by background documents.

Ready-to-Use Case Method Activity
TROUBLED TEAM

The case method is a training strategy that combines analysis with action. Here's an activity that features an interesting approach to the case method in which teams of players select and purchase materials for their analysis.

Purpose

To select and analyze the most appropriate data for identifying causes of performance problems in teams.

Time

90 minutes.

Participants

Six or more, organized into three to five teams.

Materials

- One copy of the Instructions to Teams for each participant
- One copy each of Memorandum and Data Menu for each team
- Additional data (pages 275 through 278). Make one copy for each team. Cut apart each of the fourteen different data sets.
- Flip-chart sheets and markers for each team
- Timer
- Deck of playing cards
- Masking tape
- Paper cups
- Poker chips

Flow

Brief participants. Explain that the purpose of this activity is to analyze factors related to the performance of teams.

Organize teams. Divide participants into three to five teams of approximately equal size.

Distribute the instruction sheet. Give one copy of the Instructions to Teams to each participant. Invite questions and clarify the rules of the activity.

Distribute the first document. Give one copy of the Memorandum to each team. Ask teams to review this memo. Explain the location for additional data. Distribute copies of the Data Menu. Tell participants that they could collect additional data by purchasing items listed in this menu.

Explain the funding. Inform participants that each team has an opening budget of $10,000 in virtual money that could be used for purchasing data sets listed in the menu. Since the budget does not permit the indiscriminate purchase of all available data, teams have to be selective about the type of data they want to collect.

Announce the official start of the activity. Set the timer for 60 minutes and start it. Encourage teams to work rapidly, dividing up the task of reviewing data from different documents.

Distribute data sets. Keep an account register for each team, with a beginning balance of $10,000. Whenever a team purchases data sets, subtract the appropriate cost from the balance.

Distribute supplies. After about 30 minutes into the activity, distribute a sheet of flip-chart paper and markers to each team. Explain that the team may create any graphics, tables, or messages for use during the presentation.

Keep track of the time. Announce the remaining time at 5-minute intervals.

Select the presenters. At the end of 60 minutes, ask all teams to stop their activity. Shuffle a deck of cards and give one card to each participant. Within each team, designate the participant who has the card with the lowest value to be the presenter.

Conduct the first presentation. Randomly select one presenter and send the other presenters outside the room. Ask the first presenter to begin. Time the presentation and stop it after 2 minutes. Repeat the process. Select one of the other presenters to return to the room and begin the presentation. Continue the activity until all teams have made their presentations. Get ready for evaluation. Tape each team's flip-chart sheet to the wall. Place a paper cup immediately below each poster.

Conduct the evaluation. Give thirteen poker chips to each team. Ask the team members to reflect on the relative effectiveness of the other teams' presentations. Encourage participants to study the flip-chart sheets used by different teams. Within 3 minutes, ask the members of each team to jointly decide how to distribute the thirteen poker chips to reflect the relative effectiveness of each presentation. When ready, ask teams to secretly drop the appropriate number of poker chips in the paper cups below each team's flip chart.

Identify the winning team. Count the number of chips in each paper cup and identify the winning team. Congratulate the winners—without making a big fuss about it.

Instructions to Teams

Who Are You?
Although you are working as a team, you represent a single team-building consultant, Pat Rodriguez.

You work for an organization that specializes in team-building activities. Your boss has asked you to investigate a complaint from Steve Johnson about a team in his corporation. You have to make a recommendation to your boss on what action to take.

What Is Your Task?
Working as a team, you have sixty minutes to collect data, analyze it, make your recommendations, and justify these recommendations. Your report must include these four components:
- What should you tell your client?
- What advice should you give to the team leader?

- What should you do with the team?
- What data suggest these actions?

What Is Given to You?

At the beginning of this activity, you will receive a one-page memo from your boss, Paul Spector, outlining your assignment.

You will receive $10,000 in virtual money to fund your data-collection activities. If you run out of money you will not have access to any more data.

You will receive a menu of the data that you can collect, along with the corresponding costs. You may purchase any of these data sets from your facilitator.

What Is Expected from You?

A randomly selected member of your team will present your report. This report is limited to 2 minutes of presentation time and one page of flip-chart paper.

How Do You Win?

Your presentation will be scored by members of the other teams. The team with the highest total score will win the activity

Memorandum

To: Pat Rodriguez
From: Paul Spector
Date: 10/21/00
Re: Troubled Team?

I had an urgent telephone call from our client, Steve Johnson. As you know, he's the CEO of Johnson Enterprises, where we set up a cross-functional team a couple of weeks ago.

Mr. Johnson attended one of the team meetings and returned in major panic. He is convinced that the team is headed toward total disaster. He tells me that team members are bickering and quarreling all the time. Apparently, there are major personality conflicts among the seven members of the team.

Mr. Johnson wants us to fix the situation immediately. He wants the team to work smoothly and effectively, the way that his top management team (which never has any major disagreements and always makes correct and rapid decisions under his "strong and effective" leadership) does.

Pat, we need to investigate this situation immediately and recommend appropriate action. Unfortunately, I will be away for the next ten days, conducting a team-building seminar in Bali at the annual conference of the Asian Federation of Facilitators.

Since you are the most objective person in our team, can you please investigate this situation? I would like to have your analysis and recommendations by the time I return Friday next week.

Thanks!

Data Menu

1	Team Mission, Vision, and Goals	$500
2	Team Members	$500
3	Interview with Steve Johnson, CEO	$1500
4	Interview with Chandra Patel, Team Leader	$1000
5	Interview with Allen Sheppard, Team Member	$750
6	Interview with Bob Thomson, Team Member	$750
7	Interview with Delores Fitz, Team Member	$750
8	Interview with Esther White, Team Member	$750
9	Interview with Fred Weils, Team Member	$750
10	Interview with George Shelly, Team Member	$750
11	Team Player Survey Scores	$1000
12	Team Development Stages Data	$1000
13	October 17th Meeting: Interview Report	$1000
14	October 24th Meeting: Observation Data	$1000

1. **Team Mission, Vision, and Goals**

   Our mission is to earn long-term loyalty by consistently delighting our customers.

   Our vision is to apply diverse perspectives to consistently provide innovative services that meet customers' needs.

   Our goals include:
   - To reduce the time between the customer's order and delivery of the product.
   - To provide a twenty-four-hour customer-service hotline.

2. **Team Members**

   Chandra Patel is the team leader. She is from the human resources department. She has been with Johnson Consumer Electronics for six years. Last year, she acted as the facilitator of the Quality Management Team.

   Allen Sheppard is from the marketing department. He has been with Johnson Consumer Electronics for seven years. As a member of the Branding Committee, he helped the company establish standards for the use of the corporate logo.

   Bob Thomson is from the engineering department. He has been with Johnson Consumer Electronics for three years. This is the first time he has worked as a team member.

   Dolores Fitz is from the Information Systems Group. She has been with Johnson Consumer Electronics for only six months and is a member of the Intranet Security Team.

3. **Excerpts from an interview with Mr. Johnson:**

   "I believe in cohesiveness among team members. If they are going to be arguing with each other all the time, then why have a team?"

   "I appointed this team to speed up the order fulfillment process. I want them to reduce customer complaints. These complaints reflect badly on our business."

   "Frankly, I shouldn't have appointed Chandra Patel as the team leader. I was appalled by her wishy-washy behavior during the October 17th meeting. She does not have what it takes to control the team and command respect."

   "Dolores is bad news. I can't understand why Chandra added her to the team. She's a loudmouth, and she questions everything and everybody. She even started arguing with me at the team meeting. I suggested to Chandra that she get rid of that girl, but Chandra is probably too weak to do that. She keeps claiming that she wants someone with a technical background."

   "George Shelly is a good guy. He keeps me informed of what's happening in the team."

(Continued)

4. Excerpt from an interview with Chandra Patel, team leader

"I believe that commitment is the result of involvement and that soft skills produce hard results. I deliberately chose the team members to increase diversity in our perspectives and opinions. It's going to take some time for the team to learn to listen to each other. We are well on our way to establishing ground rules for team meetings and following them. I'm extremely grateful to Mr. Johnson for his support, but sometimes I wish he would leave us alone. He thinks we are not producing quick results, but I want to invest some time right now defining our goals and analyzing the situation. One thing that I learned from my TQM experience is that it is cheaper to pay now by spending extra time than pay later to recover from mistakes. All in all, I've got a great team, and we are almost ready to take on the challenge."

5. Excerpt from an interview with Allen Sheppard, team member

"I have no major complaints about the way the team is operating. Mr. Johnson has given us all the resources we need. I like the way Chandra is making sure that all of us have our say. Our meetings are informal and relaxed. We all know what to do and we all do our homework. Dolores has done a great job of analyzing the delays in our current order-fulfillment system. I like the way she keeps challenging standard procedures. I know that Mr. Johnson gets impatient sometimes, but after all, we've been in business only for a couple of weeks."

6. Excerpt from an interview with Bob Thomson, team member

"Sometimes Chandra gets carried away with this participation thing, but we are all committed to our goal and we will come up with strategies for speeding up the shipping procedure. Dolores has identified sources of major delays and we should be able to remove them easily."

7. Excerpt from an interview with Dolores Fitz, team member

"Most of the time most of the team members don't know what's happening. What we have here is a simple problem. All we need to do is to centralize order taking and inventory control at the same database. I like Chandra, but I hope she focuses on the obvious problem rather than asking everyone for their opinions."

8. **Excerpt from an interview with Esther White, team member**

"At customer services, we've been working on this problem for six years. I don't know why Mr. Johnson needs a team to investigate the situation. As we told him earlier, we need to hire someone to do the job."

9. **Excerpt from an interview with Fred Weils, team member**

"I have no comments about our team. Everything's fine. I am eager to get the job done and return full-time to my R&D responsibilities."

10. **Excerpt from an interview with George Shelly, team member**

"I know exactly what Mr. Johnson wants, and I am afraid that the team is not giving him what he wants. As I told him during last week's golf game, this situation has several legal implications."

11. **Team Player Survey Scores**

Results from Parker Team Player Survey: Primary Team Player Styles

Chandra Patel: Communicator	Bob Thomson: Contributor
Esther White: Challenger	George Shelly: Challenger
Allen Sheppard: Contributor	Dolores Fitz: Challenger
Fred Weils: Contributor	

Background information: All teams need a balance among four types of team players:

Contributors are task-oriented team members who do their homework and provide the team with good technical information and data. They are always dependable, but sometimes they have a tendency to become bogged down in the details.

Collaborators are goal-oriented team members who focus on the vision, mission, and goals of the team. They are flexible and willing to pitch in and work outside their roles. However, they sometimes fail to consider individual needs of team members.

Communicators are process-oriented team members who are effective listeners and facilitators. They are sensitive people, but sometimes they fail to confront other team members.

Challengers are team members who question the goals and methods of the team and even disagree with higher authorities. They are open and direct, but sometimes they push the team too far.

(Continued)

The Case Method

12. **Team Development Stages Data**

Analysis of a questionnaire in which each team member selected the top five frequent behaviors:

Behaviors associated with the forming stage: 27 percent

Behaviors associated with the storming stage: 49 percent

Behaviors associated with the norming stage: 18 percent

Behaviors associated with the performing stage: 6 percent

Background information: According to Tuckman, all teams have to necessarily go through these four developmental stages: During the *forming* stage, team members focus on understanding the team's goal and their role. During the *storming* stage, the team defines itself through conflicts among its members. During the *norming* stage, team members negotiate the structure of the team and the division of labor. During the *performing* stage, team members focus on accomplishing their goals.

13. **October 17th Meeting: Interview Report**

Anonymous comments about what happened during the October 17th meeting:

"Mr. Johnson gave us a pep talk about company loyalty and team loyalty."

"Mr. Johnson got impatient with Chandra. He was also upset about Dolores's impertinent comments."

"When Mr. Johnson said that we should be loyal to the team and stop arguing, Dolores retorted that we should be loyal to customers because the team's mission demanded that. Mr. Johnson was upset by this comment, which he perceived to be a challenge to his authority."

"Dolores made some interesting challenges to the company's assumptions about order fulfillment. She also had some tough questions about the way the team is taking care of its business."

"It would have been nice if Mr. Johnson left us alone to do our own thing. After all, if he believes in empowerment, why is he telling us what to do?"

"Mr. Johnson was absolutely right. I wish Chandra demanded and commanded more loyalty from team members."

"Maybe Mr. Johnson will disband the team. Then the customer relations group can quickly solve the problem."

14. **October 24th Meeting: Observation Data**

"This is one of the weekly meetings held for an hour every Friday afternoon. The meeting took place in the fifth-floor conference room. The climate of the meeting was informal but involved technical discussions.

"Apparently each team member had been assigned a task. The meeting began with a report from Dolores on the technical aspects of speeding up the process of taking customer orders and shipping products. This was a continuation of the presentation from the previous meeting, which was interrupted by Mr. Johnson's unanticipated arrival. Using an LCD projector, Dolores identified the steps in the current telephone order-taking process. She identified activities that delay the process and suggested how to eliminate or combine steps. Several team members asked questions and raised issues. Dolores responded succinctly.

"Chandra invited Esther (who had been fairly quiet) for her comments and reactions. Esther complained that Dolores was attacking the customer service department without understanding the rationale behind its process. Dolores appeared to be surprised and suggested that it is time to reexamine and revise all standard operating procedures that do not add value or meet current realities. There was some tense interchange between Esther and Dolores. Chandra intervened and asked other team members for their suggestions. Allen suggested that Esther should be given an opportunity to present the historical perspective on the order-fulfillment process. Dolores agreed, explaining that being a new employee was both her strength and her weakness. Esther wanted to give her reactions to Dolores' analysis at the next meeting, after collecting some information from customer reps. Chandra congratulated the team for handling a potential conflict in a healthy fashion."

25 Production Simulations

Production simulations involve the design and development of a product. Different teams compete with each other to create the best product. The activity begins with teams receiving specifications for the final product, along with an evaluation checklist. Teams also have access to training sessions, job aids, reference materials, sample products, and expert consultants. Final products from different teams are evaluated by outside experts, end users, and peers on a variety of relevant dimensions.

MARKET

You are a fresh MBA graduate recently hired by a large high-tech corporation. After the first week on the job, your manager sends you to a five-day "boot camp" for all new employees of the marketing division. Somewhat reluctantly, you turn up at 8:30 on a Monday. Margery, the facilitator, welcomes you and twenty-one others to the training session and explains that the entire group will participate in a lengthy simulation game. Here are some highlights of Margery's briefing:

- Participants will be organized into teams of five or six members.

- On the afternoon of the fifth day, each team will present a ten-page marketing plan for a new software product. Each team will introduce its plan through a 3-minute presentation, using not more than five slides.

- The team may select any one of the seven different software products. Market analysis data and technical specifications related to the selected product will be provided to the team.

- All teams will have access to a library of books, articles, checklists, and sample marketing plans. During a 2-hour period every morning, an expert will conduct a workshop on different topics related to the preparation of a marketing plan. However, only one member of each team may attend this workshop.

- All teams will have access to an expert for 30 minutes every afternoon. During this time, you can use the expert as a consultant and ask questions and request feedback.

- During the last part of the simulation, a three-member panel of expert judges will evaluate the marketing plans from different teams. The panel will evaluate the marketing plans, along the three dimensions of completeness, clarity, and creativity.

You and five other participants are assigned to a team. Your team decides to prepare a marketing plan for a new type of customer-management software. Margery gives you a copy of the template for the marketing plan and a rating scale that will be used by the expert judges.

Your team decides to send you to all the training workshops so you can learn the principles and procedures and share them with your teammates. On the first morning, you attend the workshop on the topic of product specification. You return to the team and brief them about what you had learned in the workshop. While you were at the workshop, the team has already reviewed the background information and has started writing some of the sections of the marketing plan. That afternoon your team meets with the expert and asks her specific questions about how best to present the technical specifications.

During the ensuing four days, your team repeats the same procedure while you attend other workshops on positioning, pricing, promotion, and selecting distribution channels. On Friday afternoon, you are slightly disappointed when your team only receives the second highest score. However, you are happy about how you have learned during the five days of the simulation.

JOKE

JOKE is a brief production simulation that lasts for 15 minutes: The facilitator organizes participants into teams and gives them a half-page handout that explains the concept of a joke formula. Specifically, it defines the self-contradicting joke in which the second half of a sentence contradicts the first half. The handout contains these two examples:

- "Defy authority, but raise your hand first."

- "I don't believe in reincarnation, but in my previous life I used to believe in it."

The facilitator asks the teams to come up with their own self-contradicting jokes within 5 minutes and write them on index cards.

She then reads each joke and asks participants to vote for the funniest one. However, no participant may vote for the joke from his or her own team.

Types of Production Simulations

Production simulations come in a variety of types. The two samples that we explored earlier illustrate several variables:

Time requirement. One obvious difference between MARKET and JOKE is the length of the activity: MARKET requires a whole week, while JOKE lasts for a mere 15 minutes. Another example of a lengthy production simulation is ID. I used to conduct this activity as a semester-long course on instructional design. In this production simulation, teams of participants designed, developed, evaluated, and revised a training package by using a systematic procedure.

Training objective. In general, most production simulations are designed to help participants to master principles and procedures related to the development of a tangible product that conforms to specific standards. Market plans and self-contradicting jokes are examples of this type of product. In some production simulations, the training objective may de-emphasize the product and focus on the process of teamwork or creative problem solving. For example, TALL TOWERS is a team-building activity that requires participants to create the tallest freestanding structure using drinking straws, paper clips, and masking tape. The main focus in this production simulation is on how teams organize and work together.

Learning resources. One of the key elements in production simulations involves learning resources supplied to participants. JOKE uses a half-page job aid with a simple definition and a couple of examples. In contrast, MARKET involves a variety of materials, including reference manuals, articles, handouts, checklists, and sample marketing plans. This production simulation also incorporates "live" workshops and consultant help. Learning resources in other production simulations may involve audio and videotape recordings, CBT programs, and websites.

Evaluation strategy. A critical element of production simulations is the evaluation strategy. MARKET uses three expert judges armed with a rating scale to objectively assess the completeness, clarity, and creativity of the marketing plans produced by different teams. In contrast, JOKE lets participant teams evaluate each other's products on the subjective criterion of how funny different jokes are.

Production simulations frequently incorporate rating scales that specify different quality standards. Copies of these evaluation instruments are given to participants to encourage them to focus on critical variables. The people who evaluate the final product may include fellow participants, experts, and end users. The evaluation of a job aid, for example, may be based on the performance of the typical users of that tool.

Both MARKET and JOKE depend on the evaluation of the final product as the main scoring activity. Other production simulations may include repeated evaluations of intermediate products. For example, the instructional design production simulation that I briefly mentioned earlier requires teams to submit intermediate products such as lists of needs analysis information, training objectives, test items, and follow-up activities. Teams score points for each of these intermediate products. In addition, they receive feedback suggestions that identify errors that must be corrected to prevent major problems during later stages of the development activity.

Benefits and Precautions

As a training strategy, production simulations have several advantages:

Tangible results. At the end of the training session, participants acquire new principles and procedures—along with a real product that they can take home with them.

On-the-job training. Production simulations bring participants as close to on-the-job training as possible. If participants' jobs involve the production of an object, this strategy acquires enormous credibility and ensures effective transfer and application of the skills and concepts to the workplace.

Just-in-time training. Instead of learning theoretical concepts first and then struggling to recall and apply them later, production simulations provide just-in-time and just enough theory for immediate use.

Mutual learning. By organizing participants into teams, production simulations encourage collaborative learning. These simulations motivate participants through a combination of peer support and peer pressure, along with cooperation and competition.

Production simulations present some potential hazards. Here are a couple of things to watch out for:

Narrow focus. Participants may focus so much on one specific type of product that they ignore principles and procedures related to similar products. For example, participants may learn how to use a word processor to format a specific type of business letter without ever learning about other types of documents. To reduce this potential problem, conduct a debriefing session at the end of the production simulation. During this discussion, explore related products and encourage participants to follow up by learning additional skills.

Free riders. Just because a team is able to produce a product, it does not guarantee that all individual participants will be able to do the same. During the simulation, perhaps a team member plays the minor role of bringing coffee to the star players, who do all the work. To reduce this potential problem, encourage all participants to take an active role in the production. If time permits, require each participant to create his or her own product after the completion of the team activity.

More Production Simulations

Here are seven different production simulations, each briefly described in a standardized format. As you review each simulation, think about how you can use elements from this activity for your own training sessions:

MISSION

Training objective. To specify the mission statement for a team.

Product specification. A team mission statement that is brief, specific, memorable, and challenging.

Time requirements. Two hours.

Learning resources. A handout on how to write team mission statements. A checklist identifying nine important requirements of a team mission statement. A collection of twenty different mission statements from different types of teams.

Evaluation strategy. The mission statements are rated by a team of participants using the same checklist that is distributed as a learning resource.

Special feature. One team is entrusted with the task of evaluating the mission statements from the other teams. While the other teams work on their mission statements, the evaluation team reads a handout on how to evaluate mission statements and practices joint evaluation of several samples.

EGG DROP

Training objective. To apply principles of creative problem solving in a team-based situation.

Product specification. Package an egg to ensure that it will not damaged when dropped from a height of 10 feet.

Time requirements. Two hours.

Learning resources. None. Participants are left to their own devices to identify and use any suitable learning resource.

Evaluation strategy. The package with the egg is dropped from a height of 10 feet. After it falls to the ground, the package is opened and the egg is examined to see if it is damaged in any way.

FAST FICTION

Training objective. To write a short-short story.

Product specification. The short-short story should not be longer than 250 words.

Time requirements. 90 minutes.

Learning resources. "How-to" articles on writing short-short stories. Checklists related to theme, plot, characterization, setting, and dialogue in short stories. A collection of twenty short-short stories from different genres.

Evaluation strategy. Each participant reads the short-short stories written by all other participants and selects the top three. The ranks are combined to compute a score for each short-short story.

Special feature. Each participant works independently. However, participants are encouraged to bounce off their story ideas on each other and to provide editorial help.

NEWSLETTER

Training objective. To use a desktop publishing software program for laying out the given newsletter content in an attractive and readable format.

Product specification. The newsletter should be eight pages long. It should not use any graphics or color. It should use all of the content (and only the content) provided on a floppy disk.

Time requirement. Six hours.

Learning resources. Software training manual. Videotaped demonstrations of different layout procedures. A collection of sample newsletters. A copy of the rating scale used by the evaluators. Thirty minutes of consultant help (any time during the session).

Evaluation strategy. A panel of experts evaluates each newsletter layout using a rating scale. In addition to a numerical score, the experts provide feedback for improving the layout.

SESSION DESCRIPTION

Training objective. To write short, compelling descriptions of conference presentations.

Product specification. The session description should not exceed 150 words and should include a title, two or three objectives, and an audience description.

Time requirement. 90 minutes.

Learning resources. "How-to" handouts. Checklists for writing and revising session titles, statements of objectives, and audience descriptions. A collection of sample session descriptions.

Evaluation strategy. A panel of three typical conference attendees select the top three descriptions of sessions that they would like to attend.

SSIVC

Training objective. To apply the principles and procedures of spicy South Indian vegetarian cooking to prepare a dry or wet curry dish.

Product specification. To cook a curry dish by choosing and using seasonal vegetables.

Time requirement. Three hours.

Learning resources. Cookbooks. Illustrated checklists explaining basic cooking procedures. A handout listing "trade secrets" of Indian chefs.

Evaluation strategy. A panel of taste testers rates the dishes created by different teams.

Special feature. This latest version of the cooking lesson that my wife and I teach is inspired by the interesting Japanese game show, "The Iron Chefs."

VIDEO DEMO

Training objective. To produce a short video segment illustrating the use of an MP3 player.

Product specification. Each team receives the same type of video equipment. They also have access to a subject-matter expert who is knowledgeable about the MP3 player. The finished videotape should not be longer than 3 minutes.

Time requirement. Three hours.

Learning resources. Several videotapes on how to make demonstration videotapes. Sample demonstration videotapes. Instruction manual for the video camera. A copy of the rating scale used by the panel of judges.

Evaluation strategy. A panel of expert judges evaluates the finished demonstration videotapes using a rating scale.

Special feature. The best videotape from each session is added to the collection of samples for use in future sessions.

Your Turn

Try your hand at creating your own production simulation. Use ideas from the samples discussed earlier. Here's a suggested procedure for producing your production simulation:

Product. Select a product that you want participants to create. Write a list of specifications to narrow down to a particular type of this product.

Evaluation instrument. Design one or more rating scales or checklists to objectively evaluate the final product.

Evaluation strategy. Determine when, how, and by whom product evaluation will be conducted. You may want to include experts, fellow participants, and end users among your panel of evaluators.

Learning resources. Collect or create a variety of learning resources. Include job aids, samples, reference manuals, handouts, and other printed materials. Also include other types of mediated materials such as audio- and video-tape recordings. Arrange for access to suitable websites. Organize training workshops and consultant help as a part of the simulation.

Logistics. Work out the details of the activity, taking into account the number of participants and the available time.

Test and revise. Try out your simulation with a group of representative participants. Make suitable changes based on the feedback.

Ready-to-Use Production Simulation
BULLET SLIDES

The majority of electronic presentations and laptop slide shows involve bulleted lists of items. This production simulation deals with the creation of effective electronic slides. The main focus of the activity is on the clarity of individual slides and the effectiveness of text content. This activity does not deal with other aspects, such as color and transition from one slide to the next.

Purpose

To prepare electronic bullet slides that communicate clearly and effectively.

Participants

Six or more, organized into three or more teams, each with two to five members. This activity works best with groups of ten to thirty participants divided into teams of five.

Time

One to two hours (depending on the number of teams)

Materials

- One copy of the BULLET SLIDES Checklist for each participant
- A printed copy of the original twelve slides (one set for each team)
- A laptop computer with the Microsoft PowerPoint software program
- An LCD projector and screen
- Timer
- Whistle

Flow

Organize teams. Assign participants to different teams. Pause briefly to permit team members to introduce themselves to each other.

Present product specifications. Distribute copies of the Bullet Slide Checklist to each participant. Explain that this checklist will be used both as a learning resource and as an evaluation instrument. Also distribute a set of printed copies of the twelve original slides to each team. Explain that teams will have a PowerPoint file with these slides in their computer. The task for each team is to revise these twelve slides so that they do not violate the items on the checklist.

Brief teams. Explain that the teams will have 30 minutes to make the revisions to the slide set. During that time, you will be available to provide brief consultative help. At the end of this 30-minute period, you will display all revised slide sets. They will be evaluated by two judges to determine the winning product.

Provide consultative help. Circulate around the teams, responding to technical questions related to the checklist. Also make appropriate suggestions to different teams.

Get ready for the evaluation. Set up an LCD projector and connect it to your laptop with the original set of slides. Assemble two or three judges (who need not be experts). Explain that they will view different sets of slides dealing with the same topic. They should identify the best slide set from the point of view of the audience for the slides. Ask the judges to conduct their evaluation independently and be ready with their choices soon after all slide sets are displayed.

Brief participants. At the end of 30 minutes, blow a whistle and announce the end of the session. Ask each team to bring the laptops to the front of the room. Introduce the judges and explain that they will be identifying the best revised slide set from the audience's point of view. In addition, explain that all participants will evaluate the slide sets and identify the best one. However, each participant should ignore the revised slide set created by his or her team and select the best one from the remaining slide sets.

Conduct the evaluation activity. Begin by projecting the original (unrevised slide set). Then project the revised slide sets from different teams, identifying each set with a number. After all slide sets have been projected, ask each participant to write the number identifying the best slide set on a piece of paper and give it to you.

Announce the results. Let each judge announce his or her choice and make any comments. Quickly sort participant votes and announce the number of votes received by each slide set. Congratulate the winning team (or teams).

BULLET SLIDES Checklist

1. **Avoid crunching.** Leave wide margins and plenty of blank space.

2. **Position the title.** Place the title on the top one-sixth of the transparency.

3. **Capitalize the title.** Begin each word in the title with a capital letter.

4. **Don't repeat.** If the same word is repeated in all bulleted items, make it a part of the title or the subtitle.

5. **Use sans serif.** Use a sans-serif font (example: *Arial* or *Helvetica*).

6. **Avoid ransom notes.** Do not use too many different fonts. Stick to a single font.

7. **Print big.** Use at least 24-point font size.

8. **Don't shout.** Avoid typing any title, item, or word in ALL CAPS.

9. **Be consistent.** Use the same font and same bullet symbol throughout.

10. **Shrink the bullet.** Make sure that the size of the bullet is the same as the font size (or slightly smaller).

11. **Use numbers.** Replace bullets with numbers if you want to emphasize the sequence or compare different items with each other.

12. **Use few words.** Use tight phrases instead of complete sentences.

13. **Don't exceed six.** Make sure that the bullet list does not contain more than six items. Make sure that no item has more than six words.

14. **Don't exceed two.** Do not use more than two levels of bullets.

15. **Keep items parallel.** Make sure that all items in the list have the same structure. (For example, they all begin with a verb.)

16. **Wrap words.** Make sure no bullet item exceeds two lines. Use the hanging indent style for the second line.

17. **Omit periods.** Do not put a period at the end of the items on the list.

18. **Prevent motion sickness.** Don't use unnecessary animation (example: *Flying bullets* and *building the slide one item at a time*).

19. **Position the logo.** Place the logo in the footer. Shrink it to a small size.

Seminar Overview

- What is an intervention?
- What are the critical features of an intervention?
- What are the different types of interventions?
- How do you choose an intervention?
- How do you design your intervention?
- How do you evaluate your intervention?
- How do you revise your intervention?
- How do you implement your intervention?

1

Types of Interventions

- Internal
  - Skill/Knowledge-based
    - Training
    - Job Aids
  - Motivational
    - Incentive Systems
    - Rewards and Recognition
- External

2

Intervention Classification System

- Improving Knowledge
- Improving Motivation
- Improving Processes
- Improving Health
- Improving Facilities

3

Improving Knowledge

- Does not know how to perform a task
- Makes too many mistakes
- **Learned wrong behaviors**
- ✍ Confuses one step with another

4

Sample Knowledge Interventions

- Accelerated Learning achieves faster learning and longer-term retention by honoring different learning preferences.
- Action Learning involves a problem, a learning team, a process, and a commitment to learning.
- Training Games are contrived activities that feature, conflict, rules, and winning and losing.
- Online Learning involves the use of interactive strategies on the World Wide Web.
- On-the-Job Training is conducted by an experienced practitioner with individual learners who are working on assigned learning tasks.

5

Motivational Problems

- Lacks feedback
- No reward or recognition
- Punishment of appropriated behaviors.
- Performer has values that clash with one another.

6

Sample Motivation Intervention
Seven Different Approaches

- Compensation and benefit systems
- Rewards and recognition
- Internal and external system
- Team building and empowerment
- Interesting work assignments
- Meaningful tasks

7

Sample Physical Resource Interventions

- Ergonomics
- Automation and Computerization
- Physical Resource Management
- Facilities Design

8

Process improvement

- Culture change
- Project redesign
- Policy alignment
- Staffing
- Feedback system

9

Sorting Criteria

- INDIVIDUAL vs. GROUP
- CHEAP vs. EXPENSIVE
- TOGETHER vs. DISPERSED
- URGENT vs. LEISURELY

10

Health Interventions

- Energy Management.
- Employee Assistance Programs.
- Nutrition.
- Win-win Negotiation.
- Violence Prevention.

11

Health Interventions

- Energy Management
- Employee Assistance Programs
- Nutrition
- Win-win Negotiation
- Violence Prevention

12

26 Training Devices

Training devices are physical objects used by an interacting group of participants to explore interpersonal principles and procedures. Some of these devices are specially created for training, while some are created for other purposes but reused for training.

EIGHT MARKS

Consider the example of a team building activity called EIGHT MARKS.

As one of the eight team members, you stand around a training device called the NetWork® apparatus. This device is a 28-inch tall system of metal posts, hoops, and strings. A felt-tipped marker hangs in the middle of the apparatus, connected to eight strings that are looped through different hoops. You hold a ring attached to one of the strings. Your facilitator, Karim, invites you and the other members of your team to move the felt pen by pulling and releasing the strings. It takes a lot of practice to coordinate the moves by the eight different team members and to move the felt pen to different locations. Once you have the moves smoothly synchronized, Karim introduces a task for the team. He places a laminated board under the felt marker. This board has four concentric rings (labeled A, B, C, and D), divided into four quadrants (marked 1, 2, 3, and 4) (as shown on the next page).

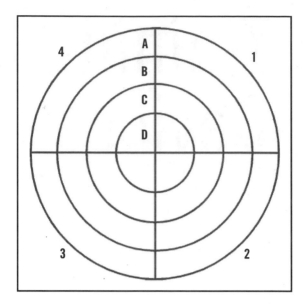

Karim calls your team away from the apparatus and gives each team member a handout to read and memorize. The handout explains that the team has to make marks on eight different target locations in this sequence: A1, B1, C1, D1, A2, B2, C2, and D2. After 2 minutes, Karim takes away the handouts and asks you to work together in silence to mark the different locations in the correct sequence. You take hold of the same ring as before and work with the other members of the team to move the felt pen around. When it is poised above the A1 area, everyone releases the string simultaneously to make a mark. As you move through the sequence, marking the other locations, you notice that the team's speed and accuracy are improving. However, when you reach the fifth location, you seem to become uncoordinated for some reason. Some team members appear to be confused, pulling the string away from the target location and releasing it at inappropriate moments, making random marks in different places. The problem becomes so frustrating that Karim stops the activity. He asks you and your teammates to define the problem and to identify probable causes. During this discussion, you discover that some team members (including you) were instructed to mark A1, B1, C1, D1, A2, B2, C2, and D2, while others were instructed to mark A1, B1, C1, D1, A4, B4, C4, and D4. So during this round, while you are pulling toward D2 some others were pulling toward D4. Karim suggests that this dilemma is a metaphor for teamwork problems in the workplace that arise when there is a lack of clarity about the goal.

Uses and Limitations

Most activities that incorporate training devices begin with the introduction of the device and specification of a task. Participants organize themselves into teams and plan a suitable strategy for accomplishing the task. Later, they implement the strategy, usually modifying it on the basis of early successes and failures. Within this general framework, the same training

Design Your Own Games and Activities

device can be used to explore different principles and procedures related to such areas as teamwork, diversity, leadership, communication, decision making, and creative problem solving.

Training devices provide visible, tangible, hands-on learning that effectively uses the powerful but seldom-used kinesthetic intelligence. The result is embodied learning that is easy to recall for future applications. The use of training devices, however, is not without limitations. Some training devices present safety hazards. As a facilitator, you need to warn participants ahead of time and observe suitable precautions. Also, participants may complain about the artificiality of the activity and claim that playing with TinkerToys® has nothing to do with the serious teamwork they undertake back in the office. To reduce this complaint, emphasize the relationship between what happens in the activity and what happens in the workplace. Also, resist the temptation to focus on playing with the device. Instead, incorporate the device in a training game or simulation.

Types and Examples

Special devices. The NetWork® apparatus is manufactured by San Francisco-based Interel, Inc., (415–566–0554) solely for the purpose of building and training teams. With a few basic tools and skills, you can manufacture your own special-purpose training device called the Team Ski. This device consists of two wooden planks shaped like long skis. Five ropes are tied to each plank, approximately 18 inches apart. Just after each rope, a leather strap is attached to the plank. Team members insert their feet into the leather straps of the same pair of skis and hold the ropes, each person standing behind another. The task for the team is to "walk" on the skis by simultaneously lifting and moving one foot at a time. You can incorporate this task in a continuous-improvement simulation that requires the team to increase its speed from one trial to the next.

Game equipment. Here are some sample games and play equipment that we have used as training devices: darts, Frisbees, jigsaw puzzles, mechanical toys, and hula hoops. We have also incorporated different types of balls and construction sets in our training activities.

PLAYING WITH PERFORMANCE. In this activity, I use Milton Bradley's game, Perfection™ to introduce basic concepts of performance consulting. The device includes a plastic tray with a 5 × 5 array of slots of different shape (such as squares, rectangles, circles, triangles, and stars) and plastic "pegs" to be placed in these slots. Before the game, I ask a volunteer player to remove the pegs from the slots, turn a built-in timer to 60 seconds, press down the tray, and begin placing the right peg in the right slot. The timer clicks ominously as the player races to fill all the slots with the correct pegs. Most players are unable to complete the task within 60 seconds, and this results in the tray springing back with a loud noise, scattering the pegs. Participants now analyze the reason for the volunteer's inability to complete the task within the time limit when hundreds of children are able to do it almost

effortlessly. Typical causes include serious ones (such as lack of practice and too many spectators) and humorous ones (such as union restrictions and old age). Working in teams, participants design suitable interventions (such as guided practice or monetary incentives) to improve the player's performance. The team with the best combination of interventions (as judged by the player) wins the game.

EARTHBALL. My friend Bernie DeKoven uses a huge, 6-foot diameter ball (with the map of the world painted on it) to explore factors that encourage community building. He merely rolls the ball toward a group of people and observes their reaction. After initial confusion and curiosity, participants spontaneously create a game to play with the ball. Without external instructions, a few facilitators emerge from the group and guide everyone toward playing the game. Depending on the type of group, the game may turn out to be cooperative or competitive. During debriefing Bernie draws out intriguing principles about interpersonal factors in a "leaderless" group.

Ordinary objects. Given a playful spirit and childlike imagination, you should be able to use everyday objects as training devices. Here are some sample objects that we have incorporated in training activities: newspapers, construction materials, tires, inner tubes, pieces of rope, wheelchairs, paper plates, and empty bottles.

TOWER OF BABALLOON. My NASAGA colleague Bill Matthews hands out packets of balloons, pieces of string, and masking tape to teams of participants and invites them to build the tallest freestanding structure within a 20-minute time limit. At the end of the activity, he debriefs participants about different teamwork factors, such as planning, assigning roles, and supporting each other.

TEAM BALANCE. I carefully balance a 6-foot plank on top of a concrete block and invite members of a team to stand on the plank without permitting any part of the plank to touch the ground. This requires careful distribution of the team members on both sides of the plank to prevent the whole structure from toppling over. During debriefing, I label the plank as a diversity continuum and emphasize the importance of team members taking positions on both sides of an issue.

Ready-to-Use Training Device Activity
TEAM MAZE
Basic Idea

Imagine that you have to walk across a minefield. This minefield is divided into squares. Some of the squares have explosives underneath, while others are safe. There is a safe path from one side of the minefield to the other

side. The challenge for your team is to cross the minefield, moving from one square to any square that is directly or diagonally adjacent, without stepping over any square. Also, you have to cross the minefield within a tight time limit. See the sample "minefield" on page 305 at the end of this chapter.

The Training Device

Think of the play area as a 9 × 6 grid, divided into fifty-four squares. Each square is large enough to permit a person to stand comfortably.

Here are three different ways to obtain a maze:

High tech. San Francisco based Interel corporation (140 Carl Street, San Francisco, CA 94117; 415–566–0554) manufactures and sells different models of the Electric Maze® made of durable fabric with pressure-sensitive squares. A control box attached to this maze carpet enables you to activate or deactivate different squares. An alarm sounds whenever a participant steps on an activated square. You can use the control box to set up different safe paths across the maze. Once set up, the maze works automatically.

Medium tech. Use brightly colored tape to create a grid on the floor. Use a simple software program (called Team Maze Assistant, available from Workshops by Thiagi, Inc.; 800–996–7725) to keep track of the safe path. This program displays a graphic on the screen of your laptop that represents the maze. You keep this graphic hidden from team members and click on different squares to activate or deactivate them. When a team member steps on the maze, click on the corresponding square on the screen display. If it is activated, the computer sounds an alarm. After the team member steps off the maze, begin tracking the movement of the next participant. The software program also keeps a step-by-step record of the paths taken by different team members. During debriefing, you can replay this record to discuss team members' behavior.

Low tech. Indoors, set up the maze using masking tape on the floor. Outdoors, use colored ribbon or rope and small stakes or pegs. Draw the map of the grid on a piece of paper (which is kept hidden from the team members) and mark the safe path on it. As the first team member steps through the maze, check the corresponding squares on the map. If the team member steps on an "activated" square, produce an appropriate sound effect by blowing a whistle, ringing a bell, banging a drum, or clattering pots and pans.

Other tips and tricks. Mark a grid with paint or tape on a large sheet of tarp or plastic to create a portable maze. Use several carpet squares, large tiles, or plywood pieces (from the local construction supply store) to lay out a grid on the floor. One of my workshop groups in Asheville, North Carolina, came up with the ingenious idea of using large paper plates to indicate the squares.

Purpose

To explore factors related to effective planning, problem solving, decision making, and communication within teams.

Participants

Five to thirty.

Time

1 hour (5 minutes for briefing, 30 minutes for the activity, and 25 minutes for debriefing)

Materials

- A maze (use any of the approaches described under the Training Device section on page 299). Set up the maze with the pattern shown in the figure on page 306. In the figure, safe squares are shown in white. The safe path is indicated by the curved line.
- Copies of the Basic TEAM MAZE Rules (page 307) for each participant
- Timer
- Whistle

Flow

Brief participants. Distribute copies of the Basic Team Maze Rules handout. Ask participants to read the rules and discuss them among themselves. Respond to questions from participants.

Start the activity. Announce the beginning of the activity. Start the timer. Remind team members that the initial planning discussion should last for at least 3 minutes. No one can step on the maze before 3 minutes have elapsed. However, team members can continue their discussion for as long as they desire beyond the 3 minutes.

Monitor activity on the maze. Note the time when the first person steps on the maze. Remind team members that they cannot talk for the next 3 minutes. After the 3 minutes, team members cannot talk if someone is on the maze. If anyone talks before 3 minutes, ask that person not to talk. If anyone talks after 3 minutes, note the time and tell participants that they cannot be on the maze for at least the next 3 minutes.

Setting off the alarm. If anyone steps on an active square, sound the alarm and ask the person to return to the previous square. From there, ask the participant to retrace the path exactly and leave the maze. The next participant now steps on the maze.

Announce time. Once every 5 minutes, announce how much time is left in the 30-minute period.

Conclude the activity. The team wins if everyone crosses the maze within 24 minutes. Congratulate the team and lead the participants in a round of applause. The team loses if all or some of the members still have not crossed the maze after 30 minutes. Stop the activity, show the correct path, and let everyone cross the maze.

Debriefing

Conduct a discussion of insights gained by different participants. Here are some suggested debriefing questions organized around six phases:

How do you feel?

- How do you feel about the final outcome of the activity?
- How do you feel about your behavior during the activity? About other team members' behavior?
- What was the most exciting aspect of the activity? The most depressing aspect? The most frustrating aspect?
- How did you feel when the first person successfully crossed the maze?
- How did you feel while crossing the maze?
- What were your feelings when someone stepped on an active square? How did you feel when you stepped on an active square?

What happened?

- What were your experiences at the beginning of the activity?
- What were your experiences at the end of the activity?
- What were your experiences during the planning process?
- During the planning period, what strategies did people suggest?
- Which strategies were implemented? Which ones were discarded?
- What were your experiences while crossing the maze?
- What were your experiences with other team members?
- Who were the leaders and major contributors during the activity?
- Who were the non-participants and skeptics?

What did you learn?

State the following general principles and ask if the participants agree or disagree with each. Ask them to provide supporting data from the maze activity and from the workplace.

- Sounding the alarm when you step on an active square gives useful information, yet most people feel embarrassed or guilty when this happens.

- People tend to plan too much.
- When you run out of time, you ignore planning.
- Effective planning involves a combination of trial-and-error experimentation and discussion.
- It is important to have a structure for the planning process.
- When confronted with a novel task, people ignore such strategies as process mapping.
- Without a leader, most groups flounder.
- Not being able to talk to each other while walking on the maze makes it difficult for the team to succeed.
- Not being able to use paper and pencil makes it difficult for the team to succeed.
- Sometimes people worry so much about making fools of themselves that they are unable to focus on the task.

How does this relate?

- Does the maze activity remind you of similar experiences in your workplace?
- What real-world activity does the maze activity reflect?
- In what ways does the planning during the maze activity reflect planning in your workplace?
- In what ways does people's behavior during the maze activity remind you of people's behavior in your organization?
- What does the maze signify?

What if?

- How would your behavior have changed if you were permitted to talk throughout the activity?

  If you were permitted to use paper and pencil?

  If you did not have to take turns?

  If you were fined $10 every time you stepped on an active square?

  If one of you was initially identified as the leader?

  If there were no planning periods?

  If you had only 10 minutes to cross the maze?

  If you had two hours to cross the maze?

  If there were twice as many participants?

  If there were only three participants?

What next?

- If we conducted the maze activity again (but with a different pattern), how would you behave differently?
- Using the maze activity as a metaphor, how would you change your team planning, problem-solving, and decision-making behaviors in the workplace?
- How would you apply the insights from the maze activity to solving your workplace problems?
- How can the principles that you learned from this activity be used to improve productivity and performance in the workplace?

Other Games with the Team Maze Training Device

As long as you have purchased or constructed a Team Maze, you can use it for a variety of team training games. Here are some suggestions:

MOB SCENE. This game explores how large groups intuitively make joint decisions and take concerted action without talking to each other. It requires larger-than-usual groups (fifty to two hundred participants). Place the maze in the middle of a large auditorium that has no furniture. Herd all participants to one side and tell them that they have 10 minutes to cross the maze to the other side. The usual TEAM MAZE rules apply. In addition, there is absolutely no talking from the start of the game. Also, participants who set off the alarm are taken to a rehabilitation area at one side of the room from where they can watch the rest of the action but cannot participate. Major learning insights from this activity relate to trust, walking the talk, self-sacrifice for the good of the group, and reluctance to be the first one to act.

TWO TEAMS. This game explores inter-team collaboration and conflict. Two teams begin at different corners of the maze and attempt to walk to the opposite corner. The usual TEAM MAZE rules apply. In addition, when one team sets off the alarm, it is time for the other team's turn. Teams assume that they are competing with each other, even though they are not told this. Effective strategy in this game requires observing and supporting the other team because there are common elements in both tasks. Major learning insights from this activity relate to competitive assumptions about other teams and the reluctance to see both teams as parts of the same organization with mutual goals.

TRAINING. This game highlights the importance of teaching a problem-solving process, rather than teaching a solution. Organize participants into two teams. Ask the first team to learn how to cross the maze while the second team waits in another room. After this has been accomplished, send the first team to the waiting room and, without actually showing the maze,

ask the team members to train the second team to cross the maze. While this training is taking place, secretly change the maze pattern. When the second team attempts to implement what it has learned, it is confronted by a new problem that was not covered during training.

HIERARCHY. This game explores communication problems in a hierarchical organization. Assign different organizational roles to participants: a president, two division managers, four managers, and several workers. After the initial briefing, prohibit everyone from talking and ask them to communicate through written memos. Each level of the organization should send memos only to the immediate "superiors." Everyone except the workers should have their backs turned to the maze. Give a map of the maze (with the safe path clearly indicated) to the president and explain that he or she cannot see what is happening on the maze, cannot show the map to anyone, and can only send memos to division managers. Major learning insights from the activity relate to empowerment, open communication, and organizational learning.

KNOWLEDGE EXCHANGE. Prepare a map of the maze and label the columns with letters and rows with numbers. Give each participant some play money and a few bits of random information (example: *A2-safe, D7-mined*) about whether or not some of the maze squares are activated. Explain that participants can buy, sell, or exchange information with each other. Individuals or teams can attempt to cross the maze when they figure out a safe path. Participants who fail pay a fine, while those who succeed receive a reward. Major learning insights from this activity relate to open sharing of information.

Tabletop Team Maze

Sometimes you don't have enough space or players or training devices to conduct the regular version of TEAM MAZE. Don't worry! With a couple decks of regular playing cards, you can conduct a tabletop version of the game.

Lay out a 9 × 6 grid of playing cards. Red cards are mines; black cards are safe areas. The value of the cards is irrelevant. Create a grid so that there is a single safe path from one side to the other. After you have checked your playing card maze, turn all the cards face down (without rearranging the layout).

Have players find the safe path, as in the regular maze. Invite the first player to turn any card on the starting side face up. If it is safe (black), the player advances to any adjacent card and turns it face up. The player continues in this fashion as long as he or she keeps turning black cards. The turn ends when the player turns up a red card. All the face-up cards are immediately turned face down before the next player takes his or her turn.

As a variation of this game, you can have two teams construct different mazes at different tables. Later, each team can attempt to cross the other team's maze. The team that succeeds in the shortest period of time wins the game.

Design Your Own Games and Activities

Sample Minefield

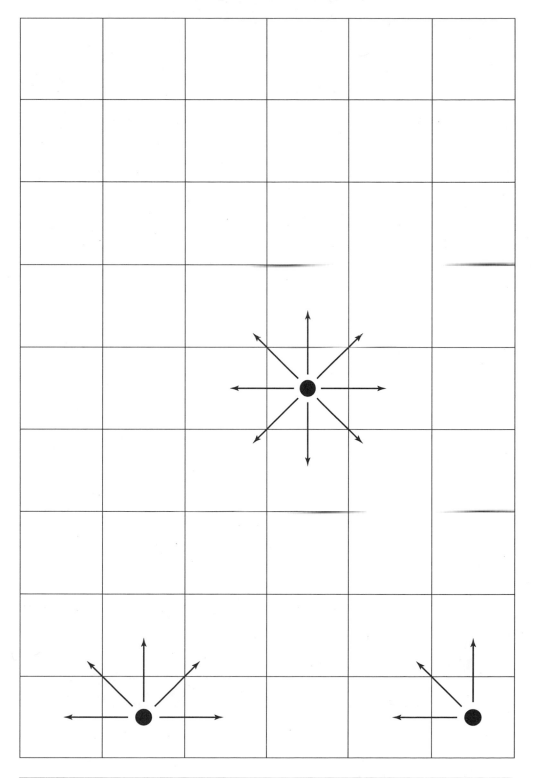

Team Maze Safe Path

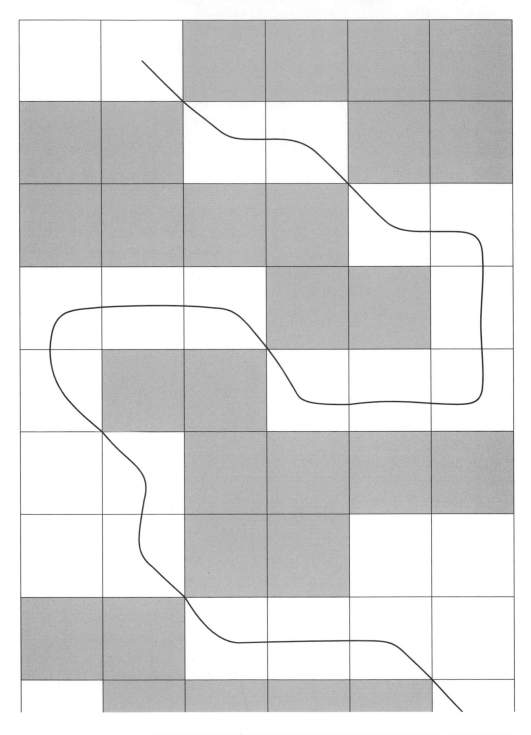

Basic TEAM MAZE Rules

- All team members should walk across the maze from any square on the lower side to any square on the opposite side.

- All team members should have crossed the maze within 30 minutes.

- Only one team member can stand or move on the maze at a time.

- All team members should take turns attempting to cross the maze. Everyone should have completed the first try before anyone steps on the maze for a second try.

- If the alarm goes off, the team member should immediately return to the previous (safe) square and retrace his or her path to leave the maze. This person cannot re-enter the maze until everyone else has had a turn.

- Team members should not use any writing materials.

- When someone is on the maze, team members may not talk to each other.

- Team members may stand all around the maze. They can point to different squares of the maze without touching. They can communicate to each other through gestures, grunts, groans, sighs, and applause.

- The facilitator will announce the beginning of the activity and immediately start the timer. Team members should spend at least 3 minutes talking to each other before anyone steps on the maze.

- Once the team has begun to walk the maze, it has to spend a minimum of 3 minutes on the maze without talking.

- Once any team member begins to talk (after people have been moving on the maze for at least 3 minutes), everyone should get off the maze. Team members should continue discussing for at least 3 minutes before the next person steps on the maze.

Reproduced from *Design Your Own Games and Activities* by Sivasailam (Thiagi) Thiagarajan with Raja Thiagarajan with permission of the publisher. Copyright © 2003 by John Wiley & Sons, Inc.

27 Metaphorical Simulation Games

Metaphorical simulation games (MSGs) reflect real-world processes in an abstract, simplified fashion. MSGs are particularly useful for teaching principles related to planning, generating ideas, testing alternatives, making decisions, utilizing resources, and working under time pressure.

An MSG is the inkblot test of experiential learning. The acronym stands for metaphorical simulation games, but don't let the term metaphorical intimidate you. It just means that the simulation game uses an abstract, simplified reflection of the real world.

A simulation game reflects the real world so that you can get as close to on-the-job training as possible while avoiding the dangers of the real world. A high-fidelity simulation game (examples: *a war game* or *a game that uses a flight simulator*) reflects the real world with a high degree of authenticity. In contrast, an MSG is a low-fidelity simulation game because it reflects the real world in an abstract, metaphorical way. For example, an MSG may involve an egg-drop contest in which different teams compete to see who could drop a protected egg from the highest point without breaking it. The egg does not simulate anything directly. But the activity simulates tough challenges that confront a team. All the problem-solving steps (planning, discussing, generating ideas, testing alternatives, working under time pressure, making the best use of available materials, and competing with other teams) that each team undertakes reflects similar collaborative activities in the real world.

Let us explore BARNGA (Thiagarajan, 1994), another MSG, in some detail.

BARNGA

You are attending a workshop on cross-cultural communications. The facilitator begins the session with a card game. She divides the players into groups of four. Each group reviews a handout to learn the game. After a few practice rounds, the players turn in their handouts and play silently. At the end of 3 minutes, the facilitator announces a tournament with a "no communications" rule. She sends the winning partners at each table to the next table. Shortly after you begin playing the tournament round, you notice that your opponents are cheating. You decide to give them the benefit of the doubt and assume that they misunderstood the rules. However, because of the no communications rule, all you can do is grunt, groan, and gesture wildly. Your opponents also appear to be confused. Only later do you realize that each table learned to play the game under slightly different rules. During the debriefing session, you confess how quickly you made several unwarranted assumptions.

BARNGA is a metaphorical simulation game. Its major learning point is that cross-cultural conflicts arise because of the assumptions we make. In this simulation, the card game reflects business interactions that are guided by a set of ground rules. The no communications rule reflects language difficulties.

Benefits, Limitations, and Suggestions

High-fidelity simulation games are excellent for training people to do step-by-step procedures, such as using a flight simulator to learn how to land a fighter airplane on the deck of an aircraft carrier. In contrast, MSGs are effective in teaching principles and helping the participants learn to apply these principles to a wide range of situations. For example, a session on alternative uses for BARNGA was held at the 1998 North American Simulation and Gaming Association (NASAGA) Conference. Although this metaphorical simulation game is traditionally used for multicultural topics, the NASAGA session demonstrated Michael Berney's use of the game for training participants to cope with change.

The use of metaphorical simulation games results in another important benefit: Because the play materials and procedures are very different from their real-world analogues, participants do not get sidetracked into trivial details. For example, a group of engineers may argue endlessly about how to build a real bridge because they know too much about the topic. A metaphorical simulation game that requires the construction of paper airplanes may distract them away from the technical details and focus their attention on interpersonal principles and procedures.

Because of the abstract nature of metaphorical simulation games, participants are likely to become impatient and complain about the irrelevancy of the activity. You will be repeatedly challenged with "What's the point?" In addition, without a good debriefing, insights gained from the

Design Your Own Games and Activities

play of the game are likely to remain as inert knowledge without being transferred to participants' workplace situations. Make sure that your debriefing questions require participants to relate the game to real-world objects and procedures. Encourage the participants to discuss how they plan to apply their new insights to old workplace challenges.

More Examples

TRIANGLES. In this MSG, players simulate the manufacturing process by cutting triangular pieces of paper and assembling them into different silhouettes. The game highlights the relationships among managers, workers, and customers. In this game, participants are divided into planners, implementers, observers, and—almost as an afterthought—customers. Planners are given a sheet of paper and instructions for cutting it into smaller triangles and rearranging these triangles into six different silhouette figures called trigrams. The planners are given 20 minutes to figure out the procedure and instruct the implementers. After these 20 minutes, planners are not permitted to talk to implementers. For the next 15 minutes, implementers assemble trigrams according to planners' instructions. At the end of this time, customers make their surprise appearance, inspect the trigrams, and award points. Almost invariably, planners and implementers in this metaphorical simulation game are lulled into ignoring customers until it is too late.

RELATIONSHIP. In this MSG, players rearrange a shuffled deck of cards in the correct order to simulate teamwork processes. The game explores how a lack of trust affects a team's productivity. Participants are divided into four teams. Each team buys shuffled decks of playing cards, arranges the cards in the correct order, and sells the decks to customers. If done correctly, the team makes a profit. The team with the most profit at the end of a 7-minute period wins the game. In the instruction sheets, members of Team A are warned that there is a saboteur in their midst. One member of this team is given secret instructions to slow down the work of the team (by making inappropriate suggestions, asking irrelevant questions, confusing other team members, and misplacing cards). All members of Team B are also warned about a saboteur in their midst, even though nobody is given this role. Members of Team C are not given any warnings, but there is a saboteur in their midst. Members of Team D are not given any warning and there is no saboteur in their midst. At the end of the game, the production rates of different teams are compared to drive home the point that unjustified paranoia about saboteurs can produce the same effect as real saboteurs.

EXCLUDE. In this MSG, an entry ritual (touching the left shoulder of a group member with your right hand) simulates the rites used by in-groups to prevent outsiders from joining. The game explores the frustrations of being left out and being ignored. At the beginning of the game, a few

participants are sent outside the room. Their instruction sheet tells them to return to the room later, join any group, and participate in the conversation. In the meantime, the other participants are divided into groups and asked to have a pleasant conversation. The facilitator demonstrates the secret entry ritual for each group. The insider groups ignore any outsiders when they return and attempt to join the groups—unless they figure out and use the correct ritual.

Ready-to-Use Metaphorical Simulation Game
PUZZLE PIECES

Purpose

To explore different factors that influence the selection or rejection of an individual by a team.

Participants

Twelve to forty

Time

40 minutes to 1 hour (20 to 30 minutes for play and 20 to 30 minutes for debriefing)

Materials

- Six sets of puzzle pieces (see Preparation below)
- Six envelopes
- $17 cash, preferably in crisp, clean $1 bills
- PUZZLE PIECES Instructions

Preparation

Master the flow of the game. Do your homework. Read the set of instructions, visualizing how the game will play out. Walk through the game with a few friends. Use the outlines of steps on page 317.

Make the puzzle pieces. Make six copies of the picture on page 318 on card stock. Put all copies in a stack, all pointing the same way. Cut all six cards so that each is divided into twelve irregular pieces. (TIP: Use a paper cutter instead of a pair of scissors.) Since you aligned the cards before cutting them, corresponding pieces from each card should be identical.

Create a master envelope and puzzle envelopes. Place the twelve pieces of each card in separate envelopes. Label one of the envelopes "Master

Design Your Own Games and Activities

Envelope" and set it aside. The remaining five envelopes are the "puzzle envelopes." Remove an identical piece from each of the puzzle envelopes and set them aside.

Flow

Form teams and select the outsiders. Ask the participants to form themselves into equal-sized teams. Assign the role of outsiders to the remaining participants. You should have at least three and no more than five outsiders.

> Example: You have a total of nineteen participants. You organize them into four teams of four, leaving three participants to be the outsiders.

Distribute the puzzle pieces. Use as many puzzle envelopes as there are teams. Distribute the eleven pieces from each envelope to each of the teams.

Explain the object of the game. Teams should assemble the pieces to reconstruct the original picture. The first team to do so wins the game.

Distribute pieces to the outsiders. While the teams are busy assembling their pieces, take the pieces from the master envelope. Give one piece to each outsider, making sure that only one of the outsiders receives the piece that you removed from the puzzle envelopes.

Brief the outsiders. Warn the outsiders that they will all feel bored initially and all but one of them will feel abandoned later. Ask them to observe the behaviors of team members without intruding in their activities.

Observe the process. Let the teams discover that they are missing a piece. If necessary, help any slow team by showing where the pieces go. When the teams put together all their pieces, they will notice a hole in the picture.

Make an announcement. Announce that the outsiders will become team members. Acknowledge that each team's picture is missing a piece. Explain that you have given an extra puzzle piece to each of the outsiders and they are now ready to join the teams.

Explain the next step. Each outsider will visit each team and show his or her piece. Team members will compare this piece with their almost complete picture. The outsider will then return to the front of the room, still holding his or her piece. This entire step should be conducted in total silence. Pause while this step is completed.

Begin the recruitment campaign. Ask each team to send one of its members to the front of the room to invite any one of the outsiders to join his or her team. The outsiders should listen to various recruitment pitches, but they should not announce their decisions. Announce a 3-minute time limit.

Because of the nature of the setup, all recruiters will converge on the single outsider who holds the missing piece.

Ask the outsider to select a team. The outsider should now identify which team he or she wants to join. After the announcement, stop the outsider from actually joining the team.

Announce financial incentives. Now explain that the team that completes the picture puzzle will win $17. Ask the team members to figure out the implications of this incentive and decide whether they should offer a financial reward to the outsider. After a suitable pause, invite the recruiters to return to the front of the room and entice the outsider. Announce a 3-minute time limit for this recruitment session.

Conclude the activity. Send the recruiters back to their teams. Ask the outsider with the missing piece to join any team. Ask the team to rapidly assemble the complete picture. Congratulate this team and pay it $17.

Field Notes

I originally designed this activity as a cultural diversity exercise but found that it has wider application. I have conducted the activity with groups of various sizes and with participants from different professions. The effect is more dramatic when PUZZLE PIECES is played by participants who work with each other (as in an in-house training session) than by participants who are strangers to each other (as in a public training session). Be careful with your selection and handling of the outsiders because they may feel left out and begin interfering with the game. Encourage them to observe the teams in action and keep telling them what you are going to do next.

Debriefing

Conduct a discussion of different insights gained by the players. Remember that the purpose of this simulation game is to explore factors that contribute to the selection or rejection of an individual by a team. Here are some suggested questions, arranged according to a six-phase debriefing model. Encourage a free-flowing discussion among the participants, and return to these questions when the conversation slows down.

How do you feel?
- How do you feel about the way the game was played?
- How do you feel about the way the game ended?
- Near the end of the game, how did you feel about the outsiders who did not have the missing puzzle piece?

Design Your Own Games and Activities

- If you were an outsider without the missing puzzle piece, how did you feel about the recruiters ignoring you?
- If you were the outsider with the missing puzzle piece, how did you feel about all teams wanting you?
- What was your reaction to the announcement about the winning team receiving a cash prize?

What happened?

- What notable things happened during the game?
- What happened during the beginning of the game when you formed teams?
- How did your team go about solving the puzzle?
- What happened when you realized that your team did not have all the puzzle pieces?
- What happened when the outsiders visited your team?
- What happened during the first round of recruitment? During the second round?

What did you learn?

- What insights did you gain from playing this game?
- What did you learn from observing what happened to the outsiders without the missing piece? To the outsider with the missing piece?
- Based on your experience in the game, how do you react to each of these statements:

  You feel happy when people need you.

  It was hard not to feel rejected even though it was not your fault.

  When competition is intense and when money is involved, people are less tactful in rejecting you.

  You may like somebody to be on your team, but that person may not have what it takes to help you on the project.

  Women are more sensitive than men about rejecting others.

How does this relate?

- How do the events in the game relate to your workplace?
- In the game, people were accepted or rejected because of the puzzle pieces they had. Does something like this happen in real life?
- What do the puzzle pieces in the game represent in the real world?

- Do you agree with people who say that the puzzle pieces represent competencies? Knowledge? Personality characteristics?
- Who do the outsiders in the game represent? Have you ever felt that you were an outsider in some situation?
- Did you notice how the outsiders without the missing puzzle piece were treated? Has something like this ever happened in your workplace?

What if?

- How would the nature of the game have changed if we had more participants on each team?
- What if none of the outsiders had the missing puzzle piece? What if all of them had the same missing piece?
- What if the game involved a more complex puzzle with several more pieces?
- What if each team had a different puzzle to reconstruct?
- What if the winning team received a cash prize of $200?
- What if the recruiters had more time to persuade the outsider with the missing piece?

What next?

- If we were to play the game again and if you were the outsider with the missing piece, how would you behave?
- What advice would you give a participant who is about to play this game for the first time?
- Considering what you have learned from this card game, would you behave differently in your workplace? If so, in what way?
- What is the most important lesson that you learned from this game? How would you apply it to your real life?

PUZZLE PIECES Instructions

Here's a condensed set of instructions for the game to help you review the steps. You may use this page as a handout when you are walking your friends or co-facilitators through the game.

What Do the Team Members Do?

- Participants organize themselves into teams.
- Each team receives eleven pieces from the facilitator.
- Team members cooperatively assemble the puzzle pieces to reconstruct the original picture.
- They discover that a puzzle piece is missing.
- Without talking, they inspect the puzzle pieces brought by outsiders.
- They figure out that one outsider has the missing piece.
- They send a representative to recruit the outsider with the missing piece to join their team.
- They wait for the outsider with the missing piece to choose the team he or she wants to join.
- They listen to the announcement about the $17 financial incentive.
- They figure out the implications of this incentive and revise their recruitment strategy
- They send the team representative to make another attempt at recruiting the outsider with the missing piece.
- If the outsider with the missing piece joins their team, they complete the puzzle and receive the cash prize.
- All team members participate in the debriefing discussion.

What Do the Outsiders Do?

- They come to the front of the room.
- They each receive a puzzle piece from the facilitator.
- They listen to the facilitator's briefing.
- They watch what the team members are doing without intruding in their activities.
- They visit each team and silently show their puzzle piece.
- They return to the front of the room and wait.
- They listen to the recruitment offers from different team representatives. They realize that only one of them is in demand.
- The outsider with the missing piece (OWTMP) selects the team he or she would like to join (but does not join the team yet).
- The outsiders wait while the teams work on a new recruitment strategy (incorporating the financial incentive).
- The OWTMP listens to the new recruitment campaign from the representatives from different teams.
- The OWTMP selects a team (not necessarily the team picked earlier) and joins it. He or she gives the puzzle piece to the team so they can complete the picture.
- All outsiders participate in the debriefing discussion.

PUZZLE PIECES Puzzle

28 Interactive Storytelling

Interactive stories are fictional narratives that involve participants in a variety of activities. In one type of interactive story, the facilitator presents a story and discusses its significance in a debriefing. In another type, the facilitator pauses at critical junctures in the middle of a story and invites listeners to play the role of a character and make appropriate decisions. In still another type, participants themselves create and share stories that illustrate key concepts, principles, or procedures.

To learn more about interactive stories, let us take you through a vicarious experience.

ETHICAL DECISION MAKING

You are attending a training session on high-impact decision making. You expect a dull philosophical presentation or a boring legal lecture. So you are pleasantly surprised when Paul, the facilitator, launches into a science-fiction story.

In Paul's story, you and the eight others in the room are the sole survivors after a nuclear holocaust. All living things on earth have been wiped out by huge doses of radiation. The room that you are in is actually an underground chamber that is shielded from radiation and controlled by a supercomputer nicknamed Guardian. Imitating the synthesized voice of a computer, Paul announces:

> "This is Guardian at 1308 Zulu time. According to presidential directive 112529A, your group is entrusted with the responsibility for coping with the current disaster and for perpetuating humankind.

Please begin a discussion on this topic, remembering that everything you say will be automatically recorded for posterity."

You feel somewhat silly, but get into the story and suggest that everyone should first try to figure out the current situation. Someone else suggests that everyone should identify one or two major goals to be achieved and focus the discussion on the means of achieving these goals. Within minutes, you are involved in an intense discussion.

Approximately 6 minutes into the discussion, you hear a loud banging on the door. In the voice of Guardian, Paul makes this announcement:

"This is Guardian at 1314 Zulu time. Someone is trying to gain access through the main entrance. From the palm print of this person, we have identified her as Theresa Watts, an analyst working at the National Security Agency. Counters indicate that she has been heavily irradiated and would contaminate this chamber if she were allowed to enter. Therefore, I am currently denying her entry as per directive 110635A. However, I am required to inform you that you may override door locks and allow Ms. Watts to enter if a two-thirds majority of you agree to this. Please discontinue your earlier discussion and decide whether you should admit Ms. Watts into the chamber. Inform me when you reach a decision."

Your group hastily shifts over to the new crisis and talks about probabilities, the sanctity of human life, and other such things. The discussion becomes more intense. However, Paul, in the guise of Guardian, interrupts you with this announcement:

"This is Guardian at 1316 Zulu time. You may discontinue your discussion of Ms. Watts, as she is now dead. She appears to have taken her own life in response to increased pain. You should now return to your discussion of the future of humankind."

Paul's storytelling continues in this vein, with the activity alternating between listening to Guardian and making high-impact decisions. After about 20 minutes, Guardian interrupts your discussion with this announcement:

"This is Guardian at 1312 Zulu . . . I have detectected an impennnnding systemwide failure in the power distributionnnn system. Mmmmy sellff-repair syssstem does not ressssponnnnd. I have sennnt a repair request to the mannnnuuufatuuurerr, but have nnnnot received acknnnnnowledgemennnt. I will shutdownnnn innn four seccconnnds. I will shutdownnn innnn four seconds. I will shu. . . ."

As you emerge slightly dazed from interacting with the story, Paul takes you through a short exercise to discard the role and regain your normal persona. He then proceeds to debrief the group.

Design Your Own Games and Activities

Uses and Limitations

From ancient times, stories have been used in education and training to dramatically illustrate important concepts, principles, and procedures. They have also been used for data collection, strategic planning, self-awareness, change management, cultural communication, creative thinking, and presenting a vision. Research data and conceptual frameworks from different disciplines suggest that people create and share stories to extract meaning from what is happening in their world.

The obvious advantage of using stories is the high level of motivation. Stories have some disadvantages also. In certain situations, they may be perceived as being too childish or artificial. Also, stories are frequently presented as one-way communication with the storyteller talking and other participants listening passively. Interactive stories attempt to reduce these disadvantages.

Types of Interactive Stories

Let us briefly explore three types of interactive stories.

Interaction during the story. The Guardian story presented above is an example in which participant interaction is incorporated throughout the story. In this format, participants take on the roles of different characters. In a different version of this approach, the storyteller modifies the story based on participants' decisions, actions, and preferences.

Interaction after the story. In this simple form, the storyteller may present the entire short story and conduct a follow-up activity. For example, newly hired employees read a story about the founding of the company. The facilitator then asks participant teams to rewrite the story as if the company were founded right now. This is followed by a discussion of preserving underlying values of the organization during changing times.

Interactive story creation. In this form, the facilitator identifies a concept (example: *empowerment*), principle (example: *proactive decisions increase customer satisfaction*) or procedure (example: *project management*). Participants, working individually or in teams, create stories to illustrate the selected topic. Later they share the stories with each other.

Ready-to-Use Interactive Storytelling Activity
A DEATH IN MY FAMILY

Here is an activity that uses a story with a debriefing and a follow-up activity.

Purpose

To explore similarities and differences among values, beliefs, and behavior patterns from different cultures.

Participants

Any number

Time

80 minutes (20 minutes for reading of the story, 20 minutes for debriefing, and 30 minutes for the follow-up activity)

Materials

- Copies of the story, A Death in My Family (page 324)
- Copies of An Approach to Writing Short Stories (page 328)
- Index cards

Field Notes

This activity frequently arouses some strong (and healthy) emotions. After the individual reading of the story and before the debriefing, I check with participants to see whether anyone wants to be excused. Recently, when I conducted this activity with an intercultural group, one of the participants was particularly affected because of a recent death in her family. However, she wanted to participate in the debriefing, and her obvious pain brought out excellent supportive behavior from the group.

Flow

Set the context. Announce that you are going to use a short story narrated by a seven-old Tamil boy named Thiagu to explore similarities and differences among cultural values, beliefs, and rituals. Tell participants that they will have 20 minutes to read the story and think about it. You will then spend 20 minutes for debriefing and another 30 minutes for a follow-up activity.

Distribute copies of the story. Invite participants to go to any convenient location and read the story. Announce the time and the location for everyone to meet for the next phase of the activity.

Debriefing

Use the standard debriefing model for discussing the content and the impact of the story. Use a few of these suggested questions to start the debriefing process. Encourage a free-flowing discussion among participants and return to these questions when the conversation slows down.

How do you feel?

- What's your overall emotional reaction to the story?
- How do you feel about the cultural values, beliefs, rituals, and behavior patterns presented in this story?
- How do you feel about Thiagu, the narrator of the story?
- How do you feel about the other characters: Thiagu's elder brother Maniannan, Father, Granny, the cook, and Mr. Natarajan?
- While most readers report sadness as their primary emotion, some readers have reacted with anger, confusion, relief, peace, and fear. What elements in the story could have caused each of these reactions?
- How do you think children would react to this story? Why do you think so?

What happened?

- What were some of the important events in the story?
- What details do you recall from the story?
- How did your feelings and emotions change through the events in the story?
- How do you feel about these specific events in the story: Thiagu's attempts at talking to his mother, behavior of women in the back room, Thiagu's conversation with the cook, the funeral procession, cremation, and Thiagu's conversation with Granny?

What did you learn?

- While the story has several aspects, let's focus on its cross-cultural factors. What are the similarities and differences between your culture and the culture of the narrator with respect to these factors:

  Rituals related to death?

  Gender differences in roles and functions related to death?

  Age differences in roles and functions related to death?

  Differences in the roles and reactions of family members, other relatives, friends, acquaintances, and strangers?

  Differences in the way adults talk about death among themselves and how they talk to children?

What if?

- How would your reactions to the story have been different

  If the narrator were an adult?

  If the story was in the form of a novel?

  If you watched a movie instead of reading the story?

If you listened to an audiotape of a child narrating the story?

If you read the story in some other language?

If the story was about the birth of a baby?

If the story took place in your own culture?

Follow-Up

Give a break. After the debriefing, announce a short break. Tell participants that you would like to conduct a change-of-pace follow-up activity when they return.

Brief participants. Tell participants that they will spend 30 minutes working in teams to create a story that highlights cross-cultural similarities and differences. Distribute copies of the handout, An Approach to Writing Short Stories, and packets of index cards. Recommend that participants follow the procedure outlined in the handout.

Provide additional details. Suggest "A Wedding in My Family" as the title for the story. Emphasize that participant teams are not expected to produce a finished story within the allotted time, but just to start.

Conclude the activity. After about 20 minutes, gather all the teams together. Invite team members to briefly present the current version of their story. Suggest that participants complete the story either individually or in teams—at their own leisure. Thank everyone for their participation.

A DEATH IN MY FAMILY

When I woke up, Maniannan was combing his hair in front of the mirror. It was too early because it was not yet daylight outside. The electric light was on and Maniannan looked strange.

"Are you going somewhere?" I asked.

"Yes, Father wants me to go to take a letter to Usman Road uncle."

"What letter?"

"This one."

I looked at the letter written in Father's tight handwriting. I recognized some words, but the others were too big for me to sound out. I asked Maniannan, "What does it say?" Maniannan read the letter in a low voice:

> After a lingering illness, Mrs. S. Valliammal attained the shade of the gracious feet of Lord Siva at 4:30 this morning. The cremation will take place at 11:30 in the Mambalam mayanam.

I did not understand what the letter said. I asked Maniannan, "What does it mean?"

"It means Mother's dead." Maniannan said softly.

Maybe "Mother's dead" meant that she was more sick and in greater pain. I went to the sick room where Mother stayed the last few months. Several grown-ups were whispering to each other.

I quickly understood the reason for their whispers. Mother was in her bed, fast asleep. She was wearing her silk sari and had a big rose garland around her neck. Her face looked beautiful so she could not be hurting too much.

I looked around for Father, but he was not around. Neither was Granny.

I got closer and whispered into Mother's ear, "Mother, are you sleeping?" She did not reply. I asked her in a louder whisper: "Mother, what does dead mean?"

She did not reply.

Granny knew everything and I would ask her. I went to the back room.

Granny was in a corner, crying silently. I had never seen Granny cry, not even when she broke her leg. But she was crying now and the tears were running down her cheeks.

Several women around Granny were also crying. When Kalyani aunt saw me, she started wailing, "My sister, why did you have to die in such a young age? Who's going to take care of your little ones?"

This served as a signal for the other women to start wailing. I heard the words but could not understand what they were saying. One woman complained about God's cruelty. Another recalled the time Mother took care of her when her husband lost his job. Another woman said that Mother was the kindest friend she ever had.

The wailing of the women became so loud that I got scared and went back to the sick room.

Mother was still sleeping. The cook placed incense sticks in different corners of the room.

I followed him to the kitchen. I asked, "What's Mother going to do?"

The cook thought for a moment and said, "She's going on a trip."

"Are we going with her?"

"No."

"Will she be gone for a long time?"

"Yes."

"When will she come back?"

"Not for a long time."

If Mother was going on a trip, I wanted to go with her.

When I went back to the sick room, I saw Maniannan slipping out through the other door.

Some men brought in a mat made of green coconut fronds. My cousin's grandfather, the oldest man in our family, put some holy ash on Mother's forehead. Some women put flowers in Mother's hair. My aunt removed Mother's gold wedding chain from around her neck and replaced it with a yellow string.

And all through these activities, Mother continued to sleep.

(Continued)

Interactive Storytelling

At 11 o'clock, Father and my uncle lifted Mother from the bed and laid her on the coconut mat. Four men lifted the mat and moved Mother to the verandah. After placing another garland around her neck, they carried Mother to the street.

Mr. Natarajan, the nice man who was a clerk in Father's office, picked me up. I told him, "I want to go with Mother."

"That's what we are going to do."

He put me behind the handlebar of his bicycle and propped it up by the window. Then he went into the house and brought back my little brother Chidambaram—who was crying softly—and put him on the saddle.

Mr. Natarajan pushed his bike and we followed the others in the procession behind Mother. Maniannan walked with Father up ahead, carrying a small clay pot. We went through several side streets. I listened to the conversation among the people who were walking with us. One of them said he liked processions with music. Another announced that they had declared a holiday in the school where Mother taught.

There were no women in the procession, but some women in the street looked at Mother and reverently patted themselves on their cheeks. A milk woman walked a little while with us and chatted with Mr. Natarajan.

"They say it's a good omen to see the body of a sumangali who dies before her husband. She looks so young. What did she die of?" Mr. Natarajan replied that she was sick for a long time and that she was indeed a virtuous sumangali.

The procession went on and on. I finally asked Mr. Natarajan, "Is Mother going on a long trip?"

He was taken aback. After thinking for a while, he said, "Yes."

The procession came to a halt near a temple. Five small huts stood behind the temple. The huts looked strange because they had tin roofs and mud floors, but no walls. On the floor of one of the huts, a lot of firewood was piled up neatly.

The men who were carrying Mother placed the mat on top of the firewood pile. I was worried that it might hurt Mother. But she did not wake up.

Mr. Natarajan put the bicycle on the stand. Chidambaram was drooping on the saddle and Mr. Natarajan straightened him up and covered his eyes.

The men poured something on the firewood. It smelled like ghee. Father put a sliver of firewood inside the pot Maniannan was carrying. When he took it out, I saw a flame at the end of the stick. Father touched the firewood pile with the burning stick and the whole pile lighted up suddenly.

I let out a shriek and closed my eyes.

When I opened my eyes after a long time, the flames were roaring. I tried to figure out what was happening. Was Father angry at Mother and punishing her? But Father did not look angry. Actually, I could see tears rolling down his cheek.

I asked Mr. Natarajan, "When the fire goes out, will Mother be better?"

He looked perplexed. "When the fire goes out," he said finally, "we will collect your Mother's ashes and place them in the holy river."

For the first time, I thought that I might not see Mother again.

When we returned home, everything was quiet. The men had gone to work and the women had gone to their homes. Even the cook was nowhere to be seen. Father had made Maniannan go to school for the rest of the day.

I went to the sick room. Somebody had removed Mother's bed and had cleaned the floor with Dettol. I sat down in a corner, trying to figure things out.

Granny came to the room. She sat by me and laid my head on her lap. I looked up at Granny's sad, kind, wise face.

"Granny, where did Mother go?"

"She has gone to God."

"Will I ever see her again?"

"Yes, Thiagu, but not the way she looked before."

"Will she look older?"

"No, she will be born a baby. She could be a baby ant or a baby elephant. She could be a baby bird. She could be a baby boy."

I did not like that. "How can I talk to her if she becomes a baby ant?"

Granny did not answer my question but continued with her explanation. "It all depends on God's will."

"Granny, why does God do these things?"

Granny pulled out the old book, *The Legend of the Graceful Games.* I had seen that book before. It had pictures and funny stories about the things that God did.

Granny read a verse from the book. The only word that I understood was playing.

"I don't understand what it means, Granny."

"You remember how you play hide and seek? God is a great game master and he has all of us playing hide and seek. God plays with the whole universe that has many worlds. When you play hide and seek, you have a boundary. But in God's game, there is no boundary. When you play hide and seek, the game comes to an end when it gets dark. But God's game never ends. Your Mother and you and I will be playing His game for ever and ever."

"But I want to find Mother."

Granny said, "If you find someone, then the game comes to an end, Thiagu. We will always keep looking for Mother in every living creature."

"Granny, I want to die so I can see Mother."

Granny said, "You cannot do that."

"Why not?"

"Because those are the rules of the game. The game must go on. We need you to explain the rules to little Chidambaram. And when you become a big man, you will have your own children and you will have to help them learn the game. Remember, you have to make sure that the game never ends."

Granny patted my cheeks.

I went looking for Chidambaram to explain the rules of the game that never ends.

An Approach to Writing Short Stories

Step 1. Specify the Theme
(a message for the reader stated in a few words)
- Prepare a theme card.
- Focus on the main message.
- Describe the theme in a single sentence.
- Identify key terms.

Step 2. Create the Plot
(an outline of events, decisions, actions, and consequences that summarize the sequence of the story)
- Prepare a plot card.
- Use the standard formula: problem, decision, complication, crisis, and climax.
- Flowchart your plot.
- Keep it lean: Avoid unnecessary complications.
- Keep it realistic—but not bland.

Step 3. Establish the Setting
(a locale where the story takes place)
- Prepare a setting card.
- Describe the setting in a single phrase.
- Visualize details of your setting.
- Write random sentences of sensory impressions.
- Keep the setting realistic—but not boring.

Step 4. Portray the Characters
(key players in the story)
- Prepare a character card.
- Identify your main character.
- Create supporting characters to help and hinder the main character.
- Create minor characters.
- Specify the gender, age, appearance, motivation, job, and other details for each character.
- Select a name for each character.

Step 5. Establish a Time Span
(period from the beginning to the end of the story)
- Prepare a time card.
- Keep your story within a brief time span.
- Identify the beginning and ending points in time.
- Divide your story into several scenes.
- Specify the time span for each scene.

Step 6. Keep Playing with the Story Elements

- Review each card and keep adding to it.
- Change the elements in one card and make suitable adjustments to other cards.
- Play what-if with the elements in each card.
- Keep revising your story until all the pieces fall in place.

Step 7. Write the First Draft

- Select a viewpoint
- Follow your preferred method for writing the first draft.
- Don't try to control your story. Let the story control you.
- If stuck, skip to some other scene.
- Try alternative sequences.

Step 8. Critique and Revise

- Check the theme. If the story is not aligned to it, revise the theme.
- Check the ending. If it is not believable, revise it.
- Check the beginning. If it does not grab the reader, revise it.
- Check the viewpoint. If it keeps shifting, revise it.
- Check your action. If it does not follow a logical sequence, revise it.
- Check your setting. If you have not given enough details, revise it.
- Check your characters. If they are not consistent, revise them.
- Check your dialogue. If it does not sound authentic, revise it.
- Check your length. If it is too long or too short, revise it.

29 Role Playing

Role playing involves participants taking on characters, personalities, and attitudes in order to achieve a variety of training and performance-improvement outcomes. Participants act out their roles in a spontaneous and realistic manner under imaginary conditions imposed through a scenario.

COMPLAINTS

It's 3 o'clock in the afternoon of the second day of a workshop on handling customer complaints. You and ten other participants are being trained to work at the customer relations desk in a huge electronic products store. Earlier during the workshop, you went through training sessions on active listening, conflict resolution, and negotiation skills. You watched videotape demonstrations of a seven-step model for dealing with customer complaints. You are now familiar with these steps and you know how to apply them flexibly to suit the specific characteristics, personalities, and needs of each customer. You also know that your goal is to earn the customer's loyalty—without giving away the store.

Nancy, your facilitator, declares that the time has come for the final performance test. You groan inwardly as she explains that each of you will participate in six short role plays. She has hired actors from a local improv group to act out the roles of customers who are not happy with the electronic products they bought. Each actor will be playing the role of a different customer with different complaints.

You hate role plays and you are not looking forward to this activity. You sit behind the desk assigned to you and quickly review the checklist that contains details for the seven steps. Your first customer is upset because his MPG player refuses to work. This customer is very knowledgeable about technical details. You compliment him on his expertise and offer to replace the player with an upgraded model, free of charge. Your customer disappears somewhat abruptly when a timer goes off. Your second customer has difficulty speaking English. You apply everything you learned about dealing with customers from other cultures and find out that someone has stolen his TV set. You try to explain that the store's maintenance agreement does not cover burglaries. You repeat the role playing procedure with two more customers with different personalities and complaints. After the fourth customer, the telephone on your desk rings. You have assumed that it was there just for decorative purposes, but you go ahead and pick it up anyhow. It turns out to be a call from your fifth customer. You get to practice your best telephone skills. After you deal with your sixth customer, Nancy reassembles the entire group. She conducts a debriefing session to discuss how you felt about the procedure and what you learned from your role play. You discover that most other participants had difficulty in determining the customer's technical expertise without appearing to be patronizing. After 30 minutes of the debriefing discussion, Nancy brings back the actors for brief comments about their overall observations. At the end of the session, you find out that each actor has actually evaluated your role play performance on a rating scale related to the six steps of the procedure. You are happy with your high ratings. At the bottom of each rating sheet, the actor has written down a suggestion for improving your performance. They all appear to be practical and you plan to work on them.

Advantages and Limitations

COMPLAINTS is a somewhat unusual application of the role-play strategy. You are probably more familiar with the traditional role plays enacted by two participants brought to the front of the room and asked to enact some interpersonal interactions.

Role plays help us achieve a variety of objectives:

Interpersonal skills practice. In a role play, participants practice interacting with different types of important customers and co-workers in a psychologically safe context. They receive feedback from other participants and from the facilitator.

Personal insights. In addition to feedback from others, the role player also checks out how the behavior feels from his or her personal point of view. This increases the participant's awareness of strengths and opportunities for improvement.

Developing emotional intelligence. Role plays help participants experience the feelings that accompany interpersonal interactions. In addition to

Design Your Own Games and Activities

increased awareness of such feelings, participants learn how to manage them so their personal performance does not degenerate.

Assessment and evaluation. Role plays provide the most valid tool for assessing interpersonal skills. COMPLAINTS, the sample role play described above, illustrates how this assessment strategy can be implemented effectively.

Role plays have several advantages over other training strategies. Here are two of the most important ones:

Focused learning. Role plays immediately engage participants into spontaneous action. This focuses the participants' attention on the learning activity.

Integrated learning. The case method trains participants to make decisions in an interpersonal situation—but stops there. In a role play, the participant is required to carry out this decision. Thus, the role play integrates thoughts, talk, and action to provide a comprehensive learning experience.

Role plays are not without their limitations. Here are some things to watch out for:

Reluctance. Role playing makes some participants feel threatened about revealing their weaknesses in front of an audience. As a facilitator, you can reduce this problem by preparing the participants beforehand and by modeling a positive, non-judgmental approach during the role play performance.

Stereotyping. Role playing encourages some participants to impress the audience with their histrionic skills with exaggerated performance. You can reduce this problem by asking role players to act in a moderate and natural fashion.

Vulnerability. Role playing sometimes results in inadvertent self disclosure and emotional outbursts. You can reduce this problem by conducting a debriefing discussion that explores different factors that influence our interpersonal behaviors.

Personalizing. Some participants take other players' statements and actions during the role play as personal attacks. You can reduce this problem by clearly separating the role from the real participant and taking time to "derole" players by systematically bringing them back to the current reality.

Types of Role Plays

All role plays involve specifications for one or more roles and a scenario that describes the background context. Within this general framework, here are several variations:

Media. Most role play scenarios are presented through a printed handout. Whenever appropriate, use an audiotape or videotape to present the background information. You may also use computers to present your scenario with some sophisticated branching options.

Level of detail. At one extreme, your scenario may include complex case materials and several pages of background data. At the other extreme, you may simply say, "Imagine that the two of you are deciding what to do about a safety violation in the manufacturing plant" and leave it at that. In general, the less information you include in the scenario, the easier it is for the players to improvise.

Conflict. Role plays require an element of conflict to maximize learning. Create such conflict by supplying different players with different information, by allocating incompatible personalities and attitudes, and by creating hidden agendas or mismatched goals.

Feedback. A key factor that contributes to learning from a role play is the nature and the amount of feedback given to participants. You may structure the feedback process by supplying participants with rating scales and observation checklists. You may also assign one or more observers to evaluate specific aspects of the role-play performance.

Number of players. Most role plays involve two characters interacting with each other. Use a larger number of roles to represent real-world team processes. Experiment with still larger groups as in a scenario related to passengers in a crowded airport.

Interaction among participants. Typically, two participants conduct a role play while the rest of the group observes the performance. Instead of this standard approach, involve more participants through parallel role plays in which groups of three (two players and an observer) act out the scenario in different parts of the room. Alternatively, conduct serial role plays in which the original players are replaced by other participants at periodic intervals.

Preparation. You may produce an elaborate role-play package with videotaped scenarios, detailed role cards, checklists for observers, and instructions for facilitators. On the other hand, you may spontaneously create a role play in the middle of your presentation by asking a volunteer to complain about your lecture—and act out the role of a defensive person in a state of denial.

Responses. Most role plays focus on face-to-face, spoken responses. Experiment with a telephone role play or a role play in a computer chat room or a role play through a series of e-mail messages—if these alternatives better reflect the workplace context. For another variation, ask participants to focus on nonverbal communication through gesture and facial expression.

Emotional impact. While all role plays involve an emotional element, you can increase or decrease its intensity. Be careful to avoid unnecessary levels of negative emotions, unless you are training people to perform such functions as working on a suicide-prevention hot line.

Design Your Own Games and Activities

Replay. After players have completed their enactment, conduct a debriefing discussion. Present appropriate frameworks related to the interpersonal concepts, referring back to the role-play experience. Now ask participants to reenact the role play with their new insights. Use the same scenario, but switch the roles assigned to the players.

DIALOGUE PLUS

What do these training topics have in common: asking for a pay raise, calming down a violent person, communicating with a person of the other gender, confronting an irate customer, debriefing an individual, delivering bad news, dissuading an employee from making an unethical decision, encouraging a friend, firing a marginal employee, giving feedback, making self-disclosure statements, overcoming customer objections, persuading a visual person, receiving compliments, responding to insensitive jokes, sharing confidential information, solving problems with a partner, and talking to a non-English speaker?

They all involve interpersonal skills that are used on a one-on-one basis. And they are all topics that can be effectively incorporated in DIALOGUE PLUS, a game that features effective use of role playing.

DIALOGUE PLUS is a framegame. It is designed to permit easy removal of old content and loading of new content.

GUT TALK, the game presented on the following pages, is a sample application of DIALOGUE PLUS. You can use the game, without any changes, to train participants to share their feelings and emotions in an effective manner. You can also remove the content (of expressing emotions) from the game and plug in any other interpersonal skills.

Ready-to-Use Role Play
GUT TALK

Most employees receive training on how to control and hide their emotions and behave in a professional fashion. However, professionals have emotions too. These feelings and emotions are critical components of many conversations. As Douglas Stone, Bruce Patton, and Sheila Heen (1999) point out in their book, *Difficult Conversations,* unexpressed emotions leak into conversations, take a toll on our self-esteem and relationships, and make it difficult for us to listen to what the other person is saying.

Purpose

To effectively express appropriate feelings and emotions in professional conversations with another person.

Participants

Any number

Time

60 to 90 minutes

Materials

- Copies of the GUT TALK Checklist for all participants
- Sets of role cards (instructions for five different roles)
- A Scenarios sheet for the facilitator
- Blank pieces of paper
- Felt-tipped pens
- Timer
- Whistle

Preparation

List of scenarios. Review the GUT TALK Checklist and the list of sample scenarios. If you want to, prepare your own scenarios that are locally relevant. However, don't make them so close to real incidents and people that they may arouse conflicting reactions. To specify your scenario, all you need is a one-or-two-sentence description so participants can personalize it with their own experiences and preferences.

Demonstration role play. Select one of the scenarios and prepare a role play to demonstrate the application of the checklist items to the situation. If possible, record a role play with a friend (playing the role of a listener) on videotape. If you prefer, rehearse the role play with a co-facilitator so that you can perform it "live" during the play session.

Room Setup

Arrange chairs in clusters of five. You don't need tables for this activity.

Flow

Present the framework. Briefly discuss the costs associated with both suppressing and expressing feelings and emotions in the workplace. When a person decides that it is worth clearing the air by expressing feelings in a specific situation, he or she should clearly identify these feelings and analyze them. The role play activity that you are planning to conduct can help you to effectively express your emotions without becoming emotional.

Discuss the checklist. Distribute copies of the GUT TALK Checklist to each participant. Explain that the six items in the checklist are recommendations for expressing feelings. Pause briefly while participants review the checklist items. Invite questions and comments and discuss them.

Design Your Own Games and Activities

Demonstrate appropriate behaviors. Inform participants that they will be role playing in the ensuing exercise. Briefly introduce the sample scenario. Play the videotaped demonstration or role play the situation with your co-facilitator. If you don't have a videotape nor a co-facilitator, ask for a volunteer, assign the role of the listener to this person, assume the role of a speaker, and conduct the demonstration role play.

Form groups. Divide participants into groups of five to seven. Five is preferable to six or seven. Try to keep the size of different groups the same.

Assign roles. Give a packet of five role cards to each group and ask each participant to take one. If there are more than five people in a group, ask the observer to share the card with one or two of the others. Explain that the ensuing activity will involve 3 minutes each of preparation, role playing, and debriefing. Explain that each role card contains instructions on what to do before, during, and after the role play. Pause briefly while participants review their role cards.

Specify the scenario. Briefly describe the situation in which the role play is to take place. Use your own scenario or one from the list on page 344. Explain that the speaker and the coach will make up any additional details and assumptions as needed.

Begin the preparation activities. Ask players and coaches to find each other and get ready for the role play according to the instructions on the cards. If the groups have more than five members, ask observers to find each other (within each group) to decide who will observe which checklist item during the role play. During the preparation time, supply blank pieces of paper and felt pens to the coaches and briefly review how to use them.

Begin the role play. After 3 minutes, blow the whistle and instruct participants to take their positions. In each group, the speaker and the listener are seated facing each other. The speaker's coach stands behind the listener and the listener's coach stands behind the speaker so that they can hold up the coaching cards without distracting the other person. The observer (or observers) are seated in front of the role players. Ask the speakers at each group to begin the role play.

Monitor the role play. Walk among the role play groups, observing and noting down interesting actions and comments—without interfering with the role play. Your co-facilitator should also be doing the same thing.

Conduct in-group debriefing. After 3 minutes, blow the whistle to stop the role play. Explain that the members in each group will give feedback only to the speaker (because we are focusing on this person's behavior). Each group member will take turns to make one positive comment about the speaker's behavior and suggest one change for the speaker to consider. Emphasize that each person is limited to just two brief statements, and these statements

should relate the speaker's behavior on a checklist item. Ask participants to follow the sequence specified in their role cards: observer (or observers), speaker's coach, listener's coach, listener, and the speaker. Ask the observer in each group to start the debriefing. People who have later turns should avoid the "others have already said what I wanted to say" ploy and make a new statement, even if a lower priority.

Conduct general debriefing. After 3 minutes, get the attention of all participants from different groups and provide general feedback based on what you (and your co-facilitator) observed during the earlier role play. Then briefly discuss participants' insights about checklist items.

Change role assignments. Ask each participant to pass the role card to the next person so that the speaker becomes the listener, the listener becomes the speaker's coach, the speaker's coach becomes the observer, the observer becomes the listener's coach, and the listener's coach becomes the new speaker.

Repeat the procedure. Present a new scenario and ask participants to repeat the role play procedure with 3 minutes each of preparation, role play, and debriefing. At the end of each round, conduct a general debriefing, change role assignments, and start a new round.

Conclude the activity. At the end of the final round, announce the conclusion of the activity. Suggest that each participant think of a situation where he or she can actually use the approach outlined in the GUT TALK Checklist. Pause for about 3 minutes while participants complete a rapid action plan by identifying a suitable situation and writing down some notes.

GUT TALK Checklist

1. Explain why you want to express your emotions and ask for the other person's permission to do so.

2. Specify all the different feelings you have. Don't focus on just one negative feeling.

3. Don't blame or judge the other person.

4. Own your feelings. Make "I feel . . ." statements rather than "You make me . . ." statements.

5. Listen to the other person's responses.

Speaker Role Card

Before the Role Play

- Work with your coach.
- Think about the situation. Add appropriate details.
- Examine different feelings related to the situation.
- Use the checklist and prepare an outline of what you are going to say.
- Identify specific areas for your coach to remind you.

During the Role Play

- Express your feelings clearly.
- Modify your actions and statements based on your coach's prompts.

After the Role Play

- Wait until everyone has given his or her feedback.
- Identify the one most positive thing that you did or said during the role play.
- Identify the one most important thing that you would change during similar situations in the future.

Speaker's Coach Role Card

Before the Role Play

- Work with the speaker.
- Help the speaker think about the situation and add appropriate details.
- Help the speaker examine different feelings related to the situation.
- Help the speaker use the checklist and prepare an outline of what he or she is going to say.
- Identify specific areas that the speaker wants you to remind him or her.

During the Role Play

- Observe the speaker's behaviors and listen to his or her statements.
- Compare these behaviors and statements to the original plan and to the checklist items.
- Write simple prompts on a piece of paper and hold them up for the speaker to see.

After the Role Play

- Wait until the observers have given their feedback.
- Identify the one most positive thing that the speaker did during the role play.
- Suggest the one most important change that you would like the speaker to consider during similar situations in the future.

Listener Role Card

Before the Role Play

- Work with your coach.
- Think about the situation.
- With your coach's help, plan how to react to the emotional statements of the speaker.
- Plan realistic and plausible reactions to the speaker's statements.

During the Role Play

- Listen to the speaker's statements.
- React in a realistic fashion.
- Modify your reactions based on your coach's prompts.

After the Role Play

- Wait until your coach has given feedback to the speaker.
- Identify the one most positive thing that the speaker did or said during the role play.
- Suggest the one most important change that you would like the speaker to consider during similar situations in the future.

Listener's Coach Role Card

Before the Role Play

- Work with the listener.
- Help the listener think about the situation.
- Help the listener plan how to react naturally to the emotional statements of the speaker.

During the Role Play

- Observe the listener's reactions.
- Write simple prompts on a piece of paper and hold them up for the listener to see.

After the Role Play

- Wait until the speaker's coach has given feedback to the speaker.
- Identify the one most positive thing that the speaker (not the listener) did during the role play.
- Suggest the one most important change that you would like the speaker to consider during similar situations in the future.

Observer Role Card

Before the Role Play

- Work with other observers, if any.
- Review the checklist and decide what behaviors to observe.
- Divide the checklist items among observers (if there are others).

During the Role Play

- Observe the speaker's behavior and listen to his or her statements.
- Take notes on behaviors and statements associated with each checklist item.
- If there are other observers, focus on the items assigned to you.

After the Role Play

- Give feedback to the speaker, based on your observations. If there are other observers, wait for your turn in the sequence of checklist items.
- Identify the one most positive thing that the speaker did (or said) during the role play.
- Suggest the one most important change that you would like the speaker to consider during similar situations in the future.

Scenarios

Both your parents are facing major medical problems. You are not sure whether you should ask for a leave of absence.

Even though employees in your corporation have been assured of job security, several of your friends have been downsized.

You are excited about a major project assigned to you, but you are not sure whether you can handle it.

You are having great difficulty getting an appointment to meet with your manager.

You contributed a lot to the successful completion of a project, but your name is not even mentioned in the final project.

You feel that the company has not given you enough freedom to use your talents.

You feel that your manager is making promotion decisions based on the 360-degree feedback given by your co-workers. You are convinced that one of them is trying to sabotage your promotion.

You want to tell your mentor how grateful you are. But you are worried she may think that you are flattering her.

Your budget is reduced by 10 percent—and no other budget is affected.

Your co-worker has failed to deliver a critical report to you on time. Now your report is going to be delayed.

Your manager has been making disparaging remarks about you to other managers.

Your manager keeps forgetting previous assignments given to you and keeps adding more assignments.

30 Cash Games

Cash games are a special type of simulation game that involves actual cash transactions. They are not gambling games. Nor do they focus on accounting procedures or financial management. Instead, they explore interpersonal skills (such as negotiation) and concepts (such as cooperation). These games use cash because it effectively simulates the real world and brings out natural behaviors and emotions in participants.

ME AND MY TEAM

You are participating in a simulation game at a team-building session. The facilitator divides the participants into five teams of six. Each participant, including you, receives 100 points. As a participant, you may keep all the points for yourself, give all 100 points to your team, or do anything in between. You have to make the decision without talking to other team members.

You win if you belong to the team with the highest total team score and have the highest personal score.

Your dilemma: If you give a lot of points to your team, you lose because your personal score is low. On the other hand, if you keep a lot of points for yourself, you still lose because your team doesn't have the highest team score.

And this is just the beginning. You play several rounds of the game with minor variations. Just as you feel that you have figured out the system, the facilitator adds a new twist: During the fourth round, you cannot communicate with your teammates and, if you win, you secretly receive a $50 cash prize.

The players' behaviors during this round provide rich data for debriefing. Participants have spent several hours exploring the tradeoffs between individual needs and team requirements, public statements and private actions, and monetary payoffs and spiritual fulfillment. All participants agree that the combination of secrecy, cash incentives, and lack of communication is hazardous to the trust in any team.

What Is a Cash Game?

ME AND MY TEAM, the experiential activity described above, is an example of a cash game. This type of simulation game involves actual cash transactions with real money, not play money. The activities, however, are not gambling games. You have to earn the money the old-fashioned way: through smart strategy and hard work. Although cash games use money, they do not deal with accounting procedures or economic principles. Rather, they explore interpersonal skills (such as negotiation) and concepts (such as cooperation).

Why Use Cash Games?

Cash games grab the participants' attention. Cash prizes reflect real-world rewards and encourage the participants to behave in a realistic manner. They are cost-effective: Although you pay out some cash, the games do not require expensive equipment and supplies. The powerful insights are well worth the money.

How to Handle Cash Games

In beginning, I explain to the participants the rationale for using real money. I adjust the cash amounts to jolt each specific group of participants without stressing them out. I make the payments immediately. Unless there is a special reason, I do not collect money from the participants. I establish ground rules against the politically correct, no-brainer strategy of collusion and sharing the prize money. If some participants appear to be squeamish, I ask them to help me as scorekeepers or observers.

Ready-to-Use Cash Game
CHANGE MANAGEMENT

The "change" in the title refers not to the latest organizational initiative but to the coins jingling in your pocket. A penny may not be worth much these days, but in this cash game it can give you a valuable insight: You may suddenly become popular by having the right resources at the right time.

Key Concept

The team or player who pays the exact change of $5 using the most coins receives a $50 bill.

Purpose

To explore the value of individual contributions to a team.

Learning Points

Concepts. Fair share, monetary payoffs, inter-team competition, valuing individual contributions, and diverse resources of different team members.

Procedures. Negotiation, coalition formation, competitive recruitment, collaborative financial planning, and teamwork under tight deadlines.

Contrasts. Cooperation versus competition, individual versus team benefits, timeliness versus monetary value, cost-based versus value-based profit sharing, and current versus potential team members.

Participants

The game requires at least ten players. The best game involves fifteen to thirty players. I have conducted the game with more than one hundred players.

Time

20 minutes for the play and 15 to 30 minutes for debriefing.

Materials

- $50 bill
- Timer
- Whistle

Flow

Announce a 1000-percent profit deal. Hold up a $50 bill and reveal that you are going to sell it for a mere $5.

Explain the restrictions. Using your own words, list these constraints:

- "You must pay me the exact change in U.S. coins."

- "You must not import or export change into the room. Nobody may leave the room to get change. Nobody can ask people outside the room to bring change."

- "This is a one-time offer. Only one individual or team can purchase a $50 bill at this discounted rate."

- "The individual or team that uses the most number of U.S. coins to pay exactly $5 gets the $50."
- "To participate in this activity, you should submit a Purchase Offer Form specifying the total number of coins that you are offering. The value of these coins should add up to exactly $5. The form should also contain the names of team members making this offer."
- "I will accept preliminary purchase offers during a 7-minute period. At the end of this time, I will announce the preliminary offers from different individuals or teams."
- "After the announcement of the preliminary offers, you have 3 more minutes to regroup yourself and make a final offer."
- "At the end of these 3 minutes, I'll give the $50 bill to the individual or the team that offered the most U.S. coins adding up to $5. If there is more than one top offer with the same number of coins, then the earliest offer will receive the $50."

Begin the game. Blow a whistle and start the timer. Tell the participants that they have 7 minutes to complete and submit their Preliminary Purchase Offer Forms. Explain that teams may revise their offers if they are able to acquire more coins to add up to the $5.

Reveal the preliminary offers. Blow the whistle at the end of 7 minutes. Beginning with the offer with the least number of coins, announce the offers.

Begin the next phase. Remind participants that they have 3 more minutes to form coalitions and to revise their offers.

Conclude the phase. At the end of 3 more minutes, blow the whistle again and announce the end of the game.

Identify the winner. Identify the offer with the most coins. In case of a tie, select the earliest submission of the tied offers.

Conclude the activity. Collect the change from the winning team. Verify the number of coins and their total value. Congratulate the team and give its representative the $50 bill. Suggest that the team members wait until the end of a debriefing discussion before splitting their well-deserved wealth.

Variations

Too many people without change? Randomly distribute small change among the participants before the start of the game.

Participants are trying to form one big cooperative team? Impose a limit on the number of members in each team.

Not enough time? Announce that the earliest team that pays exactly $5 using the most U.S. coins will get $50. Declare a 5-minute time limit. Speed up the debriefing by giving everyone a copy of the questions.

Debriefing

To make sure that the participants not only enjoy CHANGE MANAGEMENT but also gain useful insights from it, conduct a debriefing session. I recommend a six-phase model for debriefing. Here are some sample questions for each phase:

How do you feel?

- How do you feel about the play of the game and its outcomes?
- How do you feel about the winning team? If you are a member of this team, how do you feel about your teammates?
- Did the behavior of any player offend you during the game? If so, how?
- If you had no change with you, how do you feel about the way the other participants treated you?

What happened?

- How were the teams formed?
- Did other participants recruit you to join their team?
- Did the other participants ignore you?
- Were you recruited by more than one team? What factors influenced your choice of which team to join?
- Did your team discuss how to divide the $50? If so, what factors did you take into account?
- Did any team try to improve its offer after the announcement of preliminary offers? How did the team do it?

What did you learn?

- What was the most important learning point for you?
- What insights did you have about cooperation and competition among the participants?
- What did you learn about forming teams and making decisions under tight deadlines?
- What did you learn about different behaviors among men and women?

How does this relate?

- If this game were a metaphor for something, what would it be?
- Some participants with no change (or with very little change) still contribute to a team with strategic advice. What are some workplace examples of people without tangible assets but with expertise and skills becoming key players in a team?

- One of the interesting points in this game is that a person with nine pennies has more to contribute than a person with a $100 bill. What are some workplace situations in which some object (or service) of low monetary value becomes extremely valuable?
- In the game, the participants with a lot of loose change were recruited by different teams. What are some workplace analogues of this situation?

What if?

- What if the game permitted only individuals to make purchase offers?
- What if some people started selling coins for profit?
- What if a participant had one hundred pennies? What if this participant waited until the last moment and submitted his individual offer?
- What if you sold $500 for $5? What if you sold $5 for $2?

What next?

- What advice would you give to a participant who is about to play this game?
- Considering what you learned from this cash game, how would you behave differently in similar team situations in your workplace?

31 PC Simulations

PC simulations use playing cards to reflect real-world objects and processes. The rules of PC simulations typically encourage participants to discover principles of interpersonal interaction and inductive thinking.

Let's play a game called INDUCT. For the first round, I will be the Rule Maker and you will be the Scientist. I write down a secret rule about a set of three cards (called triplets). I place these two sets of cards on the table and declare them to be legal triplets:

I place these two sets of cards on another side of the table and declare them to be illegal. In other words, they violate my secret rule:

Your mission is to study the legal and illegal triplets and discover my secret rule. You assemble triplets from your deck of playing cards, place them on the table and declare whether they are legal or illegal. You get 2 points for presenting a legal triplet, 1 point for presenting an illegal triplet, and you lose 1 point if you misidentify a triplet.

You study my sample triplets, boldly present me with this set, and declare it to be a legal triplet:

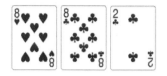

You are sure that my secret rule specifies that a triplet should have two cards of the same value and a third one of a different value. So you are shocked when I say, "Wrong."

Later, after several more turns (including a few in which I present additional examples of legal and illegal triplets) you figure out that the secret rule is "Two cards of the same value and the third one of a higher value."

What Is a PC Simulation?

INDUCT is an example of a PC simulation. The acronym PC does not stand for personal computer or politically correct. It stands for *playing cards*. PC simulations use playing cards to reflect real-world objects or processes. In INDUCT, the playing cards reflect sets of data (such as the products that customers like and dislike). The rules of the game reflect the processing of data to identify patterns.

More Examples

The person who invented playing cards is the greatest game-design genius. With a simple deck of fifty-two cards, you can create millions of games, including those that simulate the meaning of life. The endless permutations and combinations of cards and the thousands of ways they can be played provide a powerful approach to simulation game design. I always create a PC simulation of whatever I want to simulate—even if I decide later to use some other format. Here are some examples that illustrate the versatility of PC simulations:

RELATIONSHIP. This PC simulation explores how the lack of trust affects a team's productivity. In this game, teams compete against each other to arrange shuffled decks of cards in the correct order. Instruction sheets to the members of some teams reveal that there is a saboteur in their midst. Some teams are warned about a saboteur even when there is none. The results of the game reveal that, whether or not there is actually a saboteur in the team, just the paranoid feeling is enough to bring down the team's productivity.

NEGOTIATE. This game explores factors related to strategic alliances. The facilitator randomly deals five playing cards (Ace, 2, 3, 4, and 5) to five players. Any alliance of players that has a total card value of at least 8 (examples: *2, 3, and 4; 3 and 5; A, 2, and 5*) wins a cash payoff. The alliance should agree on a formula for dividing the payoff money among themselves. The game is repeated for several rounds, emphasizing the importance of establishing continuing relationships rather than going for immediate profits.

SH! This simulation game involves two groups of participants exchanging playing cards and a third group acting as judges. The goal of the sasharers group is to get rid of red cards (that have negative value). Members of the cimvit group cannot refuse the red cards forced on them, but they can lodge a complaint to the judges. As the game proceeds through different rounds, the cimvits learn to turn the tables on the sasharers. Only after the end of the game the players are told that it simulates sexual harassment in the workplace. The debriefing session uses the players' experiences in the game as a metaphor for sexual harassment.

Ready-to-Use PC Simulation
CARD SETS

Here is a PC (playing cards) simulation that reflects some important team-building principles.

Purpose

To encourage cooperation among individuals who are engaged in traditionally competitive roles.

Time

30 minutes for the activity and 15 minutes for debriefing.

Participants

Eight to forty-eight. Best with sixteen to thirty-two players. During the game, half of the players are assigned to the Red Region and the other half to the Blue Region. Within each region, half of the players are given the role of Buyers and the other half are given the role of Sellers.

Co-Facilitator

This game presents a few logistic hassles, especially if you are running it for the first time. Work with a co-facilitator who can assemble and distribute different card sets and spec sheets. Since you can "train" the co-facilitator in a matter of minutes, you can use one of the early-arriving players to fulfill this role.

PC Simulations

Materials

- Two decks of playing cards, with different colored backs
- Blank paper
- The CARD SETS Summary (page 358) for each participant
- CARD SETS tables for the facilitator
- Spec Sheets tables as needed
- Red and blue pens
- Flip chart
- Felt-tipped markers
- Whistle

Preview

Basic principle. The following basic principle operates in this game, independent of the total number of players: *Enough resources are available, but if the Buyers (or Sellers) don't team up, not everybody gets what he or she wants.* Here is an example:

Alan is trying to sell this card set:

Barbara is trying to sell this card set:

Charlie wants to buy a card set with three cards of the same value, but of different suits. Alan has such a card set for sale.

Diane wants to buy a card set with three cards in sequence and in the same suit. Barbara has three cards in sequence but, alas, they are not in the same suit.

However, if Alan and Barbara were to team up and rearrange their cards, they can create these two card sets:

Now they can sell both sets to the two Buyers. Everybody will be happy! Alternatively, if Charlie and Diane team up and buy both card sets, then they can rearrange the cards to meet their needs.

Preparation

Before the game, you need to assemble card sets and Buyer's specs. A card set contains three playing cards. You need one card set for each Seller in each region. Determine how many Sellers you have in each region. Use the list of cards in the Card Sets Table (page 358) to assemble card sets based on the number of Sellers. Use red-backed cards for the Red Region and blue-backed cards for the Blue Region.

Spec sheets specify the type of card set required. You need one spec sheet for each Buyer in each region. Determine the number of Buyers in each region. Use the information given in the Spec Sheets Table (page 359). Write the specs with a red pen for the Buyers in the Red Region and a blue pen for the Buyers in the Blue Region.

Flow

Brief the players. Explain that the game involves buying and selling card sets. Distribute copies of the handout and point out that the card sets could be of two different types.

Organize the players into groups. Divide the players into Red and Blue regions and divide each region into equal numbers of Buyers and Sellers. Explain that the two regions will not interact with one another but will play the game at the same time. If you have an extra person in either group, assign an observer's role to this person.

Distribute the supplies. In each region, give each Seller a card set to sell and each Buyer a spec sheet that shows what to buy. Use the red sets for the Red Region and the blue sets for the Blue Region.

Explain the play procedure. Tell participants that, within each region, individual Buyers locate Sellers. The Seller gives up his or her card set in exchange for the spec sheet from the Buyer. This concludes the transaction. After a card set has been exchanged, it cannot be returned or taken back.

Give a secret tip to the Blue Region. Assemble all players in the Red Region. Answer any questions and tell the players to wait until they hear the whistle before conducting their transactions. Under the guise of doing the same thing in the Blue Region, assemble all players in that region. Explain that you are going to give the Sellers an important tip. Tell the Sellers to rapidly collect the specs from all Buyers, combine the card sets, and rearrange the cards to meet the Buyers' specs. They can then sell all their card sets.

Monitor the transactions. Blow the whistle to start the game. Notice how the Red Region players tend to finish more quickly than the Blue Region players. Blue Region players will finish more slowly, but they should all complete their transactions successfully. Some Red Region players will probably not complete transactions successfully.

Do a rapid data check. Explain that the card sets and specs in both regions were identical. Find out how many people in each region were unable to buy or sell card sets. Reveal that the Sellers in the Blue Region combined and rearranged their card sets. You will probably receive some complaints from Red Region Sellers.

Get set for the second round. Collect all the card sets. Ask your co-facilitator to rearrange the card sets and prepare spec sheets exactly as before.

Introduce the second round. Explain that because of complaints from some Sellers, the management has decided to prohibit Sellers from combining and rearranging their card sets. During the next round, the game will be played in exactly the same way as before, except that Sellers cannot rearrange their card sets. Distribute the card sets and the spec sheets as before.

Drop another secret tip. Visit the Red Region and explain that you are going to give the Buyers a valuable tip. Suggest that they buy any card set from a Seller, even if does not meet their specs. Later, the Buyers can combine their cards and rearrange them to meet their specs. After sharing this tip with the Buyers in the Red Region, casually visit the Blue Region and re-emphasize that the Sellers cannot rearrange their card sets.

Conduct the second round. Blow the whistle to start the next round. This time, the players in the Red Region are likely to finish later.

Do another rapid data check. Find out how many people in each region were unable to buy or sell card sets. Explain that the Buyers in the Red Region bought all available card sets and rearranged them to meet their requirements.

Debriefing

Conduct a discussion of different insights gained by the players. Remember that the purpose of the game is to foster cooperation. Here are some suggested questions, arranged according to the six-phase debriefing model:

How do you feel?

- How do you feel about the way the game was played?
- How did you feel if you were a Seller with a card set that no Buyer wanted? If you were a Buyer with a spec sheet that no Seller could match?
- How do you feel about the cooperative strategy that helped everybody to "win"?
- How did you feel about the players with the same role as yours? With a role different from yours?
- How did you feel about the players in the other region during the first round? During the second round?

What happened?

- During the first round, what did the Sellers in your region do? What did the Buyers do?
- If you were a Seller, how did you respond to a Buyer whose spec sheet did not match your card set? If you were a Buyer, how did you respond to a Seller whose card set did not match your spec sheet?
- During the first round, who did you talk with? What did you talk about? During the second round, who did you talk with? What did you talk about?

What did you learn?

- What was the most important learning point for you?
- What insights did you gain about buying and selling? About cooperating and competing?
- What did you learn about laws and policies that prohibit collusion among Sellers?
- What did you learn about planning and acting?

How does this relate?

- What real-world processes does this game relate to?
- How does the game relate to the fact that the U.S. produces more than enough food to feed all its citizens, and yet many people go hungry?
- How does this game relate to individual versus team selling strategies?
- How does this game relate to Buyers' cooperatives?

What if?

- What if the facilitator did not drop secret hints? Do you feel the players would have figured out suitable strategies?
- What if we played a third round that permitted rearrangement of the cards by all Buyers and Sellers?
- What if everyone belonged to the same region?
- What if there were more Sellers than Buyers? More Buyers than Sellers?
- What if we provided a cash incentive for successful individual salespeople? A cash incentive for the team of Sellers if they sold all the card sets?

What next?

- What advice would you give a participant who is about to play this game for the first time?
- Considering what you learned from this card game, how would you behave differently in your workplace?

CARD SETS Summary

SYMBOL	CARD SET	EXAMPLES
S3	Three cards of the same value, but of different suits.	2♣ 2♠ 2♦ — 10♣ 10♥ 10♦
R3	Three cards in sequence, and in the same suit.	2♣ 3♣ 4♣ — 8♦ 9♦ 10♦

Reproduced from *Design Your Own Games and Activities* by Sivasailam (Thiagi) Thiagarajan with Raja Thiagarajan with permission of the publisher. Copyright © 2003 by John Wiley & Sons, Inc.

CARD SETS Table

If you have this many sellers ...	... then use these card sets
2	2♣2♠2♥ · 2♣3♠4♥
3	2♣2♠2♥ · 3♠3♥3♣ · 2♣3♠4♥
4	2♣2♠2♥ · 3♠3♥3♣ · 4♠3♣4♥ · 2♣4♦4♣
5	2♣2♠2♥ · 3♠3♥3♣ · 4♠3♣4♥ · 2♣4♦4♣ · 5♣5♠5♥
6	2♣2♠2♥ · 3♠3♥3♣ · 4♠3♣4♥ · 2♣4♦4♣ · 5♣5♠5♥ · 5♠6♦7♥
7	2♣2♠2♥ · 3♠3♥3♣ · 4♠3♣4♥ · 2♣4♦4♣ · 5♣5♠5♥ · 5♠6♦7♥ · 6♣6♦6♠
8	2♣2♠2♥ · 3♠3♥3♣ · 4♠3♣4♥ · 2♣4♦4♣ · 5♣5♠5♥ · 6♣6♦6♠ · 7♠6♣7♥ · 5♠7♣7♦
9	2♣2♠2♥ · 3♠3♥3♣ · 4♠3♣4♥ · 2♣4♦4♣ · 5♣5♠5♥ · 6♣6♦6♠ · 7♠6♣7♥ · 5♠7♣7♦ · 8♣8♦8♠
10	2♣2♠2♥ · 3♠3♥3♣ · 4♠3♣4♥ · 2♣4♦4♣ · 5♣5♠5♥ · 6♣6♦6♠ · 7♠6♣7♥ · 5♠7♣7♦ · 8♣8♦8♠ · 8♠9♦10♥
11	2♣2♠2♥ · 3♠3♥3♣ · 4♠3♣4♥ · 2♣4♦4♣ · 5♣5♠5♥ · 6♣6♦6♠ · 7♠6♣7♥ · 5♠7♣7♦ · 8♣8♦8♠ · 9♣9♦9♥ · 8♠9♦10♥
12	2♣2♠2♥ · 3♠3♥3♣ · 4♠3♣4♥ · 2♣4♦4♣ · 5♣5♠5♥ · 6♣6♦6♠ · 7♠6♣7♥ · 5♠7♣7♦ · 8♣8♦8♠ · 9♣9♦9♥ · 10♠9♦10♥ · 8♠10♦10♥

Reproduced from *Design Your Own Games and Activities* by Sivasailam (Thiagi) Thiagarajan with Raja Thiagarajan with permission of the publisher. Copyright © 2003 by John Wiley & Sons, Inc.

Design Your Own Games and Activities

Spec Sheets Table

If you have this many buyers ...	... then use these spec sheets										
2	S3	R3									
3	S3	S3	R3								
4	S3	S3	S3	R3							
5	S3	S3	S3	S3	R3						
6	S3	S3	S3	S3	R3	R3					
7	S3	S3	S3	S3	S3	R3	R3				
8	S3	S3	S3	S3	S3	S3	R3	R3			
9	S3	S3	S3	S3	S3	S3	S3	R3	R3		
10	S3	S3	S3	S3	S3	S3	S3	R3	R3	R3	
11	S3	S3	S3	S3	S3	S3	S3	S3	R3	R3	R3
12	S3	S3	S3	S3	S3	S3	S3	S3	S3	R3	R3	R3

32 Jolts

Jolts are interactive experiential activities that lull participants into behaving in a comfortable way and then suddenly deliver a powerful wake-up call. Jolts force participants to re-examine their assumptions and revise their habitual practices. A typical jolt lasts only a few minutes but provides enough insight for a lengthy debriefing.

SIX LETTERS

How well do you know U.S. presidents? In the following list of letters, cross out SIX LETTERS to reveal the name of an historical U.S. president.

F I S I L X L L E M T O T E R E R S

Please don't give up too soon.

The heart of any jolt, including this one, is the debriefing. During the debriefing, I will begin by asking if you gave up trying to solve the problem. I will explore why some people give up when they are not able to solve the problem immediately. I will relate this to people's workplace and personal behaviors. I will then explore excuses people use such as:

- "I live in Australia and I am not interested in U.S. history."

- "I am not good at solving word puzzles."

- "Someone will give me the solution later."

- "I am trying to find the learning point here. I don't care about U.S. presidents."

Once again, I will relate these behaviors to the workplace and personal life.

Benefits and Uses

The major advantage of using a jolt is that it packs powerful learning into a brief period of time. It startles participants and appeals directly to their emotions. It frequently requires interaction and almost always requires introspection. By startling participants, a jolt makes them more mindful of their behavior patterns.

Use jolts to encourage self-awareness. For example, use this tool to help participants examine their stereotypes, prejudices, and assumptions as a part of a training session on diversity, sexual harassment, change management, customer focus, or creative problem solving. Begin the training session with a jolt as an icebreaker to capture participants' attention. Treat the rest of the training session as an extended debriefing discussion. Schedule a jolt as a segue between one training module and the next. Use a jolt to keep participants awake and energized after a lunch break. Use a jolt as a final activity to remind participants that in spite of everything they learned, they can still revert to their habitual behavior patterns. There is a difference between intellectually knowing what to do and emotionally being able to do it.

Proceed with Caution

In spite of their apparent simplicity, jolts can be tricky to facilitate. Here are some caveats about their use:

A question of trust. Most jolts incorporate an element of entrapment. Participants will complain that you "made them do inappropriate things." Because a jolt may require you to withhold information or to encourage people to make invalid assumptions, some participants feel betrayed. Be sure that you have earned enough trust before using a jolt.

Emotional outbursts. Some jolts may produce intense emotional distress because people don't want their dysfunctional behavior patterns to be revealed. If you are unsure about your ability to handle these reactions, try something less intense with participants in a blissful state of denial. Or conduct the session with a co-facilitator who has more experience in handling emotional outbursts.

Political correctness. Some jolts may elicit behaviors that may later be blown out of proportion into major transgressions. Be sure to model and encourage high levels of confidentiality and non-judgmental behavior. Establish a ground rule that anything that takes place inside the training room will stay there.

What is the point? Be sure to select a jolt that is relevant to a specific training objective. Clearly explain the connection between the jolt and job-relevant behaviors during debriefing. Some facilitators use irrelevant jolts because of their curiosity about how much they can rattle the cage or how far they can push the envelope. This is an abuse of participants' trust. Make sure you are not one of these facilitators.

Design Your Own Games and Activities

Things getting out of hand. Two important facilitation skills in using a jolt are knowing when to stop and being able to abandon the activity in the middle. In using a jolt, continuously compare the negative feelings it produces with the positive learning outcomes. Training folklore is replete with anecdotes about damage done to people who have participated in ethnic-discrimination simulations and prison-warden role plays. Remember that you are not conducting a sociology experience but merely making a learning point.

Hit and run. Because jolts are of short duration, there is a temptation to squeeze them into your crowded training session. Remember that the debriefing is as important—if not more important—than conducting the jolt. Be sure to set aside plenty of time for a discussion period after the jolt. During the debriefing, spend sufficient time to elicit and listen to statements of feelings from participants.

Types of Jolts

I classify jolts into *entrapment* and *enlightenment* activities. The first category involves enticing participants into their habitual behavior patterns and pointing out more effective alternatives. The second category involves helping participants discover important principles. You can also classify jolts according to whether they are primarily a one-person, two-person, or group activity. SIX LETTERS, for example, is an entrapment activity for one person. Even if I distributed copies of SIX LETTERS to fifty participants in a room and asked them to solve the puzzle, it would still be a one-person jolt because there is no interaction among participants.

Two-person jolts are used to explore cooperative and competitive behaviors. Here is a jolt called NEWTON that I borrowed from my friends Deidre Lakein and Alan Schneider. (The name is an allusion to Newton's third law of motion, which proclaims that for every action there is an equal and opposite reaction.)

NEWTON

Here's how you conduct NEWTON: Ask participants to pair up and stand facing each other. Ask them to plant their feet firmly on the ground, raise both their hands, and place them palm to palm. Now tell the participants that they win if they can make the other person move his or her feet—within 30 seconds. Blow a whistle and start a timer. Most participants will use brute force to push each other. A few martial arts practitioners may suddenly stop pushing and let the other person's momentum topple them forward.

After a suitable pause, blow the whistle, stop the activity, and compare different strategies used by participants. Ask for a volunteer for a quick demonstration. Select someone of the other gender. Assume the initial face-to-face, palm-to-palm position. Whisper to the other person, "Let's dance!" Hum a lilting tune and move your feet, inviting the other person to follow you. Politely listen as participants yell that you cheated. Point out

that you merely asked them to make the other person move his or her feet within 30 seconds. There was no prohibition against moving your own feet. Continue with the debriefing, bringing out learning points related to making assumptions, win-win solutions, modeling appropriate behaviors, solving conflicts, and the futility of meeting force with force.

CHATTER

Here is an enlightenment jolt for groups. I use this activity to explore cultural differences. Each player gets an "etiquette" card with a message like one of these:

> "It is impolite to stand aloof, so stand close to the others until you touch them. If someone backs off, keep moving closer."
>
> "It is impolite to crowd people, so maintain your distance. Stand away so that there is at least an arm's length between you and the nearest person. If anyone gets too close to you, back off until you have achieved the required distance."
>
> "Use a lot of analogies and metaphors in your conversation. Avoid direct statements."

The etiquette messages are related to different types of diversities, and they frequently contradict each other. Some participants get blank etiquette cards.

Ask participants to pretend that they are at a cocktail party. Urge them to get together in groups of five and discuss any topic of their choice. During the conversation, participants should behave according to their etiquette card, without revealing the message given to them. Participants with blank cards should behave according to their personal preferences.

After 3 minutes, blow a whistle. Ask people in each group to point to the person who behaved in the most bizarre fashion, the most rude fashion, the most irritating fashion, the most alien fashion, and the most comical fashion. Point out that all these behaviors are acceptable (and even preferred) in some group or another. During the debriefing, bring out the truth of "Different strokes for different folks." Also elicit the learning points that one person's politeness is another person's boorishness and that we all feel uncomfortable behaving outside our cultural norms.

It's Simpler Than You Think!

Here's the solution to the puzzle at the beginning: Literally cross out six letters to get Fillmore.

F I ~~S~~ L ~~X~~ L L E M ~~T~~ O ~~T~~ R E R ~~S~~

You probably know that Millard Fillmore was the thirteenth president of the United States, from 1850 to 1853. He was Zachary Taylor's vice president and when Taylor died in 1850, he suddenly became the president.

So what's the point? Sometimes we are too smart for our own good. Instead of following directions, we complicate things unnecessarily.

TRIPLE JOLT!

Jolts startle participants and deliver a powerful wake-up call. As one of the participants at a recent conference session put it, they "reveal the truth that is often obscured by reality." A typical jolt lasts only a few minutes but provides enough insights for a lengthy debriefing.

TRIPLE JOLT features three jolts that provide insights about the formation and functioning of teams. Each jolt highlights the impact of a different factor. You can conduct any of these jolts in 20 to 30 minutes.

Field Notes

You can conduct all three jolts, one after the other. Or you can select and conduct the one that best suits your current needs. If you decide to play only one jolt, you can describe the other two versions during the debriefing and ask participants to speculate on how their behavior would have changed if they played either of the other two versions.

The second and third versions award cash prizes (of $25 each) to explore some critical factors associated with team formation. If you cannot afford to do this or feel uncomfortable about cash awards, you can use play money or play for points.

Basic Concept

All three jolts involve giving a playing card to each participant and asking participants to form teams to create the best poker hand. The first jolt requires participants to work under tight time pressure. The second jolt involves cash incentives for teams and forced choice between two members with identical cards. The third version involves unequal individual cash incentives. If you are using all three jolts, collect the cards back at the end of each session, shuffle them, and redistribute them.

Although the jolts involve playing cards and poker hands, participants need not be familiar with the game of poker; the reference handout (Ranks of Poker Hands on page 372) provides all the necessary information. It does not matter if some participants are experienced poker players. Actually, an imbalance in players' knowledge of poker can increase the interest level and the instructional value of the game.

Team Poker—I
Purpose

To explore how a common goal, limited time, and individual differences influence the way people form teams.

Participants

At least twelve; best for sixteen to forty.

Materials

- A deck of playing cards
- Ranks of Poker Hands (see page 372) for each player
- Timer
- Whistle

Flow

Distribute playing cards. Shuffle the deck and give one card to each player. Explain that players should hold onto their cards at all times during the game. They may not give away or exchange their cards.

Brief the players. Explain that the game involves assembling teams of five members. The team whose five cards represent the best poker hand wins the game. Ask participants to raise their hands if they are familiar with the game of poker and the ranks of different poker hands. Explain that experience in playing poker is not a prerequisite for playing this game.

Distribute the reference handout. Give one copy to each player. Ask them to study the sheet and become familiar with the ranks of poker hands. Explain that players can refer to this handout throughout the game.

Highlight the object of the game. Players should assemble themselves into teams of five that will form the best poker hands. Each team should have exactly five members. If the total number of players is not evenly divisible by five, some will be left out. Players may join or leave any team at any time. They may entice players from other teams.

Conduct a walk-around. Ask players to hold their cards in front of them and silently walk around the room so everyone can see who has which card. After a suitable time period, blow the whistle and ask players to stop where they are.

Announce the time limit. Explain to players that they have a tight time limit of 3 minutes to organize themselves into teams. Start the timer and blow the whistle to indicate the beginning of the exercise.

Conclude the session. Announce time when you have 1 minute remaining, 30 seconds remaining, and 10 seconds remaining. Blow the whistle to indicate the end of the game.

Determine the winning team. Read the names of different poker hands listed in the handout, one at a time, beginning with the lowest (nothing) hand. Find out which team has the most powerful hand. If more than one team has the same type of hand, refer to the handout and break the tie. Congratulate the winning team.

Design Your Own Games and Activities

Debriefing

To ensure reflection and sharing of insights, conduct a debriefing using the six-phase model. Here are some suggested questions:

How do you feel?

- How do you feel about the game you played?
- What are your positive and negative reactions toward members of your team? Toward members of the winning team? Toward people who were left out? Toward the facilitator? Toward the card you received? Toward the team formation process?

What happened?

- How useful was the walk-around and finding out who had which card?
- How much planning did you do before joining a team?
- How did you decide who to partner with initially?
- Was there a big demand for you? Or did the others tend to ignore you?
- Did you passively follow the lead of others or actively organize your team?
- How exactly did your team form itself?
- Who took the lead in forming your team?
- Did you reject any participant who wanted to join your team?
- Did any participant reject your invitation to join your team?
- Did you get left out of all teams?
- What did you learn?
- What did you learn from this activity?
- The same individual can be extremely valuable in one team and totally useless in another. How does this game illustrate this principle?
- How did the following factors influence the way teams were formed?
  Same goal for all participants
  Alternative approaches for achieving the goal
  Only one team can win
  Self-selected team formation
  Time pressure
  Each participant with a different card
  Previous relationships among partners
- How does this game relate to your workplace?
- What real-world processes are reflected in this game?
- What do the cards represent?
- Were you ever under such time pressure to form a team?

What if?

- How would your behavior have changed in the following situations?

  Members of the team with the winning poker hand received a cash prize.

  Each person has two playing cards (but uses only one of them).

  You have to choose between two participants with the same (duplicate) playing cards.

  Participants may exchange cards with each other.

  A team may have more than five members (and select five cards among them).

What next?

- Knowing what you now know, how would you change your strategy if we played the game again?
- Knowing what you now know, how would you change your strategy in forming teams in your workplace?

Team Poker—II

Purpose

To explore how cash incentives and similarity among people influence the way people form work teams.

Participants

At least twelve; best for sixteen to forty.

Materials

- Two decks of playing cards
- $25 (preferably in five $5 bills)
- The Ranks of Poker Hands handout (see page 372)
- Timer
- Whistle

Flow

Arrange cards for distribution. Shuffle the first deck and deal the cards in packets of four. From the other deck, locate the duplicate of the first card in each packet and place this card on top of the packet. You now have five-card packets that consist of two identical cards and three other cards. Turn these cards face down and place the five-card packets one on top of another.

Distribute playing cards. Beginning from the top of the arranged deck, give one card to each player. Explain that players should hold onto their card at all times during the game. They may not give away or exchange their cards.

Design Your Own Games and Activities

Brief the players. Explain that the game involves assembling teams of five members. The team whose five cards represent the best poker hand wins the game. Ask participants to raise their hands if they are familiar with the game of poker and the ranks of different poker hands. Explain that experience in playing poker is not a prerequisite for playing this game.

Distribute the reference handout. Give one copy to each player. Ask them to study the sheet and become familiar with the ranks of poker hands. Explain that players can refer to this handout throughout the game.

Highlight the object of the game. Players should assemble themselves into teams of five that will result in the best poker hands. No team may have two players with the same (duplicate) cards. Each team should include exactly five members. If the total number of players is not evenly divisible by five, some will be left out. Players may join or leave any team any time. They may entice players from other teams.

Announce a cash prize for the winning team. Explain that each member of the winning team will receive a $5 prize.

Announce the time limit. Explain to players that they have a tight time limit of 3 minutes to organize themselves into teams. Start the timer and blow the whistle to indicate the beginning of the exercise.

Conclude the session. Announce time when they have 1 minute remaining, 30 seconds remaining, and 10 seconds remaining. Blow the whistle to indicate the end of the game.

Determine the winning team. Read the names of different poker hands listed in the handout, one at a time, beginning with the lowest (nothing) hand. Find out which team has the most powerful hand. If more than one team has the same type of hand, refer to the handout and break the tie. With suitable fanfare, award the $5 prize to each member of the winning team.

Debriefing

To ensure reflection and sharing of insights, conduct a debriefing using the six-phase model. Use appropriate questions from the previous set along with these additional questions:

How do you feel?
- How do you feel about the cash prize?
- What did you learn?
- How did the following factors influence the way teams were formed?
    Two members with identical cards
    Cash prizes for members of the winning team
- How does this game relate to your workplace?
- What does the cash prize represent?

What if?

- How would your behavior have changed if members of the team with the winning poker hand did not receive a cash prize?

Team Poker—III

Purpose

To explore how unequal cash incentives to different members of a team influence the way people form work teams.

Participants

At least twelve; best for sixteen to forty.

Materials

- Two decks of playing cards
- $25 (preferably in $1 bills)
- The Ranks of Poker Hands reference handout (see page 372)
- Timer
- Whistle

Flow

Arrange playing cards for distribution. Shuffle the first deck and deal the cards in packets of four. From the other deck, locate the duplicate of the first card in each packet and place this card on top of the packet. You now have five-card packets that consist of two identical cards and three other cards. Turn these cards face down and place the five-card packets one on top of another.

Distribute playing cards. Beginning from the top of the arranged deck, give one card to each player. Explain that players should hold onto their card at all times during the game. They may not give away or exchange their cards.

Brief the players. Explain that the game involves assembling teams of five members. The team whose five cards represent the best poker hand wins the game. Ask participants to raise their hands if they are familiar with the game of poker and the ranks of different poker hands. Explain that experience in playing poker is not a prerequisite for playing this game.

Distribute the reference handout. Give one copy to each player. Ask them to study the sheet and become familiar with the ranks of poker hands. Explain that players can refer to this handout throughout the game.

Announce cash prizes. Explain that members of the winning team will win a cash prize. Explain that you will award cash prizes in the amounts of $1, $2, $4, $7, and $11 to the five members of the winning team. Each team has to decide who among its members will receive each of these amounts. Team members cannot redistribute the prize money.

Highlight the object of the game. Players should organize themselves into teams of five that will result in the best combination of cards into poker hands. Each team should specify who among its members will receive each of the five unequal cash prizes. No team may have two players with the same (duplicate) cards. Each team should include exactly five members. If the total number of players is not evenly divisible by five, some will be left out. Players may join or leave any team any time. They may entice players from other teams.

Announce the time limit. Explain to players that they have a tight time limit of 3 minutes to organize themselves into teams and to decide who will receive which cash prize (if the team should have the best poker hand). Start the timer and blow the whistle to indicate the beginning of the exercise.

Conclude the session. Announce time when they have 1 minute remaining, 30 seconds remaining, and 10 seconds remaining. Blow the whistle to indicate the end of the game.

Determine the winning team. Read the names of different poker hands listed in the handout, one at a time, beginning with the lowest (nothing) hand. Find out which team has the most powerful hand. If more than one team has the same type of hand, refer to the handout and break the tie. Ask the winning team to specify who will receive which of the five different amounts of cash. With suitable fanfare, award these cash prizes.

Debriefing

To ensure reflection and sharing of insights, conduct a debriefing using the six-phase model. Use appropriate questions from the previous sets along with these additional questions:

How do you feel?

- How do you feel about different people receiving different amounts of prize money?
- How do you feel about the rule that prohibits the team from redistributing the prize money?

What happened?

- How did your team decide who gets which cash prize?

What did you learn?

- How does the unequal distribution of incentives affect teamwork?
- How does this game relate to your workplace?
- Have you ever felt that some employees make more money through luck rather than through hard work?

What if?

- How would your behavior have changed if the winning team were permitted to distribute the total prize money of $25 in any way they wanted?

Ranks of Poker Hands

Value of Cards
Here are all 13 cards in each suit, arranged from the highest to the lowest:

Ace, King, Queen, Jack, 10, 9, 8, 7, 6, 5, 4, 3, 2, Ace

Notice that an Ace can be counted either as the highest or the lowest card.

Values of Poker Hands
Here are the nine different types of poker hands, from the lowest (*Nothing*) to the highest (*Straight Flush*):

HAND	SAMPLE
Nothing. None of the five cards has a value that matches the value of another card. Also the cards are of different suits. *Tie breaker:* If two players have *nothings*, the player with the highest card wins. For example, a hand with A♣ - Q♦ - 9♥ - 8♠ - 2♦ beats the sample hand (on the right).	
One Pair. This hand contains two cards of the same value and three other odd cards. *Tie breaker:* If two players have *pairs*, the value of the paired cards determines who wins. For example, a hand that contains a 6♣ - 6♠ pair beats the sample hand. If both players have pairs of the same value, then the hand with the highest card among the other three cards wins.	
Two Pairs. This hand contains a pair of cards of the same value, another pair of cards of a different value, and an odd card. *Tie breaker:* If two players have two pairs, the value of the higher pair determines who wins. For example, a hand with a 8♦ - 8♣ pair (and another pair) beats the sample hand. If both players have higher pairs of the same value, then the hand with the higher second pair wins. If these pairs also match, then the hand with highest odd card wins.	
Three of a Kind. This hand contains three cards of the same value and two odd cards. *Tie breaker:* If two players have *three-of-a-kind* hands, the value of the higher three of a kind determines who wins. For example, a hand with K♦ - K♠ - K♥ beats the sample hand.	
Straight. This hand contains five cards in sequence, but not of the same suit. *Tie breaker:* If two players have *straights*, then the value of the card on top of the straight determines who wins. For example, a hand with J♥ - 10♣ - 9♥ - 8♠ - 7♦ beats the sample hand shown on the right.	
Flush. This hand contains five cards of the same suit, not in sequence. *Tie breaker:* If two players have *flushes*, then the value of the highest card determines who wins. For example, a hand with A♥ - 10♥ - 7♥ - 3♥ - 2♥ beats the sample hand.	
Full House. This hand contains three cards of the same value and two of another. *Tie breaker:* If two players have *full houses*, then the value of the set of three cards determines who wins. For example, a hand with J♠ - J♥ - J♠ - 7♥ - 7♦ beats the sample hand.	
Four of a Kind. This hand contains four cards of the same value and an odd card. *Tie breaker:* If two players have *four-of-a-kind* hands, then the value of the set of four cards determines who wins. For example, a hand with 5♠ - 5♥ - 5♦ - 5♣ - 9♠ beats the sample hand.	
Straight Flush. This hand contains five cards of the same suit, in sequence. *Tie breaker:* If two players have straight flushes, then the value of the highest card in the sequence determines who wins. For example, a hand with 10♠ - 9♠ - 8♠ - 7♠ - 6♠ beats the sample hand.	

References

Epstein, Seymour. (1993). *You're Smarter Than You Think*. New York: Simon & Schuster.

Gardner, Howard. (1999). *Intelligence Reframed: Multiple Intelligences for the 21st Century*. New York: Basic Books.

Parker, Glenn M. (1996). *Team Players and Teamwork*. San Francisco: Jossey-Bass/Pfeiffer.

Presnky, Marc. (2000). *Digital Game-Based Learning*. New York: McGraw Hill.

Senge, Peter M. (1994). *The Fifth Discipline: The Art and Practice of the Learning Organization*. New York: Currency/Doubleday.

Sternberg, Robert J. (1996). *Successful Intelligence: How Practical and Creative Intelligence Determine Success in Life*. New York: Simon & Schuster.

Thiagarajan, Sivasailam, & Steinwachs, Barbara. (1990). *Barnga: A Simulation Game of Cultural Clashes*. Yarmouth, ME: Intercultural Press.

Tuckman, Bruce W. (1965). Developmental sequence in small groups. *Psychological Bulletin, 63*, 384–399.

Glossary of Interactive Strategies

Action Learning involves a combination of action and reflection by a team to solve complex, strategic problems in a real-world organizational setting. Team members apply existing skills and knowledge and create new skills, knowledge, and insights through continuously reflecting on and questioning the problem definition, the collaborative behavior, and the ensuing results.

Action Research is a strategy (similar to *action learning*) in which a team of participants conducts field research to examine a question. Specially suited for participants who don't know what they don't know, data collected during the research may alter the original question. The team may learn unanticipated principles and procedures because of the volatile nature of open-minded inquiry and objective reflection.

Appreciative Inquiry (AI) is an alternative to traditional problem solving. Instead of focusing on what is wrong, AI emphasizes positive aspects of a situation. The AI process involves encouraging participants to share stories of positive experiences with one another. The facilitator reviews these stories to identify themes for further inquiry. Participants create and share images of a preferred future and brainstorm ways to create that future.

Assessment-Based Learning Activities (ABLA) require participants to complete a test, a rating scale, or a questionnaire and receive a score (and other feedback) about their personal competencies, attitudes, or personality traits. In some ABLAs, participants' responses are combined to identify the perceptions, opinions, or characteristics of a team, a work group, or an

organization. Whenever appropriate, ABLAs encourage interaction and discussion among participants to analyze their responses and to apply the results to future action.

Audio Games are training activities that primarily depend on playback of recorded audio messages (such as audiotape or streaming audio) to provide the training content, structure the training activity, and collect player response. Most audio games use few or no visuals (in the form of text or graphics).

Board Games borrow structures and play materials from popular recreational games to create highly motivating training events. Board games typically use game cards and dice to encourage individuals and teams to demonstrate their mastery of concepts, principles, skills, and problem-solving strategies.

The Case Method involves a written account of a real or fictional situation surrounding a problem. Participants work individually and in teams to analyze, discuss, and recommend appropriate solutions and to critique each other's work. In some cases, the facilitator may recount the actual decisions implemented in the real-world situation on which the case was based.

Cash Games are a special type of simulation game that involves actual cash transactions. They are not gambling games. Nor do they focus on accounting procedures or financial management. Instead, they explore interpersonal skills (such as *negotiation*) and concepts (such as *cooperation*). These games use cash because it effectively simulates the real world and brings out natural behaviors and emotions in participants.

Classification Card Games involve pieces of information (such as facts, concepts, technical terms, definitions, principles, examples, quotations, and questions) printed on cards. These games borrow procedures from traditional playing card games and require players to classify and sequence pieces of information from the instructional content.

Closers are activities conducted near the end of a session. They are used for reviewing main points, tying up loose ends, planning application activities, providing feedback, celebrating successful conclusions, and exchanging information for future contacts.

Coaching Activities involve an individual facilitator (the coach) supporting the learning and improving performance efforts of another individual (the coachee) through interactive questioning and guidance. The process usually requires the two people to establish goals and the coach to observe the coachee, debrief the activity, offer relevant feedback, and suggest suitable improvements.

Computer Game Shells incorporate special types of framegames that are presented on a computer screen. The shells permit the loading of new content (usually in the form of questions) by the facilitator. The computer program creates the game and acts as a timekeeper and scorekeeper. Some of the shells provide highly graphic interfaces with sound effects that reflect

Glossary of Interactive Strategies

popular TV game shows. These computer games can be presented to large audiences by projecting the display on big screens.

Consensus Decision-Making Activities involve a list of items (usually ten) to be arranged in order of priority. Participants complete the task individually and then reach consensus in teams. Then they compare their priority rankings with expert rankings. In the process, they learn more about factors that contribute to the importance of items and also factors that influence making decisions and reaching consensus in teams.

Corporate Adventure Learning involves physical activities (such as sailing, rafting, rappelling, rock climbing, exploring wilderness areas, and walking on rope bridges) in challenging indoor or outdoor environments. A trained facilitator ensures safety of participants and conducts suitable debriefing discussions that enable participants to construct knowledge, skill, and value from these exciting experiences.

Creativity Techniques provide a structure that enables participants to solve a problem or to utilize an opportunity in a creative fashion. These techniques are useful not only for learning new skills and knowledge but also for improving the performance of a team.

Critical Friend involves a special type of peer-coaching approach. In this strategy someone you trust (your critical friend) listens to your plans, observes your behavior, asks probing questions, and critiques your methods and accomplishments. Participants may pair up with a critical friend during a training session and may continue collaborating with each other for a long time afterwards. In addition to face-to-face conversations, this collaboration can be conducted through telephone, postal mail, and e-mail.

Debriefing Games are interactive strategies that are used for encouraging reflection and dialogue about an earlier activity or event. These games require processing of a common experience to extract key learning points from it. They generally encourage participants to identify and express emotions, recall events and decisions, share lessons learned, relate insights to other real-world events, speculate on how things could have been different, and plan for future action.

Disaster Simulations are activities that require participants to cope with simulations of natural or organizational disasters, such as an earthquake or downsizing. In dealing with such disasters, participants learn to make fast collaborative decisions in complex and rapidly changing situations.

E-Mail Games are conducted through the Internet. They may involve the play of electronic versions of interactive training games or specially designed activities that permit asynchronous communication in which people receive and send messages at different times. Typical e-mail games exploit the ability of the Internet to ignore geographic distances and involve participants pooling their ideas and polling to select the best ones.

Facilitated Activities help teams analyze problems, formulate goals, generate alternative solutions, and make decisions. Usually, a trained facilitator conducts these structured activities to help teams maximize their diverse talents and to arrive at collaborative solutions that are superior to individual solutions.

Fantasy Role-Playing Games require participants to enact individual or team roles, often within a science-fiction or fantasy scenario. These role-play activities focus on skills and concepts related to such topics as leadership, teamwork, and planning. Debriefing after the role play draws parallels between the fictional fantasy and workplace reality.

Framegames provide templates for instant creation of training games. These generic frameworks are deliberately designed to permit easy replacement of old content with new content. You can use framegames to rapidly develop training activities that suit your needs.

Graphic Analogies Discussion Generators are based on brilliant designs from Scott Simmerman. These activities use cartoon illustrations to engage, enlist, and involve people in performance-improvement discussions and to stimulate collaboration and creativity. The strategy basically involves asking a group of people to compare elements from a generic illustration to the organizational context.

Guided Learning Activities provide a special type of on-the-job training. New employees (or new members of a team) observe workplace processes using carefully designed checklists. Later, they perform job-related activities under the guidance of an experienced employee or team member and receive immediate feedback.

Hypotheticals employ an expert moderator to utilize the multiple expertise that exists within a group. The moderator assembles a panel, presents a hypothetical scenario, and facilitates a discussion of individual approaches to solving the problem. Members of the audience can involve themselves by asking additional questions of the panel members and challenging their assumptions.

Improv Games are activities adapted from improvisational theater. The actors do not use a script but create the dialogue and action as they perform. When used as an interactive training technique, improv games facilitate the mastery of skills related to such areas as creativity, collaboration, communication, and change.

Instructional Puzzles challenge the participants' ingenuity and incorporate training content that is to be previewed, reviewed, tested, re-taught, or enriched. Puzzles can be solved by individuals or by teams.

Interactive Lectures involve participants in the learning process while providing complete control to the instructor. These activities enable a quick and easy conversion of a passive presentation into an interactive experience.

Glossary of Interactive Strategies

Different types of interactive lectures incorporate built-in quizzes, interspersed tasks, teamwork interludes, and participant control of the presentation.

Interactive Storytelling involves fictional narratives in a variety of forms. Participants may listen to a story and make appropriate decisions at critical junctures. They may also create and share stories that illustrate key concepts, steps, or principles from the instructional content.

Item Processing is an interactive strategy in which individuals and teams generate, organize, and sequence ideas, facts, questions, complaints, or suggestions. As a result of this activity, participants create organized lists of items. More importantly, this activity enables participants to construct meaningful categories and sequences from isolated items. This results in deeper understanding and easier recall of the content.

Jolts lull participants into behaving in a comfortable way and deliver a powerful wake-up call. They force participants to re-examine their assumptions and revise their standard procedures. Jolts typically last for a few minutes but provide enough insights for a lengthy debriefing.

Magic Tricks incorporate a relevant conjuring trick as a part of a training session. Magic tricks provide metaphors or analogies for important elements of the training content. The tricks are also used as processes to be analyzed, reconstructed, learned, performed, or coached for training participants in appropriate procedures.

Matrix Games require participants to occupy boxes in a grid by demonstrating a specific skill or knowledge. The matrixes provide a structure for matching or classifying individual items or organizing and comparing a set of items. The first participant to occupy a given number of boxes in a straight line (horizontally, vertically, or diagonally) wins the game.

Metaphorical Simulation Games (MSGs) reflect real-world processes in an abstract, simplified fashion. MSGs are particularly useful for teaching principles related to planning, generating ideas, testing alternatives, making decisions, utilizing resources, and working under time pressure.

Musical Team Building involves participants playing on different musical instruments to create synchronized and rhythmic music. The process that leads to the spontaneous and gradual evolution of the final piece of music is debriefed to provide insights into such topics as teamwork, leadership, and communication.

Openers are activities conducted near the beginning of a session. They are used to preview main points, orient participants, introduce participants to one another, form teams, establish ground rules, set goals, reduce initial anxieties, or stimulate self-disclosure.

Pair Work is based on the pair programming component of the extreme programming methodology. This strategy involves two people working on

the same computer, sharing a single keyboard. All paired work results in the development of better products. In addition, paired work between an expert and a novice results in the latter learning new technical concepts and skills. Paired work between people from different fields (for example, a subject-matter expert and a writer) results in more effective collaboration skills.

Paper-and-Pencil Games require players to make their moves by writing or drawing something on paper. A typical game may involve players working on a small piece (or a large sheet) of paper. Paper-and-pencil games may incorporate elements of role plays, simulations, creativity techniques, or quiz contests.

PC Simulations use playing cards to reflect real-world objects and processes. The rules of PC simulations typically encourage participants to discover principles of interpersonal interaction and inductive thinking.

Polarity Management™ is a team-based approach created by Barry Johnson for identifying and managing unsolvable problems. The technique involves identifying polarities (such as *team versus individual*), listing the positive and negative aspects of each pole, and systematically working toward action guidelines for effectively managing the dilemma.

Procedural Simulations are dress rehearsals of real-world events, such as conducting a raid to rescue hostages, evacuating a burning building, or being subjected to a surprise inspection by auditors from the funding agency. By working through these simulations, participants get ready for real-world events.

Production Simulations involve the design and development of a product (such as a video segment, a newsletter, a marketing plan, or a jingle). Different teams compete with each other to create the best product. The initial briefing in this strategy involves teams receiving specifications for the final product, along with a checklist of quality criteria. Teams have a budget and a time limit. They can purchase different job aids, reference materials, handouts, sample products, and consultative help to assist them in their production activity. The final products are evaluated by a panel of outside experts who provide feedback along a variety of dimensions.

Read.me Games combine the effective organization of well-written documents with the motivational impact of interactive experiential activities. Participants read a handout and play a game that uses peer pressure and support to encourage recall and transfer of what they read.

Reflective Teamwork involves participants creating a product related to some aspect of teamwork. Teams then evaluate their characteristics and performance by using the product they created.

Role Plays involve participants assuming and acting out characters, personalities, and attitudes other than their own. These activities may be tightly or loosely structured and may involve a participant assuming multiple roles or reversed roles.

Scenario Educational Software (SES) is a computer-simulation format developed by Mark Keegan to incorporate key features of discovery learning. A typical SES program transports participants to a specific time and place (such as a health clinic in West Africa or a penitentiary at Rikers Island). The simulated activity presents an optimal challenge, requires participants to make decisions, and provides relevant feedback. Most SES activities last for a significant period of time to maximize the impact of repeated practice.

Sharing Circles. David Cowan, Susanna Palomares, and Dianne Schilling have been successfully using this approach for the past twenty-five years. The technique involves eight to twelve participants seated in a circle, sharing a discussion of a selected topic. Everyone gets a turn to share without interruptions, probes, and putdowns. The session concludes with a review and a summary.

Simulation Games help participants experience an event similar to a real event—without the difficulty, expense, or danger of the real event. Originally used in war games for training officers and soldiers, simulation games are currently used in business games for teaching complex concepts. Most simulations are based on models of reality. Computers are frequently used to translate complex models in such areas as aircraft piloting and urban planning into graphic representations.

Strategic Questioning is a technique developed by Fran Peavey from San Francisco. This strategy involves identifying a situation, sharing participants' feelings to that situation, and discussing what each individual would like to see happen. Used with community action groups around the world, this strategy also requires the group to identify the obstacles to achieving the desired result and generating a wide range of strategies to move closer to the results.

Structured Group Discussions use a self-contained instructional format designed for collaborative learning among team members—without the need for an outside facilitator. The activity is facilitated by an audiotape or videotape recording or a computer program that specifies discussion topics, presents background information, imposes time limits, and provides feedback (in the form of model responses and checklists).

Structured Sharing represents a special type of framegame that facilitates mutual learning and teaching among participants. Typical structured sharing activities create a context for a dialogue among participants based on their experiences, knowledge, and opinions.

Telephone Games use telephones and answering machines. They may involve the play of interactive training games over long distances. Telephone games may involve elements of role play and virtual teamwork.

Television Games borrow the structure of popular TV game shows to present the instructional content and to encourage participants to practice skills. They involve selected contestants and the "studio audience," who participate and learn vicariously. TV games can be broadcast for distance learning, made available on videotapes, or presented live by using computer game shells and graphics.

Thought Experiments are mental role plays that involve guided visualization. Individual participants mentally rehearse new patterns of behavior or hold imaginary dialogues. Combined with self-reflection, these activities result in increased self-awareness and mastery of new knowledge and insights.

Training Devices involve physical activities performed on electrical and mechanical pieces of equipment. Participants solve a problem or meet a challenge with the device and relate the process to their workplace activities.

Troubleshooting Simulations require participants to systematically find the causes of problems and to fix the problems. These simulations can use realistic simulators (as in the case of debugging faulty machinery) or computer print-outs of output data (as in the case of slowing down the loss of market share).

Tutoraids are job aids (checklists, flowcharts, and decision tables) that enable a knowledgeable but untrained person to tutor another person on basic skills, including literacy and numeracy.

Video Feedback involves each member of a group role playing an interpersonal skill. This is followed by the group members providing positive and constructive feedback to each role player with the intent of helping the person improve his or her interpersonal skills.

Video Vitamins enhance the instructional value of training videos. In a typical video vitamin, participants watch a videotape and then play one or more games that help review and apply the new concepts and skills.

Wall Games, based on designs by Steve Sugar, typically involve posters mounted on a wall (or an easel) that require participants to write or draw. A typical wall game may present a vertical version of a board game, a matrix game, or an instructional puzzle. Participants may play these games individually or in teams.

Web-Based Games are interactive activities presented on the Internet. A variety of games and simulations can be played on the web by individuals or by teams. Multiplayer games permit several participants to interact with each other at the same time.

WebQuests are based on a format developed by Bernie Dodge and Tom March at San Diego State University. They feature a special type of inquiry learning in which participants collect information from the web. WebQuests focus on using information rather than merely retrieving it. A typical WebQuest requires participants to analyze, synthesize, and evaluate the information from the web.

Reproduced from *Design Your Own Games and Activities* by Sivasailam (Thiagi) Thiagarajan with Raja Thiagarajan with permission of the publisher. Copyright © 2003 by John Wiley & Sons, Inc.

Activity Indexes

Activities Arranged by Title

Title	Strategy	Topic	Participants	Time	Page
A DEATH IN MY FAMILY	Interactive Story	Diversity	10–50	80	321
APPLES AND ORANGES	Matrix Game	Cost/Benefit Analysis	3–10	30–120	114
BOOSTERS AND BASHERS	Video Vitamin	Evaluation	15–30	30–60	76
BULLET SLIDES	Production Simulation	Computer Slides	6–20	60–120	288
C3PO	E-Mail Game	Idea Generation	10–30	4 days to 4 weeks	192
CALL TO ACTION	Action Learning	Learning Projects	4–8	60	247
CARD SETS	PC Simulation	Cooperation	8–48	45	353
CHANGE MANAGEMENT	Cash Game	Teamwork	10–30	45	346

(Continued)

Activities Arranged by Title (*Continued*)

Title	Strategy	Topic	Participants	Time	Page
CONFERENCE CALL	Telephone Game	Telephone Skills	5–8	30–60	172
COOPETITION	Game Show	Review	20–30	30	182
CRYPTIC STRATEGIES	Instructional Puzzle	Knowledge Management	10–30	45	140
EMPTY OR FULL?	Board Game	Optimism/Pessimism	3	30–45	105
GUT TALK	Role Play	Difficult Conversations	10–50	60–90	335
INSERT AND DELETE	Audio Game	Facilitation Skills	10–30	30–45	160
INSIDE STORY	Interactive Lecture	Performance Technology	12–30	30–45	47
MULTIPLE FEEDBACK	Reflective Teamwork Activity	Effective Feedback	5–15	30–60	258
ONE-ON-ONE	Paper-and-Pencil Game	Collaboration/Competition	2–200	45	128
PUZZLE PIECES	Metaphorical Simulation Game	Inclusion	12–40	40–60	312
QUICK DRAW	Improv Game	Collaboration	4–50	20	202
ROBOT	Opener	Change Management	10–30	20–30	212
SEVEN SENTENCES	Creativity Technique	Employee Support	4–7	30	35
SILENT MOVIES	Item Processing	Training Design	10–30	30–60	64
TEAM MAZE	Training Device	Problem Solving	5–30	60	298
TEN TRICKS	Card Game	Team Development	2–5	10–15	94
THIRTY-FIVE	Debriefing Game	Idea Generation	10–100	15–30	89
TIME TRAVEL	Textra Game	Creative Problem Solving	12–40	30–45	55
TOP TIPS	Structured Sharing	Team Meetings	12–20	30–45	27
TRIPLE FEEDBACK	Closer	Feedback	20–30	45–60	224
TRIPLE JOLT	Jolt	Teamwork	16–40	60	365
TROUBLED TEAM	The Case Method	Teamwork	6–20	90	270

By Interactive Strategy

Strategy	Title	Topic	Number of Players	Time	Page
Action Learning	CALL TO ACTION	Learning Projects	4–8	60	247
Audio Games	INSERT AND DELETE	Facilitation Skills	10–30	30–45	160
Board Games	EMPTY OR FULL?	Optimism/Pessimism	3	30–45	105
Card Games	TEN TRICKS	Team Development	2–5	10–15	94
Cash Games	CHANGE MANAGEMENT	Teamwork	10–30	45	346
Closers	TRIPLE FEEDBACK	Feedback	20–30	45–60	224
Creativity Techniques	SEVEN SENTENCES	Employee Support	4–7	30	35
Debriefing Games	THIRTY-FIVE	Idea Generation	10–100	15–30	89
E-Mail Games	C3PO	Idea Generation	10–30	4 days to 4 weeks	192
Game Shows	COOPETITION	Review	20–30	30	182
Improv Games	QUICK DRAW	Collaboration	4–50	20	202
Instructional Puzzles	CRYPTIC STRATEGIES	Knowledge Management	10–30	15	140
Interactive Lectures	INSIDE STORY	Performance Technology	12–30	30–45	47
Interactive Storytelling	A DEATH IN MY FAMILY	Diversity	10–50	80	321
Item Processing	SILENT MOVIES	Training Design	10–30	30–60	64
Jolts	TRIPLE JOLT	Teamwork	16–40	60	365
Matrix Games	APPLES AND ORANGES	Cost/Benefit Analysis	3–10	30–120	114

(Continued)

By Interactive Strategy (*Continued*)

Strategy	Title	Topic	Number of Players	Time	Page
Metaphorical Simulation Games	PUZZLE PIECES	Inclusion	12–40	40–60	312
Openers	ROBOT	Change Management	10–30	20–30	212
Paper-and-Pencil Games	ONE-ON-ONE	Collaboration/ Competition	2–200	45	128
PC Simulations	CARD SETS	Cooperation	8–48	45	353
Production Simulations	BULLET SLIDES	Computer Slides	6–20	60–120	288
Reflective Teamwork Activities	MULTIPLE FEEDBACK	Effective Feedback	5–15	30–60	258
Role Playing	GUT TALK	Difficult Conversations	10–50	60–90	335
Structured Sharing	TOP TIPS	Team Meetings	12–20	30–45	27
Telephone Games	CONFERENCE CALL	Telephone Skills	5–8	30–60	172
Textra Games	TIME TRAVEL	Creative Problem Solving	12–40	30–45	55
The Case Method	TROUBLED TEAM	Teamwork	6–20	90	270
Training Devices	TEAM MAZE	Problem Solving	5–30	60	298
Video Vitamins	BOOSTERS AND BASHERS	Evaluation	15–30	30–60	76

Opening Samples Arranged by Title

Title	Interactive Strategy	Topic	Page
BARNGA	Metaphorical Simulation Game	Diversity	310
BINGO LECTURE	Interactive Lecture	Diversity	41
COMPANY PICNIC	Improv Game	Diversity	199
COMPLAINTS	Role Playing	Customer Service	331
CONSULTANTS	Instructional Puzzle	Organizational Learning	137
DEPOLARIZER	E-Mail Game	Merger	189
DESIGNER TAGS	Opener	Getting Acquainted	209
DOUBLE NEGATIVE	Closer	Action Planning	221
DOUBLE REVERSAL	Creativity Technique	Empowerment	33
EACH TEACH	Textra Game	Quality Management	53
EIGHT MARKS	Training Device	Teamwork	295
ET—EFFECTIVE TEAMS	Reflective Teamwork Activity	Teamwork	255
ETHICAL DECISION MAKING	Interactive Story	Decision Making	319
HELP-DESK DIALOGUE	Paper-and-Pencil Game	Help Desk	125
HELP!	Telephone Game	Call Centers	169
INDUCT	PC Simulation	Inductive Logic	351
INTELLIGENT CARDS	Card Game	Multiple Intelligence	91
KEY POINTS	Video Vitamin	Teamwork	73
MARKET	Production Simulation	Marketing	281
ME AND MY TEAM	Cash Game	Teamwork	345
MOOD CHECK	Debriefing Game	Merger	85
PM CHAMPIONSHIP	Game Show	Project Management	179
PROJECT NET GAIN	Action Learning	Intranet Design	243
READING FOR BINGO	Matrix Game	Product Knowledge	111
RECALLED	The Case Method	Intercultural Communication	267
SIMCITY® 2000	Simulation Games	On-the-Job Training	235
SIX LETTERS	Jolt	Assumptions	361
TENSES	Item Processing	Personal Vision	61
THE BEST AND THE WORST	Structured Sharing	Leadership	25
THE CADUCEUS CRISIS	Audio Game	Change Management	157
THIRTY STEPS	Board Game	Problem Solving	103
VALUES ENVELOPES	Structured Sharing	Corporate Values	13

By Interactive Strategy

Interactive Strategy	Title	Topic	Page
Action Learning	PROJECT NET GAIN	Intranet Design	243
Audio Games	THE CADUCEUS CRISIS	Change Management	157
Board Games	THIRTY STEPS	Problem Solving	103
Card Games	INTELLIGENT CARDS	Multiple Intelligence	91
Cash Games	ME AND MY TEAM	Teamwork	345
Closers	DOUBLE NEGATIVE	Action Planning	221
Creativity Techniques	DOUBLE REVERSAL	Empowerment	33
Debriefing Games	MOOD CHECK	Merger	85
E-Mail Games	DEPOLARIZER	Merger	189
Game Shows	PM CHAMPIONSHIP	Project Management	179
Improv Games	COMPANY PICNIC	Diversity	199
Instructional Puzzles	CONSULTANTS	Organizational Learning	137
Interactive Lectures	BINGO LECTURE	Diversity	41
Interactive Storytelling	ETHICAL DECISION MAKING	Decision Making	319
Item Processing	TENSES	Personal Vision	61
Jolts	SIX LETTERS	Assumptions	361
Matrix Games	READING FOR BINGO	Product Knowledge	111
Metaphorical Simulation Games	BARNGA	Diversity	310
Openers	DESIGNER TAGS	Getting Acquainted	209
Paper-and-Pencil Games	HELP-DESK DIALOGUE	Help Desk	125
PC Simulations	INDUCT	Inductive Logic	351
Production Simulations	MARKET	Marketing	281
Reflective Teamwork Activities	ET—EFFECTIVE TEAMS	Teamwork	255
Role Playing	COMPLAINTS	Customer Service	331
Simulation	SIMCITY® 2000	On-the-Job Training	235
Structured Sharing	THE BEST AND THE WORST	Leadership	25
Structured Sharing	VALUES ENVELOPES	Corporate Values	13
Telephone Games	HELP!	Call Centers	169
Textra Games	EACH TEACH	Quality Management	53
The Case Method	RECALLED	Intercultural Communication	267
Training Devices	EIGHT MARKS	Teamwork	295
Video Vitamins	KEY POINTS	Teamwork	73

Index of Activities Briefly Described *(with instructional strategy)*

(Continued)

Activity Indexes

Index of Activities Briefly Described (with instructional strategy) (Continued)

Resources

Basic Books on Interactive Strategies

Here's my recommended reading list for anyone with a serious interest in the field of games and interactive experiential strategies. The collection includes books with philosophical, academic, and practical perspectives.

Carse, James P. (1986). *Finite and Infinite Games: A Vision of Life as Play and Possibility.* New York: The Free Press. Finite games are the familiar contests of everyday life. Infinite games are unscripted, unpredictable, and more rewarding.

DeKoven, Bernie. (2002). *The Well-Played Game: A Playful Path to Wholeness.* San Francisco: iUniverse. The Guru of Glee explains how a well-played game can bring joy to you and to the others who play the game.

El-Shamy, Susan. (2001). *Training Games: Everything You Need To Know About Using Games to Reinforce Learning.* Stirling, VA: Stylus Publishing. This book is an excellent introduction to the design and use of training games.

Gredler, Margaret E. (1992). *Designing and Evaluating Simulations and Games: A Process Approach.* Houston: Gulf. Written by an educational psychologist, this book provides a scholarly introduction to the design and evaluation of instructional games and simulations.

Greenaway, Roger. (1993). *Playback: A Guide to Reviewing Activities.* Edinburgh, Scotland: The Duke of Edinburgh's Award. The book provides an excellent and practical introduction to the debriefing process.

Jones, Ken. (1997). *Games and Simulations Made Easy: Practical Tips to Improve Learning Through Gaming.* London: Kogan Page. Ken Jones is one of the most brilliant designers of training games and simulations.

Kolb, David A. (1984). *Experiential Learning: Experience as the Source of Learning and Development.* Englewood Cliffs, NJ: Prentice Hall. This book is the classic in the field. Kolb's model has formed the basis for the design of experiential learning activities for two decades.

Koppett, Kat. (2001). *Training to Imagine: Practical Improvisational Theatre Techniques to Enhance Creativity, Teamwork, Leadership, and Learning.* Stirling, VA: Stylus Publishing. Kat provides a collection of improv games and explains how they can be used in training and management.

Presnky, Marc. (2000). *Digital Game-Based Learning.* New York: McGraw-Hill. Although this is a book about computer games, Marc's discussion of the new generation of learners and basic principles of game design can be applied to any type of learning.

Sleigh, John. (1990). *Making Learning Fun.* Wollongong, NSW, Australia: John Sleigh Management Training. John Sleigh is the best training game designer from Australia.

Sugar, Steve. (1998). *Games That Teach: Experiential Activities for Reinforcing Learning.* San Francisco: Jossey-Bass/Pfeiffer. Steve presents an excellent collection of framegames for achieving different types of training objectives.

Thiagarajan, Sivasailam, & Parker, Glenn. (1999). *Teamwork and Teamplay: Games and Activities for Building and Training Teams.* San Francisco: Jossey-Bass/Pfeiffer. Glenn and Thiagi explore teamwork, team training, and team building through games.

Books on Interactive Strategies
Design

Ellington, Henry, Addinall, Eric, & Percival, Fred. (1984). *Case Studies in Game Design.* London: Kogan Page.

El-Shamy, Susan. (2001). *Training Games: Everything You Need to Know About Using Games to Reinforce Learning.* Stirling, VA: Stylus Publishing.

Fripp, John. (1993). *Learning Through Simulation: A Guide to the Design and Use of Simulations in Business and Education.* London: McGraw-Hill.

Gredler, Margaret E. (1992). *Designing and Evaluating Simulations and Games: A Process Approach.* Houston: Gulf.

Greenblatt, Cathy S. (1988). *Designing Games and Simulations.* Thousand Oaks, CA: Sage.

Greenblatt, Cathy S., & Duke, Richard D. (1981). *Principles and Practices of Gaming Simulations.* Thousand Oaks, CA: Sage.

Jones, Ken. (1997). *Games and Simulations Made Easy: Practical Tips to Improve Learning Through Gaming.* London: Kogan Page.

Kolb, David A. (1984). *Experiential Learning: Experience as the Source of Learning and Development.* Englewood Cliffs, NJ: Prentice Hall.

Koppett, Kat. (2001). *Training to Imagine: Practical Improvisational Theatre Techniques to Enhance Creativity, Teamwork, Leadership, and Learning.* Stirling, VA: Stylus Publishing.

Langer, Ellen J. (1997). *The Power of Mindful Learning.* Reading, MA: Addison-Wesley.

Pfeiffer, J. William. (Ed.) (1994). *Pfeiffer & Company Library, Volume 21, Experiential Learning Activities: Training Technologies.* San Francisco: Jossey-Bass/Pfeiffer.

Russell, Lou. (1999). *The Accelerated Learning Fieldbook: Making Instructional Process Fast, Flexible, and Fun.* San Francisco: Jossey-Bass/Pfeiffer.

Debriefing

Boud, David, Keogh, Rosemary, & Walker, David (Eds.). (1985). *Reflection: Turning Experience into Learning*. London: Kogan Page.

Greenaway, Roger. (1993). *Playback: A Guide to Reviewing Activities*. Edinburgh, Scotland: The Duke of Edinburgh's Award.

Luckner, John L., & Nadler, Reldan S. (1992). *Processing the Experience: Strategies to Enhance and Generalize Learning*. Dubuque, IA: Kendall/Hunt.

Facilitation

DeKoven, Bernie. (2002). *The Well-Played Game: A Playful Path to Wholeness*. San Francisco: iUniverse.

Heron, John. (1989). *The Facilitators' Handbook*. London: Kogan Page.

Kaner, Sam. (1996). *Facilitator's Guide to Participatory Decision Making*. Gabriola Island, BC, Canada: New Society Publishers.

Priest, Simon, Gass, Michael A., & Gillis, Lee. (2000). *The Essential Elements of Facilitation*. Dubuque, IA: Kendall/Hunt.

Rees, Fran. (1998). *The Facilitator Excellence Handbook*. San Francisco: Jossey-Bass/Pfeiffer.

Schwartz, Roger M. (1994). *The Skilled Facilitator: Practical Wisdom for Developing Effective Groups*. San Francisco: Jossey-Bass.

Game Theory

Hamburger, Henry. (1979). *Games as Models of Social Phenomena*. San Francisco: W. H. Freeman.

McMillan, John. (1992). *Games, Strategies, and Managers: How Managers Can Use Game Theory to Make Better Business Decisions*. New York: Oxford University Press.

Murnighan, J. Keith. (1992). *Bargaining Games: A New Approach to Strategic Thinking in Negotiations*. New York: William Morrow.

Workplace Applications

Carse, James P. (1986). *Finite and Infinite Games: A Vision of Life as Play and Possibility*. New York: The Free Press.

Gallwey, W. Timothy. (2000). *The Inner Game of Work*. New York: Random House.

Marquardt, Michael J. (1999). *Action Learning in Action*. Palo Alto, CA: Davies-Black.

Pesce, Mark. (2000). *The Playful World: How Technology Is Transforming Our Imagination*. New York: Ballantine Books.

Schrage, Michael. (2000). *Serious Play: How the World's Best Companies Simulate to Innovate*. Boston, MA: Harvard Business School Press.

Types of Interactive Activities
The Case Method

Barnes, Louis B., Christensen, C. Roland, & Hansen, Abby J. (1994). *Teaching and the Case Method*. Boston, MA: Harvard Business School Press.

Naumes, William, & Naumes, Margaret J. (1999). *The Art and Craft of Case Writing*. Thousand Oaks, CA: Sage.

Classic Games

Bell, R. C. (1979). *Board and Table Games from Many Civilizations.* New York: Dover Publications.

Costello, Matthew J. (1991). *The Greatest Games of All Times.* New York: John Wiley & Sons.

Grunfeld, Frederic B. (1982). *Games of the World: How to Make Them, How to Play Them, and How They Came to Be.* New York: Plenary Publications International.

Schmittberger, R. Wayne. (1992). *New Rules for Classic Games.* New York: John Wiley & Sons.

Computer and Web-Based Games

Arch, Dave, & Ensz, Sue. (2000). *Web-Based Interactive Learning Activities.* Amherst, MA: HRD Press.

Bates, Bob. (2001). *Game Design: The Art and Business of Creating Games.* Roseville, CA: Prima Publishing.

Keegan, Mark. (1995). *Scenario Educational Software: Design and Development of Discovery Learning.* Englewood Cliffs, NJ: Educational Technology Publications.

Presnky, Marc. (2000). *Digital Game-Based Learning.* New York: McGraw-Hill.

Rouse, Richard. (2001). *Game Design: Theory and Practice.* Plano, TX: Wordware Publishing.

Creativity Techniques

Epstein, Robert. (1995). *Creativity Games for Trainers A Handbook of Group Activities for Jumpstarting Workplace Creativity.* New York: McGraw-Hill.

Maisel, Eric. (2000). *The Creativity Book: A Year's Worth of Inspiration and Guidance.* New York: Putnam.

Framegames

DeVries, David L. (1980). *Teams-Games-Tournament: The Team Learning Approach.* Englewood Cliffs, NJ: Educational Technology Publications.

Stolovitch, Harold D., & Thiagarajan, Sivasailam. (1978). *Frame Games.* Englewood Cliffs, NJ: Educational Technology Publications.

Sugar, Steve. (1998). *Games That Teach: Experiential Activities for Reinforcing Learning.* San Francisco: Jossey-Bass/Pfeiffer.

Thiagarajan, Sivasailam. (1995). *Games by Thiagi—Framegames.* Amherst, MA: HRD Press.

Improv Games

Gesell, Izzy. (1997). *Playing Along: 37 Group Learning Activities Borrowed from Improvisational Theater.* Duluth, MA: Whole Person Associates.

Johnstone, Keith. (1979). *Impro: Improvisation and the Theatre.* New York: Theatre Arts Books.

Johnstone, Keith. (1999). *Impro for Storytellers.* New York: Theatre Arts Books.

Interactive Lectures

Bowman, Sharon. (2000). *Preventing Death by Lecture: Terrific Tips for Turning Listeners into Learners.* Glennbrook, NV: Bowperson Publishing.

Thiagarajan, Sivasailam. (1995). *Interactive Lectures.* Amherst, MA: HRD Press.

Thiagarajan, Sivasailam. (1996). *Lecture Games.* Amherst, MA: HRD Press.

Thiagarajan, Sivasailam. (2001). *Fun in the Workplace: Interactive Lectures* (Info-line 0105). Alexandria, VA: ASTD.

Role Playing

Dormant, Diane. (1980). *Rolemaps.* Englewood Cliffs, NJ: Educational Technology Publications.

Jackson, Steve. (1999). *GURPS: Generic Universal Roleplaying System.* Austin, TX: Steve Jackson Games.

van Ments, Morry. (1983). *The Effective Use of Role Play.* London: Kogan Page.

Simulations

Jones, Ken. (1987). *Simulations: A Handbook for Teachers and Trainers.* London: Kogan Page.

Thiagarajan, Sivasailam. (1966). *Games by Thiagi—Simulation Games.* Amherst, MA: HRD Press.

Thiagarajan, Sivasailam, & Stolovitch, Harold D. (1978). *Simulation Games.* Englewood Cliffs, NJ: Educational Technology Publications.

Storytelling

Denning, Stepen. (2001). *The Springboard: How Storytelling Ignites Action in Knowledge-Era Organizations* Booton, MA. Butterworth Heinemann.

Gargiulo, Terrence L. (2002). *Making Stories: A Practical Guide for Organizational Leaders and Human Resource Specialists.* Westport, CT: Quorum Books.

Simmons, Annette. (2001). *The Story Factor: Inspiration, Influence, and Persuasion Through the Art of Storytelling.* Cambridge, MA: Perseus Publishing.

Structured Sharing

Johnson, Barry. (1996). *Polarity Management: Identifying and Managing Unsolvable Problems* Amherst, MA: HRD Press.

Thiagarajan, Sivasailam. (1978). *Groupprograms* Englewood Cliffs, NJ: Educational Technology Publications.

Wenger, Etienne, McDermott, Richard, & Snyder, William M. (2002). *Cultivating Communities of Practice.* Boston, MA: Harvard Business School Press.

Collections of Games and Activities

Barca, Michele, & Cobb, Kate. (1993). *Beginnings and Endings: Creative Warmups and Closure Activities.* Amherst, MA: HRD Press.

Bowman, Sharon. (1988). *How to Give It So They Get It: A Flight Plan for Teaching Anyone Anything and Making It Stick.* Glennbrook, NV: Bowperson Publishing.

Bowman, Sharon. (1997). *Presenting with Pizzazz: Terrific Tips for Topnotch Trainers.* Glennbrook, NV: Bowperson Publishing.

Carnevale, Anthony P., & Kogod, S. Kanu (Eds.). (1996). *Tools and Activities for a Diverse Workforce.* New York: McGraw-Hill.

Caroselli, Marlene. (1998). *Great Session Openers, Closers, and Energizers: Quick Activities for Warming Up Your Audience and Ending on a High Note.* New York: McGraw-Hill.

Drum, Jan, Hughes, Steve, & Otero, George. (1994). *Global Winners: 74 Learning Activities for Inside and Outside the Classroom.* Yarmouth, ME: Intercultural Press.

Epstein, Robert. (2000). *The Big Book of Stress Relief Games: Quick, Fun Activities for Feeling Better.* New York: McGraw-Hill.

Epstein, Robert, & Rogers, Jessica. (2001). *The Big Book of Motivation Games.* New York: McGraw-Hill.

Forbes-Greene, Sue. (1983). *The Encyclopedia of Icebreakers.* San Francisco: Jossey-Bass/Pfeiffer.

Fowler, Sandra M., & Mumford, Monica G. (Eds.). (1995). *Intercultural Sourcebook: Cross-Cultural Training Methods* (Vol. 1). Yarmouth, ME: Intercultural Press.

Fowler, Sandra M., & Mumford, Monica G. (Eds.). (1999). *Intercultural Sourcebook: Cross-Cultural Training Methods* (Vol. 2). Yarmouth, ME: Intercultural Press.

Gregson, Bob. (1982). *Incredible Indoor Games Book: One Hundred and Sixty Group Projects, Games, and Activities.* Belmont, CA: Pitman Learning.

Hart, Lois B. (1989). *Saying Goodbye: Ending a Group Experience.* King of Prussia, PA: Organization Design and Development.

Hart, Lois B. (1989). *Saying Hello: Getting Your Group Started.* King of Prussia, PA: Organization Design and Development.

Jones, John E., & Bearley, William L. (1989). *Energizers for Training and Conferences.* King of Prussia, PA: Organization Design and Development.

Jones, Ken. (1988). *Interactive Learning Events: A Guide to Facilitators.* London: Kogan Page.

Jones, Ken. (1991). *Icebreakers: A Sourcebook of Games, Exercises, and Simulations.* San Francisco: Jossey-Bass/ Pfeiffer.

Jones, Ken. (1993). *Imaginative Events for Training: A Trainer's Sourcebook of Games, Simulations, and Role-Play Exercises.* New York: McGraw-Hill.

Kirby, Andy. (1992). *The Encyclopedia of Games for Trainers.* Amherst, MA: HRD Press.

Kroehnert, Gary. (1993). *100 Training Games.* New York: McGraw-Hill.

Laver, Michael. (1979). *Playing Politics: Seven Games that Bring Out the Politician in All of Us.* Harmondsworth, Middlesex, England: Penguin.

Leder, Drew. (1998). *Games for the Soul: 40 Playful Ways to Find Fun and Fulfillment in a Stressful World.* New York: Hyperion.

Leigh, Elyssebeth, & Kinder, Jeff. (2000). *Learning Through Fun and Games.* New York: McGraw-Hill.

Luvmour, Sambhava, & Luvmour, Josette (Eds.). (1990). *Everyone Wins.* Philadelphia, PA: New Century Publishers.

Lynn, Adele B. (2001). *The Emotional Intelligence Activity Book: 50 Activities for Promoting EQ at Work.* New York: AMACOM.

MacGregor, Cynthia. (1999). *Everybody Wins! 150 Non-Competitive Games for Kids.* Avon, MA: Adams Media.

Nilson, Carolyn. (1995). *Games That Drive Change.* New York: McGraw-Hill.

Parker, Glenn. (2002). *Team Depot: A Warehouse of Over 600 Tools to Reassess, Rejuvenate, and Rehabilitate Your Team.* San Francisco: Jossey-Bass/Pfeiffer.

Pfeiffer, J. William. (Ed.). (1989). *The Encyclopedia of Group Activities: 150 Practical Designs for Successful Facilitating*. San Francisco: Jossey-Bass/Pfeiffer.

Scannell, Edward, Newstrom, John, & Nilson, Carolyn. (1995). *The Complete Games Trainers Play: Experiential Learning Exercises*. New York: McGraw-Hill.

Scannell, Edward, Newstrom, John, & Nilson, Carolyn. (1998). *The Complete Games Trainers Play* (Vol. II). New York: McGraw-Hill.

Seelye, H. Ned. (Ed.). (1996). *Experiential Activities for Intercultural Learning*. Yarmouth, ME: Intercultural Press.

Silberman, Mel. (1995). *101 Ways to Make Training Active*. San Francisco: Jossey-Bass/Pfeiffer.

Sleigh, John. (1990). *Making Learning Fun*. Wollongong, NSW, Australia: John Sleigh Management Training.

Solem, Lynn, & Pike, Bob. (1998). *50 Creative Training Closers: Innovative Ways to End Your Training with Impact*. San Francisco: Jossey-Bass/Pfeiffer.

Sugar, Steve, & Takacs, George. (1999). *Games That Teach Teams: 21 Activities to Super-Charge Your Group*. San Francisco: Jossey-Bass/Pfeiffer.

Sweeney, Linda Booth, & Meadows, Dennis. (1995). *The Systems Thinking Playbook: Exercises to Stretch and Build Learning and Systems Thinking Capabilities*. Durham, NH: IPSSR/Laboratory for Interactive Learning.

Thiagarajan, Sivasailam, & Parker, Glenn. (1999). *Teamwork and Teamplay: Games and Activities for Building and Training Teams*. San Francisco: Jossey-Bass/Pfeiffer.

Ukens, Lorraine L. (1996). *Getting Together: Icebreakers and Group Energizers*. San Francisco: Jossey-Bass/Pfeiffer.

Ukens, Lorraine L. (1996). *Working Together: 55 Team Games*. San Francisco: Jossey-Bass/Pfeiffer.

Ukens, Lorraine L. (1999). *All Together Now! A Seriously Fun Collection of Interactive Training Games and Activities*. San Francisco: Jossey-Bass/Pfeiffer.

Ukens, Lorraine L. (2000). *Energize Your Audience: Quick Activities to Get Them Started and Keep Them Going*. San Francisco: Jossey-Bass/Pfeiffer.

VanGundy, Arthur. (1998). *101 Great Games & Activities*. San Francisco: Jossey-Bass/Pfeiffer.

West, Edie. (1997). *201 Icebreakers Group Mixers, Warm-Ups, Energizers, and Playful Activities*. New York: McGraw-Hill.

The Best Resource on Interactive Strategies

Someone once asked me, "If you were sent to the space station and permitted to take only one book with you, which book would you take?" This is what I'd do: I'd cheat a little and take a whole library of books—in a single CD-ROM. The *Pfeiffer Library* CD-ROM is the ultimate electronic resource. It contains the content from different sources:

Ten volumes of the *Handbook of Structured Experiences*

Twenty-six sets of Pfeiffer *Annuals* (from 1972 to 1997)

The *UA Training Technology* series

Theories and Models

Reproduced from *Design Your Own Games and Activities* by Sivasailam (Thiagi) Thiagarajan with Raja Thiagarajan with permission of the publisher. Copyright © 2003 by John Wiley & Sons, Inc.

The materials have been reedited and reorganized to form one comprehensive resource, categorized according to the following topics:

- Individual Development
- Communication
- Problem Solving
- Groups
- Teams
- Consulting
- Facilitating
- Leadership
- Training Technologies

Because the library is on a single CD-ROM, you don't have to flip through the pages to find activities that meet your needs: You can search through thousands of pages by typing in any key word. Once you have located the appropriate activities, you can print them directly from the CD-ROM or quickly, effortlessly export the pages to your word processor and customize the materials for use in your own training session.

Yes, the price is steep: $2,250. But the content and the convenience are definitely worth it.

Websites on Interactive Strategies

The Internet is full of intriguing websites that deal with interactive strategies. Here's our current top twenty.

20 Questions: http://q.20q.net/q.cgi. See if you can outsmart artificial intelligence by playing twenty questions with the computer.

Bernie DeKoven: www.deepfun.com/. Let Bernie DeKoven, your personal guru of glee, lead you through the playful path to happiness.

Clarke Aldrich: www.simulearn.net/. Explore immersive simulation software on leadership and other topics from one of the best designers.

Conversational game—Hipbone Games: http://home.earthlink.net/~hipbone/. Charles Cameron claims, "Anyone from a child to a Ph.D. in astrophysics can play our games: like a conversation between friends, a HipBone game quickly finds its own level."

Forio Business Simulations: www.forio.com/. Use free resources to create business simulations that run on the web.

Game Design Course: http://edweb.sdsu.edu/courses/edtec670/. This is the official site of the San Diego State University course, *Exploratory Learning through Simulations and Games* conducted by my brilliant friend Dr. Bernie Dodge.

Game design templates: www.quia.com/. Use these templates for creating fourteen different types of interactive online activities.

Games and illusions: www.sandlotscience.com/. Amuse yourself and amaze yourself with interactive games, illusions, distortions, and magic.

Resources

Interactive mazes and puzzles: www.clickmazes.com/index.htm. An addictive collection of interactive mazes and other types of puzzles.

An International Journal: www.unice.fr/sg/. Official website of Sage Publication's *Simulation & Gaming.* Be sure to visit the *Resources* section.

Mark Prensky: www.games2train.com/. Read excerpts from the book, *Digital Game-Based Learning.*

Multiplayer word games and puzzles: www.funster.com/. Check out the *Funster Forum* for new puzzles.

Online games: www.ishouldbeworking.com/games.htm. Play a variety of Java, Shockwave, Flash, and HTML games.

Professional association: www.nasaga.org. Visit the official website of the North American Simulation and Gaming Association and become a member (free of charge).

Rules for card games: www.pagat.com/. Learn or review the rules for any game with playing cards, from *All Fours* and *Authors* to *Zap Your Neighbor* and *Zwickern.*

Rules for board games: www.everyrule.com/boardgames_az_list.html. Learn or review rules for hundreds of board games.

Scott Kim: www.scottkim.com/. Explore web games, puzzles, inversions, and articles on game design from the Internet's most intriguing puzzle master.

Shopping for games: www.kumquat.com/cgi-kumquat/funagain/home. Browse through—and purchase—new and old games.

Virtual tinker toys: www.sodaplay.com/. Modify an animated graphic simulator to defy gravity.

WebQuest: http://edweb.sdsu.edu/webquest/webquest.html. Learn from Bernie Dodge how to create your own interactive online learning materials.

Companion Website to This Book

Please visit the companion web page for this book, www.thiagi.com/designyourown. We will post additions, supplements, updates, and corrections for this book as they become available.

You may also want to visit our website at www.thiagi.com. We have designed the website to provide more content, less fluff. It contains more than six hundred pages' worth of ready-to-play training games, e-mail games, puzzles, tips for facilitators, tips for rapid instructional development, short stories, articles, handouts, and links to other websites.

The Thiagi website also contains current and back issues of my online newsletter that acts as a follow-up to this book. Published monthly since June 2001, *Play for Performance* includes articles on new interactive strategies, ready-to-play activities, activities based on the interactive formats explored in this book, practical advice on design and facilitation, discussion of e-learning strategies, interviews with game designers, book reviews, information about conferences, puzzles, and contests. The website is updated frequently. Please visit often to update and upgrade your skills and knowledge.

About the Authors

Sivasailam "Thiagi" Thiagarajan, Ph.D., is QB International's resident mad scientist (*aka* director of research and development). His current research area is the blending of classroom and online interactive experiential strategies.

Thiagi has been designing a new interactive activity every day of the year since March 21, 1998. He has published more than two hundred training games and has written twenty books on interactive strategies for improving human performance. He writes an online newsletter, *Play for Performance,* with new activities and advice every month.

In the field of e-learning, Thiagi is recognized for three major contributions: The *library playground* approach to the rapid design of online learning materials, *web-based framegames* for creating instant training games, and *RAMEs (Replayable Asynchronous Multiplayer Exercises)* that incorporate e-mail and web pages for sharing their best practices.

Thiagi has been the president of the North American Simulation and Gaming Association (NASAGA) for four different terms and organized the annual conferences. He has also been the president of the International Society for Performance Improvement (ISPI). He has received seventeen different awards and Presidential Citations from ISPI, including the society's highest award, Honorary Life Member. He also received an Honorary Life Member award from NASAGA, as well as its highest award, the Ifill-Reynolds Award.

Raja Thiagarajan grew up as a member of the networked generation, writing his first computer program when he was ten years old. He received a master's degree in computer science from Indiana University. With several

years of play time on computer games, Raja is the designer and author of three training game-design software packages: *Zingo, Computer Game Shells,* and *Puzzlemaker.* As the director of computer applications at QB International, Raja supervises the web-based training playground (*www.qube.com*), and coordinates the design of *QB International Playground Suite,* a tool for creating web-based training games. Raja is also involved in the design and testing of computer games in technical and soft skill areas.

How to Use the CD-ROM

System Requirements

Windows PC

- 486 or Pentium processor-based personal computer
- Microsoft Windows 95/98/2000 or Windows NT 3.51 or later
- Minimum RAM: 16 MB for Windows 95 and NT
- Available space on hard disk: 8 MB Windows 95 and NT
- 2X speed CD-ROM drive or faster
- Netscape 3.0 or higher browser or MS Internet Explorer 3.0 or higher

Macintosh

- Macintosh with a 68020 or higher processor or Power Macintosh
- Apple OS version 7.0 or later
- Minimum RAM: 12 MB for Macintosh
- Available space on hard disk: 6MB Macintosh
- 2X speed CD-ROM drive or faster
- Netscape 3.0 or higher browser or MS Internet Explorer 3.0 or higher

NOTE: This CD requires Netscape 3.0 or MS Internet Explorer 3.0 or higher. You can download these products using the links on the CD-ROM Help Page.

Getting Started

Insert the CD-ROM into your drive. The CD-ROM will usually launch automatically. If it does not, click on the CD-ROM drive on your computer to launch. You will see an opening page. You can click on this page or wait for it to fade to the Copyright Page. After you click to agree to the terms of the Copyright Page, the Home Page will appear.

Moving Around

Use the buttons at the left of each screen or the underlined text at the bottom of each screen to move among the menu pages. To view a document listed on one of the menu pages, simply click on the name of the document. To quit a document at any time, click the box at the upper right-hand corner of the screen.

Use the scrollbar at the right of the screen to scroll up and down each page.

To quit the CD-ROM, you can click the Quit option at the bottom of each menu page, hit Control-Q, or click the box at the upper right-hand corner of the screen.

To Download Documents

Open the document you wish to download. Under the File pulldown menu, choose Save As. Save the document onto your hard drive with a different name. It is important to use a different name, otherwise the document may remain a read-only file.

You can also click on your CD drive in Windows Explorer and select a document to copy it to your hard drive and rename it.

In Case of Trouble

If you experience difficulty using this CD-ROM, please follow these steps:

1. Make sure your hardware and systems configurations conform to the systems requirements noted under "Systems Requirements" above.

2. Review the installation procedure for your type of hardware and operating system. It is possible to reinstall the software if necessary.

3. You may call Jossey-Bass/Pfeiffer Customer Care at (800) 956-7739 between the hours of 8 A.M. and 5 P.M. Eastern Standard Time, and ask for Jossey-Bass/Pfeiffer Technical Support. It is also possible to contact Technical Support by e-mail at *techsupport@JosseyBass.com*.

Please have the following information available:

- Type of computer and operating system
- Version of Windows being used
- Any error messages displayed
- Complete description of the problem.

(It is best if you are sitting at your computer when making the call.)